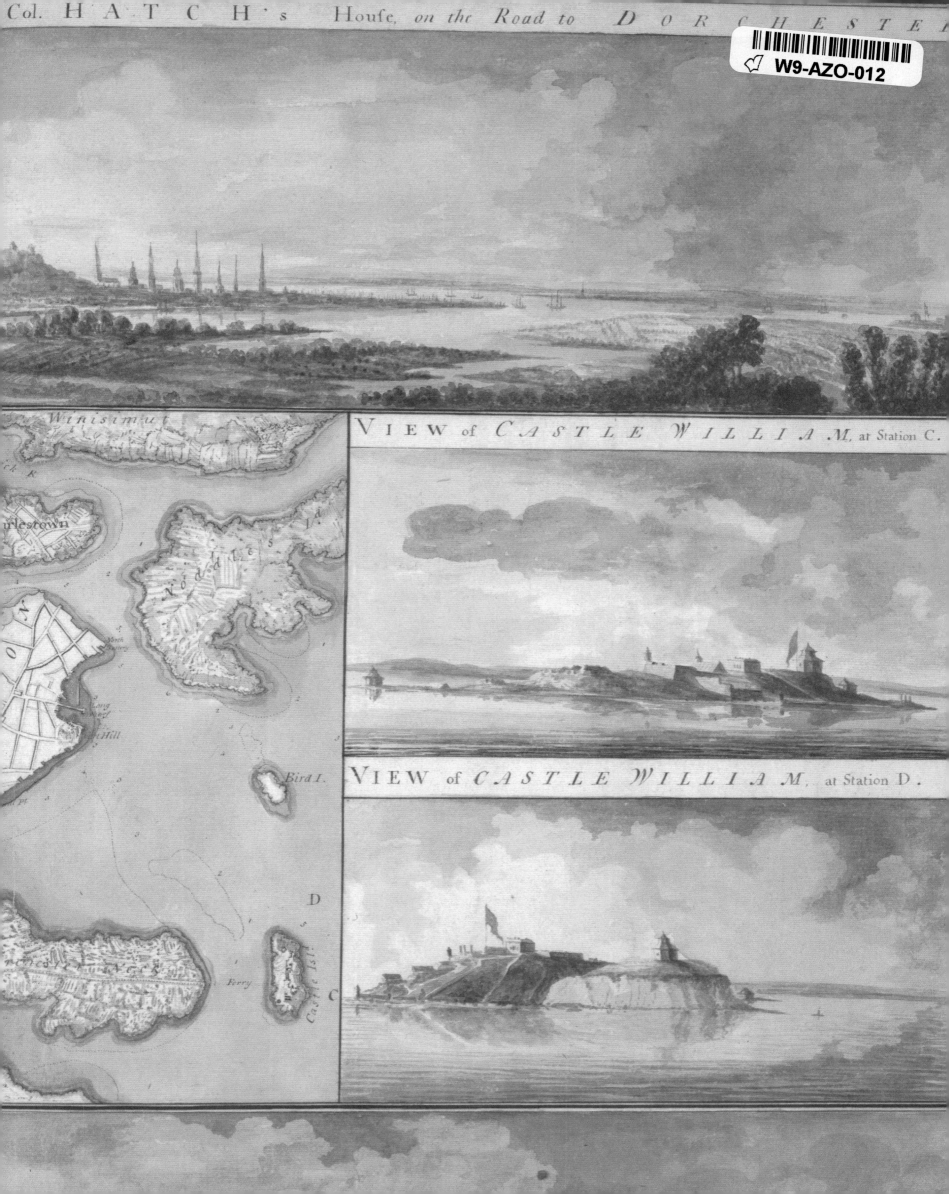

Col. H A T C H's Houſe, on the Road to D O R C H E S T E R

VIEW of CASTLE WILLIAM, at Station C.

VIEW of CASTLE WILLIAM, at Station D.

THE AMERICAN
Revolution

THE AMERICAN
Revolution

The global struggle
for national independence

BRENDAN MORRISSEY

THUNDER BAY
P·R·E·S·S

SAN DIEGO, CALIFORNIA

Thunder Bay Press

An imprint of the Advantage Publishers Group

5880 Oberlin Drive, San Diego, CA 92121-4794

www.advantagebooksonline.com

All notations of errors or omissions should be addressed to Thunder Bay Press, editorial
department, at the above address. All other correspondence (author inquiries,
permissions) concerning the content of this book should be addressed to Salamander
Books Limited, 8 Blenheim Court, Brewery Road,
London N7 9NY, England.

ISBN 1-57145-541-8

Library of Congress Cataloging-in-Publication Data available upon request.

Printed and Bound in Italy by G. Canale & C

1 2 3 4 5 01 02 03 04 05

CREDITS

Editorial Director: Charlotte Davies

Art Director: John Heritage

Production: Phillip Chamberlain

Reproduction: Media Print (UK) Ltd

Produced for Salamander Books by
D.A.G. Publications Ltd

Special thanks to
Roberta Wiener and James R. Arnold

Title page:

The Storming of Redoubt 10 at Yorktown by American troops.
This painting captures the dash and bravery of the assault of
14/15 October 1781. For the loss of nine dead and 31 wounded,
the light infantry killed or captured all 70 members of the garrison.
(Virginia State Library)

CONTENTS

The Siege of Yorktown. This and the painting on the following two pages were reputedly executed from eyewitness reports by a French engineer officer named Berthier (who later became Napoleon's chief of staff). In the first painting a French regiment in column of platoons passes one of the abandoned British outer redoubts on its way to the trenches in the middle distance. The British defences are shrouded in smoke and the black dot just above the horizon is a falling British shell (from which the horsemen are taking cover). (Musée de Versailles, Paris)

PREFACE

Before I agreed to write this book, I asked myself what there was to say about the American War of Independence, or Revolutionary War, that was either new, or that could be presented in a different way. What would attract the casual reader, or the lover of history new to this particular subject, yet still hold the attention of the "grizzled veteran" who has seen the same facts and figures rehashed a dozen times?

The idea that I found most appealing was to show that this was a global struggle—a world war in the truest sense. While the fundamental objective—independence for the Thirteen Colonies—inevitably led to a focus on operations in and around North America, I believe that it is vital to any understanding of those events, and the reason behind the outcome, to consider the war in the context of the dynastic and imperial struggles of eighteenth-century Europe. For the British in particular, the maritime struggle with their European foes had as much, if not more, influence on the final outcome as the indecisive clashes of small armies in North America.

In doing so, I also wished to continue the seemingly endless task of confronting some of the worst myths that still surround the war, especially those resulting from the misconceptions concerning contemporary British society (a society to which most contemporary Americans believed they rightfully belonged), so beloved of the media. However, some of these have been a long time a-dying and have survived the onslaught of far more talented and persuasive authors …

On a final note, I have deliberately chosen to refer to the opposing groups of white Americans as Rebels and Loyalists, since the terms "patriot" or "American" can just as easily be applied to either. The term "black" is used in juxtaposition to "white" purely for brevity and simplicity.

The author would particularly like to thank the staff of D.A.G. Publications for their patience and perseverance, and above all, his wife Nora, without whose unfailing support and love, he would never get anything done.

Brendan Morrissey

INTRODUCTION

On both sides of the Atlantic Ocean, two widely held misconceptions remain concerning the American Revolutionary War, or War of Independence as it is known in Europe. One is that the main cause of the conflict was taxation; the other is that the military struggle consisted of a series of land battles, from Canada to the Carolinas, in which one side blundered about in bright red coats and talcum-powdered hair, while the other hid behind trees and rocks, picking off their opponents at long range. In fact, there were several reasons why some inhabitants of North America took up arms against Great Britain, just as the tactics used by both sides were considerably more complex than those described above. Equally, there were other theaters of operations, to the extent that North America itself became a sideshow for everyone except Americans (after 1778, even the British were placing more emphasis on Europe and the Caribbean). By the time hostilities were ended formally, in 1783, the conflict had involved countless tribes and races—including some who had never heard of America—across four continents and half a dozen seas and oceans.

Cornwallis's army marching out of Yorktown to the Surrender Field. Note that the British are in three ranks, rather than the two ranks used in battle. The French are in three ranks and the Americans in two. (Musée de Versailles, Paris)

THE FOURTEEN COLONIES

Although traditionally referred to as the "Thirteen Colonies," there were actually fourteen areas of North America between the Province of Quebec and the Floridas that owed allegiance to the British crown. From the south, they were Georgia, South and North Carolina, Virginia, Maryland, Delaware, Pennsylvania, New Jersey, New York, then the New England Colonies of Connecticut, Rhode Island, New Hampshire, and Massachusetts Bay (which then included modern-day Maine), and finally Nova Scotia, populated by a mixture of native Englishmen—mainly from Yorkshire—and New Englanders. Of the thirteen "American" Colonies, nine were Crown Colonies with Royal governors appointed in London; Maryland and Pennsylvania were, in essence, privately owned; and Connecticut and Rhode Island were chartered Colonies with elected governors. External trade was governed by the Navigation Acts, which encouraged the Colonists to buy luxury goods (silver, china, paint, and glass) and essentials (fabrics, woolen cloth, and guns) from the mother country and to ship their raw materials—and, occasionally, their own manufactured goods—to ports in Great Britain and Ireland.

In 1760, the population was about 1,300,000, whites, 220,000 Native Americans, and 325,000 black slaves. By 1775, the totals were nearer 2,000,000, 200,000 and 500,000, respectively, compared with 8,000,000 in Great Britain and Ireland. Well over ninety percent of the population lived in the countryside and only four conurbations—Charleston, Boston, New York, and Philadelphia—had more than 10,000 inhabitants, although Philadelphia's 35,000 made it the second largest city, after London (750,000), in the British Empire.

The vast majority of whites were of British stock; however, by the 1760s, third or fourth generation Colonists saw themselves—if only subconsciously—as Americans (though not in a nationalistic sense, but rather as other Britons might state they were English, Welsh, Scots, or Irish: when Paul Revere rode into the Massachusetts countryside, he warned that the Regulars were coming, not "the British"). The rest of the white population was mainly German, Dutch, or Swiss, with small groups of Scandinavians and French Huguenots; many of these Europeans had emigrated to escape either persecution, or prosecution. Overall, there was still an unusually high proportion of males in the white population, especially among the younger age groups, reflecting the highly selective nature of emigration. Many of the young men were "indentured servants"—virtually slaves, except that their service was limited in time—who had usually been tricked into "apprenticeships" in order to pay their passage across the Atlantic. A high proportion were unwilling residents: it has been estimated that about one in four of all white males arriving from Great Britain before 1775 were criminals sentenced to penal servitude.

Among the Native American population, except for a few small tribes, the indigenous population of British North America lived north and west of the 1763 Proclamation Line. Historically, the French had been more successful than the British in securing their friendship, as might be surmised from the use of the term "French and Indian Wars" to cover conflicts prior to 1754. The major exception were the six nations of the Iroquois, whose traditional enemies had all allied with France. Other tribes particularly hostile to the Colonists (though less so to the British, as time passed) were those of the northwest (Chippewa, Delaware, Miami, Fox, and Shawnee) and the southeast (Cherokee, Creek, Chocktaw and

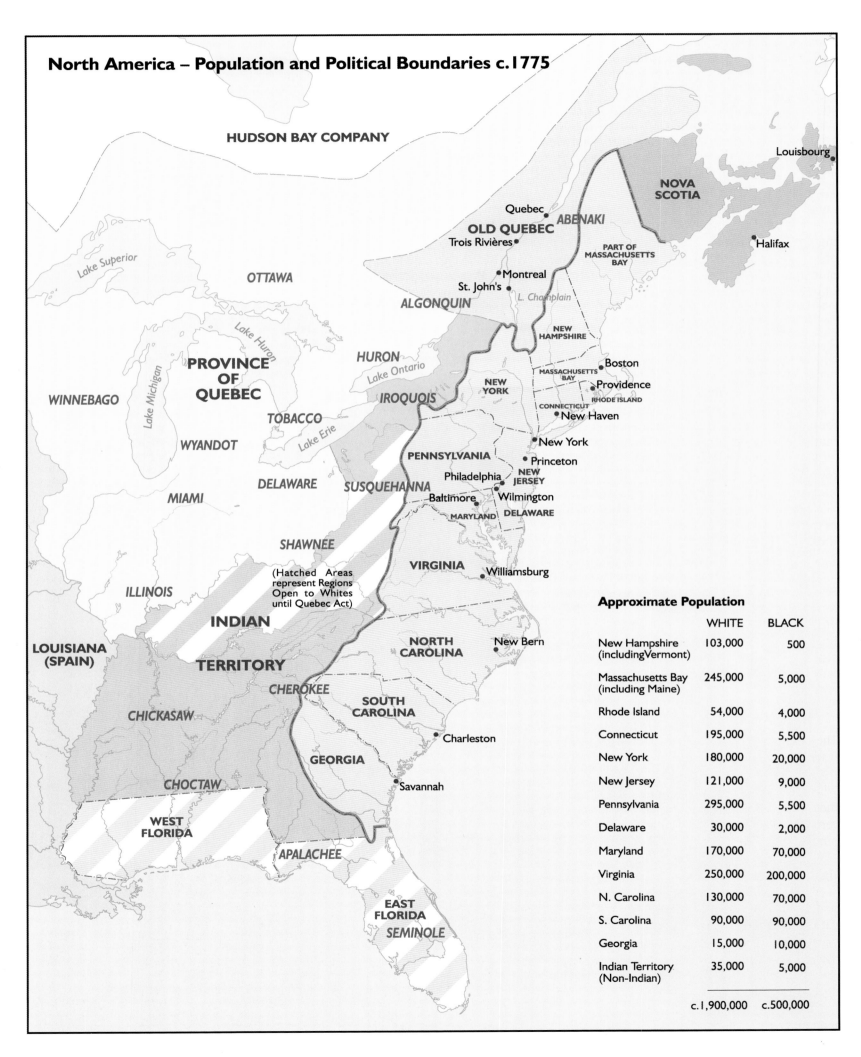

North America – Population and Political Boundaries c.1775

HUDSON BAY COMPANY

Louisbourg

NOVA SCOTIA

Quebec
ABENAKI
OLD QUEBEC
Trois Rivières
PART OF MASSACHUSETTS BAY
Halifax

Montreal
St. John's
L. Champlain
NEW HAMPSHIRE

Lake Superior

OTTAWA

ALGONQUIN

Lake Huron

HURON
Lake Ontario

PROVINCE OF QUEBEC

WINNEBAGO

Lake Michigan

IROQUOIS

NEW YORK

MASSACHUSETTS BAY
Boston
Providence
RHODE ISLAND
CONNECTICUT
New Haven

TOBACCO

Lake Erie

WYANDOT

DELAWARE

SUSQUEHANNA

PENNSYLVANIA
New York
Princeton
NEW JERSEY
Philadelphia
Baltimore
Wilmington
MARYLAND
DELAWARE

MIAMI

SHAWNEE

VIRGINIA
Williamsburg

ILLINOIS

(Hatched Areas represent Regions Open to Whites until Quebec Act)

INDIAN

LOUISIANA (SPAIN)

TERRITORY

NORTH CAROLINA
New Bern

CHEROKEE

SOUTH CAROLINA

CHICKASAW

Charleston

GEORGIA

CHOCTAW

Savannah

WEST FLORIDA

APALACHEE

EAST FLORIDA
SEMINOLE

Approximate Population

	WHITE	BLACK
New Hampshire (including Vermont)	103,000	500
Massachusetts Bay (including Maine)	245,000	5,000
Rhode Island	54,000	4,000
Connecticut	195,000	5,500
New York	180,000	20,000
New Jersey	121,000	9,000
Pennsylvania	295,000	5,500
Delaware	30,000	2,000
Maryland	170,000	70,000
Virginia	250,000	200,000
N. Carolina	130,000	70,000
S. Carolina	90,000	90,000
Georgia	15,000	10,000
Indian Territory (Non-Indian)	35,000	5,000
	c.1,900,000	c.500,000

Seminole), who were constantly being squeezed out of their ancestral homelands by the westward migration of white settlers.

Between the early 1600s and the late 1760s, some 400,000 Africans had been imported into British North America as slaves, reaching a peak of 10,000 per year by the 1750s. Of the half a million black inhabitants in 1775, the vast majority were still slaves, almost two-thirds of them living in Maryland, Virginia, and the Carolinas. In South Carolina, they formed the majority of the population; in the rest of the South it was about one-third; moving north, they formed ten percent of the population of New York (the only colony outside the South with more than 5,000 slaves), but just five percent in New England, where most free blacks lived. Paradoxically, the blacks who made most impact on the machinery of colonial society were the slaves—primarily because of the threat posed by their numbers. In the South, there had been a number of slave revolts, usually limited in geographical extent and most quickly put down. However, their legacy was a much more efficient and mobile militia than was to be found in the North, where large-scale threats to communities had receded over the previous 100 years.

Despite this volatile ethnic mixture, concerted revolts had always seemed unlikely, because the cultural differences between the Colonies, let alone the different races and nationalities, invariably resulted in a lack of consensus, whatever the subject. In fact, there was constant bickering—often violent—between neighboring Colonies, typified by the arguments over the Ohio Valley (New York and Pennsylvania) and Vermont (New Hampshire and New York). It would need something exceptional to bring such a disjointed group together; unfortunately, the King's unwitting ministers were about to provide it.

COLONIAL RULE

There has been much debate in the past two centuries as to whether a rift between Great Britain and its North American Colonies was inevitable, or whether there was a specific moment or event that made the move toward that rift irreversible. What is certain, is that those Colonies had been founded by men who had come to the New World seeking religious, political, or economic freedom—in short, the right to govern their own affairs.

Prior to the French and Indian Wars, the Colonists had enjoyed precisely this right—although it must be said that this was almost entirely by default, and had occasionally even proved to be a double-edged sword. Geographical distance and the inherent inertia of eighteenth-century government had discouraged British politicians and civil servants from taking much interest in colonial affairs (unless it put money into their pockets) and few would have both-

ered to invest the time needed—six months to a year—actually to visit the colonies. Indeed, it is not impossible that the lack of Royal and Parliamentary interference in local affairs was responsible for the good relations that did exist.

As the North American Colonies grew in size, they became increasingly self-sufficient (or usurped the powers of Parliament, depending on the observer's allegiance). However, they had done so largely from necessity, rather than devious design. For example, time and distance made them self-reliant in matters of defense, with direct British aid often limited to naval or logistic support (only in the French and Indian Wars did substantial numbers of regular troops appear); a cry for help to London might not produce a response for six months or more. As a consequence, the military organizations of the colonies became substantially different from the militia in England.

After the Treaty of Paris, in 1763, the Colonists assumed that normal service, in the form of govern-

Below: *George III (1738–1820) had succeeded his grandfather as king in 1760, at the age of twenty-two. Extremely religious, his one failing was obstinacy, and he refused to shift on the questions of the right of Parliament to tax the American Colonies, and later the acceptance of their independence. However, despite the hyperbole of the Declaration of Independence, he was no tyrant and vigorously opposed the "hawks" in his Cabinet who wanted to crush the Colonists. (National Portait Gallery)*

Above: *Frederick, Lord North (1732–92) has been portrayed as a bumbling incompetent as a result of the outcome of the War yet, like the king, he preferred conciliation to confrontation, but had to accept that an armed struggle was inevitable. Despite intense opposition, he remained prime minister until 1782. (National Portrait Gallery)*

Above right: *William Legge, 2nd Earl of Dartmouth (1731–1801) was a gentle, pious man and the stepbrother of Lord North. He became Secretary of State for the Colonies in 1772, but was replaced by Lord George Germain in November 1775. Despite holding strong views on the supremacy of Parliament, he was a friend of the Colonists. (National Portrait Gallery)*

ment by omission, would be resumed. However, Parliament saw the recent—and massive—enlargement of the Empire as a situation demanding the consolidation of political control and an overhaul of the entire administrative process. Following the shock of Pontiac's Rebellion, with the deaths of over 400 soldiers and colonists, the Proclamation Act of 1763, fixed the western boundaries of the Thirteen Colonies (thus ending the cosy fiction that each colony simply continued westward until the Pacific Ocean got in the way). The Act was enforced through the chain of forts built originally to protect the Colonists from the French; however, with the garrison commanders (much to their own discomfort) often required to double as governors of the local population, the continued presence of troops prompted some leading Colonists to resurrect the old English fear of standing armies as a threat to liberty.

TAXATION WITHOUT REPRESENTATION

Like all British colonies, those in North America existed to serve British interests. The Seven Years' War had left Great Britain with a massive national debt (over £130 million) and with 10,000 troops still in North America, needing to be paid, housed, equipped, clothed, and fed, it was still growing. The king's chief minister, George Grenville, felt it was

time to share the tax burden more evenly, and when the Colonies refused to pay even half the cost of keeping troops in North America, they were taxed in various ways. The Stamp Act, in particular, outraged the Colonists, and mobs calling themselves "Sons of Liberty" rampaged through Boston and New York, suggesting that those interested in selling stamps should choose a safer career, and tarring and feathering those who ignored such warnings.

Despite being seen as far more conservative than New England, New York led the antitax lobby, hosting the Stamp Act Congress and producing the first bloodshed of the Revolution in the bizarrely named "battle of Golden Hill" (which resulted in sore heads, but no fatalities). The extra troops sent to end this violence and enforce the acts became increasingly unpopular in New York, especially after a Quartering Act allowed them to occupy private property if barracks were unavailable (a common enough measure in England). Four regiments were sent to Boston and were immediately subjected to political intimidation; and fights between soldiers and civilians were common, especially when the soldiers offered themselves as cheap labor.

On March 5, 1770, a crowd attacked a sentry outside the Custom House; the guard was called out and, in the confusion, opened fire, killing five of the mob and wounding five more. Despite the immediate depiction of the so-called "Boston massacre" as a brutal assault on peaceable civilians, all but two of the soldiers involved were acquitted (the two "guilty" men being branded and dismissed from the service). Outside Boston, there were calls to end "mobbing" and disband the "Sons of Liberty."

Grenville (who died soon after his legislation was enacted, leaving others to pick up the pieces) was succeeded by Lord North, who was much closer to the King. North looked toward conciliation, repealing every tax, except that on tea. The ensuing lull suggested that the worst was over, but in June 1772, the Royal Navy schooner *Gaspée* was burnt by Rhode Island smugglers, and British tea—dubbed "the beverage of traitors"—was boycotted. North sought to defuse the situation (and save the failing East India Company) by reducing the tax on tea until it was cheaper than the Dutch variety being smuggled into America. However, radicals such as Boston's Samuel Adams continued to focus on the principle of Parliament's right to tax the Colonists. In December 1773, Adams and John Hancock—one of several wealthy merchants whose lucrative smuggling of foreign tea was under threat from the cheaper British product—organized the "Boston Tea Party", an event emulated in ports large and small throughout the Colonies.

The response from North's ministry included a succession of Acts of Parliament, all of them designed to punish the miscreants: they included the closure of the port of Boston, Royal control of all public appointments in Massachusetts, and the instalation of the senior Army officer, General Thomas Gage, as its new Governor; a new Quartering Act, and the Quebec Act, which extended that province southward to the Floridas, further preventing westward migration and awakening the ever-present fear of a Catholic conspiracy.

The Acts, known collectively in North America as the Intolerable, or Coercive Acts, achieved something that no natural disaster, or threat from the French and their Native American allies, ever had. They

Below: *A contemporary view of the center of Boston, showing the Old State House (center) which remained the hub of Massachusetts government until the early 1800s, and the Customs House (extreme right, with the four steps leading up to the front door). (Massachusetts Historical Society)*

Right: *A gound plan of the Boston Massacre. This was also drawn by Revere, for the trial of the soldiers, and accurately shows the soldiers hemmed against the corner of the Customs House, and the places where the five "victims" were standing when they were shot. The figure at far left, in the alleyway, was an innocent bystander, mortally wounded by a stray bullet. (Massachusetts Historical Society)*

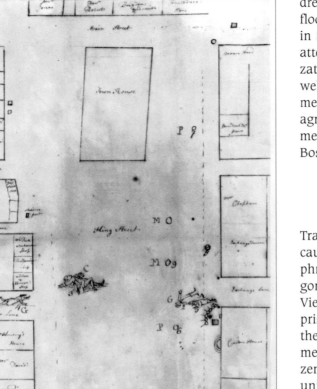

Right: *The Boston Massacre. This is the famous "cartoon" version prepared by Revere (and rumored to have been stolen by him from another artist). This was the version for distribution as propaganda in Great Britain and elsewhere in the Colonies, showing confident troops firing into an apparently harmless group of civilians. (Anne S. K. Brown)*

drew the Colonies together for the first time: aid flooded into Boston from all over North America, and in September 1774, a Congress in Philadelphia was attended by every colony except Georgia. The organization was amateurish in the extreme, and about as well controlled and attended as a typical militia drill-meeting. However, it did agree a nonimportation agreement, and threatened a nonexportation agreement as well, if the legislation closing the port of Boston was not repealed at once.

THE CAUSES OF UNREST

Traditionally, taxation is always cited as the main cause of dissatisfaction with British rule and the phrase "no taxation without representation" has gone into American folklore (although during the Vietnam War, Britons working in America were surprised to learn that they were liable to be drafted into the US armed forces, without exemption or deferment, despite enjoying none of the rights of US citizens). Almost certainly this is because taxation is universally loathed and thus presents a positive image of those who dissented, whereas some of the other factors involved make less pleasant reading. It is highly debatable whether representation in Parliament would have made any difference. Even

Left: *The Boston Massacre. This later version, despite wrongly showing the soldiers as grenadiers, gives a much more accurate idea of the troops being penned in and surrounded by an aggressive mob, some of whom cried "Fire!" and struck the soldiers' muskets with their clubs. The officer at left tries to prevent his men from firing—again an accurate depiction. (Anne S. K. Brown)*

allied to British Whigs, American MPs would probably have been outvoted.

It must also be borne in mind that few Americans ever had to pay these iniquitous taxes. The most hated—Stamp Duty—had existed in England and other parts of the Empire for years, while low rates of literacy and owner-occupancy of land, would have left only the requirement for stamps on packs of playing cards affecting the vast majority. Typically, between five and ten percent of the white, adult (over sixteen years of age) males in each colony would have paid stamp duty, or other taxes on luxury goods—virtually the same demographic group (nearer twenty percent in more egalitarian New England) allowed a vote in their local and colonial assemblies. Such people—invariably the wealthiest members of society—were, at worst, being asked to bear a tax burden equivalent to one-fiftieth of that being paid by their British cousins (it has even been suggested that the Colonists had the lowest tax burden of any white people in the world at that time) to finance less than half of the cost of keeping troops in North America to defend them.

What affected ordinary Colonists, especially as land in the original colonies became scarcer and more immigrants arrived from Europe, was the increasing restriction on westward migration into the Indian territories. For many poor people, this was the only opportunity to own their own homes and work the land for themselves, rather than for the benefit of landlords. For a few rich people—such as

Left: *Paul Revere (1735–1818) was unknown until the 1860s, when a highly romanticized account of his famous ride conveniently ignored his early capture and the more effective exploits of his companions, Dawes and Prescott. Revere was a silversmith who became the leader of the Boston "mechanics" (a contemporary name for skilled laborers) and a trusted messenger for the Massachusetts Committee of Safety. He took part in the Boston Tea Party and commanded the artillery at Penobscot Bay in 1779. (Museum of Fine Arts, Boston)*

George Washington and Israel Putnam—it put an end to lucrative land speculation in areas such as the Ohio and Tennessee valleys (that would, in any event, have effectively ended the dream of home ownership for many immigrants). The reinforcement of the 1763 Proclamation Line by the Quebec Act created even more anger on this subject, but also brought another unpleasant aspect of colonial life to the fore.

The vast majority of the Colonists, whatever their nation of origin, were generally happy as the subjects of George III, as he was a Protestant king.

However, with the capture of New France and the Floridas, the British Empire acquired a Roman Catholic dimension hitherto limited entirely to Ireland. This did not please the great and the good of North American society, who found their world bounded by Catholics to the north (Quebec), to the west (Louisiana—secretly ceded by France to Spain in 1763), and to the south (the Gulf of Mexico and the Franco-Spanish islands of the western Caribbean). For good measure, religious tolerance in Maryland meant that another pocket of Papists effectively split the colonies in half. When the Quebec Act

Right: *Samuel Adams (1722–1803) was a talented agitator who sought to provoke trouble between Great Britain and its North American Colonies, and founded the first Committee of Correspondence to coordinate opposition. (Museum of Fine Arts, Boston)*

guaranteed the laws, customs and religions of the Canadians there was outrage. In October 1774, John Jay (later envoy to Catholic Spain and one of the five peace commissioners) published a pamphlet claiming that not only would French-Canadian Catholics be armed and used to subdue and devastate the English-speaking colonies, but also that, if successful, this force would then be transported across the Atlantic to achieve the same in Great Britain. Jay acted with the approval of the First Continental Congress, which, at the same time, was seeking support from French-Canadian society for its stance over the closure of Boston's port, and inviting French-Canadians to join the fight for liberty!

Another factor influencing colonial minds at the time, was smuggling. Freed from the need to fight the French and Spanish, the Royal Navy was now in a position to crack down on this pastime, which was virtually a tradition in English—and now American—society (possibly because the taxation system focused much more on luxuries than land and income, as elsewhere in Europe). This was a major headache for merchants, such as John Hancock, of Massachusetts, and Abraham Whipple,

Left: *John Hancock (1737–93) had inherited one fortune at the age of twenty-seven, and soon made another from smuggling. A vain man, who relentlessly sought popularity, his social status was a valuable asset to radicals, such as Adams, who was constantly at his side. Despite a complete lack of military experience, he expected to be appointed commander-in-chief of the Continental Army, and was visibly upset when Washington was chosen. (Massachusetts Historical Society)*

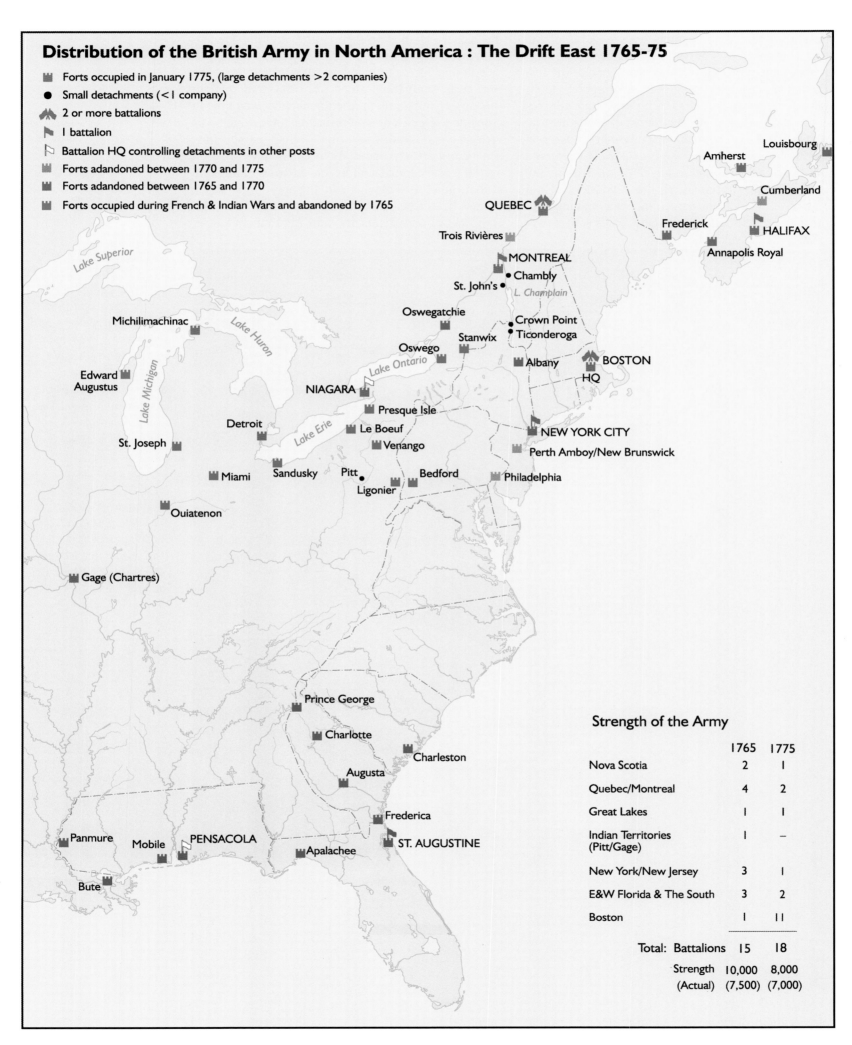

Distribution of the British Army in North America : The Drift East 1765-75

Forts occupied in January 1775, (large detachments >2 companies)

Small detachments (<1 company)

2 or more battalions

1 battalion

Battalion HQ controlling detachments in other posts

Forts adandoned between 1770 and 1775

Forts adandoned between 1765 and 1770

Forts occupied during French & Indian Wars and abandoned by 1765

Louisbourg

Amherst

Cumberland

QUEBEC

Frederick

HALIFAX

Trois Rivières

Annapolis Royal

MONTREAL

Chambly

St. John's

L. Champlain

Oswegatchie

Crown Point

Stanwix

Ticonderoga

Michilimachinac

Oswego

Lake Ontario

Albany

BOSTON

Edward Augustus

Lake Huron

HQ

Lake Superior

Lake Michigan

NIAGARA

Presque Isle

Detroit

Lake Erie

Le Boeuf

NEW YORK CITY

St. Joseph

Venango

Perth Amboy/New Brunswick

Miami

Sandusky

Pitt

Bedford

Philadelphia

Ligonier

Ouiatenon

Gage (Chartres)

Prince George

Charlotte

Charleston

Augusta

Frederica

Panmure

Mobile

PENSACOLA

Apalachee

ST. AUGUSTINE

Bute

Strength of the Army

	1765	1775
Nova Scotia	2	1
Quebec/Montreal	4	2
Great Lakes	1	1
Indian Territories (Pitt/Gage)	1	–
New York/New Jersey	3	1
E&W Florida & The South	3	2
Boston	1	11
Total: Battalions	15	18
Strength	10,000	8,000
(Actual)	(7,500)	(7,000)

of Rhode Island, much of whose wealth derived from tax evasion and illicit imports of highly sought after (and hence, highly priced) goods from outside Great Britain and its Empire.

There was also the question of slavery. Abolitionism was growing in Great Britain and also in certain Colonies in North America, particularly New England, and more than one contemporary writer commented acidly on the demands for "liberty" and "freedom" by those who owned hundreds, in some cases thousands, of slaves (white as well as black). The 1772 case of *Re: Somerset* effectively abolished slave ownership in England and Wales (in 1778, a similar case did the same in Scotland) and it is notable that very few slave-owners in the South were Loyalists, most that were having chosen that route more from dislike of their neighbors. Even before fighting broke out, there were widespread fears in the South that the British would free, or even arm the slaves, or else encourage slave uprisings.

CIVIL–MILITARY RELATIONS

The traditional view of Colonial attitudes to the Army is one of growing hatred (fully reciprocated) that contributed directly to the outbreak of hostilities. The Army is depicted as a tangible, everyday symbol of ministerial oppression, whose presence and actions rekindled the ancient Anglo-Saxon resentment of standing military forces (a view more often based on cost than on moral principle). The reality was not only more complex, but was surprisingly often at variance with this image.

While attacks—both verbal and physical—on the soldiery did provide a convenient outlet for Colonial

frustration, the Army was also a source of valuable income (and manpower) for many sections of American society. The Army brought an estimated £3 million each year into the North American economy, especially around New York and other ports of entry.

Away from major conurbations (especially Boston, where the Army threatened the power of the "mobility" and its political manipulators) soldiers and civilians generally lived together happily. Some enlisted men had skills that were scarce in rural areas; others provide much-needed labor at harvest time, or other busy periods. In fact, the quality of local life and the number of men marrying local women made it difficult to move troops away from American without a plague of desertions. By the same token, when regiments were sent home, there was no shortage of volunteers for "drafting" (a process whereby the departing regiment transferred enlisted men to its successor, so as to bring it up to full strength).

Following the conclusion of the war with France, the Army was accepted—even fêted—throughout North America. Even the clergy were heard extolling the virtues of the soldier from the pulpit. Undoubtedly, there were those in all walks of Colonial life who disliked the Army for personal reasons, genuine or petty; yet even this group was prepared to trade with the Army when it suited (Boston brick manufacturers used troops to break strikes that threatened their businesses, but then refused to sell the Army bricks to build barracks for the winter). Even the "Boston Massacre" did not create a rift that was beyond reconciliation: within months of that event—well before the truth had caught up with the propaganda—a threat of war between Great Britain

Above: *British troops arriving in Boston in 1768. The quartering of two regiments in Boston undoubtedly increased tension between the Colonists and the North ministry. (New York Public Library)*

THE NORTH BATTERY, BOSTON.

Built in 1646, on the spot now occupied by Battery Wharf, by Maj. Gen. John Leverett, afterwards Gov. of Mass.

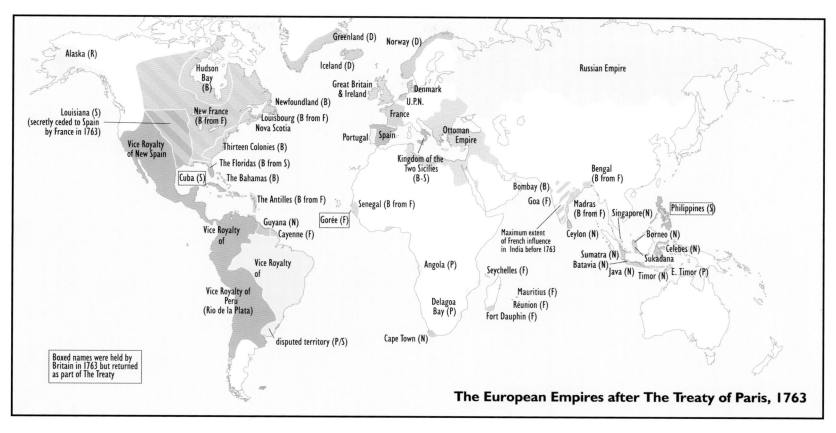

The European Empires after The Treaty of Paris, 1763

Above left: *Encampment on Boston Common. Although this shows the Common in 1768, the scene would have changed little by 1775, as the Bostonians refused to provide quarters for the troops, or materials for them to build their own. The large house belongs to John Hancock, and on the right is Beacon Hill with its signal post. (New York Public Library)*

Left: *The North Battery. An engraving by Paul Revere, showing part of the defenses of Boston harbor. (Massachusetts Historical Society)*

and Spain over the Falkland Islands saw hundreds of Americans offering to serve in Provincial units, and even enlisting as Regulars (one regiment recruited over fifty men in a month). Regiments leaving New Jersey for Ireland in the early 1770s were given tearful sendoffs and the officers presented with ornate gifts by the local community.

Friction, however, arose in the mid-1760s, as the Army's role shifted visibly from defending frontier settlements against the Indians, to defending the latter by policing the Proclamation Line. In frontier areas, this problem was exacerbated by the *de facto* authority exercised—usually with reluctance—by regimental officers, in the absence of any recognizable civilian government (a grievance removed, ironically, by the need to send the troops back east to perform the type of policing role that made the Army so unpopular in Great Britain and Ireland).

THE WORLD OF COMMERCE

Underlying all of the above was the role of international trade in the eighteenth century. Even before the evolution of the nation state, the capacity to trade—including moving goods (especially by sea, to maximize the number of accessible markets) and protecting them in transit—had been a major determinant of status and power. As power blocs evolved across Europe and made it increasingly difficult for states to extend their metropolitan borders permanently, so overseas expansion became the main route to economic and political growth, and the merchant fleets and their military escorts a projection of a nation's power.

Commercially, empires provided the mother country with vital, and occasionally rare, raw materials (as well as denying them to rivals), and with captive markets for its own goods. This was far more valuable than the potential for population growth (desirable as that might be for military purposes), or the mere occupation of territory—"coloring the map red" as it were. In wartime, the most costly and elaborate plans would be entertained if they were designed to rob an enemy of a colony that produced particularly valuable resources, while the ensuing peace negotiations might witness vast tracts of uninhabited (and thus uncultivated) land offered for the return of a valuable spice island, or a sheltered harbor on one of the major shipping routes.

By 1775, the possession of a large—and very successful—trading empire had made Great Britain the most powerful nation in the world, with its diplomats the favored guests of royal palaces and courts around the globe. Much of this success had been achieved at the expense of France and Spain—the two colonial superpowers of the day and Great Britain's main commercial rivals. Defeat in a succession of dynastic wars throughout the eighteenth century, and humiliation in the most recent, the Seven Years' War, left both nations burning for revenge. The revolt of Great Britain's North American Colonies offered them precisely the opportunity they sought and their involvement—at first covert, then later as cobelligerents—would ensure that the struggle spread to other theaters. Indeed, it can be argued that not only was the American Revolutionary War a global conflict in its own right, it was virtually a continuation of the Seven Years' War—itself often described as "the first world war."

Boston, 1775: Washington surveys the lines. (MARS)

THE COMMANDERS

The military outcome of the American Revolutionary War was determined by the acts and decisions of a small number of men from Great Britain, her North American Colonies, France, Spain, and the various minor German states. A quick glance at the careers and characters of the most prominent of these men shows that virtually all of them were regarded—at least within their own communities—as "gentlemen." It was this attribute, rather than any inherent, or acquired, military skill, that usually determined whether or not a man could become an army officer during the *ancien régime* (naval officers had similar social requirements, but were normally expected to acquire technical skills before they could be commissioned). Any promotion beyond the regiment (or the ship), would depend on "interest" or political patronage—sometimes allied to merit, sometimes irrespective of it. Today, this seems barely credible, but it made some sense in a world in which the military academy—and professional training generally—was still the exception rather than the rule.

Gentlemen were generally better educated and were used to giving orders. They also understood the concept of honor and how essential it was to being accepted both by their peers, and by those whom they would lead into battle (it was also linked to the concept of *noblesse oblige*—power begetting responsibility). Activities such as hunting taught them fieldcraft, horsemanship, weapons handling (especially firearms, which were very expensive), and a vital "eye for ground." Nor should the notion of heredity be dismissed out of hand, as it contributed to the physical strength and mental facility required for active service.

Their social upbringing also allowed them to fit into a military hierarchy, while maintaining social equality and fraternal familiarity. Almost all senior military officers in Europe and North America were Masons—interestingly, it was rumored that Arnold, alone of all the Continental Army's major generals, was not.

Such professional camaraderie was important, as the military world of the eighteenth century was very small and many career paths crossed—some more than once. Gates, for example, had begun his career serving alongside Germain (and Wolfe), and later joined Burgoyne during the Jacobite Rebellion: interestingly, both Burgoyne and Gates were also rumored to be the illegitimate sons of noblemen. Washington, Lee, and Gates had all been with Braddock at Monongahela, Lee and Gates both being wounded. During the Seven Years' War, both Clinton and Von Riedesel were aides-de-camp to the Duke of Brunswick, while Lee fought under Burgoyne in Portugal, and Carleton and Sir William Howe were battalion commanders at Quebec. Some senior Hessian officers had served with the British Army in 1745, and between 1759 and 1763.

Links with royal households and the civil power, via governorships and other public offices, also made the armed forces more reliable politically. The Howe brothers were reputed to have blood links to George III, while Carleton, Clinton, and Cornwallis were all former Foot Guards officers. D'Estaing and La Fayette both began their military careers in the famous *Mousquetaires*. In more authoritarian nations, senior officers often doubled as government ministers; in Great Britain, they were often Members of Parliament. This created a vested interest in the status quo that made a *coup d'état* less likely.

Men from other social strata did become officers—indeed, it was far more common than is generally supposed. However, it was rare for them to progress very far, as they were usually already advanced in years and seldom possessed the finance or patronage to gain promotion. While there were notable exceptions in all armies, senior rank tended to be the preserve of the well connected, often involving service in regiments associated with the royal household. Equally, every service had its contingent of foreign officers, some of whom joined as individuals (usually with the consent of their own government and often bringing valuable experience), while others were recruited into special units, often made up largely or entirely of their fellow-countrymen.

THE CONTINENTALS

General George Washington (1732–99), descended from a seventeenth-century English settler, was the only officer on either side to hold a senior command throughout the War. His appointment as commander-in-chief is usually ascribed to the political imperative of involving the Southern colonies, but few other candidates had a comparable military résumé. After his victory at Great Meadows and subsequent surrender at Fort Necessity had sparked off the French and Indian Wars, he served as aide-de-camp to Braddock at Monongahela and, at twenty-

three, took command of the Virginia militia. He later served under Bouquet and Forbes, and was the only native-born American to have commanded above regimental level prior to 1775.

Limited, but increasingly radical, involvement in politics led him to become a delegate at both Continental Congresses. He made little impact, but did advocate urgent preparation for a military struggle that—unlike many contemporaries—he saw as inevitable. He also understood the weaknesses of the militia and the consequent necessity of a standing army, although he was no tactician. In six years he won no major battles and suffered unnecessary

defeats; even successes such as Trenton tend to illustrate motivational skill rather than military capability. What he did understand were the limitations of the Continental Army and the need to avoid major actions until it was capable of opposing the Regulars on equal terms, and this was his real value to his cause.

He was brave on the battlefield and not afraid to delegate command (although he was luckier than his opponents in being able to choose, or at least recommend, his preferred candidates). He was also a capable administrator who reorganized an army under the nose of his enemy more than once. The respect accorded to him by all ranks allowed him to mold contingents from colonies with a history of rivalry into a homogeneous fighting force and it is a testament to his integrity that an often antimilitary Congress felt able to delegate executive power to him on several occasions. He dealt skilfully with various mutinies, the Conway Cabal, and the Newburgh Addresses, and maintained good relations with his former enemies, the French. After the war, he retired briefly from public life, but served two terms as president (and declined a certain third); ironically, his last military duty was to resume his role as commander-in-chief in anticipation of war with France, in 1798.

Major General Nathaniel Greene (1742–86) was born into a Quaker community in Rhode Island, where his family had an iron foundry. He served as a deputy to the colony's General Assembly and, in 1774, helped to establish a militia company (which he was forced, due to an infirmity, to join as a private). When fighting broke out, he was a surprise choice to command the Rhode Island militia brigade and, at thirty-three, was the youngest of the first batch of brigadier generals appointed to the Continental Army. Promoted to major general in August 1776, he missed the New York campaign through illness, but returned in time to serve at Trenton.

Early in 1777, he appeared before Congress, on Washington's behalf, to answer complaints about the army, then commanded a division at Brandywine and Germantown. In 1778, he was at Monmouth and Newport. In October 1780, he replaced Gates in the South and, within a year, had achieved a major strategic success without winning a single tactical victory. Deploying militia to protect his scarce Continentals, and making full use of partisan corps and irregulars, he showed a complete understanding of the forces at his disposal and, by the end of the War, had a reputation second only to that of Washington.

Greene's abilities included a talent for logistics; as an able (if reluctant) Quartermaster General, he improved the transport and depot systems. However, many in Congress felt that he had too much influence over Washington and were upset when he challenged De Coudray's promotion. In 1780, he had to resign as Quartermaster General—and only narrowly escaped expulsion from the army. His predecessor, Mifflin, alleged financial irregularities and incompetence, and Greene's sensitivity to criticism prompted debate over his monetary dealings. He could also be hasty and overconfident (for example, advising Washington to hold the forts on the Hudson, in 1776). He was one of those who supported the war effort financially, as well as physically, and his losses forced him to resettle near Savannah on land confiscated from Loyalists.

Major General Charles Lee (1731–82) was educated in England and Switzerland, before entering the Army in 1747. He fought under Braddock and then in the Mohawk Valley (where he was adopted by the Mohawks and married a Seneca), before being wounded at Ticonderoga and serving at Fort Niagara and Montreal. In 1761, he served in Portugal under Burgoyne and became a colonel in the Portuguese army after his success at Villa Velha, before retiring as a disgruntled halfpay major at the end of the Seven Years War.

From 1765, he was an aide to the King of Poland and observed the Russo-Turkish conflict, before coming to America in 1773. His military career, and numerous publications in support of the Whigs, ingratiated him with Congress, which appointed him third-in-command, after Washington (whom he regarded as a talentless amateur) and Ward. After providing useful advice on the investment of Boston, he organized the defenses of Rhode Island, New York City and, as commander of the Southern Department, Charleston. Returning to New York, he advised against holding the Hudson forts, but his failure to come to Washington's aid in the retreat into New Jersey raised suspicions of jealousy and ambition. Captured in December 1776, he spent eighteen months as a prisoner, during which he secretly pre-

Below: *Nathaniel Greene. (Independence National Historical Park)*

sented Howe with a plan to end the war, which was ignored (and probably unworkable).

After his exchange, he led the vanguard at Monmouth Court House. When he failed to press home an attack that he—and others—had consistently opposed, Washington replaced him on the spot. (In fairness, Lee had always believed in the superiority of citizen militia over paid regulars and was probably unaware of how the Continentals had improved in his absence.) Infuriated by this public humiliation, Lee demanded a court-martial, which found him guilty and suspended him from command for one year. Hearing a rumor that he was to be dismissed, he wrote Congress such an offensive letter that it was forced to do just that.

Lee was a well-educated and intelligent, but solitary and eccentric man, whose appearance, sharp tongue, and unpleasant personal habits—as well as an annoying habit of eventually being proved right—guaranteed him enemies (his behavior in 1778 provoked one duel and almost led to two others). His military experience led others to tolerate these shortcomings, but eventually his vanity and personal ambition caused his downfall.

Major General John Sullivan (1740-1795) was a native of New Hampshire and trained as a lawyer before becoming heavily involved in the political life of the colony and a major in the militia. Prior to the outbreak of hostilities, he was an active Whig and helped to organise and lead the raid on Fort William and Mary, Portsmouth, in December 1774. He then served at the second Continental Congress and was subsequently appointed a brigadier general on the creation of the Continental Army.

In 1776, he led the relief column into Canada and took command on the death of Thomas, but was replaced by Gates after the disastrous retreat to Crown Point. He received another command at New York, but was superceded again, this time by Putnam. Captured at Brooklyn, he was released to take a message to Congress from the Howes that instigated the peace talks of September 1776. He fought in the New Jersey and Pennsylvania campaigns and was investigated—but cleared—by Congress over a failed attack on Staten Island and alleged misconduct at Brandywine.

Like Greene and Knox, Sullivan threatened to resign over the promotion of De Coudray and may also have been involved in the Conway Cabal. Chosen for the Rhode Island command by default, he failed to work closely with the French, but political connections allowed him to survive and command the expedition against the Iroquois, in 1779. As a result of illness brought on by the expedition, he resigned his commission and entered Congress. He chaired the committee of enquiry into the mutiny of January 1781, and later became governor of New Hampshire and a federal court judge.

The length of Sullivan's military career is surprising, given that he seems to have achieved so little of any note and there is more than a suggestion that this longevity owed much to political influence (though Washington appears to have thought highly of him). Undoubtedly brave, and a good organiser, Sullivan courted popularity among officers and men and was rather too easily impressed by flattery. He was also guilty of over-confidence, yet would quickly fall into despair in times of adversity.

Major General Philip Schuyler (1733–1804) was born into a distinguished Dutch *patron* family. In the French and Indian Wars, he fought at Lake George, but discovered an aptitude for logistics. In 1757, he established depots at Fort Edward and Fort Ann, and organized a supply line to Fort Oswego, before resigning his commission and earning a substantial income supplying provisions. In 1758, he returned to service as a major and deputy commissary, and saw action at Fort Ticonderoga and Fort Frontenac.

After the Peace of Paris, he inherited large estates along the Mohawk and the Hudson. In 1768, he was elected to the New York Assembly, where he was equally vociferous in opposing government policy and mob violence. When Congress needed to appoint a major general from New York, Schuyler was chosen to command the Northern Department and the invasion of Canada. However, his insistence on discipline

Below: *John Sullivan. (Independence National Historical Park)*

and proper preparation made him enemies among the "liberal" New Englanders, and delayed the start of the campaign. Before he could advance, an attack of gout forced him to hand command to Montgomery, and he remained in Albany to organize supplies and build the Lake Champlain fleet.

In January 1777, the New England lobby in Congress found an excuse to replace him with Gates. Typically, Schuyler saw this as an attack on his integrity; although he won the first round, perceived indecisiveness in defending Fort Ticonderoga led to his removal and he had to wait until October 1778 for a court-martial to acquit him of incompetence. He then resigned and spent the rest of the War handling Indian and administrative affairs, and improving cooperation with the French. After the war he participated in public life until 1798.

Schuyler understood better than anyone, on either side, the need for reliable logistics in the northern wilderness. His tactical abilities were never properly tested, yet he displayed talent as a strategist; the supply system he created in the Northern Department, and the "scorched earth" policy used to delay Burgoyne, provided the foundations for the victory at Saratoga. Although his stern, patrician

Left: *Philip Schuyler. (Metropolitan Museum of New York)*

Right: *Horatio Gates. (Independence National Historical Park)*

manner was widely disliked, he was a man of integrity and never shirked a task, if he believed it necessary and an appropriate one for a gentleman.

Major General Horatio Gates (1727–1806) was the son of a housekeeper and godson of Horace Walpole. He joined the 20th Foot in 1744, serving alongside Germain and Wolfe, and then transferred into a regiment raised for the Jacobite Rebellion whose mess included one John Burgoyne. Gates served in Canada, before buying the captaincy of an Independent Company in 1754, and later fought at Monongahela, Fort Herkimer, and Martinique, before retiring as a halfpay major.

Settling in Virginia, Gates impressed Washington, who made him adjutant general in 1775. In 1776, as a major general, he went to the Northern Department, before returning for the New Jersey campaign. Early in 1777, he was sent to command Fort Ticonderoga, but when the appointment was rescinded, Gates made such an exhibition of himself in front of Congress that he almost ended his career. However, he eventually replaced Schuyler for good and with victory at Saratoga coinciding with defeats in Pennsylvania, he provided a perfect figurehead for the Conway Cabal, becoming president of the Board of War, as a preliminary to replacing Washington as commander-in-chief.

The year 1780 was not his best: in addition to the disaster at Camden, his son died and he retired to his estates to await an inquiry. Strangely, he was cleared of any misconduct in 1782 and returned to active service; he became involved in the Newburgh Addresses, but ended up supporting Washington. Widowed in 1784, he remarried in 1786, freed his slaves, and moved to New York. He served briefly in the legislature and used his wife's money to help veterans.

Like Schuyler, Gates was better at running an army than leading it into battle and Camden suggests that his "do nothing" approach at Saratoga was luck, rather than good judgment. Much of the subsequent criticism, however, was undoubtedly manufactured by Schuyler's supporters in revenge for attacks on the latter by the New Englanders (who later supported Gates). Yet the suggestion that Gates was motivated by hatred of the British class system is totally unsubstantiated, nor was he snubbed by fellow officers, or overlooked for promotion in British service. Rather than being overly ambitious, he seems to have been susceptible to flattery and allowed himself to be used by the Conway and Newburgh cliques.

Below: *Benedict Arnold. (Frick Art Reference Library)*

Major General Benedict Arnold (1741–1801) was born in Connecticut. At fifteen, he ran off to fight in the French and Indian Wars, but a year later was posted as a deserter; he re-enlisted, only to desert again in order to complete an apprenticeship to a druggist. By 1775, he was a prosperous merchant and captain of Connecticut militia, and marched his men to Cambridge on hearing the news of Lexington. He convinced the authorities to let him lead the planned attack on Fort Ticonderoga, but Ethan Allen refused to accept him. A successful attack on St. John's was followed by an argument over seniority and charges of financial irregularities—a sequence of events that would become all too familiar.

Recognizing his skills, Washington chose him to lead part of the force invading Canada, but Arnold underestimated the distance and the terrain. Barely half his force reached Quebec and during the attack on the city, he was wounded in the leg. After convalescing, he took command of the Lake Champlain fleet (amid more quarrels with fellow officers) and despite losing at Valcour Island, stopped Carleton reaching Ticonderoga and Albany before winter.

Embittered at subordinates being promoted over him, he resigned in July 1777. Washington persuaded him to accept a post in the Northern Army, but he later clashed with Gates, who relieved him of command. During the year he spent convalescing from the wounds incurred at Saratoga, Arnold became military governor of Philadelphia, where he married the daughter of a prominent Loyalist. But once again he was accused of financial irregularities and this possibly decided him to make contact with the British.

Even under British colors, he was never trusted completely and met considerable public disdain when he came to England. After the War, he turned to privateering, then commerce, and even moved to Canada to start afresh. Nevertheless, he died deep in debt, leaving his wife to raise their four sons (all of whom joined the Army).

Arnold was a complex man: brave and resourceful on the battlefield, jealous, avaricious, and insecure away from it. It is difficult to know for certain, but his treachery was probably prompted by a combination of greed, pique at being overlooked for promotion, and genuine disaffection with the aims of the War.

THE ALLIES

Major General Marie Joseph Paul Yves Roch Gilbert du Motier, Marquis de La Fayette (1757–1834) was the son of a French officer killed at Minden. At thirteen, he was orphaned, inherited enormous wealth and estates and entered the army. At sixteen, he married into the influential De Noailles family and the following year (with their encouragement) began to take a deep, if somewhat romanticized interest in the political and military

conflict in America. Through the Comte de Broglie and "Baron" De Kalb, he made contact with Silas Deane, who agreed to recommend that Congress make both La Fayette and de Kalb major generals.

La Fayette was nineteen, spoke little English and had no military experience; Congress welcomed him coolly and he received his appointment, but no command. Fortunately, Washington took a liking to him and, at Brandywine, he received a wound that raised his standing. He supported Washington during the Conway Cabal. Chosen to lead the aborted invasion of Canada, he rejoined the Main Army in time to serve at Monmouth and Newport (attempting—with little success—to repair Franco-American relations).

In January 1779, he returned to France and after lobbying vigorously, but unsuccessfully, for various projects, did succeed in having a corps sent to serve under Washington (although he failed to secure command of it and Rochambeau subsequently kept him at arm's length). In 1780, he went back to America and took command of the Continental troops in Virginia. Eluding Cornwallis (who referred to him disparagingly as "the boy") through the summer of 1781, he led the light infantry division at Yorktown and then returned home. He was assembling a Franco-Spanish army to invade England when the War ended.

Initially, La Fayette was motivated by a search for glory, boredom, and hatred of the English, only later espousing the ideology of the War. Nevertheless, his

Above: *The Marquis de La Fayette. (Independence National Historical Park)*

Above left: *Comte D'Estaing. (Anne S. K. Brown Military Collection)*

Above right: *Comte de Rochambeau. (Independence National Historical Park)*

financial contribution was considerable: he declined his salary and spent $200,000 of his own money, although Congress did award him 11,000 acres in Louisiana in 1803. He revisited North America in 1824, attracting—and greatly enjoying the adulation of—huge crowds wherever he went.

Admiral Charles-Henri-Théodat, Comte D'Estaing (1729–94) was born in Auvergne, into one of the leading noble families of France. Entering the army, he became a colonel at sixteen and a brigadier general at twenty-seven, but transferred to the navy during the French and Indian Wars. He served with some distinction in the East Indies and Europe, and was captured twice, as a result of which he was imprisoned for allegedly breaching his first parole and developed a near-pathological hatred of the English. After the Peace of Paris, he was appointed governor of Sainte Domingue and the Leeward Islands.

Although the navy had no great opinion of his abilities, he was appointed vice-admiral and in April 1778, left Toulon for North America. He arrived too late to trap the British forces in the Chesapeake, and a planned attack on New York also came to nothing. He then joined Sullivan at Newport, but damage to his ships from shore batteries, an enemy fleet, and a hurricane, persuaded him to withdraw to Boston. This effectively ended the siege, causing considerable rancor between the allies; however, his presence contributed to Clinton's decision to abandon Philadelphia.

After capturing several islands in the Caribbean, D'Estaing attempted to restore confidence in the alliance by threatening Georgia and South Carolina.

Unfortunately, sloth and overconfidence allowed the British to fortify Savannah and the subsequent siege failed, with heavy casualties, D'Estaing himself being wounded. Despite abandoning his forces to their fate, he returned to France a hero and supported La Fayette's call to send a corps to North America. In 1782, the fleet D'Estaing was assembling for American service was instrumental in persuading the British to sue for peace. After the War, he was granted United States citizenship and 20,000 acres in Georgia, but was guillotined in 1794, having tried to court favor with both sides during the French Revolution.

D'Estaing appears to have been the stereotypical eighteenth-century French nobleman, whose arrogance and callousness made him unpopular with his allies—yet he possessed considerable intellect, composing poetry and writing plays. He was extremely ambitious and did not shun hard work, but does not seem to have been particularly competent, or lucky.

Lieutenant General Jean Baptiste Donatien de Vimeur, Comte de Rochambeau (1725–1807) was born at Vendôme and, as a third son, was destined for a career in the Catholic Church, when his older brother died. He joined the army in 1740, serving in a cavalry regiment and fighting in Bohemia, Bavaria, and the Rhineland. He was promoted to colonel at the age of twenty-two and a year later was aide-decamp to the Duc d'Orléans. In 1749, he became governor of Vendôme and, during the Seven Years' War, fought at Minorca and in Germany. Now commanding an infantry regiment, he was commended for his skill and bravery in the action at Clostercamp, during which he was wounded several times. In 1761, he was appointed Inspector General of Cavalry, and worked hard to improve both tactics and the welfare of the ordinary soldier.

In 1776, he was made governor of Villefranche-en-Roussillon and, in 1778, he took part in the famous exercises of the army assembled to invade England, in the course of which he illustrated the superiority of linear tactics and firepower over the more traditional column formations. As a result of this performance, in 1780 he was asked to command the corps earmarked for North America. With no knowledge of either the English language or North America, Rochambeau had to overcome his hosts' traditional dislike of Frenchmen and repair the damage caused by his predecessor D'Estaing. He also had to curb the overenthusiastic Marquis de La Fayette and deal with the problems caused by the administrative failures that left over 3,000 of his 8,000-strong command stranded in France.

Rochambeau was happy to serve under Washington, and his cooperation in moving his force to the Hudson, and then south into Virginia, made the victory at Yorktown possible. Unsurprisingly, he served as a politician during the French Revolution, and later became a marshal of France. Unlike many other officers who served in North America, he escaped the guillotine—though only as a result of Robespierre's death.

His administrative skill and hard work, together with his tact and courtesy (especially having seen at first hand the state of the Continental Army), improved the Franco-American alliance at a time when it could easily have fallen apart, after the disasters at Newport and Savannah.

Rear Admiral François Joseph Paul, Comte de Grasse (1722–88) was born in the family castle, in Provence, and attended the naval school at Toulon, before becoming a page to the Grand Master of the Knights of Saint John, at Malta. In 1740, he returned to France and was wounded and captured in the action off Cape Finisterre in 1747. For three months, he was a prisoner in England, where he learned much about the Royal Navy and made many friends. During the Seven Years' War, he served in Canada and the Caribbean, and afterwards against the Barbary pirates, before taking command of the marine brigade at St. Malo, in 1773.

In 1778, he was promoted to commodore, commanded a division at Ushant, and later served at Savannah and Martinique, assuming command in the West Indies when D'Estaing went back to France. However, ill-health forced De Grasse to hand over to De Guichen and return home himself. Despite attempts to persuade the King to let him retire, he was promoted to rear admiral and sent back to the Caribbean with full discretion to support France's allies as he saw fit (reflecting the high esteem in which he was held). After the indecisive action off Martinique against Hood, he

Above: *Comte de Grasse. (National Maritime Museum)*

berated his captains for failing to obey his orders. Unfortunately, influence at court counted more than seniority in the French navy and he would regret this lecture. After further minor actions, he sailed north in August and sealed the fate of Cornwallis by forcing Graves's fleet away from Yorktown. Returning to the Caribbean, he was captured at The Saints, in April 1782, on his way to attack Jamaica. Further captivity in England resulted in his becoming an intermediary in the peace negotiations.

In 1784, he stood trial for The Saints defeat and, despite being acquitted, was banished to his estate at Tilly. His family was forced to flee to the United States when his château (including Yorktown memorabilia) was destroyed by Revolutionary mobs. Standing over six feet tall, handsome, intelligent, and hot-tempered, De Grasse was a brave and talented man whose achievements were ignored by France—though not by the United States—for the next 150 years.

Pierre André de Suffren de Saint-Tropez (1729–88) was a native of Provence who joined the Navy in October 1743, seeing action at Toulon, in the

West Indies, and at Cape Breton, before being captured by the British in 1747. After brief service in the galleys of the Order of Malta, he was present at the siege of Minorca, in 1757, before being captured again by the British, this time in neutral waters off Lagos. He then fought the Barbary pirates before re-entering the service of the Order of Malta in 1767, becoming a Commander of the Order in 1771. Returning to French service, he was involved in the revitalization of the French Navy.

When France entered the War, he served under D'Estaing at Newport and Grenada; despite openly criticizing his commander, D'Estaing recommended Suffren for promotion. On his way to reinforce the Dutch at the Cape of Good Hope, Suffren attacked a British squadron in neutral waters off the Cape Verde Islands (no doubt recalling his own experience at Lagos), thereby serving notice that he was not in the same mold as other French admirals. After saving Cape Colony, he sailed on to India where he won a series of four actions against Sir Edward Hughes and was preparing a new offensive when news arrived of the Treaty of Paris.

A superb strategist, he won respect for the French Navy by disdaining the negative, defensive tactics of his colleagues. Unfortunately, he was not such a brilliant tactician and while he was undoubtedly let down by a poor set of captains and a shortage of trained crews, he expected too much of them and did not have the ability to improve their performance. During his return journey home, he was fêted at every port of call (not least by his opponents) and a special vice-admiral's post was created for him. He died in 1788, on his way to take command of the fleet at Brest; ostensibly, his demise resulted from a notoriously overindulgent diet and stress brought on by violent fits of temper, but rumors circulated that he had been killed in a duel.

Bernardo de Galvez (1746–86) was born into a distinguished and influential family and attended the military college at Avila, before serving in Portugal and Algiers during the Seven Years' War. Posted to New Spain, he distinguished himself in action against the Apaches, and in diplomacy with other tribes. These successes and his family connections won him the command of the Louisiana garrison in 1776, and he became acting governor in January 1777.

Prior to 1779, he did everything within his power to assist the Rebels, allowing them the freedom of New Orleans and seizing ships and cargoes from British merchants trading illegally with Spanish colonists along the Mississippi. He also organized large loans and stockpiled shipments of arms from Spain. He almost overreached himself by granting sanctuary to Rebels who had raided West Florida and authorizing the sale of their plunder at public auctions, but his diplomatic skills averted the worst of British wrath. Given prior notice, by his uncle, of Spain's entry into the war, De Galvez was able to attack the Floridas before the British were ready, cleverly augmenting his few Regular troops with black volunteers, local militia, and friendly Chocktaws. Although delayed briefly by a hurricane, he quickly seized the British forts at Manchac, Baton Rouge, and Natchez, before taking Mobile the following year.

The capture of Pensacola, in 1781, saw him ennobled, promoted to lieutenant general, and made governor of Florida. His performance, from the moment he opened the siege by taking control of the Spanish flagship from its timid commander, through his honorable treatment of prisoners and his personal bravery (he was twice wounded leading attacks) covered the spectrum of military virtues. Had the planned invasion of Jamaica not been thwarted by the presence of the Royal Navy, his name might be more widely known in military circles.

Contrary to the popular image of Spanish colonial rulers, De Galvez was an efficient and popular civil administrator. As governor of Louisiana and, later, Viceroy of New Spain (where he succeeded his father), he improved relations with the Indians, modernized infrastructure and military defenses, and (learning from events elsewhere) liberalized trading laws. He married into the Creole community, before returning briefly to Spain and advising King Carlos III on colonial matters. He was subsequently appointed Captain-General of Cuba and supreme commander of Spanish forces in the Americas, before succeeding his father as Viceroy of New Spain.

THE BRITISH

Admiral Richard Howe (1726–99) went to sea at fourteen, in Anson's ill-fated voyage around the world. He served in the Caribbean until 1744, then in British waters during the Jacobite Rebellion, being severely wounded in an action off the Scottish coast. In 1755, he sailed to North America, where his ship fired the first naval shots of the Seven Years' War. He later served at Rochefort, and commanded the amphibious expeditions against St Malo and Cherbourg, during which he formed an unfavorable opinion of Germain. In 1759, his ship was first into action at Quiberon Bay. After the Peace of Paris, he became Treasurer of the Navy and—astonishingly for the time—refused to profit from it.

In 1776, he took command of the naval forces in North America, with power to negotiate with the enemy. He provided good support to the Army in the New York and Philadelphia campaigns, but resigned in 1778 after disagreements with the government (though he stayed long enough to thwart the French attacks on New York and Newport). His performance as Treasurer of the Navy suggests that the allegations that he and his brother prolonged the war for their own gain were just political mischief.

The change of government in 1782 saw him recalled and he also entered the House of Lords, having been MP for Dartmouth since 1757. The relief of Gibraltar earned him widespread acclaim (not least from his enemies and casual observers, such as Frederick the Great). In 1783, he became First Lord of the Admiralty and handled the post-war demobilization. His subsequent service included the Glorious First of June (for which he received the Order of the Garter) and the sensitive handling of the Spithead mutiny. He eventually became Admiral of the Fleet and General of Marines.

Best described as being abreast of his age, rather than ahead of it, Howe was a competent tactician and highly regarded by contemporaries and successors, including Nelson, especially for his work on signaling. Tall, dark, and taciturn, "Black Dick" had a shy, awkward manner. He appeared generous to friends, haughty and morose to his enemies. Like his brothers, he enjoyed a good relationship with the lower ranks (who, in turn, enjoyed his grim eccentricities), and his sensitive handling of the Spithead mutiny, in 1797, typified his approach.

Admiral George Brydges Rodney (1719–92) entered the Royal Navy at thirteen. He was commended for gallantry off Ushant, in 1747, and became governor of Newfoundland two years later. During the Seven Years' War, he served at Louisburg and later destroyed stores and invasion barges in several French ports. In October 1761, he took command of the Leeward Islands and after the Peace of Paris, returned to England as a vice-admiral. He was created a baronet in 1764, and the following year became governor of Greenwich Hospital.

Unfortunately, his political career (he was elected to Parliament in 1751, 1761, and 1768) and lifestyle were financially ruinous. After failing to secure the governorship of Jamaica, in 1775 he fled to France to escape creditors, but further extravagance forced him to borrow heavily, creating suspicion that he was offered a command by the French. However, confirmation of a promotion and receipt of several years' back pay helped him to discharge his debts, although his enmity with Lord Sandwich meant that he did not receive a command until the end of 1779.

He showed aggression in the moonlit battle off Cape St. Vincent, but soon gave evidence of another side to his character, blaming his captains for De Guichen's escape (the ill-judged "pursuit" to New York generating only a row with Arbuthnot over seniority and prize money). His obsession with the rewards of St. Eustatius probably prevented him concentrating his forces to keep De Grasse away from North America. After several months' leave, he returned as a vice-admiral, but his incomplete victory at The Saints was criticized and, based on his previous performance, a replacement had already been sent. Out of embarrassment, the government awarded him a barony and a pension, and ended the inquiry into the St. Eustatius affair. His finances secure, but his health failing, he retired to the country.

Rodney was a man of delicate appearance and bad health, made worse by financial pressures. This in turn made him greedy and selfish in his quest for prize money and he was unscrupulous in claiming credit from others and blaming them for his own errors. Yet he was also brave and talented, and was popular with the public. As such, he has been described as the com-

Above left: *Richard, Lord Howe. (National Maritime Museum)*

Above right: *George Brydges Rodney. (National Maritime Museum)*

plete eighteenth-century English aristocrat—arrogant and avaricious, yet spirited and adept.

Lieutenant General Sir William Howe (1729–1814) entered the Army in 1746, served in the 20th Foot with Wolfe, and commanded a regiment at Louisburg. He commanded the light infantry at Quebec, and later fought at Montreal, Belle Isle, and Havana (where he was adjutant general). In 1758, he succeeded his brother George as member of parliament for Nottingham and in 1768, became governor of the Isle of Wight. In 1772, he was promoted major general and two years later took charge of training the Army's reconstituted light infantry companies.

As a Whig, Howe opposed government policy toward the Colonies and stated he would not serve against them, but later accepted a command on the basis that he could not, in all conscience, refuse his country's call. Although often criticized, he chose the correct tactics at Bunker Hill; given the effect of that day on his later campaigns, it is worth considering how much more decisive he might have been subsequently had that first attack succeeded. His failure to destroy Washington's army in New York and Pennsylvania raised questions as to his loyalty and

motives. Having already tendered his resignation due to the government's refusal to send him more troops, he found himself being blamed for Burgoyne's defeat and returned to England to defend himself.

In Parliament, he suffered the wrath of Germain who was defending himself against attacks over Burgoyne's defeat. A pamphlet war and a Parliamentary inquiry both petered out, but left Howe the victim of a whispering campaign. Nevertheless, in 1782, he became Lieutenant General of the Ordnance and later held various commands during the French Revolution.

Howe's hesitancy may have been a product of his lack of success, rather than its cause, but he was as notoriously indolent and indecisive away from the battlefield as he was brave and energetic on it. If the war was won or lost before 1778, then Howe must stand accused of failing to win it (though perhaps not actually losing it). This view may be tempered by the fact that he and his brother had to undertake simultaneous military and political missions that were often incompatible, with decreasing political backing and increasingly conflicting orders.

Lieutenant General Sir Henry Clinton (1738–95) was the only son of Admiral George Clinton, governor of New York from 1741 to 1751, and was briefly a New York militia officer. On coming to England, he joined the 2nd Foot Guards and served in Germany during the Seven Years' War, distinguishing himself in action and becoming aide-de-camp to Ferdinand, Duke of Brunswick. After the cessation of hostilities, he entered politics, forming useful and powerful connections and served briefly at Gibraltar, where he gave the first indications of being a difficult and tactless subordinate. In 1772, he became a major general and an MP, but almost suffered a mental breakdown after the death of the wife he adored.

In North America, he showed awareness and personal bravery at Bunker Hill, but again proved a problematic subordinate, and Howe constantly sought opportunities to send him away. Disgusted with Howe's indecisiveness and refusal to listen to his ideas, and angry that Germain accepted Parker's version of the Charleston fiasco, Clinton returned to England and proffered the first of many resignations. Germain placated him and, in 1778, Clinton became commander-in-chief in North America.

Yet his talents as a field commander—typified by the capture of Charleston in 1780—were too often submerged by his inability to give clear, concise orders and sensitivity to criticism. Ironically, the man who was such a difficult deputy was persistently plagued by the politics and failings of his own subordinates (especially the naval officers), by government interference, and by some appalling bad luck. He was especially disconcerted by the "dormant commission" of Cornwallis and increasingly felt it was more politic

Below: *Sir William Howe. (National Army Museum)*

to make polite requests of the latter, rather than give him direct orders. Although widely blamed for Yorktown, he was refused an inquiry to clear his name. However, his re-election to Parliament in 1790, promotion to general in 1793, and the governorship of Gibraltar the following year, all indicate that some form of rehabilitation took place.

Unlike Howe and Carleton, Clinton had only seen active duty in Europe and, although usefully fluent in German, he tended to dismiss the value of American service, which may also have contributed to his failure to understand how vulnerable the "seaboard strategy" was should the enemy acquire local naval superiority. It is difficult to say whether his lack of achievement was due to caution, or merely a recognition of what was possible in the circumstances. He certainly felt that he was expected to achieve as much as Howe, but with fewer troops and naval support, and in the face of increasing intervention by France and Spain.

Lieutenant General Charles, Earl Cornwallis (1738–1805) joined the 1st Foot Guards at seventeen and served as a staff officer in Germany. He returned to England and became a member of parlia-

Below: *Sir Henry Clinton. (National Army Museum)*

Above: *Charles, Earl Cornwallis. (National Portrait Gallery)*

ment in 1760, but saw more fighting in Germany before entering the House of Lords in 1762. Although a Whig, he became aide-de-camp to the king and was promoted to major general in 1775, having indicated he was prepared to serve in North America.

He was severely criticized for his failure to corner Washington in New Jersey and particularly for being fooled so easily before and during the Princeton action. A delay in his return to England meant that he missed the negotiations that surrounded Burgoyne's proposals and Clinton's resignation. In fact, Cornwallis supported Howe's plan for the attack on Philadelphia and defended the late start of the 1777 campaign, in which he commanded a division made up of élite British and German units.

In 1778, he returned to England again, was promoted to lieutenant general, and returned to America as Clinton's second-in-command, with a "dormant commission." This was merely to prevent a more senior German officer becoming commander-in-chief if Clinton were killed or incapacitated; but Clinton, because of his paranoia and his knowledge of Cornwallis's correspondence with Germain, failed to give Cornwallis clear orders. When Cornwallis took command in the South, he used this as an excuse to pursue his own strategy. Despite defeating Gates,

Above: *Sir Guy Carleton. (National Archives of Canada)*

General Sir Guy Carleton (1724–1808) came from an old Irish Protestant family and joined the Army in 1742, later transferring to the 1st Foot Guards. Arriving in North America in 1758, he served at Louisburg, became Quartermaster General under Wolfe, and was wounded leading the grenadiers at Quebec. He later served at Belle Isle, Port Andro, and Havana, and, in 1766, became lieutenant governor of Quebec. In 1770, he returned to England and was promoted to major general two years later. In 1774, he presented Parliament with the Quebec Act, which it is believed he drafted, and returned to Canada to become governor of Quebec.

When Gage was ordered home, Carleton was given the independent command of all troops in Canada. Unfortunately, his enthusiastic welcome had led him to overestimate the extent of Canadian support for Great Britain and having sent most of his troops to Boston, he was forced to declare martial law when Montgomery invaded. After a heroic defence of Quebec City, reinforcements (led by Burgoyne) allowed him to take the offensive in 1776, but poor weather, difficult terrain, and Arnold's fleet conspired to prevent him reaching Ticonderoga before winter. When Burgoyne went back to England, his subtly understated criticisms fueled Germain's existing hatred of Carleton, who found himself a scapegoat and his attempt depicted as a failure.

In 1777, Carleton was promoted lieutenant general and, in summer 1778, handed over the governorship to Haldimand and returned to England. In 1782, the new government needed someone to deal with the rampant corruption in New York City and immediately made him commander-in-chief in North America. He later supervised the evacuation of British forces and Loyalists. After the War, he was reappointed governor of Quebec and created Baron Dorchester; he retired to England in 1796.

Carleton was much maligned during and after the War, which probably explains why his vital defense of Canada has never been properly acknowledged. He demonstrated considerable military talent against superior forces, talents matched by his abilities as a civil administrator. The fate of Burgoyne's expedition suggests that Carleton's cautious approach to the advance into New York was not ill-judged—except perhaps from a government desk 3,000 miles away. As well as being an honest administrator, he also possessed considerable common sense, recognizing that respect for the Catholic faith and French systems of local government were vital to the retention of British control over Quebec.

Cornwallis was outfought by Greene (whose strategic awareness and tactical limitations made them virtual opposites). Although he was badly let down by the Royal Navy, Cornwallis's obsession with Virginia contributed greatly to the defeat at Yorktown—yet he returned to England a hero, while Clinton took the blame.

Cornwallis was not only personally brave, but also—except for the incident in New Jersey—proved himself one of the ablest battlefield commanders on either side. However, he needed a strong superior to control him and it is ironic that his one independent command was in a situation where boldness and aggression were not the answer. After the war, he served in India from 1786 to 1793, acquiring a reputation in both military and civil duties; a second posting, however, resulted in his death. In between, he was appointed governor-general and commander-in-chief in Ireland, where he brought a touch of humanity to the 1798 revolt and resigned when the government ignored his proposals for Catholic emancipation.

Major General John Burgoyne (1722–92) entered the Army at fifteen and served in the War of the Austrian Succession, but saw no action. He resigned his commission in 1751 after eloping with the daughter of the Earl of Derby, but was subsequently reconciled with his father-in-law, whose patronage re-established his military career. He set up the first

light horse units in the Army and saw his first action in 1759, serving at St. Malo, Cherbourg, and Belle-Isle, before leading the famous raid on Alcantara, in Portugal. Promoted to major general in 1772, he arrived in Boston in May 1775, but went home that winter to tend his sick wife. In 1776, he sailed to Canada, where he constantly pestered Carleton with plans for operations into upper New York.

His wife's death took him back to England for another winter, during which he sold his ideas to Germain. In February 1777, he submitted his idea for isolating New England with an attack down Lake Champlain to Albany, combined with similar thrusts along the Mohawk Valley, and up the Hudson from New York City. Germain recommended the plan to the King and, with some amendments it was approved, Burgoyne being chosen to command the main thrust from Canada. However, once in the field, his confidence soon evaporated, while his dilatory and indecisive manner led to vital delays and mistakes—which he later tried to blame on col-

leagues and subordinates. Condemned in Parliament for the defeat at Saratoga (though not by the public, who blamed Howe), he saw no further action in the War, but was briefly commander-in-chief in Ireland, before being ousted by political opponents. He retired from military service and became involved in the theater.

Burgoyne's other career, as a playwright, showed through in the flowery and verbose texts of his military communications. Ironically, both careers were built upon a single, spectacular success among otherwise very average efforts. Although brave and witty, he was superficial and vain, addicted to public gestures and—like so many British officers of the time—the bottle. He was not a friend who could be relied upon, yet his treatment of the enlisted man was progressive and earned him the nickname "Gentleman Johnny." His pronouncements before and during the Saratoga campaign show that he clearly misunderstood the nature of the rebellion.

Above: *John Burgoyne. (Frick Art Reference Library)*

1775

"If they mean to have a war, let it begin here"

CAPTAIN JOHN PARKER

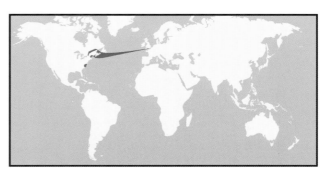

RED INDICATES FIGHTING, INCLUDING PRIVATEERING ON SHIPPING LANES

The Battle of Bunker Hill (June 17, 1775)

While the first Continental Congress was debating a response to the Intolerable Acts, it made another decision that had far-reaching (and perhaps not entirely foreseen) military consequences. It was proposed that each colony's own provincial congress should set up a "committee of safety" to ensure that the actions agreed were properly understood and observed by the local population. Inevitably, the committees came to be dominated by the more radical and zealous Whigs, who lost no time in "persuading" Tories to change their views and to reorganizing the militia, in order to bring it to a higher level of readiness should an armed struggle become necessary.

Massachusetts took the lead, forcing all officers to resign and stand for re-election by the rank-and-file (thereby removing the pro-Tory senior officers). At the same time, it began selecting, training, and equipping the one man in four chosen to be "minutemen" through purchases abroad, removal of items from public arsenals and theft from the Boston garrison. The Committee of Safety soon had substantial stockpiles of cannon, muskets, and powder (the last being priceless in a country with no facilities for its large-scale manufacture) at Worcester and Concord. Soon, Connecticut, Rhode Island, and New Hampshire were following suit.

MASSACHUSETTS

One of the measures taken to punish Massachusetts for its lead in opposing the sovereignty of Parliament was to make Lieutenant General Thomas Gage—commander-in-chief in North America since 1763—Governor of Massachusetts. In response, the General Assembly formed an alternative government—the Provincial Congress—with John Hancock as its president. Just before he returned to North America from a period of leave in England (his first since 1763), Gage had—rather uncharacteristically for such a cautious man—boasted that he could subdue Boston with four regiments. By August 1774, he had trouble controlling the town with twice that number, while his second-in-command, Major General Sir Frederick Haldimand, calculated that the Provincial Congress could mobilize 30,000 men without difficulty.

Bostonians now openly attacked officers and soldiers in the street, stole weapons and equipment, and encouraged desertion. The courts discriminated against the Army, levying disproportionate fines for trivial offenses, while dismissing charges brought by soldiers against civilians unless there were independent civilian witnesses. The Boston Port Act made hundreds of men redundant, yet no labor could be found for projects for the Army or the Royal Navy, and the unemployed made excellent spies, such that Gage could do nothing without it becoming common knowledge.

Gage, however, had his own sources of intelligence, which almost certainly included Dr. Benjamin Church, a leading member of the Provincial Congress, and militia Major General William Brattle. On September 1, he sent 250 men to seize two brass cannon at Cambridge, and the contents of the Charlestown powder house. The militia were caught unprepared, although false tales of atrocities galvanized 4,000 men to gather in Cambridge the following day, and another 6,000 militia marched on Worcester, two days later.

Unfortunately, this minor success backfired as the Provincial Congress set up a system of "alarm riders" to rouse the countryside whenever the Regulars left Boston. Just one week later, troops sent to retrieve guns from Charlestown returned empty-handed. Stores began to disappear from public arsenals throughout Massachusetts and, despite reinforcements raising Gage's strength to 3,000, the problem was fast spreading throughout New England. In December, cannon and ammunition were removed from Fort William and Mary, in Portsmouth, New Hampshire, and forty-four cannon were taken from Fort George, in Newport, Rhode Island.

Throughout all this, Gage tried to maintain good relations with the Bostonians, but merely alienated his own men. Even attempts to keep the troops out of trouble by marching them into the countryside simply allowed his opponents to practice their response. When the Castle William garrison went to seize cannon at Salem, in late February, local militia dismantled a bridge and blocked their path until the guns had been removed to safety. On March 30, Brigadier General Lord Percy's brigade was twice forced to retire on finding bridges either broken down, or covered by artillery. Such incidents convinced the militia that the Regulars would always back down, and although both sides were under strict orders not to fire first, it could only be a matter of time before blood was shed.

As more and more information reached London, the North ministry made one last attempt at reconciliation. In February 1775, a proposal was submitted based on self-taxation by the Colonists, but still including restrictions on trade and fishing in the seas off Newfoundland. With so many New Englanders—wealthy or otherwise—relying on the sea for their livelihoods, it was inevitable that the approach would be rebuffed. Lord Dartmouth, Secretary of State for the American Colonies, sent Gage instructions to take all necessary steps to disarm the militia and deal with any armed disturbances that might follow. If war was inevitable, better that it begin sooner rather than later, when the opposition would be better prepared.

Gage sent officers to survey the area around Boston; two of them explored Worcester and Suffolk counties, narrowly escaping capture. On March 20, the same officers reconnoitered Middlesex County, learning of the stores being kept at Concord. Aware that the

Left: *Lieutenant General the Hon. Thomas Gage (1719–87) found himself in the unfortunate position of being a soldier trying to control a civilian population, and inevitably ended up being ridiculed by both sides. Eventually, his military and civil governorships descended into inefficiency, inactivity, and indecision that saw him nicknamed "Old Tom" and "Granny Gage" by his own men. (Firle Collection, Firle Place, Sussex)*

Right: *Lieutenant Colonel Francis Smith (1723–91) had an undistinguished career before and after the events of April 19. His selection to command the expedition to Concord probably had much to do with him being a longstanding friend of Gage and sharing the latter's views on the sanctity of private property. (National Army Museum, London)*

Provincial Congress would soon disperse, Gage made preparations for an expedition to seize those stores.

On the afternoon of April 18, Gage dispatched mounted officers to patrol the roads between Cambridge and Concord, and that night, 700 light infantry and grenadiers from the regiments in Boston, under Lieutenant Colonel Francis Smith, set out for Concord. A local silversmith, Paul Revere, arranged· to have lanterns hung in the Old North church to signal their departure (which was already the worst kept secret in Boston) and then rode to Lexington. There he met William Dawes and Dr. Samuel Prescott, and all three set off to rouse the countryside. Revere was captured almost immediately, but was later released and returned to Lexington.

As the Regulars arrived in Lexington, a group of armed men were visible on the common. The group was ordered to disperse, but as they did so shots were exchanged and blood was spilt. A war had begun. The Regulars marched on toward Concord,

Left: *Brigadier General Hugh, Lord Percy (1742–1817) was a progressive officer, who introduced good conduct and long-service awards among his troops. His wit and charm made him popular with both sides, and he was often entertained by John Hancock. (The Percy family and The Fusiliers Museum, Northumberland)*

LEXINGTON: APRIL 19, 1775

On learning that the Regulars—perhaps 2,000 strong—were approaching, the leader of Lexington's militia, Captain John Parker, formed up his men (most of them fresh from the local tavern) in a two-deep line on the village green. At the same time, Revere and ten others escorted Hancock and Adams from the tavern and north towards Bedford.

The Regulars were expecting trouble by now, having been told that hundreds of militia had been roused and having had several men fire blanks at them from close range. The two leading companies passed either side of the Meeting House and deployed into line, their commander ordering the militia to lay down their arms. Parker ordered his men to disperse, but to keep their weapons.

At this point, a number of shots rang out; the Regulars replied with a massed volley and then, as a dozen of Parker's men attempted to return the fire, followed up with the bayonet. Eight militiamen were killed and ten wounded, while one Regular was hit in the hand and an officer's horse in the side. It was just after 5:00 a.m.

The initial shot, or shots, do not appear to have been fired by anyone on the green. In the tavern earlier, Parker and his men had agreed to do nothing to provoke the redcoats. It seems odd that a veteran of the French and Indian Wars should then place between forty and eighty men (many friends or relatives) in such an exposed and tactically useless spot. The explanation may lie in the activities of Samuel Adams, who was seen talking to Parker, and several others who were not subsequently seen on the green. His comment, "Oh, what a glorious morning this is!" as he escaped to Bedford hints that Fate may have had more than a helping hand that April morning.

Above: *The Battle of Lexington. One of four images drawn from eyewitnesses accounts just days after the event. Note that all of the militia are shown dispersing, to make it appear that the British are shooting them in the back. This image worked so well that those men who did fire back at the Regulars later had trouble proving the fact. (Anne S. K. Brown Collection)*

CONCORD: APRIL 19, 1775

Three of the seven light infantry companies (about 120 men) detached by Smith to follow the militia halted at the North Bridge, one on the town side and two on the far bank. The other four crossed over and marched on for two miles, searching houses in the area.

By 9:00 a.m., 500 militia were on a hill overlooking the North Bridge. Seeing smoke rising from houses in the town, and fearing the worst, they advanced. The Regulars fell back across the bridge, but the rapid advance of the militia prevented Smith from removing the planks of the bridge, or forming up his men properly so they did not mask one another's fire. The Regulars opened fire, but caused just two fatalities; the militia then fired back, killing two soldiers and wounding ten more, including half of the officers. They then swarmed across the bridge and forced the light infantry a quarter of a mile back down the road into the town. Only the arrival of Smith with three companies of grenadiers ended the pursuit. Uncertain what to do next, Smith returned to Concord.

Other groups of Regulars scattered around the town had also heard the firing and fell back, pulling up the planks of the South Bridge and commandeering horses, carriages, and bedding for the wounded. At the same time, the troops sent off to search the distant houses returned and crossed North Bridge back into Concord unmolested, having found no stores and heard no gunfire (only becoming aware of events when they found a dead soldier beside the bridge).

At noon, Smith decided it was time to leave and sent out flank guards to cover the main column. Seeing this, the militia set off across the fields to the north of the town, with other groups joining them at regular intervals, until there were over 1,000 militia in the surrounding fields as Smith left Concord. As his flanking parties briefly rejoined the column to cross a small bridge, they were shot at and fired a desultory volley in return. The fire they then received left two of them dead and several lying wounded around the stream, and gave a foretaste of what the sixteen miles back to Boston had in store.

being met on the way by local minutemen, who promptly turned about and led them into the town, each group's fifes and drums playing merrily. The militia then fell back across a bridge over the Concord River. Smith sent the light infantry after them and ordered the grenadiers to search the town. Unfortunately, while burning some of the stores, fire spread to two houses and, though extinguished immediately, the flames and smoke were visible for some distance.

The flames caused one group of militia to attack some of Smith's men, and with more militia appearing he decided to withdraw. As his column marched back to Lexington, it was continually ambushed and sniped at from behind stone walls, trees, rocks, farm buildings, and houses; occasionally, the Regulars hit back, the flank guards circling around the ambushers and catching the militiamen unawares. At one point, the troops exchanged fire again with Parker's company (albeit with much less effect) and by the

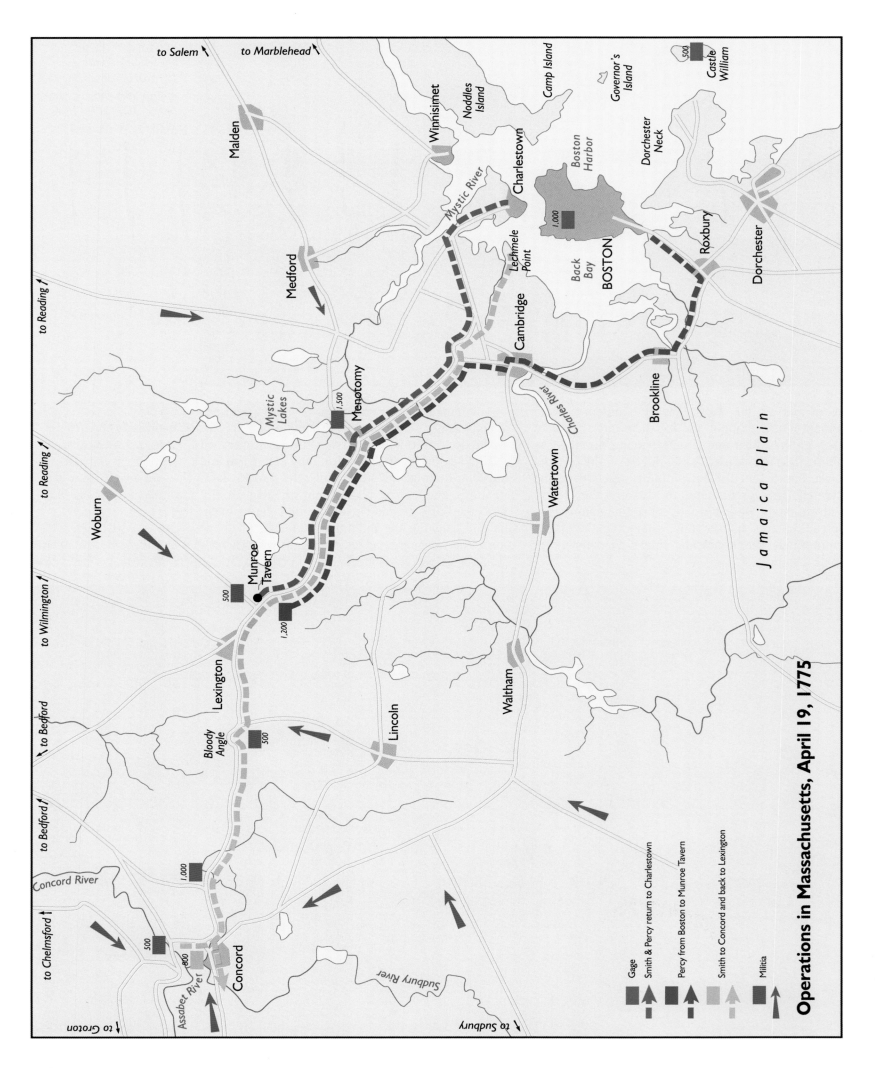

Operations in Massachusetts, April 19, 1775

Left: *A View of the South Part of Lexington. Percy's brigade begins the withdrawal to Boston, having sent Smith's exhausted men on ahead. Note the British flanking parties and the militia firing from behind walls. (Anne S. K. Brown Collection)*

Below: *Retreat to Boston. This illustrates the close-quarter nature of the fighting along the road back to Boston. Despite popular myth, the militia were not outstanding marksmen: it has been estimated that it required at least 200 rounds to cause each British casualty. (Anne S. K. Brown Collection)*

time the column reached Lexington, Smith himself had been wounded and order was disintegrating under the heavy musketry and the fatigue of ten hours' marching. At one point, officers blocked the road and presented their bayonets to restore order.

Just beyond Lexington, the troops found Percy's brigade waiting for them. By 3:00 p.m., groups of militia were gathering behind walls and buildings, so Percy ordered his two guns to open fire, deployed marksmen in front of his line and had six buildings set alight to prevent their use as cover. Around 3:30 p.m., the Regulars left Lexington, with Smith's exhausted men in the lead and Percy's four battalions taking turns to cover the flanks and rear. They passed through Menotomy and Brookline, which saw the heaviest fighting of the day; in one house, eleven

minutemen were killed in a single room. Knowing that the road through Cambridge was longer and the only bridge might be guarded (as indeed it was), Percy headed for Charlestown, arriving just after 7:00 p.m. While Smith's men were rowed back to Boston, Gage ordered defenses built across Boston Neck and on Bunker's Hill.

The militia had lost 49 dead, 41 wounded and five missing (excluding the casualties at Lexington); the British had 73 dead, 174 wounded and 26 missing (mostly prisoners), but the greatest casualty was the belief that the militia would not stand against them. Had the militia been coordinated above company level (a general was present but decided merely to "observe") and had they been better shots (it took an estimated 300 rounds to cause each British casualty), none of the Regulars might have escaped. In his report, Gage remarked that, throughout the action, the militiamen had shown martial virtues that had seldom been displayed against the French and Indians, while Percy reported that they were not the cowards of popular Tory belief.

Over the next two days, 20,000 men gathered around Boston, forcing Gage to withdraw his outposts—against the advice of his subordinates, who recommended holding Dorchester Heights and Charlestown. He then began negotiations with the Provincial Congress for Bostonians to leave (without arms) in return for Loyalists being allowed through the American lines, only to realize that this left the Rebels free to bombard Boston. With more militia arriving from other parts of New England, the Provincial Congress formed an "army of observation" under Major General Artemas Ward, who made his headquarters at Cambridge. His officers surveyed the hills around Boston and recommended works to cover the roads out of Boston and a strong redoubt, with cannon, on Bunker's Hill.

On May 13, 3,000 Connecticut troops marched across Charlestown Neck and on to Breed's Hill, where they taunted the crews of the British warships in the harbor (the remaining inhabitants of Charlestown sensibly slipped away that night). Short of fresh food, Gage sent thirty men in an unarmed schooner to secure forage from one of the islands; the rebels failed to intercept them, but took care to burn the rest of the hay. On May 24, the Committee of Safety ordered all livestock removed from Hog Island and Noddle's Island (where most of the naval stores were kept). Gage found out, but did nothing and four days later Rebel troops burned the barns and pastures, and killed any livestock they could not remove. On June 8, he finally sent over 200 light infantry, but nothing of value remained.

At the end of May, Gage received reinforcements,

including three major generals—Sir William Howe, Henry Clinton, and John Burgoyne—and orders to place all of Massachusetts under martial law. This he did on June 12, offering pardons to all opposed to Royal authority (except Hancock and Adams). At the same time, a major attack across Boston Neck and through Roxbury was planned for June 18, but news was leaked to the Committee of Safety. On June 16, Ward convened a council of war; despite personal misgivings, he gave way to the bellicose majority and ordered the occupation and fortification of Bunker's Hill on the Charlestown peninsula.

The detachment, under Colonel William Prescott, arrived on Bunker's Hill, but his officers then debated whether to construct the defenses there, or on Breed's Hill, which was nearer to Boston. The latter course was chosen, work beginning around midnight and—amazingly—continuing undisturbed until 4:00 a.m. when lookouts on one of the warships in the harbor saw them and opened fire, killing one man (at which digging promptly stopped so that he could be buried). Other vessels joined in and at 9:00 a.m. the battery on Copp's Hill, on the north side of Boston, commenced a steady fire, which continued all day, but did little damage, due to the extreme range.

Gage called a council of war that included the three major generals and the senior naval officer in North America, Vice Admiral Samuel Graves. There was unanimous agreement that the works posed a threat and that, being incomplete and isolated, they should be attacked. However, the only feasible approach was by water and there were only enough boats for 1,000 men (barely half the number needed) and none capable of carrying horses or artillery. With the tide ebbing and a westerly wind, the outward trip would be long and slow, so any landing site had to be close. Moulton's (or Morton's) Point appeared the obvious choice. Howe would command the assault,

Below: *View of Charlestown from the Copse [sic] Hill Battery. This image shows the British camps set up after the battle, but demonstrates the view from the battery and its field of fire. (Massachusetts Historical Society)*

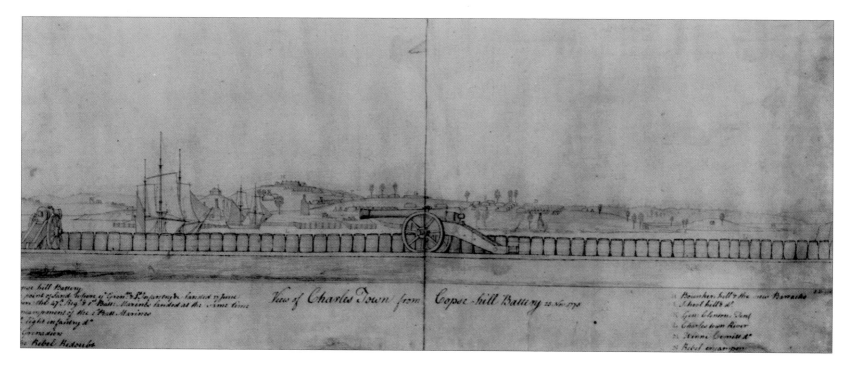

with Clinton supervising reinforcements in Boston. Graves, whose ships were all seriously undermanned, realized that the low water would render the larger warships useless, and transferred their men to smaller vessels with shallower drafts.

Under pressure from the Committee of Safety to support Prescott, Ward had sent him 4,000 men, and as many more to Putnam on Bunker Hill. With every man and gun now committed, he had nothing left to support Major General John Thomas, whose men were hurriedly fortifying Roxbury. Fortunately, Gage had no fresh troops (and little inclination to use any) and merely bombarded Roxbury from Boston Neck all afternoon.

BUNKER HILL: JUNE 17, 1775

The smaller warships and gondolas bombarded Moulton's Point and the Neck (none having the range or elevation to hit the redoubt at low tide), while the ships' boats brought over 2,500 men in two waves. Howe formed them into two divisions, one led by himself and the other by Brigadier General Robert Pigot. The Rebel line seemed stronger than it had from Boston: a redoubt with a 100-yard breastwork covering its north side; three *flêches* hastily built from fence material; and a rail fence leading to a ten-foot-high bluff overlooking the Mystic River. The intervening ground appeared flat, but was rocky and uneven, with hidden gulleys, stout rail fences, clumps of trees, and some brick kilns, all of which would disrupt an advance. Howe decided to bypass the redoubt and take Bunker Hill, isolating Breed's Hill. His division would punch through the rail fence and roll up the enemy line, while Pigot made a feint against the redoubt.

As the light infantry moved along the beach to outflank the rail fence, Colonel John Stark's New Hampshiremen rose up from behind a stone wall and opened a deadly fire. At the rail fence, the gunners found they had the wrong ammunition, while the rough ground halted the grenadiers, who merely returned the Rebel volleys before pulling back. Pigot's men exchanged fire with Prescott's defenders before retiring, having done little damage. Meanwhile, the ships had set fire to several houses in Charlestown that were being used by snipers annoying Pigot's left; by 4:00 p.m. most of the town was ablaze.

Howe modified his plans, moving the light infantry inland to cover the rail fence, while he attacked the *flêches*. This attack was also repulsed, by a constant stream of fire lasting nearly thirty minutes. Concerned at the growing enemy strength on Bunker Hill, Howe ordered reinforcements from Boston (which were brought over by Clinton) and planned a third attack. This time, the surviving light infantry feinted against the rail fence, while the gunners (now with the correct ammunition) enfiladed the breastwork, forcing the defenders into the redoubt. As the rest of Howe's division attacked the *flêches* and breastwork, Pigot hit two sides of the redoubt (during which Major John Pitcairn was mortally wounded) and both Prescott and Stark ordered their men to retire, pursued by Clinton. At this point, the men on Bunker Hill—who still outnumbered Howe—fled, except for a few who withdrew in good order, using walls, fences, and hedges to delay the Regulars, while Putnam rode away carrying valuable entrenching tools.

Around 5:00 p.m., Howe ordered a halt, due to his heavy losses (especially among the officers). Clinton's rapid advance had trapped many Rebels in copses and houses all over the peninsula, and mopping up continued for several days. In two hours, Howe lost over 1,000 dead and wounded and Ward around 500 (ignoring the hundreds of militia who simply went home during and after the battle).

Cyclorama of the Battle of Bunker Hill. In its entirety, the work represents Howe's third assault around 4:30 p.m. and is generally accurate, except for making the warships too large and having too few defenders in the redoubt— both sides had around 2,000 men. As would happen so often at crucial moments, nature favored the Rebel cause: the westerly breeze and ebbing tide were the exact opposite of what the Royal Navy needed to maneuver its ships and to row the boatloads of troops over from Boston. The cyclorama panels continue overleaf. (The Bostonian Society)

Fear, dense smoke from hundreds of black-powder weapons, and the claustrophobic nature of the fighting around the redoubt created a myth that the action occurred in intense heat, whereas records show that humidity was low and the temperature—64 degrees Fahrenheit in the morning and around the mid-80s by 4:30 p.m.—was typical for a June day in Boston. (The Bostonian Society)

The redoubt and breastwork were roughly built and incomplete when the British attacked. Both were about six feet high with a ditch in front and a firing platform inside. Despite criticism of Howe's tactics, only ill-luck with artillery ammunition and fate, which placed Stark, one of the few competent American officers, at the most vulnerable part of the line, prevented either of the first two attacks from clearing the field. (The Bostonian Society)

Although Charlestown's wharves and jetties would have offered a perfect landing place, they were commanded by the guns in the redoubt and the troops would have had to fight their way through the town, negating their superior discipline and firepower. Occupying Charlestown Neck would have been equally difficult, as a mill dam and marshes prevented boats from landing guns and horses, and the longer journey would have left the former unsupported for almost two hours. (The Bostonian Society)

On June 18, Howe built a large fortification on Bunker Hill and Clinton urged Gage to occupy Dorchester Heights. However, Gage did nothing until June 24 and even then, a planned attack was canceled when it was thought that the enemy had learned of it.

Meanwhile, the second Continental Congress, which had convened in Philadelphia in May to discuss a common response to the events in Massachusetts, had been persuaded to adopt the "army of observation" as its own. On June 14, it had announced the formation of a "Continental Army," allocated 22,000 men to the siege of Boston, and appointed George Washington of Virginia the first commander-in-chief. On July 3, Washington arrived in Cambridge to assume command from Ward and begin organizing the new force. The following months saw no more major battles, but various minor raids and demonstrations were undertaken to aid training—a task made easier by the increasingly lethargic response of the enemy.

Unsurprisingly, Gage was recalled to London and Howe replaced him as commander-in-chief in North America. Howe was keen to leave Boston, recognizing that it had no military value, but an early (and fierce) winter and a shortage of transports prevented him. The garrison suffered from shortages of food, clothing, and firewood and were increasingly forced to undertake foraging raids.

In the Rebel lines, the picture was no brighter: desertions and sickness from the lack of warm accommodation and the expiration of enlistments at the end of December eventually left Washington outnumbered. Recruiting for the new Continental Army was proving difficult. Officers and men rejected attempts to create "national" regiments, preferring to serve with men from their own colony. In terms of re-enlistments, there were enough officers and Washington was able to choose regimental commanders, who in turn selected their subordinates. It was then up to the junior officers to encourage the men to reenlist, but by December 30, only 9,649 men had done so, with another 2,800 rejoining in January. Washington was forced to urge the New England assemblies to organize drafts and allow free

Above: *British troops surveying Breed's Hill. This watercolor by a British officer, painted soon after the battle, probably shows the flèches on the north slope of Breed's Hill and the steepness of the ground over which the British Regulars advanced. (New York Public Library)*

Below: *Entrance to Boston Harbor. Castle William is on the island to the left. This would have been the final view of Howe's army as it evacuated Boston on March 17, 1776. (National Maritime Museum)*

A Panorama of Boston and its Environs. The view is from Beacon Hill and the work was executed in the fall of 1775 by two officers of the Boston garrison.
Top: In the right foreground is Boston's North End, with Charlestown peninsula to its right; the British lines on the Neck, their camp on Bunker Hill and the captured redoubt on Breed's Hill, can be seen above the burned ruins of Charlestown.
Bottom: The islands to the northeast of Boston, in the main harbor. (British Library)

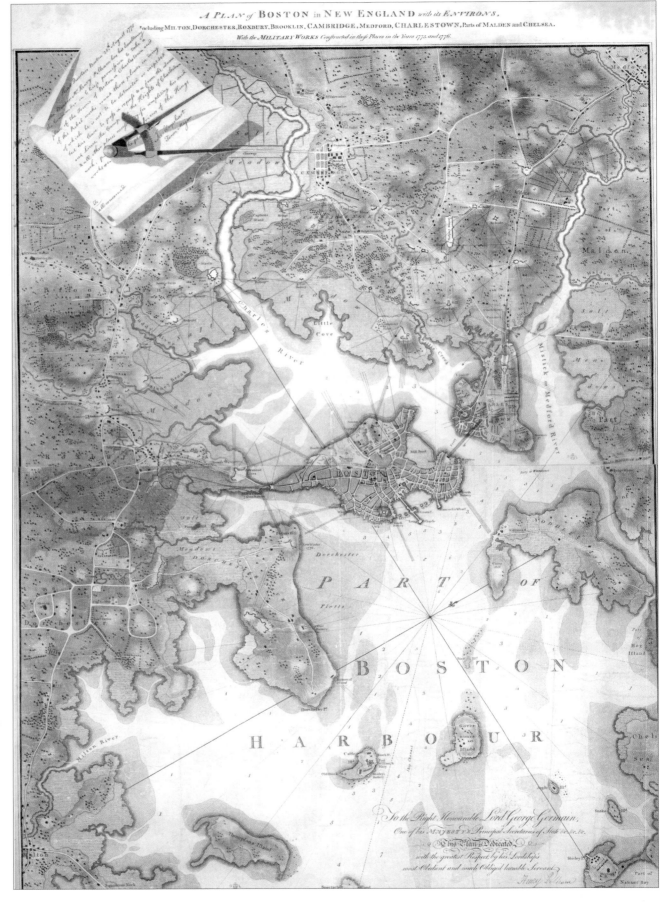

negroes to re-enlist, and in the last four months of the siege, the militia had to be called out.

By March, however, things were looking better and the "Continentals" had 14,400 officers and men. Nevertheless, there was a desperate need for supplies, especially muskets, and men refusing to re-enlist had

theirs confiscated. Given these shortages and the struggle to attain basic efficiency despite constant reorganization, it was fortunate that Washington's army did not have to face their opponents in open battle.

In mid-January, a council of war decided that the Rebels had to attack before more Regulars

Right: *The Old South Meeting House. The scene of antigovernment demonstrations each year on the anniversary of the Boston Massacre, it inevitably became a target for the Regulars once the siege of Boston confined them to the town. A cavalry regiment removed the pews and used the building as a combined riding school, pigsty, and officers' mess. (Author's collection)*

arrived in the spring, but to do this they needed heavy artillery. This arrived in the shape of sixty guns and mortars (three weighing over a ton each), which Washington's senior gunner, Colonel Henry Knox, had transported the 350 miles from Ticonderoga. On February 16, Washington proposed an attack across the frozen Back Bay; his staff, however, considered his estimate of the odds—16,000 to 5,000 in his favor—too optimistic, and proposed instead to occupy Dorchester Heights, which commanded the main harbor. The works were virtually finished in one night, under cover of a heavy bombardment (digging noises were reported to Smith, but he did nothing). Bad weather forced Howe to cancel a planned night attack and although an attempt to extend the fortifications was beaten off, Howe's guns could not elevate sufficiently to hit the Rebel works and the harbor was now unsafe.

Washington agreed not to attack if Howe did not burn the town and on March 17, 12,000 troops, sailors, and 1,000 Loyalists, sailed out into Nantasket Roads and on to Halifax, Nova Scotia. The Rebels seized 100 cannon, the entire British medical store, and 3,000 blankets; since taking command in July 1775, Washington had forced the Royal army to evacuate Boston at a cost of just twenty dead.

NEW YORK

In 1775, New York covered more than 50,000 square miles—including present-day Vermont—but this was mostly wilderness, with few white settlements beyond Fort Dayton in the west, or Fort Ticonderoga at the southern end of Lake Champlain—one of the two main trade routes between Canada and the Colonies. New York City was the second largest in the Colonies, after Philadelphia, with 22,000 inhabitants. It had a diverse population that included 150,000 whites (one in four of whom were not from Great Britain or Ireland), 20,000 blacks, and 10,000 Indians, mainly Iroquois (also known as the Six Nations).

The geography of the upper half of the colony had made it a frequent battleground in previous conflicts and the population included many veterans who had received land grants after the French and Indian Wars. However, fifteen years of peacetime neglect had left the military infrastructure, especially the once-great forts of Ticonderoga and Crown Point, on the point of collapse.

On April 30, Benedict Arnold (who had marched his militia company to Boston on hearing the news of Lexington and Concord), met the Massachusetts Committee of Safety to discuss the seizure of much-

Above: *Two plates from the Panorama of Boston and its Environs.*
Top: Boston Neck, with the Blockhouse half way along, and Boston Common, still in use as a military camp, in the foreground. The large house in the right foreground belonged to John Hancock; the town of Roxbury is immediately above it, with Rebel entrenchments and tents on the hillside to the right. Bottom: Rebel encampments and the town of Cambridge are just visible on the hills west of Boston. The huts in the foreground are ropewalks and to their left is the infamous Mount Whoredom. In the middle distance are more Rebel defenses and encampments, including a signaling post.

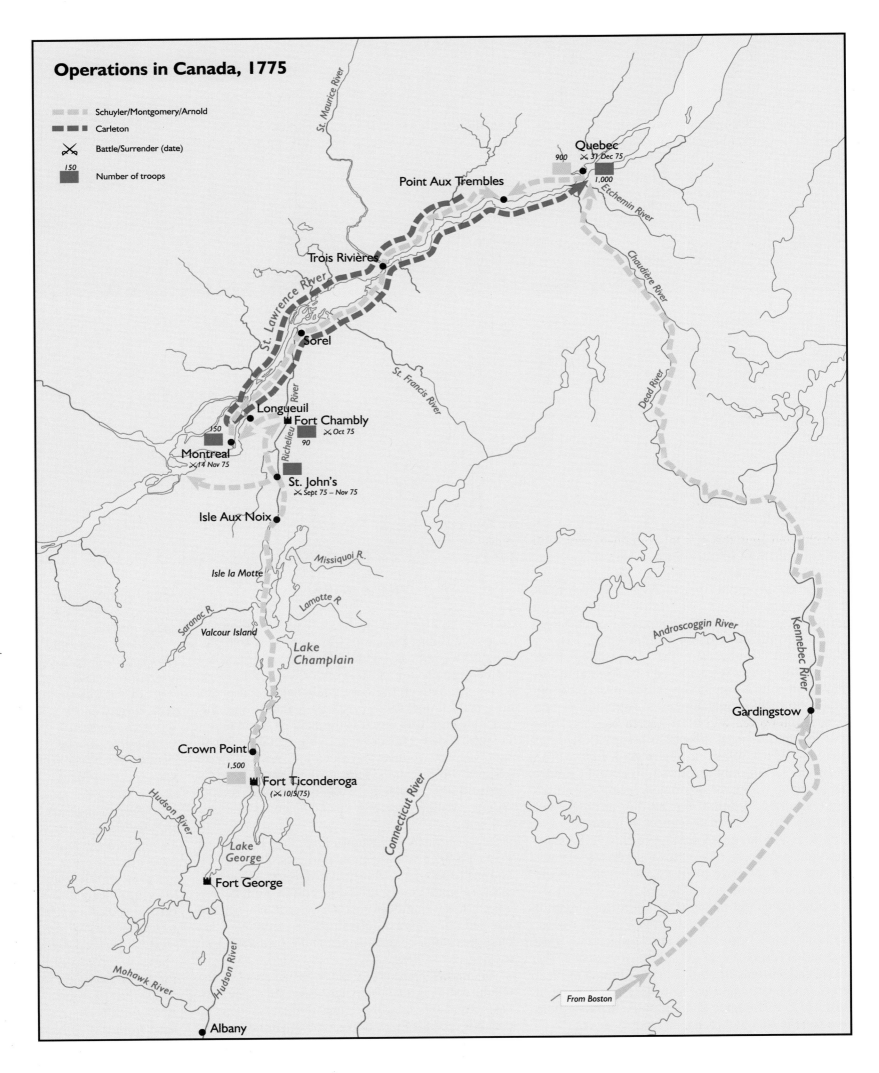

Operations in Canada, 1775

Schuyler/Montgomery/Arnold

Carleton

Battle/Surrender (date)

150 Number of troops

St. Maurice River

Quebec
900
✕ 31 Dec 75
1,000
Etchemin River

Point Aux Trembles

Trois Rivières

Chaudière River

St. Lawrence River

Sorel

St. Francis River

Dead River

Richelieu River

Longueuil
Fort Chambly
150
✕ Oct 75
90
Montreal
✕ 14 Nov 75
St. John's
✕ Sept 75 – Nov 75

Isle Aux Noix

Missiquoi R.

Isle la Motte

Lamotte R.

Saranac R.

Valcour Island

Androscoggin River

Kennebec River

Lake Champlain

Gardingstow

Crown Point
1,500

Fort Ticonderoga
(✕ 10/5/75)

Connecticut River

Hudson River

Lake George

Fort George

Mohawk River

Hudson River

From Boston

Albany

needed heavy artillery from Fort Ticonderoga. A week later, with the rank of colonel, he was given 400 men to take the fort and bring the guns back to Boston. Another expedition, however, was also on its way, led by a land speculator called Ethan Allen, with a party composed of "Green Mountain Boys"—a quasi-military group formed to protect the inhabitants of Vermont from the colonial authorities in New York (which had recently been awarded ownership of the region in a longstanding dispute with New Hampshire).

Allen's party of around 220 had moved up to the southern end of Lake Champlain, opposite the fort, when Arnold arrived and insisted on taking command. After several heated discussions, Allen was confirmed as leader of the group, with Arnold allowed to join and march at his side. The fort's garrison consisted of forty-two men, mostly infirm or aged veterans expecting to live out a quiet retirement. They and the ninety guns stored inside were taken without bloodshed in the first aggressive act of the war, coinciding with the opening day of the second Continental Congress. After the capture of the fort, more of Allen's men arrived and began looting and drinking; appalled, Arnold made another attempt to take command and shots were fired by Allen's men.

Another Vermonter, Seth Warner, led a party of fifty men upriver and seized Crown Point—also now a shadow of its former self—the following afternoon. The garrison comprised nine soldiers and ten women and children, but the arsenal contained over 100 guns. A third group, this time made up of Arnold's men, seized a prominent local Tory, Major Philip Skene, and the schooner that he kept on Lake Champlain. Arnold fitted it with four cannon and some lighter armament and, on May 17, raided the fort at St. John's in Quebec, surprising the fifteen-man garrison and capturing a sixteen-gun sloop.

Both Arnold and Allen then made representations to the Continental Congress that they could successfully invade Canada with under 2,000 men. Congress, however, wisely considered both men too headstrong and uncontrollable. Once Washington had approved the concept of an invasion based on Fort Ticonderoga, they gave the command to Major General Philip Schuyler of New York, the fourth senior officer of the Continental Army and commander of the newly formed Northern Department.

Further south, the militia in New York City greeted the news of Lexington by seizing the arsenal and two ships at anchor in the harbor loaded with provisions and supplies for the Regulars in Boston. Within weeks, a Provincial Congress had been formed and numerous watch companies set up to patrol and police the city. The harbor had also been closed, although the presence of some remaining warships meant that citizens had to live under the guns of the Royal Navy for the time being. By July, New York as a whole had raised 3,000 Continentals and over 2,000 men were drilling in the city.

CANADA

Congress saw a British-controlled Canada as a threat and the 60,000 French colonists, or Canadians, as the opportunity to remove it. But although the Canadians were far from proud, patriotic subjects of George III, they were less than impressed with the anti-Papist credentials of many members of Congress.

On June 27, Congress ordered Major General Philip Schuyler to invade Canada. From his experiences in the French and Indian Wars, Schuyler understood only too well how important supply lines were to an army, and also how difficult it was to supply an army in the sparsely inhabited wilderness of upper New York and Quebec. He also suffered from chronic gout, which kept him away from his troops to such an extent that the task of leading them into Canada was given to his second-in-command, Brigadier General Richard Montgomery.

Montgomery immediately moved north up Lake Champlain toward the British fort at St. John's (which had been recaptured, since Arnold had seized it in May). He was then rejoined by Schuyler, who promptly ordered a withdrawal, believing the Royal garrison to be too strong, then reversed his decision and launched an attack, which failed. He finally handed command back to a doubtless relieved Montgomery, who opened the siege on September 16. The British commander, Major Preston, held out for seven cold, wet weeks until, with just three days' provisions remaining, he was forced to surrender. For once, the bravery of the garrison was not in vain and the delay was to have serious repercussions for the Rebels, who were running short of supplies, had no winter clothing and were only signed up to serve until December 31.

Further north, other Rebel groups were having mixed fortunes. Allen had succeeded to some extent in finding recruits—both English and French—for the Canadian regiments being raised for Congress by James Livingston and Moses Hazen. On September 25, Allen had tried to capture Montreal, but was beaten off by Loyalist militia. In October, a Rebel force (including Canadian recruits) had captured Fort Chambly and its seventy-eight defenders. Eventually, Montgomery marched on Montreal and forced the governor of Quebec, Major General Guy Carleton, to flee to Quebec City, leaving Montreal to surrender on November 12.

Meanwhile, the irrepressible Arnold had persuaded Washington to give him command of another force being sent into Canada, this time via northern Massachusetts (now Maine). Leaving Boston on September 13, Arnold led more than 1,000 men overland to Newburyport, then by water to Gardinerstown at the end of the Kennebec River. The plan was to travel up the Kennebec in 200 bateaux, cross the promontory known as "Height of Land" and then continue down the Chaudière River that

Above: *View of Quebec from the Ferry House. (National Archives of Canada)*

flowed into the St. Lawrence opposite Quebec City. The route had apparently been surveyed in advance and compared favorably with that taken by Montgomery.

In fact, Arnold had miscalculated both the distance to be traveled and the time the journey would take. His men found themselves carrying the bateaux through swamps and over rapids in an absolute wilderness, with their supplies dwindling. On October 25, some 300 men voted to turn back after four days of constant rain. The remainder pressed on and just over 600 reached Point Levi on November 9. They crossed the river by canoe on November 13 and pitched camp a mile from the walls, but pulled back twenty miles to Point-aux-Trembles on news of a suspected sortie by the garrison.

Here they were joined by Montgomery and 300 men from Montreal. However, with no artillery heavy enough to breach the defenses, and with enlistments soon due to expire, it was clear that a conventional siege was out of the question. The two men agreed that the only option was an all-out assault.

QUEBEC: DECEMBER 31, 1775

The plan was to wait for a blizzard to hit the city, which it duly did on New Year's Eve. Arnold would then lead his 600 men along the bank of the St. Charles River and through the suburb of St. Roche, while Montgomery would take his 300 troops along the narrow path beside the St. Lawrence, passing under the Cape Diamond bastion at the southern end of the city walls. Having entered the Lower Town from two sides, the Rebels would set fire to the mainly wooden buildings and, in the ensuing confusion, capture the citadel from below.

Inside the city, Carleton had only seventy Regulars, but the militia, and the marines and sailors from the two Royal Navy warships trapped by the ice, augmented his total available force to around 1,200 men. But without knowing where the enemy would strike, he had to defend the entire city. The Rebels could virtually guarantee that—initially, at least—they would outnumber the defenders at the point of contact.

The attack began at 4:00 a.m., as Arnold managed to get past the Palace Gate, but was held up by a barricade that the defenders had erected across the main road into the Lower Town, the Sault au Matelot. Early on, Arnold was wounded in the leg and had to be carried to the rear, and Brigadier General Daniel Morgan took over command, as the attack became bogged down in street fighting. Carleton managed to gather 200 men, whom he sent to cut off their retreat. Without assistance from Montgomery, Morgan's men would be surrounded and captured.

Unfortunately, by that time Montgomery was dead and the rest of his command had fled. The leading elements of his column had arrived at a barricade that Carleton had erected in anticipation of just such an attack. The Rebels were challenged and Montgomery was killed in the first volley of canister and hand grenades. Morgan's men held out as long as they could, but finally surrendered when dawn showed the hopelessness of their position. The Rebel losses were sixty killed and wounded and over 400 captured; Carleton's casualties were five dead and thirteen wounded.

Above: *View of Quebec from the Île d'Orléans. The hill on the left is the Cap Diamond Bastion under which Montgomery's group passed on their way into the Lower Town. (National Maritime Museum)* **Below:** *Plan of the siege of Quebec. (British Library)*

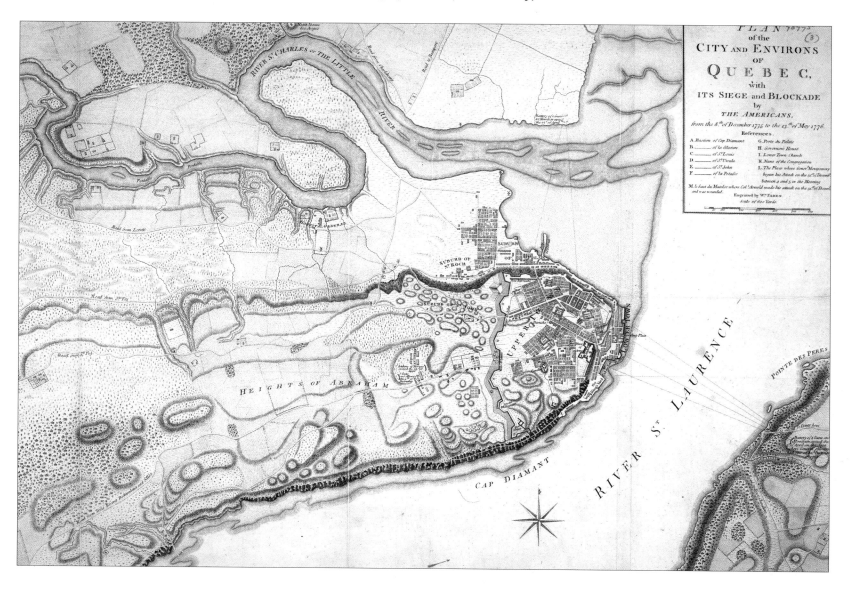

Laid low by injury, and with his force reduced to 500 through casualties and expiration of enlistments, Arnold called for more men and a replacement commander. In April, Montgomery's second-in-command and temporary governor of Montreal, Brigadier General David Wooster, arranged to swap places with Arnold to allow him to recover. Arnold agreed, but made no secret of his personal and professional contempt for the man who had antagonized the *Canadiens* by closing the churches on Chirstmas Day. With smallpox and desertion further reducing the besiegers, there were no further attempts made to capture Quebec City, only a hope that the spring thaw would come late and the garrison would be starved into surrender. It did not happen and this was as near as the Rebels would come to conquering Canada.

VIRGINIA

Virginia, oldest and largest of the Thirteen Colonies (covering over 30,000 square miles), contained almost twenty percent of the entire population of British North America. Of these, around 200,000 were slaves—almost as many as the other colonies put together—and only South Carolina had a lower ratio of whites to blacks outside the Caribbean. This had resulted in a militia that was alert and pro-Whig, but organized primarily to combat slave

John IV Earl of Dunmore
Captain in Regiment of Foot Guards
1755. Governor of Virginia 1770.

Left: *Lord Dunmore (1732–1809). John Murray, 4th Earl Dunmore, had been appointed governor of Virginia in 1771, having previously been governor of New York. Initially popular with Virginians, his fall from grace began when he dissolved the House of Burgesses in 1773 in response to the rising tide of anti-government sentiment. (Scottish National Portrait Gallery)*

revolts. Not that Virginians were slow to display their anger toward others: only the previous year, the Royal governor—Lord Dunmore—had defeated a Shawnee uprising (known as Dunmore's War) and there was a history of disputes with Pennsylvania over the Ohio Valley.

Ironically, the political unity forged by Dunmore's War had aided Virginia's political representatives in supporting the New Englanders in their dispute with Great Britain. On April 20, Dunmore seized twenty barrels of gunpowder at Williamsburg. A lawyer named Patrick Henry called out the militia, in reply to which Dunmore outlawed him and threatened to arm the slaves. The moderates on both sides regained control, but only after Dunmore had to pay for the powder from his own pocket. When news of Lexington arrived, Dunmore was faced with threats to take him hostage and, on June 8, sought refuge aboard a Royal Navy vessel anchored in the York River.

This river was one of four major waterways (the others being the James, the Rappahanock, and the Potomac) that snaked across Virginia. Each was navigable for some distance inland, while a network of creeks and smaller rivers ensured that almost every town and plantation was accessible by water—a feature of which Dunmore made good use. He assembled a small flotilla and, reinforced by a detachment of Regulars from Florida, had seized or destroyed over seventy cannon, in addition to other military supplies, by the end of October.

On November 7, he declared martial law and offered freedom to those slaves or indentured servants who would serve the King. Within days, over 100 "loyal Ethiopians" had joined him and, together with the Regulars, the little army marched to Great Bridge, some twelve miles from Norfolk. Their approach caused 300 militia to flee in panic, but a force of Continentals compelled Dunmore to withdraw to Great Bridge.

The causeway at Great Bridge was the main land route into Norfolk and Dunmore had his troops construct a small wooden fort beside it. He soon discovered, however, that the Rebels were about to be reinforced with artillery and, believing they were only 300 strong, he decided to take the offensive. On December 9, he ordered his Regulars to attack across the causeway. In fact, the enemy had over 1,000 men and the result was a slaughter, the Regulars losing seventeen dead and forty-nine wounded from 130 officers and men. With more enemy troops arriving daily, Dunmore decided to abandon Norfolk and put the remaining troops aboard his flotilla. On January 1, he bombarded Norfolk, whereupon the starving garrison went on a two-day rampage that ended with the town being burned. Although this was done to prevent Dunmore's troops from sheltering there, his bombardment was blamed for all the damage and the "Norfolk incident" was cited as an argument for independence.

As the Rebel forces increased, they also became more active and eventually Dunmore found it impossible to establish a base anywhere on the Chesapeake. Consequently he was obliged to cruise the Potomac, burning plantations and seizing stores, until the following August, when he learned of the abortive attack on Charleston, South Carolina, and headed for New York.

EUROPE

The political conflict between Great Britain and the Colonies soon became a talking point in clubs and *salons* across Europe. News of British plans and strengths had filtered through via French agents who had penetrated the Admiralty, in London, although little information of this was yet being passed to the Americans.

At home, opinion in Parliament was divided, the Whigs welcoming American successes and courting favor with their London agents, while the Tories predictably condemned them. On October 26, the king opened a new session of Parliament and declared that decisive measures were needed to end the disorder in North America, for which purpose the senior commanders of Royal forces on the far side of the Atlantic would be given the power to accept the submission of any colony that wished to return to normality. The opening debates saw the government achieve comfortable two-thirds majorities in both the House of Commons (176 votes to 72) and the House of Lords (76 votes to 33), while a proposal to repeal the Intolerable Acts as a first step to conciliation was roundly rejected.

Among the general public, though, there was no outcry or patriotic demonstration; after all, it was not their fight. Recruiting actually fell, due to the prospect of being sent to fight in North America, forcing the government to look to Europe. Empress Catherine II of Russia was approached for 30,000 men (the idea being that their lack of English and natural subservience would forestall any sympathy for the Rebels), but she declined, due to a war with the Turks. Great Britain's oldest ally—Portugal—was not interested (and probably did not boast troops of an appropriate quality), while her main European ally in the previous conflict, Prussia, was positively hostile, Frederick still smarting over his perceived betrayal by "perfidious Albion."

Certain minor German states, however, saw a rare chance to fill the national coffers and offered to supply men. Initially, they were politely dismissed, but as the North ministry considered ways of ending the rebellion, it soon became painfully apparent that Great Britain did not, and never would, have enough men to do the job. Consequently, the first quarter of 1776 saw a flurry of activity between the palace of St. James and the courts of Hesse-Kassel, Brunswick-Wolfenbuttel, and sundry other principalities.

Left: *Patrick Henry (1736–1799). Henry had urged armed resistance to Dunmore and marched on Williamsburg with a unit of militia when Dunmore seized the public arsenal. As colonel of the first provincial regiment raised by Virginia in 1775, he was technically commander-in-chief of all military forces in the colony. Denied the opportunity to exercise control over the militia by opponents within his own party, he resigned from military life in February 1776. (Independence National History Park)*

1776

"These are the times that try men's souls"

THOMAS PAINE

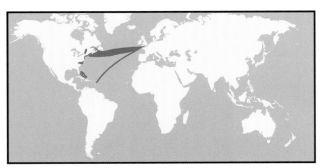

RED INDICATES FIGHTING, INCLUDING PRIVATEERING ON SHIPPING LANES

The evacuation of Boston (March 17, 1776). (Anne S. K. Brown Military Collection)

The strategy of the North ministry for 1776 was to overawe the Rebels with a massive (by British standards) show of force. Despite the views of Gage, it was still felt that the conflict was the work of a few agitators, who had somehow stirred up the passions of the ordinary people (few of whom had ever been affected by the Stamp Act or taxes on luxury goods). At worst, it was akin to the Jacobite Rebellion of 1745, in which support had been sporadic and localized. In fairness, this view appeared to be borne out by the constant references to the "Ministerial" forces (rather than the King's men) in Rebel propaganda and genuine expressions of alarm at the growing influence of the independence party.

The "grand design" involved clearing Canada, then moving down Lake Champlain to join the main army at the Hudson River, and moving north after establishing New York City as the main British base in North America. The two armies would then unite and strike eastward at Boston. Both forces would set up fortified posts along the length of the Hudson valley, effectively creating a military "buffer zone" between New England—widely seen as the source of discontent—and the remaining colonies, which were assumed to be predominantly loyal.

It is quite probable that a swift, successful campaign, leaving New England isolated, would have led even hardliners to question the wisdom of continuing

Right: *George Sackville, Lord Germain (1716–1785) was Secretary of State for the American Colonies from November 1775 until February 1782. Though widely considered the architect of British defeat in the war, in fact he was responsible for the successful buildup of British forces in America in 1776. His biggest failure was in understanding the nature of the war and the confusion that followed his attempts to direct it from London. (The Courtauld Institute and Knowle Estates)*

the struggle. As events transpired, it might also have avoided the widespread disaffection of Loyalists and neutrals by confining plundering to overwhelmingly pro-Rebel Massachusetts and Connecticut. However, the plan needed considerable coordination to stand a chance of success—a difficult proposition given that the starting points were over 500 miles apart, with most of the intervening territory either held by the enemy, or impenetrable wilderness. It also required commanders who were bold, energetic, and—perhaps most important of all—lucky.

CANADA

The Separate Army, now commanded by Arnold, maintained its siege of Quebec City, despite the failure of the assault on New Year's Eve. Prospects, however, were bleak: there were no trained gunners or engineers; enlistments were expiring; provisions and military supplies were running short; and there were too few doctors to treat the recent outbreak of smallpox. Support from the local population, already dwindling, was further diminished by the efforts of local priests and the lack of gold in the military chest, forcing the Rebels to issue a proclamation that anyone refusing to accept paper currency would be treated as an enemy. In Montreal, the garrison was threatening to withdraw once the ice melted.

On May 6, a British relief force (led by the 29th Foot—the infamous "vein openers" of the Boston "Massacre") arrived outside Quebec City, forcing Thomas, who had replaced the convalescing Arnold, to withdraw to Sorel. There, the Rebel army—now known as the Northern Army—received reinforcements led by Major General John Sullivan, who took over command.

On June 6, Sullivan attempted a surprise assault on the British camp at Trois Rivières, believing it to be held by just 800 men (in fact there were 6,000). After a two-day journey by bateaux to within three miles of his objective, 1,500 men moved off, led by a *Canadien* guide. Either by accident or design, they ended up in a large swamp and were exhausted when they reached the British camp. After driving in the advanced posts, they attacked the main entrenchments and were driven off, with some loss. Carleton deliberately let the remainder escape, as he did not wish to be burdened with prisoners (although he still ended up with almost 250, including the senior officer, Brigadier General William Thompson). The Rebels retreated through the swamp, pursued by Indians, *Canadiens*, and mosquitoes. Barely 1,100 survivors arrived back at Sorel three days later. The British lost eight dead and nine wounded.

Sullivan wanted to remain at Sorel, but his subordinates overruled him. Short of food, riddled with smallpox, and thoroughly disheartened by its recent experiences, the Northern Army withdrew to Crown Point. The speed and distance of their retreat surprised Carleton, who arrived at Sorel on June 14, to find it deserted, as was Fort Chambly, whch he reached four days later. In the intervening twelve miles, Sullivan had had all the bridges destroyed and trees felled across the roads in the dense woods. When the British arrived at Île-aux-Noix, at the head of Lake Champlain, they found enemy corpses riddled with smallpox putrefying in the heat.

Carleton spent the next few months constructing a freshwater fleet capable of controlling Lake Champlain, transporting his troops and keeping them supplied. This took longer than anticipated, not least due to the sheer number of vessels—almost 700—that he believed were needed to ensure superiority over the fleet being built by Arnold at the southern end of the lake. The vessels had to be built from scratch, which meant finding large supplies of seasoned timber and craftsmen willing to do the work.

Above: *Montreal from the mountain. Unlike Quebec, Montreal saw no fighting during the invasion of Canada. (British Library)*

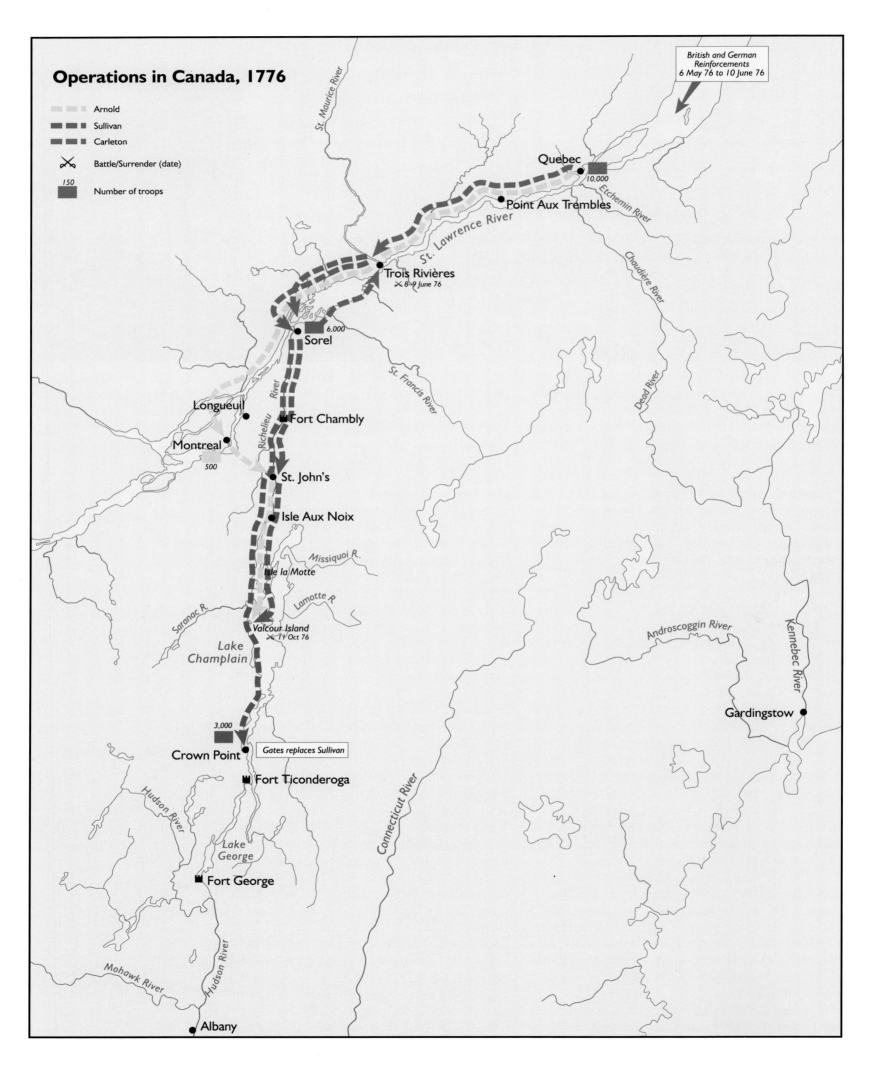

Operations in Canada, 1776

Arnold
Sullivan
Carleton

Battle/Surrender (date)

150 Number of troops

British and German Reinforcements 6 May 76 to 10 June 76

Quebec
10,000

Point Aux Trembles

St. Maurice River

St. Lawrence River

Etchemin River

Chaudière River

Trois Rivières
8–9 June 76

Sorel
6,000

St. Francis River

Dead River

Longueuil

Fort Chambly

Montreal
500

Richelieu River

St. John's

Isle Aux Noix

Missiquoi R.

Isle la Motte

Lamotte R.

Androscoggin River

Kennebec River

Saranac R.

Valcour Island
11 Oct 76

Lake Champlain

Gardingstow

Crown Point
3,000

Gates replaces Sullivan

Fort Ticonderoga

Connecticut River

Hudson River

Lake George

Fort George

Mohawk River

Hudson River

Albany

The weather, too, was far from kind, with heavy rain through August and September, and increasingly cold nights. Yet despite these problems, Carleton was criticized for not pressing ahead to Crown Point and Fort Ticonderoga, which were being hurriedly rebuilt and reinforced by the enemy.

Eventually, he sent his brother, Thomas, south with 400 Indians on September 10 (later reinforcing them with 100 Canadians and 1,300 Germans), and moved his Advance Guard, under Brigadier General Simon Fraser, to within five miles of the New York border. This left Burgoyne in command of the main body on Île-aux-Noix, with Carleton leading his recently completed flotilla on to the lake on October 4.

Meanwhile, Arnold had moved his smaller fleet north up Lake Champlain, close to the border, in early September. Threatened by Indians, he withdrew to Cumberland Head, and then to a secure anchorage at Valcour Island, on September 23. It was there, on October 11, that Carleton's fleet found him. In the ensuing action, Arnold's force was largely destroyed; however, his movements—indeed, his mere presence on the lake—had bought valuable time.

After the defeat at Valcour Island, the Rebels were forced to abandon Crown Point, which Carleton then occupied, but the British did not move against Fort Ticonderoga, despite the advice of many junior commanders. Carleton felt that winter was too close (in fact, it came early and was extremely bitter, even by local standards) to besiege a fortress which, so rumor had it, was well garrisoned and had been restored to something approaching its former strength. He decided to retire to St. John's for the winter, to rest and organize for the inevitable campaign of the following spring. His many enemies in London—including Germain—ensured that the version of events that reached the king was highly detrimental. It overlooked the problems of moving into unknown territory controlled by an enemy who could still give a good account of himself, and that without capturing Fort Ticonderoga, Carleton could not remain on Lake Champlain. His decision might have been colored by memories of Abercromby's disastrous attack in 1758; certainly he was unaware that the garrison's supplies there were all but exhausted. In addition, his engineers had strongly advised against wintering at Crown Point, where every building (including the vital saw mills) had been burned by Sullivan. Without shelter or defenses, Carleton would have suffered heavy losses to the weather and have left himself vulnerable to raids.

As for the Rebel forces, it is quite probable that their expulsion from Canada actually benefited them in the long-term, by removing what would undoubtedly have become a major drain on scarce resources. Despite pressure from displaced Canadians, such as Moses Hazen, plans for another invasion were rejected in 1778, 1780, and 1781, due to shortages of men and material, the logistical requirements, the strength of the enemy, and a lack of interest from the French that was not entirely unwelcome to their allies, many of whom were not keen to see New France re-established.

THE CAROLINAS

As events deteriorated in New England through the second half of 1775, Dartmouth and then Germain (the latter with rather more reservations) began to consider an expedition to the South. Much of this was driven by economic considerations, particularly the need for tobacco to fulfil contracts with European buyers. Although the four Royal governors had all been expelled by strong Rebel forces, they had managed to convince the Government that substantial Loyalist elements existed and the appearance of a force of Regulars would soon restore the status quo.

Most persistent and optimistic was Josiah Martin of North Carolina, who felt that the large Scottish contingent and people from the "back-country" (known as Regulators) who were politically opposed to the Whig plantation owners, were ready to flock to the Royal cause. The plan was to land troops from

Below: *Canadian farmer. In 1775, there were 75,000 French-speaking Canadians and both sides were eager to secure their support. However, few ordinary people were interested in fighting for either side. (New York Public Library)*

VALCOUR ISLAND: OCTOBER 11–13, 1776

On the morning of October 11, Carleton passed Cumberland Head, aware that Arnold's fleet was near. Due to the strong winds, he overshot Valcour Island by two miles, but one of Arnold's vessels had already spotted the British and Arnold decided to use his four fastest vessels (including his own "flag-ship" *Congress*) to draw Carleton into the southern end of the channel, which he blocked by arranging the rest of his fleet in line of battle. However, on seeing the strength of Carleton's command, he returned to the channel, which required him to beat against a heavy wind, made more unpredictable by the surrounding cliffs and pine forests. The wind forced the *Royal Savage* aground on the southern tip of Valcour Island, where she was attacked and crippled by the leading British schooner, *Carleton*, which also fell foul of the wind. The ship was heading straight into the Rebel line when her commander dropped anchor and, using a spring in the cable, swung the vessel back broadside on to the enemy.

The other British sailing vessels were unable to make headway, but several gunboats (which were being rowed) came up to support *Carleton* and the two sides traded shots for over an hour, until the spring was shot away from her cable (throughout the action, Indians poured musket fire into Arnold's line from both shores, but with little effect). Around 2:00 p.m., Carleton's line began to withdraw, two gunboats towing the *Carleton* to safety. Meanwhile, the *Royal Savage*, trapped on the beach, was boarded by the crew of the *Thunderer* who were in turn driven off by gunfire from other Rebel vessels. A rescue attempt was thwarted by the crew of the *Maria* who set fire to the *Royal Savage*, which blew up after dark. About 5:00 p.m., as dusk fell, the *Inflexible* came up to support the gunboats and silenced the remainder of Arnold's vessels.

Carleton assumed he had Arnold trapped and would finish him off the next day, but a northeasterly breeze allowed the latter to slip away into the lake. It took three hours for the vessels to pass through the British line and move far enough down the lake to be able to use their oars. Unfortunately, the wind then turned, preventing Arnold's vessels from making good their escape, and a stop for essential repairs (during which two gundalows and the *Jersey* had to be abandoned) further reduced their lead. Both sides spent much of October 12 rowing against the wind, and by dawn on October 13, Arnold's surviving vessels were twenty-eight miles from Crown Point, having covered just six miles. Another change in the wind gave an initial benefit to Carleton, who closed the gap to one mile, forcing the *Washington* to surrender and the *Lee* to run ashore, leaving just *Congress* and four gundalows. After a brief, one-sided fight, Arnold ordered his crews to beach on the Vermont shore, where they burned their vessels and fled overland to Crown Point. With only 200 men remaining, Arnold decided to abandon the post and he burned the buildings before retreating to Fort Ticonderoga.

Arnold had fifteen (possibly sixteen) of his nineteen vessels present at the battle, of which eleven were lost over the three days. Of his 750 crewmen, sixty became casualties during the battle, another twenty during the pursuit, with 100 more taken prisoner from the *Washington* (these men returning so full of praise for their treatment by Carleton that they were sent home to avoid damaging morale!). Out of Carleton's force of four sailing ships, one "radeau" (a huge, two-masted raft), twenty gunboats and four armed rowing boats, only the two largest sailing vessels and the gunboats were engaged (around 670 crew and 200 infantry serving as marines). His losses are not known, but given the limited damage done to the worst-hit vessel, the *Carleton*, they must have been extremely light.

Right: *Battle of Valcour Island (October 11, 1776). Another view of the battle, this time from Arnold's line of gunboats as the British approach. (Library of Congress)*

Below right: *Battle of Valcour Island (October 11, 1776). The view from the south as Carleton's fleet rounds the southern end of Valcour Island. (The Royal Collection 2001 © Her Majesty Queen Elizabeth II)*

Below: *Carleton's fleet at Valcour Island. Carleton's flotilla was gathering at St. John's and a number of vessels, including the three-masted sloop* Inflexible, *had to be moved around the rapids on the Richelieu River. Carleton tried to move the sloop on rollers, but the ground was too soft and it had to be dismantled, carried down to St. John's in pieces, and reassembled. (Library of Congress)*

Opposite page, top:

Commodore Sir Peter Parker (1721–1811) commanded the Royal Navy element of the Charleston expedition. Despite considerable experience, Parker did not handle his ships well and negligent pilots compounded his problems by running three of his ships aground. He and Clinton blamed each other for the fiasco. (National Maritime Museum)

Opposite page, bottom:

Attack on Charleston as seen from on board the Bristol (June 28, 1776). Drawn by an artillery officer who witnessed the action. Fort Sullivan is at the extreme right. (Beverley R Robinson Collection)

Right: *Aftermath of the battle (October 13, 1776). After Arnold had slipped past Carleton on the night of October 11, the following day saw a chase down Lake Champlain. By dawn on the third day, the British appeared to be gaining and Arnold's men decided to beach their vessels and escape across country.*

Boston and Ireland at Cape Fear, North Carolina, in mid-February, to help local Loyalists regain control of Virginia, the Carolinas, and Georgia. Having accomplished this, the Regulars would move north to reinforce Howe, who should by then have occupied New York City.

Unfortunately, Martin made the error of assuming that all would go to plan. In early February, he called out the Loyalists and sent two Scottish Regular officers to organize and lead them. However, the Regulators held back and the others became disillusioned and began to drift home, leaving 1,400 men—mainly Highlanders—of whom barely half were armed. Meanwhile, the Rebel militia had assembled and one group managed to maneuver the Loyalist "army" toward another militia force at Moore's Creek Bridge, blocking the Loyalists' route to the sea. Dismantling the bridge and fighting from behind prepared defenses, the Rebels easily defeated the Loyalists, who retreated and were later captured. All suspected Loyalists in the region were then disarmed, effectively neutralizing them for the rest of the War.

Meanwhile, overall command of the main force was given to Clinton (not least so as to remove him from Howe's presence), and he left Boston on January 20 with just 100 men in three ships. However, he had conflicting orders: to move as rapidly as possible to the rendezvous, but also to stop at various ports along the way. On February 4, he arrived at New York City, where Governor Tryon had had to seek refuge aboard a Royal Navy ship in the harbor. He then met with Governor Dunmore, also living aboard ship, in Hampton Roads, on February 17. Delayed by bad weather, Clinton finally arrived at Cape Fear on March 12, where Governors Martin and Campbell brought him news of various disasters, not least the defeat at Moore's Creek Bridge. Worse, there was no news of the 3,000 troops from Ireland under Major General Lord Cornwallis and the squadron under Commodore Sir Peter Parker, which was supposed to arrive in early February. In fact, Parker had only left Cork on February 13; delayed by contrary winds, he reached Cape Fear on April 18 and Cornwallis two weeks later, with stragglers still arriving in late May.

Finding Cape Fear unsuitable as an anchorage, and with discretion from Germain to attack elsewhere if North Carolina was held by large Rebel forces, Clinton considered establishing raiding posts along the Chesapeake, but Parker and Campbell persuaded him instead to attack Charleston. Unfortunately, Congress and the South Carolina Assembly had anticipated such a move and had raised substantial numbers of troops and improved the city's defenses, especially the forts and batteries

on the islands guarding the entrance to the harbor. In addition, Washington had sent Lee to supervise the preparations and take command (characteristically, he did little except criticize the efforts of others).

The British plan involved a preliminary assault on the unfinished fort on Sullivan's Island, but their four-week preparation allowed the defenders to complete the two sides facing the main channel. When Clinton landed on neighboring Long Island, he found the crossing point to Sullivan's Island (which had not been sounded) too deep and had to abandon the plan to cut the garrison's line of retreat. Unfavorable winds delayed Parker's attack another five days and he decided to go ahead without Clinton's help. By then, the Rebels had 7,000 troops available and the fort mounted twenty-five guns.

June 28 was not one of the Royal Navy's better days: as the leading vessels engaged the fort, more tried to slip past and outflank it, but three immediately ran aground (one of which could not be refloated and had to be burned). This saved the Rebels; for had those ships continued upriver they could have fired directly into the fort over the unfinished west face. As it was, the completed sections—sixteen feet thick and faced with palmetto logs—proved impregnable to the ten-hour British bombardment. Return fire from the fort inflicted 200 casualties, a third of them killed, against twelve dead and twenty-five wounded among the garrison. Deciding against any further attempts, the British force sailed for New York City, arriving on August 2. The real damage, however, was the humiliating nature of the defeat and the freedom of action it gave the Rebels, knowing that the South was secure.

British bungling alone had averted a major disaster for Rebel arms: the arrival of the British ships on

Above: *Colonel William Moultrie (1730–1805) was a recognized military leader in South Carolina, having participated in expeditions against the Cherokees. In 1775, he was appointed colonel of one of the two South Carolina Continental regiments and held Fort Sullivan against the attack by the Royal Navy. (Independence National Historical Park)*

June 1 caused panic among the civilian population and Lee had genuine concerns about the defensibility of Fort Sullivan. The attack demonstrated several inherent weaknesses that would haunt British efforts throughout the war: the paralyzing effect of conflicting orders from military commanders and politicians; the lack of reliable maps and charts of operational areas; and poor cooperation between the Army and the Royal Navy (both Clinton and Parker accused each other of failing to support the attack). It was these shortcomings, rather than a lack of intelligence (military or cerebral), that would defeat otherwise workable plans in the years ahead.

NEW YORK

Meanwhile, Sir William Howe—who had been forced to remain at Halifax until June because of a lack of provisions—had finally sailed for New York. Arriving at Sandy Hook, he resolved to seize control of the narrow channel between Staten Island and Long Island, which he rightly saw as the key to the harbor. He established posts on Staten Island, which had been secured as a naval base by his brother, Lord Richard Howe, the senior naval commander in American waters. However, nothing further happened in July and well into August. Sir William Howe cited the risk of sickness among the troops from overexertion in the heat, and the numbers of the enemy (especially in artillery) and the strength of their defenses on Long Island.

In fairness, the seasons were more extreme in North America than in Europe (during the siege of Boston, Lee compared the heat of summer with that in Spain). It was also true that, even if Howe's men were invincible, they were certainly not immortal. Like Marlborough before him, and Wellington later, he had Great Britain's only army and could not afford to lose it. A colleague, General Murray (then commander of the Minorca garrison), suggested that Washington's best plan was to lose a battle each week until the Royal forces were destroyed! Benjamin Franklin was equally sanguine about tactical defeats, believing that America could absorb losses, whereas a British defeat would be decisive.

In the meantime, as reinforcements dribbled in from Great Britain and Ireland, and Clinton returned from Charleston, the Howe brothers devoted themselves to their role as mediators and tentatively opened negotiations with representatives of Congress. They published their intent in a Proclamation that offered pardons and consideration of a fairer form of government for the Colonies. (Unfortunately, because the covering letter was sent to Washington as a private individual, rather than as commander-in-chief of the Rebel army, he refused to receive it.) In any event, the recent Declaration of Independence meant that only military defeat would now bring Congress to the negotiating table, although it is unclear whether that occurred to the Howes. Possibly their brief, their views of the Colonists, or both, stopped them realizing that such a drastic measure was the only option remaining.

Driven by civil, rather than military, imperatives, and admittedly against his own better judgment, Washington had scattered his forces around Long Island and Manhattan to defend New York City. The Howes have been criticized for not landing on Manhattan and cutting him off entirely; however, without knowledge of the enemy dispositions, and controlling only one side of the channel into the harbor, this would have been extremely risky, relying on southerly winds for success (which, for most of the summer, were from the north). As it was, they proceeded with the capture of Long Island and on August 22, 15,000 troops landed, unopposed, at Gravesend Bay. Four days later, Sir William Howe defeated Putnam in the Battle of Brooklyn, inflicting

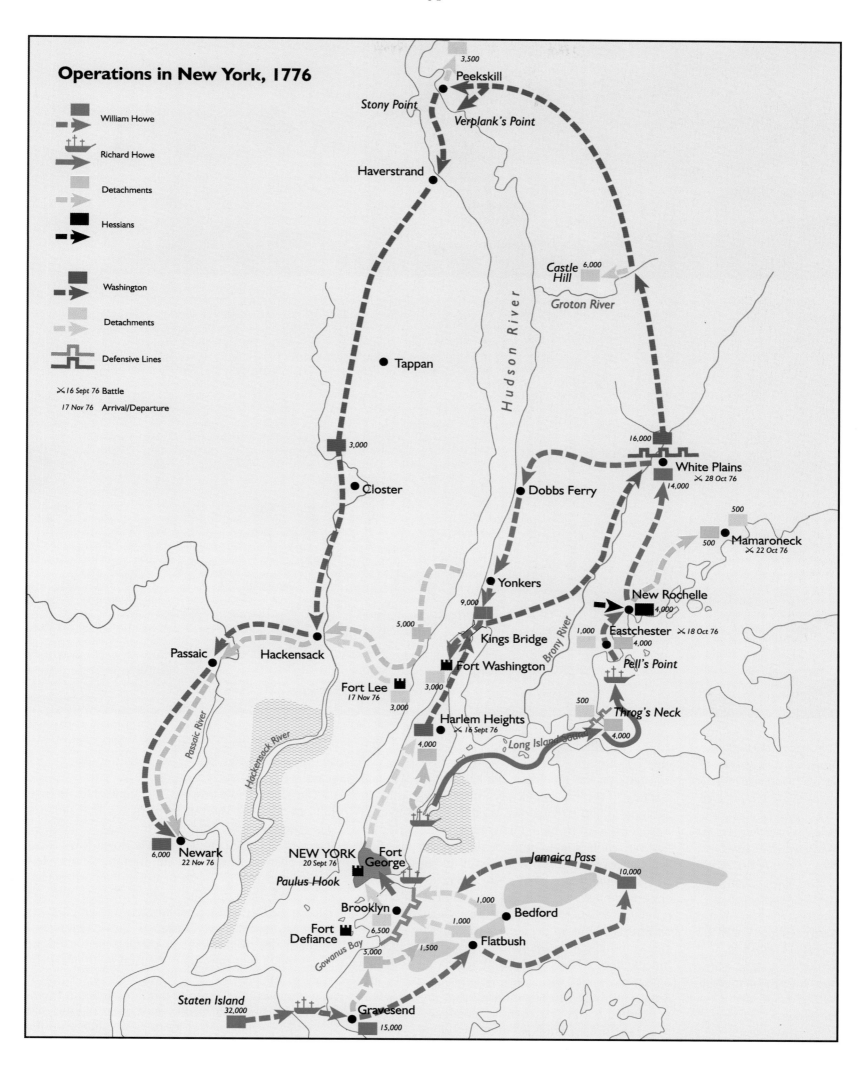

Operations in New York, 1776

Legend:
- William Howe
- Richard Howe
- Detachments
- Hessians
- Washington
- Detachments
- Defensive Lines
- ✕ *16 Sept 76* Battle
- *17 Nov 76* Arrival/Departure

Peekskill 3,500

Stony Point

Verplank's Point

Haverstrand

Castle Hill 6,000

Groton River

Hudson River

Tappan

16,000

White Plains ✕ *28 Oct 76*
14,000

Closter

Dobbs Ferry

3,000

Mamaroneck 500 ✕ *22 Oct 76*
500

Yonkers

9,000

New Rochelle 4,000

5,000

Kings Bridge

Bronx River

Eastchester 1,000 ✕ *18 Oct 76*
4,000

Passaic

Hackensack

Fort Washington

Pell's Point

Fort Lee *17 Nov 76*
3,000
3,000

Harlem Heights ✕ *16 Sept 76*

Throg's Neck 500

Long Island Sound
4,000

4,000

Passaic River

Hackensack River

Newark *22 Nov 76*
6,000

NEW YORK *20 Sept 76*
Fort George

Paulus Hook

Jamaica Pass 10,000

Brooklyn

Bedford 1,000

Fort Defiance 6,500

1,000

Flatbush

Gowanus Bay 5,000 1,500

Staten Island 32,000

Gravesend 15,000

2,000 casualties (ncluding prisoners) and suffering only 300 himself.

Brooklyn was the first major battle of the War and a sound, if incomplete, victory for the Royal army. In addition to battle casualties, Washington's army was further depleted by militiamen returning home for the harvest, while some Continentals decided their first experience of war was one too many and deserted.

The Royal troops then spent the next two weeks sleeping rough on Long Island, while Lord Howe approached Congress for a meeting, which took place on Staten Island on September 11. However, neither side could agree on the status of the Declaration of Independence, Howe arguing that he could not recognize Congress, as it was not recognized by the King, while Congress maintained that an independent United States was more economically beneficial to Great Britain than a set of sulky colonies. Unable

to progress beyond this impasse, the meeting broke up; they were the last peace negotiations for six years.

The Howes now renewed the campaign, though still not with the level of ruthlessness that perhaps was required. With control of the channel between Staten Island and Long Island, the Royal Navy could now operate around Manhattan. This left Washington's army—most of which was concentrated around Harlem, with only Putnam's division holding the City and harbor—exposed to amphibious landings in his rear. However, these required a northerly tide to counteract the strong currents in the East River, and a full night of darkness to allow the boats to get past the enemy batteries in the city. A plan proposed by Clinton to land in the South Bronx area and block Washington's retreat was rejected, but 4,000 troops did land at Kip's Bay, halfway up the

BROOKLYN: AUGUST 26–27, 1776

Although painfully aware that his army was stuck on two islands without naval support, Washington was forced to fortify Brooklyn Heights, as they overlooked New York City harbor. He committed two of his five divisions (about 10,000 of his 28,000 men) to Long Island, giving command to Major General Nathaniel Greene. Unfortunately, Greene fell ill and his deputy, Sullivan (now back from Canada) was superseded by the more senior—but less able—Major General Israel Putnam.

The Rebel forces were divided into two groups, one occupying entrenchments on Brooklyn Heights, the other holding the Heights of Guan, to the southeast. The Guan ridge was intersected by four passes; they were, from south to north: Gowanus Road, Flatbush Road, Bedford Pass, and Jamaica Pass. The first three were guarded by units under William Alexander (also known as Lord Stirling) and Sullivan, but Putnam had neglected Jamaica Pass, on the far left of his line.

Howe soon learned of this and led his main force of 10,000 on a night march north across the Rebel front, then turned southwest to move through Jamaica Pass. Early the next day, Sullivan's men at Flatbush Road and Bedford Pass found themselves outflanked and fled, with Sullivan being taken prisoner. At the same time, the remaining 5,000 Royal troops under James Grant were advancing towards Stirling's men at Gowanus Road. Grant deliberately moved slowly, encouraging Putnam to keep Stirling's men in place long enough for Howe to arrive in their rear and force them to surrender. Stirling and virtually all of his 1,600 men were killed or captured.

Washington now crossed the East River and took command. Recognizing that he could not hold Brooklyn Heights, but still reluctant to abandon New York City, he brought over more men to bring his force back to almost 10,000 strong. For a brief moment, Howe could have captured half the Rebel army and its commander-in-chief, but chose a more cautious approach—perhaps reminded of the losses at Bunker Hill the previous year. There is little doubt that he acted out of concern for the lives of his own men, rather than those of his enemy, as has been suggested; he may also have believed that a second line of defenses stood behind those on Brooklyn Heights. Many of Howe's regiments were fresh from Europe and had not engaged the Rebels before, and there is evidence that he wanted to avoid any setback in this first battle, so as to maintain their clearly superior morale. Whatever the reasons, he balked at a frontal assault and his men began preparing formal siege works, but progress was slowed by heavy rain.

On August 29, after a council of war recommended withdrawal to Manhattan, Colonel John Glover's Marbleheaders rowed Washington and his army back over the East River. Howe has been much criticized by historians for his caution, but at the time, even his own officers were divided on the wisdom of a direct assault.

Left: *Battle at Gowanus Creek. In a desperate attempt to avoid being cut off by Howe's flank march, Stirling's men ford Gowanus Creek to reach the Brooklyn Heights. (Anne S. K. Brown Collection)*

east side of Manhattan, to cut off the city. Warships raked the beach and forced the militia defenders to flee, but Putnam still managed to escape up the west side of Manhattan, albeit without his artillery.

On September 16, British and Hessian advance guards pushed too far ahead and were withdrawn by Clinton; it was a minor check, of little significance to Howe, but the "battle" of Harlem Heights gave a much-needed boost to the morale of Washington's army. Instead of pushing on, Howe decided to occupy New York City, which he entered unopposed, and proceeded to consolidate with a line of redoubts across Manhattan and an outpost at Paulus Hook, protecting the harbor. In his defense, Howe cited the need to obtain intelligence of the surrounding country and the less than enthusiastic reception of the local population. His position was not improved by the fire that broke out in the city on the night of September 20, almost 600 houses being destroyed before troops and civilians extinguished the flames. (There is doubt whether or not the fires were started deliberately: what they did do was to deny a large number of billets to Howe's army during the coming winter.)

It was October 12 before the Royal army moved again. First, it landed on Throg's Neck, a large peninsula behind Washington's left flank. However, this was a poor choice tactically, as the Rebels held the bridge linking the neck to the mainland. After six days, Howe re-embarked his men and landed at Pell's Point. In two more skirmishes at Eastchester and Marmaroneck, the Rebel rearguards again gave a good account of themselves, despite being forced back. The slowness of the advance, however, allowed Washington to leave garrisons in Fort Washington (guarding the northern tip of Manhattan) and Fort Lee (overlooking the Hudson on the New Jersey side) and concentrate his forces in a prepared position at White Plains.

Howe spent three days preparing to attack the main Rebel entrenchments, but was thwarted by

Above: *General Israel Putnam (1718–1790) was a New England legend even before the Revolution, having served in Rogers Rangers during the French and Indian War and Pontiac's War. He took command of the troops on Long Island after Greene fell ill, but was simply not competent as a field commander and was later sent home to train recruits. He retired in 1779, after a stroke. (Anne S. K. Brown Collection)*

WHITE PLAINS: OCTOBER 28, 1776

Howe, now with over 20,000 men, approached Washington's main force, which by this time numbered 16,000. It was only at this point that Washington and his subordinates saw that their position was dominated by Chatterton's Hill. This hill was actually a ridge on the far side of the Bronx River, at the right of the Rebel line. Running north–south, about a mile long and almost 200 feet high, it dominated Washington's entire line. Sending two militia regiments over to occupy it, Washington ordered 1,500 Continentals forward to skirmish with the approaching British and Hessians and buy time for the militia to prepare earthworks. But Howe's men steadily outflanked this advance guard and eventually forced it back on to Chatterton Hill, where an impetuous attack by Hessian grenadiers—eager to show the British their mettle—was beaten off.

Washington now sent another 1,300 Continentals, under the command of Brigadier General Alexander McDougall, and two guns to further reinforce the defenders, as Howe's main force came up and virtually paraded before the Rebel line. Eventually, eight battalions and twelve guns moved forward to attack the hill, while the rest of the Royal forces stood and watched. The British guns soon dominated the action, but the infantry had trouble crossing the river, swollen by recent rain. The Hessians, led by Colonel Johann Rall, began building a bridge, but the British—under Major General Alexander Leslie—crossed via a nearby ford, determined to embarrass their allies.

A bayonet charge by the two leading British regiments was repulsed, partly due to the junior officers in charge of the attack stopping to use their firearms, and the men following suit. A Hessian regiment then advanced on their left, crossing a burning field with cartridge boxes held above their heads to stop their ammunition igniting, but it was also thrown back. More British troops joined the line and a mass attack was stopped in its tracks by heavy fire from the Continentals.

However, Rall's Hessians—who had been crowded over to the extreme right of the Rebel position—now found themselves facing the two militia regiments. Their attack, backed up by a charge by the British light dragoons, caused the militia to panic and rout. This uncovered the right flank of the Continental regiments, which were forced to retire one by one to the main Rebel lines. A small rearguard kept the pursuing British infantry at bay and further attacks were discouraged by heavy artillery fire from the main Rebel position.

Having captured the key to Washington's line, the British and Hessians then halted and made no further attempt at pursuit. Howe, having made no attempt to launch a simultaneous attack on the main position in support of the assault on Chatterton's Hill, simply began preparing artillery positions for a future assault that never took place. Casualties were up to 350 on the Rebel side and 231 British and Hessians.

Above: Phoenix *and the* Rose *with fireships. On July 12, a number of Royal Navy ships broke through the incomplete defenses in the Hudson River and attacked Washington's lines of communications for more than a month. On August 16, Washington ordered an attack by galleys and fireships, which succeeded in destroying one of the smaller vessels. (Anne S K Brown Collection)*

Opposite page, bottom: *Phoenix passing the batteries in the Hudson. Following the attack by fireships on August 16, the flotilla returned, running the gauntlet of the Rebel batteries once more with minimal damage. (National Maritime Museum)*

heavy rain; by the time he was ready, Washington had slipped away. Unwilling to pursue his enemy much further northward, Howe turned south toward Fort Washington. Greene had persuaded Washington that the fort was defensible and the garrison could escape across the Hudson River at will. But a deserter had given away the plans of the fort and although an assault from two sides by British and Hessian troops was again delayed by rain, it went ahead on November 16. The outer lines were quickly stormed and the 2,800-strong garrison was forced to surrender (the largest Rebel loss in a single action until the capture of Charleston, four years later). Unsure as to whether Howe would head north to link up with Carleton, or south to take Philadelphia, Washington left Lee and 7,000 men at Castle Hill and dispatched Heath with 4,000 more to Albany. He then led his remaining 2,000 men across the Hudson at Peekskill, to join Greene at Fort Lee, from where he had the dubious pleasure of watching the disaster at Fort Washington.

Meanwhile, Howe had sent Clinton (against the latter's wishes) to seize Rhode Island. Clinton's fears that the Rebels might have fortified Newport, leaving him to commence a siege in the depths of winter, proved unfounded, and on December 8, he seized Newport without a fight. This provided the Royal Navy with an excellent base and staging post for transatlantic convoys; but it also meant that the Royal army had to detach men to provide a garrison capable of holding it.

NEW JERSEY

After the capture of Fort Washington, Howe sent Cornwallis across the Hudson to take Fort Lee, but this time Greene had the good sense to evacuate the garrison (though much valuable material was left behind). Cornwallis set off in pursuit of Washington, his troops leaving behind their tents and baggage train in an attempt to quicken their pace. He passed through Newark on November 28 and reached New Brunswick on December 1, where he halted to await reinforcements, on Howe's orders. The pursuit was eventually resumed and Cornwallis's advance guard

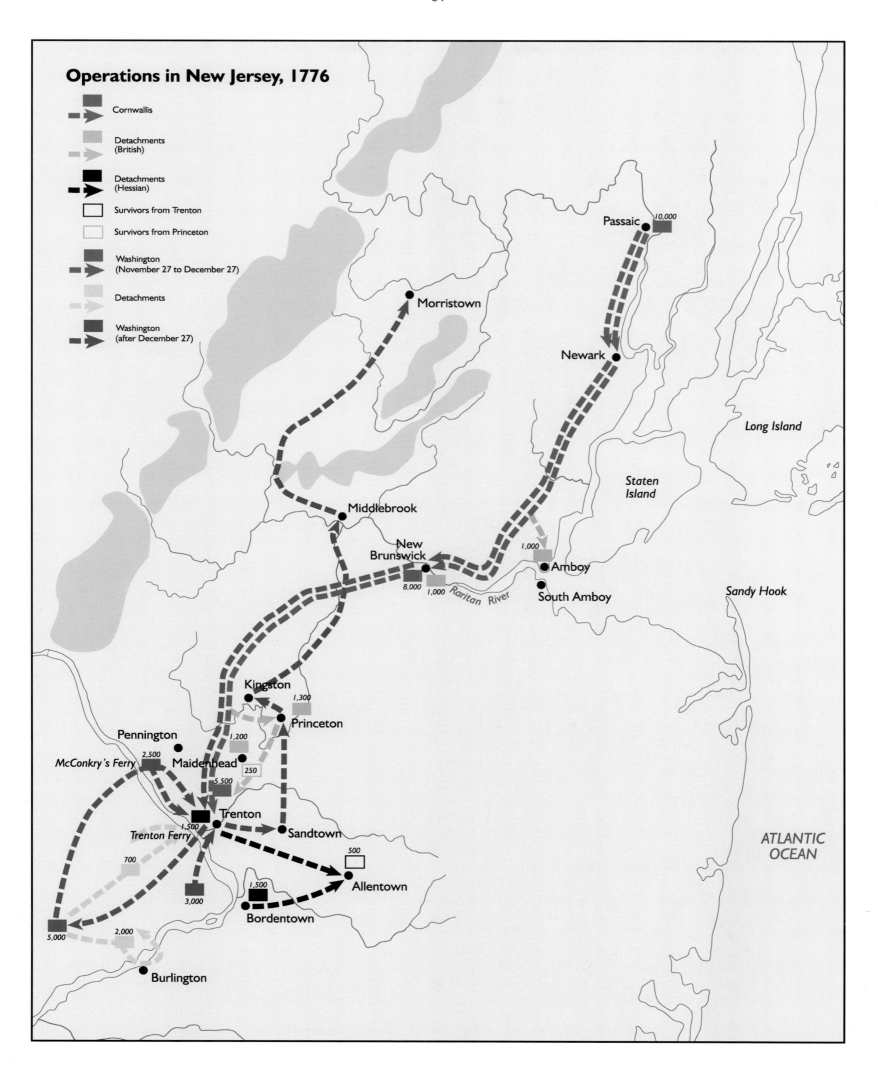

Operations in New Jersey, 1776

Cornwallis

Detachments (British)

Detachments (Hessian)

Survivors from Trenton

Survivors from Princeton

Washington (November 27 to December 27)

Detachments

Washington (after December 27)

Passaic   *10,000*

Newark

Long Island

Morristown

Staten Island

Middlebrook

New Brunswick   *1,000*   Amboy

8,000   *1,000*   *Raritan River*

South Amboy

Sandy Hook

Kingston

1,300

Pennington   Princeton

1,200

McConkry's Ferry   *2,500*   Maidenhead

5,500   *250*

1,500   Trenton

Trenton Ferry   Sandtown

700   *500*

ATLANTIC OCEAN

3,000   *1,500*   Allentown

Bordentown

5,000   *2,000*

Burlington

arrived at Trenton on December 8, only to find that the Rebels had taken or destroyed all the boats along that stretch of the Delaware River. Despite the speed of Cornwallis's march, Howe decided that it was too late in the season to reach Philadelphia and sent his army into winter quarters. Impressed by the numbers of Loyalists (whom he felt obliged to protect) and with the enlistments of Washington's troops due to expire on New Year's Eve, Howe confidently dispersed his forces across New Jersey, in order to spread the demand for food, forage, and firewood.

Desperately short of Continentals, Washington tried to recall Lee, who was now in northern New Jersey. Lee refused—possibly due to his dislike of Washington and a desire to see him fail—citing the problem of moving through enemy-occupied territory and the potential benefit of a substantial force in the enemy's rear. Worried about this force, Howe had ordered a reconnaissance to discover its strength and intentions, and one party under Lieutenant Banastre Tarleton surprised and seized Lee at White's Tavern. Ironically, this may have been a turning point for Washington as Lee's capture left Sullivan (recently returned in an exchange of prisoners) the senior officer, and he immediately brought the remaining men—about 2,000—south.

Yet Howe was also experiencing problems. Clinton had returned from Rhode Island and was suggesting that the Royal forces were too extended, while looting and pillaging by the troops (who saw all Americans as Rebels) were shifting the allegiance of the civilian population firmly toward the enemy.

By the end of December, Washington had managed to bolster his dwindling forces with volunteers from Pennsylvania and some New Jersey militia (though the latter were disappointing, both in numbers and quality). On December 25, he crossed the Delaware and attacked Trenton, which was held by 1,500 Hessians. The non arrival of some of his troops meant that a further attack on Princeton had to be rejected, but the Hessian garrison at Bordentown panicked and fled, abandoning its baggage. This allowed Washington to cross to the north bank of the Delaware again on December 27. This time he was pursued by Cornwallis, who forced the Rebel army to withdraw through Trenton on January 2, 1777, leaving the two sides facing each other across Assunpink Creek. Knowing that he was cut off from the Delaware ferries, Washington conducted a night-march toward Princeton.

Washington could not capitalize on his success at Princeton, as more and more of his men left on

TRENTON AND PRINCETON: DECEMBER 25, 1776 AND JANUARY 2, 1777

On the night of December 24, Washington crossed the Delaware with 2,400 troops at McConkey's Ferry. He divided his command into two columns, under Greene and Sullivan; the former circled round to the north of Trenton, while the latter approached from the east, along the river. Both columns drove in the pickets posted on the road and arrived at the outskirts of Trenton just before 8:00 a.m.

Despite warnings, and in contravention of accepted practice, the Hessian commander, Rall, had failed to fortify the town or provide redoubts in which his men could rally to repulse a surprise attack. Caught offguard after celebrating Christmas Eve, the Hessians were unable to resist Washington's superior numbers, especially the Rebel artillery, which broke up several bayonet charges—neither side being able to use their muskets to any great effect because of the cold and damp. After a last stand in an orchard southeast of the town, Rall surrendered. Almost 500 of his 1,400 men escaped, but he lost twenty-two dead and over 900 captured. Washington lost four dead and eight wounded.

After the battle, Washington learned that two other columns—700 men under Brigadier General James Ewing, sent to seize the bridge over Assunpink Creek (sealing off the south end of Trenton), and 2,000 militia mounting a diversionary attack on neighboring Bordentown—had failed to cross the Delaware.

* * * * *

Washington recrossed the Delaware into New Jersey on December 27. By the afternoon of January 1, however, he found himself being chased through Trenton and over Assunpink Creek by Cornwallis, with the best elements of the Royal army. Leaving his campfires burning, Washington slipped away and headed for Princeton, where Cornwallis had left a single British brigade as a rearguard.

Arriving in the early hours of the morning, the Rebels found two of the three British regiments, under Lieutenant Colonel Charles Mawhood, marching off to rejoin Cornwallis with their baggage train, and the other stationed in the town. Mawhood saw the leading Rebel brigade, under Brigadier General Hugh Mercer, and one regiment withdraw with the wagons while the leading unit attacked. An exchange of volleys and a bayonet charge broke both Mercer's troops and a supporting brigade of militia, before Washington personally led forward a brigade of Continentals and steadied the line. By now assailed on all sides, Mawhood ordered another bayonet charge and his regiment fought its way through, although hardly a man was left unwounded and many were captured in the brief pursuit.

Washington then turned his attention to the troops in Princeton. A single gun was brought forward and after two shots were fired into Nassau Hall, they surrendered. The Rebels found large quantities of military supplies and also looted the town (claiming the inhabitants were all Loyalists), before escaping north. They had lost twenty-three dead (including Mercer) and twenty wounded; the Royal forces had twenty-eight dead, fifty-eight wounded and 323 captured.

the expiry of their enlistments. He headed north to Morristown, where the surrounding hills provided a secure position for winter cantonments. Howe, on the other hand, had lost over 1,000 men inside a week, although there was a view that the Rebel efforts were borne of despair, rather than strength. (In fact, there was much truth in this—Washington's reason for crossing the Delaware was to "do or die" in securing a vital, morale-boosting victory; it also made it harder for some of his troops to return home on the expiry of their enlistments.) He had been forced to pull back to the line of the Raritan River, making any attack on Philadelphia the following spring that much more difficult. And a proclamation offering amnesty to all who took an oath of allegiance to the King was made to sound very hollow: many who had taken it now decided to take a similar one pledging allegiance to Congress—just in case.

EUROPE

Meanwhile, the British were facing problems at sea. Delays in the dockyards had affected the attack on Charleston; shortages of merchant ships and escorts had prevented an earlier evacuation of Boston—and seriously affected its efficiency when it did occur. Also, the Rebel war effort was entirely dependent on material imported from Europe, usually via the Caribbean (until the end of 1777, this included ninety percent of all the gunpowder available). A well-planned blockade would effectively strangle that effort. However, the general ill-preparedness of the Royal Navy and the need to keep one eye on Europe, despite the absence of official hostilities, prevented that. There were only thirty-three ships in the American squadron, against an estimated requirement of fifty; more particularly, they were not the small, well-armed, and speedy vessels needed to catch blockade-runners, but often obsolete frigates (either too slow, or undergunned) and the smaller line-of-battle ships that had been "retired" from the Channel fleet. By mid-1776, the number had risen to five warships and another eight brigs and schooners under Admiral Howe, but these resources were dissipated by the need to supply—and in the early days transport—the Army, a relationship that came under increasing attack from naval officers as leading the Army to expect too much.

The Royal Navy also had to protect convoys from the swarms of privateers that had appeared from the seagoing communities of New England and the middle colonies. Some 500 Highlanders were captured off Boston, while so many new uniforms for the troops in Canada and New Jersey were captured en route that both armies had to take the field in improvised "service dress" using worn-out clothing. Lord Howe refused to restrict the activities of fishermen, for fear of forcing them to become privateers,

Right: The First Salute (November 16, 1776). As the privateer Andrea Doria *entered the harbor of the Dutch Caribbean colony of St. Eustatius, the crew fired a salute. The governor of the island, Johannes de Graaf ordered an eleven-gun salute to be fired in return. This was the first occasion on which a vessel representing the United States received such an honor.*

although he was more heavily criticized for allowing the Colonies to continue trading. This omission he justified on the grounds that it showed goodwill in the peace negotiations then occurring—a clear example of the conflict between the military and political imperatives of British war aims, as well as demoralizing the commanders of the smaller vessels in his command.

However, although the number and spirit of the privateers would increase through the War, it would be an officer of the Continental Navy who would have the most dramatic effect (psychologically, if not actually) on British commerce. In 1776, a Scotsman

named John Paul Jones took part as a junior officer in a raid on Nassau in the Bahamas. He was rapidly promoted to the command of his own vessel, with which he began to get a taste for capturing British merchantmen.

Nevertheless, Howe's victories over Washington, however incomplete, had produced a noticeable response in the capitals of Europe. In Great Britain, the North ministry experienced a surge in popularity, while the Congressional representative in Paris, Silas Deane, suddenly found it much harder to obtain credit. Many diplomats, unfamiliar with the nature of warfare in North America, assumed that

the fall of New York City heralded the collapse of the Rebel cause.

All this was lost once the news of Trenton and Princeton arrived in Europe. These successes indicated a hitherto unsuspected level of resilience among the Rebel forces, which went down well at the courts of Louis XVI of France and his uncle, Charles III of Spain. With only one exception (who felt that internal political reform would benefit France more), his ministers were all in favor of taking every advantage of the war in North America—especially once the size of the British war effort, and the consequent debilitating effect on the defenses of the British Isles, was clear.

1777

"Determined to conquer or die"

BRIGADIER GENERAL JOHN GLOVER

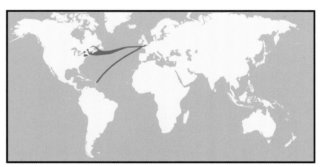

RED INDICATES FIGHTING, INCLUDING PRIVATEERING ON SHIPPING LANES

Burgoyne surrenders to Gates at Saratoga. (Yale University Art Gallery)

After the disappointing victories (and even more disappointing defeats) of the previous year, the coming year had to be successful for the King's commanders. While their position was far better than it had been in 1776, there was a feeling that little impact had been made outside of New York and New Jersey and that other areas with greater potential had been sacrificed, such as Florida (from where the handful of Regulars who could have exercised control had been removed) or Maryland (where no Regulars had been sent, leaving the militia free to intimidate disaffected Loyalists and political abstainers from the religious minorities).

Howe saw a single decisive battle as the quickest way to end the war; however, this required a concentration of forces that was beyond Great Britain's resources. His opponents also lacked the manpower—and the logistical and administrative capabilities—to mount a serious offensive and were limited to reacting to him, but they were still sufficiently strong locally to require substantial garrisons in strategic locations, such as Quebec and Rhode Island. They could also move troops quickly from one theater to another by land, whereas the Royal forces could transfer men only by sea.

There was a further problem: historically, politicians had allowed commanders in North America considerable latitude, due to the vast distance that separated London from the theater of operations. However, this only worked where everyone was following an agreed plan; where two or more commanders were determined to go their own way, or had their own ideas about how success was to be achieved (and measured), such a free rein was a recipe for disaster. And such a free rein was exactly what Germain was about to give Howe and Burgoyne.

Burgoyne returned to Canada in May with a letter from Germain approving the plan presented to the King during the winter and ordering Carleton to support him. Carleton was to remain in Canada with 3,700 men, while Burgoyne with 8,000 would move down Lake Champlain, and a separate force of 2,000 was to invade the Mohawk Valley and join Burgoyne at Albany. Here they would await the arrival of Howe from New York, with another 10,000 men. Germain, however, had also approved Howe's proposal to invade Pennsylvania and Virginia, then move on to Georgia and the Carolinas for the winter. He had even offered 5,500 extra troops—far fewer than Howe wanted, which led the latter to amend his plan simply to the capture of Philadelphia. Germain had stressed that Howe must return in time to aid Burgoyne, but had only sent Howe a copy of Burgoyne's plan, with no further directions. Howe wrote to Carleton in April, stating that a force from Canada should not rely on him, but could—if necessary—be supported from New York City.

Washington was also keen to learn what the Royal commanders were planning, having reduced the likely options to a thrust up the Hudson River to Albany (the Northern Department's supply center), or an attack on his Main Army and Philadelphia. He considered a twin thrust to isolate New England beyond their capabilities, believing that any advance from Canada would be blocked by Fort Ticonderoga—"the Gibraltar of the wilderness." Schuyler, who commanded the Northern Department, knew that neither the fort, nor its inadequate garrison, would stop a determined thrust, but could not convince Washington.

PENNSYLVANIA

As the year began, Howe's army was still reeling from the twin defeats at Trenton and Princeton and was finding it difficult to obtain supplies and suitable winter accommodation. By comparison, Washington's army had practically ceased to exist, those remaining being badly clothed, underfed, and exposed to the weather, many of them suffering from smallpox. Nevertheless, he managed to move from Morristown to Middlebrook in order to block any attack on Philadelphia and, between March and May, numbers increased from 3,000 to 9,000.

Eager to bring Washington to battle, Howe was repeatedly frustrated by bad weather and the poor health of his own troops. By the time he was ready, Washington was in a position of strength, such that any battle would be on terms and ground of his own choosing. Howe diverted himself with a raid on Peekskill in the Hudson Highlands in March, and on Danbury, Connecticut, in April (the latter a particularly hard-fought affair that was almost foiled by Arnold). In mid-June, Howe made one last attempt at luring Washington out of his lines, but it did not work. Faced with the prospect of fighting his way across New Jersey, which would require large detachments to protect his sole supply line—through New Brunswick—Howe decided to move to Philadelphia by water.

Having made his decision, Howe inexplicably waited until July 9 to embark his men and then did not sail until July 23, having awaited news from Burgoyne. He left New York City in the charge of Clinton, who had just 7,000 men—including 3,000 untrained Loyalists—to defend the 100 miles from Long Island, via Manhattan to Paulus Hook and New Jersey: the only reinforcements to arrive in Howe's absence were 1,700 untrained Regulars in September. Once at sea, Howe was becalmed for two days and lost another to fog and storms, before false intelligence that Washington was ready to oppose any landing from the Delaware River forced him to choose a longer route, through the Chesapeake. His convoy rounded the Virginia Capes on August 17 (at which point the weather suddenly became extremely hot) and eight days later, after a month aboard ship, the troops finally disembarked at Head of Elk—only to be caught in a severe storm before their tents were unloaded.

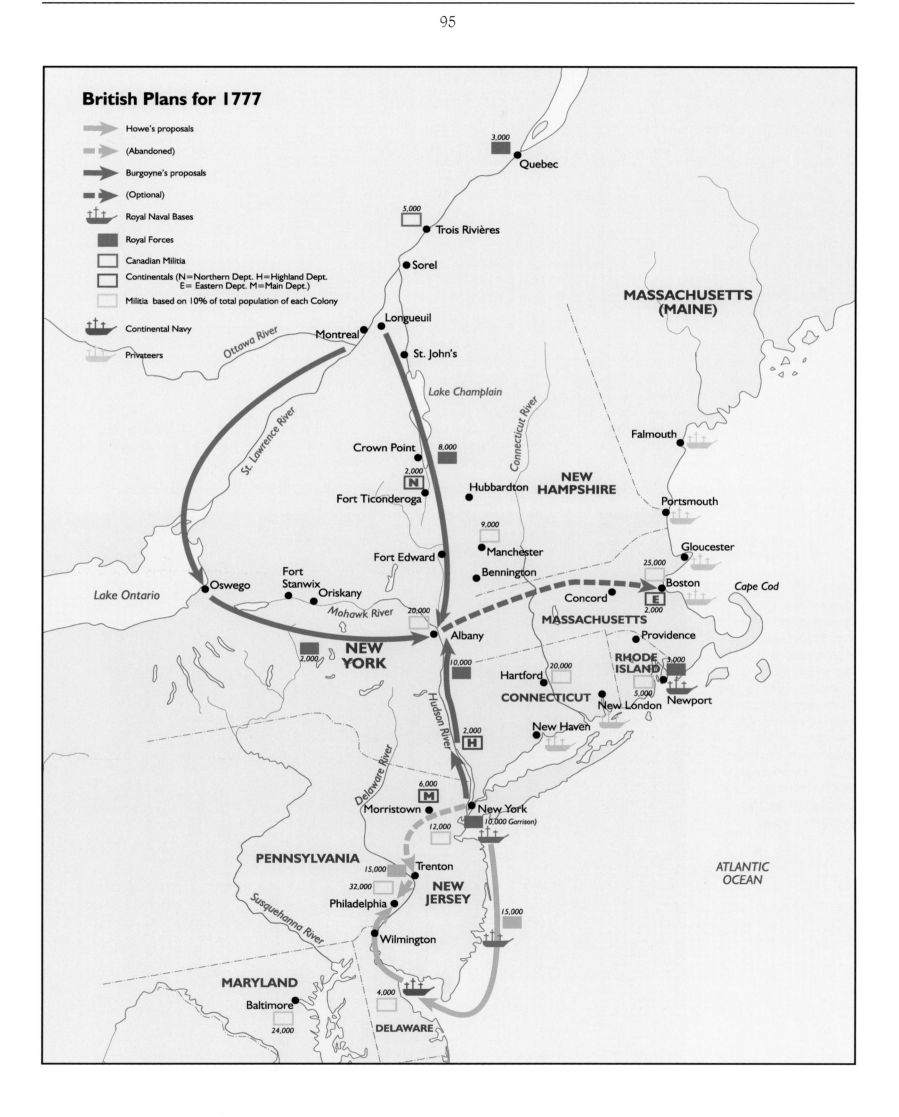

British Plans for 1777

Howe's proposals

(Abandoned)

Burgoyne's proposals

(Optional)

Royal Naval Bases

Royal Forces

Canadian Militia

Continentals (N=Northern Dept. H=Highland Dept.
E= Eastern Dept. M=Main Dept.)

Militia based on 10% of total population of each Colony

Continental Navy

Privateers

Quebec 3,000

Trois Rivières 5,000

Sorel

Ottawa River

Montreal

Longueuil

St. John's

Lake Champlain

Connecticut River

St. Lawrence River

Crown Point 8,000

Fort Ticonderoga 2,000 [N]

Hubbardton

NEW HAMPSHIRE

MASSACHUSETTS (MAINE)

Falmouth

Portsmouth

Gloucester

Manchester 9,000

Fort Edward

Bennington

Lake Ontario

Oswego

Fort Stanwix

Oriskany

Mohawk River

20,000

Albany

Boston 25,000 [E] 2,000

Cape Cod

Concord

MASSACHUSETTS

Providence

NEW YORK

2,000

10,000

Hartford

20,000

RHODE ISLAND 3,000

CONNECTICUT

New London 5,000

Newport

Hudson River

2,000 [H]

New Haven

6,000 [M]

Morristown

New York (10,000 Garrison)

12,000

PENNSYLVANIA

15,000

Trenton

NEW JERSEY

Susquehanna River

32,000

Philadelphia

15,000

Delaware River

Wilmington

ATLANTIC OCEAN

4,000

MARYLAND

Baltimore 24,000

DELAWARE

BRANDYWINE: SEPTEMBER 11, 1777

Washington placed his 11,000 men (of whom 3,000 were militia and the rest Continentals) on the east bank of Brandywine Creek, which was impassable except at a handful of fords. He deployed his best troops—Greene's division—at Chadd's Ford on the main Philadelphia Road, with Sullivan's men on his right and the Pennsylvania militia on the left.

Howe ordered Lieutenant General Wilhelm von Knyphausen to make a feint with 5,000 men against Chadd's Ford, while he led the remainder of the Royal army—about 8,000 troops—northward, to outflank Washington. Knyphausen drove back the Rebel pickets and occupied some high ground opposite the ford, from where his artillery opened fire.

Meanwhile, Howe and Cornwallis had crossed the unguarded fords upstream and headed for Osborne's Hill, to the rear of Washington's right flank, covering seventeen miles in about eleven hours in the intense heat. Initial reports of this movement reached Washington and he briefly contemplated a counterattack against Von Knyphausen; however, one contradictory message led him to dismiss the previous information and he held his position until the Royal army appeared on Osborne's Hill. Howe delayed his attack, possibly to give his men time to rest, giving Washington time to realign Sullivan's troops and prepare Greene's division to move to their support.

Howe and Cornwallis attacked around 4:30 p.m. and immediately overran one of Sullivan's brigades. Greene's division then began to arrive—some elements having marched four miles in three-quarters of an hour—and occupied a plowed hill near the village of Birmingham. Washington arrived around 5:30 p.m., but left Sullivan in charge of the battle. After ninety minutes of fierce fighting, the British eventually drove Sullivan's troops back and Greene's men were forced to withdraw to avoid being surrounded. Hearing the firing, Von Knyphausen had advanced across Chadd's Ford and drove back Washington's center, capturing all of his artillery. The two wings of Howe's army eventually linked up just after 7:00 p.m., as darkness fell.

Washington disengaged his troops and fled eastward, unhindered by any pursuit from the Royal army (though in Howe's defense, the loss of so many horses on the voyage had greatly reduced the effectiveness of his cavalry). He had lost over 1,200 men, including 400 prisoners; Howe had lost 577 dead and wounded—of whom forty were Hessians.

Right: *The Paoli "Massacre" (September 21, 1777). Washington had left Wayne as a rearguard to shield his main force from the victorious (if somewhat dilatory) Howe. Convinced that his presence was still a secret, Wayne was caught off guard by a night attack by Major General Sir Charles Grey—known ever after as "No Flint Grey" for removing the flints from his men's muskets and making them rely on the bayonet. (Valley Forge Historical Society)*

After resting his men and the few horses that had survived the voyage, Howe set off for Philadelphia. Washington, his army now equipped with new weapons from France, harassed Howe all the way, and there were sharp skirmishes at Elkton on August 28, Wilmington three days later, and Cooch's Bridge on September 3. Finally, Washington decided to block their progress at Brandywine Creek, about halfway between Head of Elk and Philadelphia. Unfortunately his position was outflanked and his army was soon heading back toward Philadelphia.

Once again, Howe had failed to win a decisive victory. At the time, he excused failure to pursue on a need to consider the wounded and prisoners, but later admitted that he had been concerned at the nature of the terrain. On September 16, the two armies clashed once again near Warren Tavern, two miles south of Washington's camp; Howe's troops were threatening both of Washington's flanks when the heavens opened, ending the action (later called the "Battle of the Clouds") and possibly saving the Rebel army from a major defeat.

Washington withdrew to Yellow Springs, and then on to Warwick Furnace to replenish his ammunition—most of which had been destroyed by rain—leaving Wayne and 1,500 men to harass Howe. However, Wayne failed to protect his camp sufficiently, and on the night of September 20, Major General Sir Charles Grey attacked him with 5,000 troops, the Rebels suffering 400 casualties, against eleven British. (As inevitably happened when Royal forces carried out a successful surprise attack, the action soon became a "massacre" in the Whig press.)

Howe had lost the opportunity to cross the Schuykill River while Washington was away and the latter soon returned, via Parker's Ford, to cover the main crossing points. However, a clever feint to the west and a rapid countermarch during the night of September 23 saw Howe across the river at Flatland's Ford and between Washington and Philadelphia. Howe entered the city in triumph on September 26 and, at first sight, had achieved his primary objective, but closer inspection of his circumstances showed a different picture. The river forts of Philadelphia were still held by Rebel troops, preventing the Royal Navy from supplying and reinforcing him by water (in fact, technically Howe was besieged). His manpower was stretched to the limits: when he sent large detachments of troops to Billingsport to clear away the militia and escort supply convoys, it left him with only 9,000 men, encamped in a poor position near Germantown, five miles north of Philadelphia. Washington attacked on the morning of October 4, but after initial gains his troops became confused in the mist and were forced to retreat.

Despite being defeated, Washington and his army took heart from the Battle of Germantown: they had maneuvered in the face of the enemy and fought him

GERMANTOWN: OCTOBER 4, 1777

Howe had not entrenched his camp at Germantown, believing that Washington's army posed no threat in its current condition. Once Washington was aware of this, he prepared an elaborate plan involving a coordinated attack by four separate columns. Two were composed of Continentals: the right, under Sullivan, would attack Howe's center, while the left, commanded by Greene, would hit his right. The other two columns were smaller and were made up of Maryland and Pennsylvania militia.

Each column was to march through the night (a major test for even the most experienced troops) and be in position by 2:00 a.m.; if successful, Howe's army would be hit from four directions at once. When the deadline arrived, only Sullivan was in place, so Washington waited until 4:00 a.m. before giving the signal to attack, assuming that the other columns would at least be close to their starting points.

Sullivan's men advanced down the Skippack Road; about five miles from Howe's camp, they encountered pickets, who put up stiff resistance, thinking they were only being attacked by a scouting party. Eventually, the pickets were forced back and 150 men took refuge in the Chew House (also called "Cliveden"), a large stone building belonging to a local judge. The leading Rebel brigades bypassed the house, but Washington was persuaded by Knox to storm it, an operation that would tie up 3,000 men and six guns for the remainder of the battle. The defenders—expecting to receive no quarter after Paoli—fought like demons and the Rebels took heavy losses; more importantly, the firing caused confusion among the units that had gone on ahead.

At this point, Greene's column entered the battle, expecting to meet the British right. Unfortunately, the speed of Sullivan's advance meant that Greene's leading brigade—whose commander was drunk—made contact with them instead, and they fired into the backs of their comrades. With some units also dressed in captured British uniforms, confusion reigned and the two groups of Continentals exchanged several volleys.

The Royal forces took the opportunity to counterattack and drove Sullivan's men back down the Skippack Road, past the Chew House. This exposed Greene's leading units, who were still advancing; finding themselves assailed on both flanks, they retreated and were pursued for ten miles, halting their attackers in a brisk skirmish at Whitemarsh Church.

British casualties were 521, while Sullivan and Greene lost 673 killed and wounded, and another 400 captured. The militia columns were not engaged: the Marylanders lost their way and failed to arrive, while the Pennsylvanians appeared on the British left, and simply halted and fired a few rounds from their guns. Washington immediately cashiered the drunken brigade commander and replaced him with La Fayette.

Above: *The Battle of Germantown (October 4, 1777). British troops can be seen filing into a stylized (and much smaller) version of the Chew House, as the Rebel columns advance down the Skippack Road. Howe can be seen on horseback in the center of the picture. (Valley Forge Historical Society)*

in the open, without the need for the protection of earthworks or forests. After a difficult—if somewhat overambitious—night march, they had come within an ace of victory. In fact, the performance at Germantown drew more admiration from observers in France than did the subsequent capture of Burgoyne's army at Saratoga.

At the same time, Howe now realized that merely entering Philadelphia had not secured it militarily, nor—as this was largely a war about ideology—was it the terminal political blow that the capture of London, or Paris, might have been in a European conflict. Howe withdrew from Germantown on October 19 and built a stronger—and much shorter—defensive line across the isthmus to the north of the city. He then set about clearing the Delaware, which was blocked by underwater obstacles (known as *chevaux de frises*) guarded by Rebel warships and two forts, Fort Mifflin (on Mud Island) and Fort Mercer (known as Red Bank and situated on a small height on the New Jersey side of the river). Fort Mifflin had been under bombardment since October 11 from batteries on Province Island, facing the less heavily fortified side of the work. On October 22, Howe sent 2,000 Hessians under Colonel Karl von Donop to capture Fort Mercer.

Von Donop immediately realized that the fort was stronger than had been suspected and that he needed heavy artillery to soften up the defenses before his men could storm them. However, he felt that his honor would be compromised if he refused to attack (the Hessians by this time having become highly sensitive to criticism from their British colleagues after the Trenton débâcle) and went ahead. His men were stopped short of the walls and, after suffering over 400 casualties—including Von Donop himself—the Hessians withdrew. To make matters worse, two British warships coming upriver to assist Von Donop went aground, one being set on fire by the guns of Fort Mercer and the other being abandoned and burned by its crew.

With provisions now running dangerously short in Philadelphia, formal siege operations began, but violent rains filled the trenches and sapped the foundations of the gun emplacements. Nevertheless, Howe's troops took their time and a six-day bombardment of Fort Mifflin led to its abandonment on November 16. This success led to a further attempt on Fort Mercer, with Cornwallis leading 3,000 men across the river at Billingsport, where he was joined by 2,000 reinforcements from New York City. The commander of the fort, Colonel Christopher Greene (cousin of Nathaniel), decided that the enemy was too numerous and ordered his 400 men to escape on November 20.

Washington was unable to take advantage of these distractions; he was awaiting reinforcements and was plagued by shortages of clothing (particu-

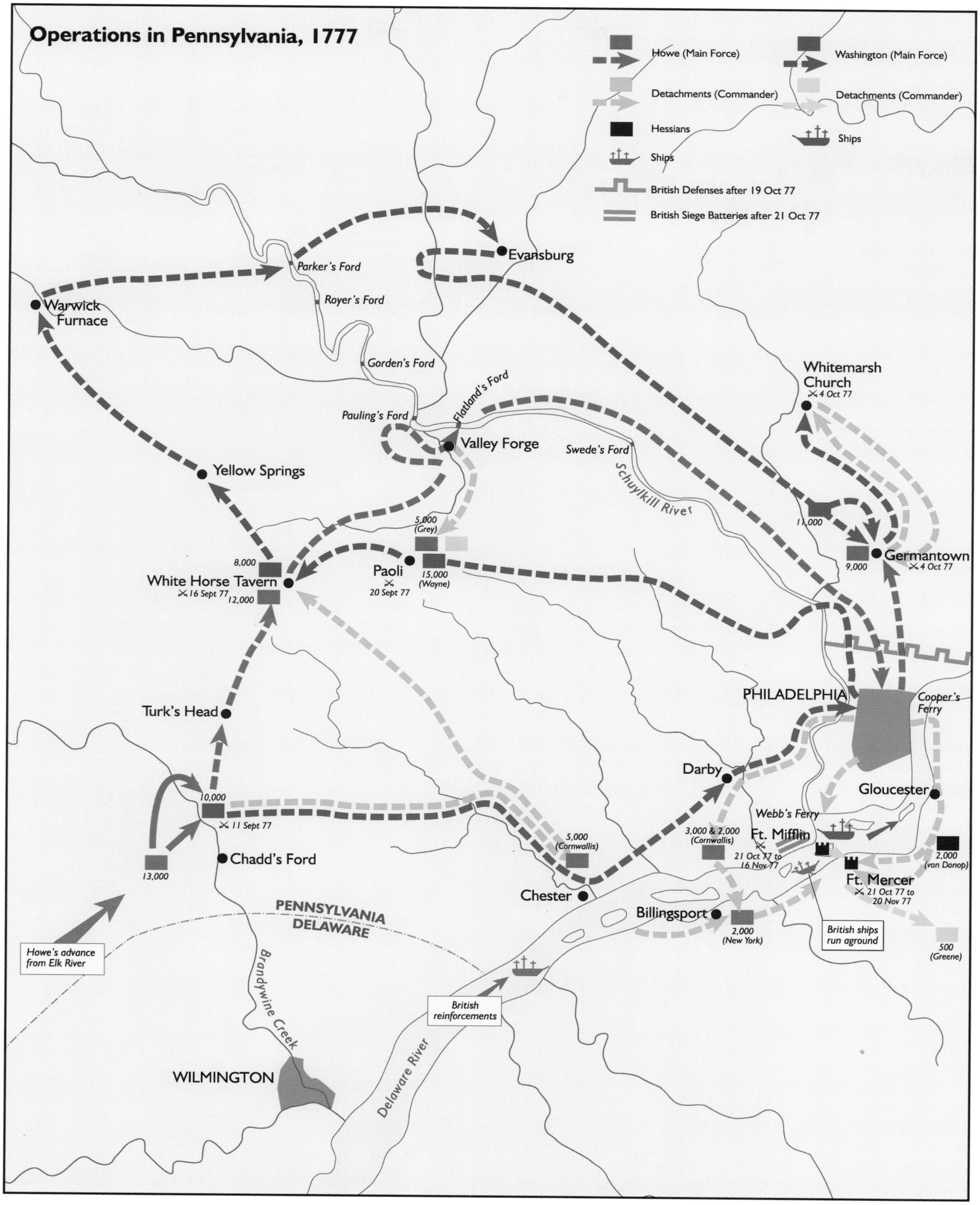

Operations in Pennsylvania, 1777

Howe (Main Force)

Washington (Main Force)

Detachments (Commander)

Detachments (Commander)

Hessians

Ships

Ships

British Defenses after 19 Oct 77

British Siege Batteries after 21 Oct 77

Parker's Ford

Evansburg

Royer's Ford

Warwick Furnace

Gorden's Ford

Whitemarsh Church
✕ 4 Oct 77

Flatland's Ford

Pauling's Ford

Valley Forge

Swede's Ford

Schuylkill River

Yellow Springs

5,000 (Grey)

11,000

8,000

White Horse Tavern
✕ 16 Sept 77
12,000

Paoli
✕ 20 Sept 77

15,000 (Wayne)

9,000

Germantown
✕ 4 Oct 77

Turk's Head

10,000
✕ 11 Sept 77

PHILADELPHIA

Cooper's Ferry

13,000

Chadd's Ford

Darby

Gloucester

Webb's Ferry

PENNSYLVANIA
DELAWARE

5,000 (Cornwallis)

3,000 & 2,000 (Cornwallis)

Ft. Mifflin
✕ 21 Oct 77 to
16 Nov 77

2,000 (von Donop)

Ft. Mercer
✕ 21 Oct 77 to
20 Nov 77

Chester

Billingsport

2,000 (New York)

British ships run aground

500 (Greene)

Howe's advance from Elk River

Brandywine Creek

British reinforcements

WILMINGTON

Delaware River

Above: *East prospect of Philadelphia. The city was the second largest in the British Empire after London, with 35,000 inhabitants. However, neither its size, nor the fact that it was the seat of Congress, added anything to its capture. (National Maritime Museum)*

Right: *Tadeusz Kosciuszko (1746–1817) was also trained at the artillery and engineering school at Mézières, in France. Finding little opportunity in his native Poland and having found an interest in the concept of liberty, he decided to go to America and helped to design the Delaware Forts. He received a Continental commission as a colonel of engineers in October 1776 and joined the Northern Department, where he selected and fortified the position at Bemis Heights. He later designed the defenses at West Point and served in the South. (Independence National Historical Park)*

Right: *Louis Lebeque de Presle Duportail (1743–1802) was born into an aristocratic family and attended the academy at Mézières before joining the Royal Corps of Engineers in 1765. By 1776, he had risen to the rank of lieutenant colonel and was one of several officers granted indefinite leave to serve in North America by Louis XVI. Given command of the Rebel engineer corps in November 1777, he was captured at Charleston, but exchanged in time to serve at Yorktown. (Independence National Historical Park)*

Below: *Attack on the Delaware Forts (October 23, 1777). The British ships* Merlin *and* Augusta *can be seen aground and on fire. The attack was poorly coordinated and a further month of fighting was needed before the river was cleared of Rebel forces. (National Maritime Museum)*

Above: *Major General Arthur St. Clair (1737–1818) was born into the Scottish gentry, served in Canada during the French and Indian Wars and then settled in Pennsylvania. An undistinguished career as a Continental officer included action at Trois Rivières and mobilizing the New Jersey militia for the Trenton campaign. However, he did well to extricate the Ticonderoga garrison in the face of stiff opposition—mostly from his colleagues. (Independence National Historical Park)*

and withdrew to Germantown, while Washington moved west to take up winter quarters at Valley Forge, on December 21. Although not a perfect post defensively, this did allow him to remain close to Philadelphia so that he could recommence the campaign in the New Year. Once again, Howe had achieved only a partial success, as he had the previous year; however, in 1777, unlike 1776, events elsewhere would eclipse even that.

NEW YORK

To the north, the same intercolonial rivalries and professional disputes that were appearing in Washington's army had already made their mark on the Northern Department. Having upset the New Englanders with his patrician attitude and insistence on proper discipline, Schuyler found himself the victim of a whispering campaign. In January, Congress had dismissed one of his staff without consulting him; when Schuyler complained, it was used as a pretext to offer him an insulting reprimand and replace him with Major General Horatio Gates in March. Schuyler visited Washington the following month and then went to Philadelphia, where he persuaded Congress to confirm Gates as his second-in-command. Gates preferred to remain as Washington's adjutant general, rather than serve under Schuyler and went before Congress himself to complain.

Such was the level of animosity between the New England lobby and Schuyler's supporters (largely from New York) that accusations were leveled against him of taking bribes from the British. This prevented him from carrying out his duties effectively: knowing the inadequacies of the defenses and the garrison at Fort Ticonderoga, he twice recommended abandoning it and received Congressional approval on both occasions. However, the political climate and the talismanic nature of "Fort Ti" made it impossible. Before the year was out, similar charges of bribery and treason (including the ludicrous allegations that silver bullets were fired into the Rebel lines as payment) would be leveled, equally unjustifiably, at other officers, such as Major General Arthur St. Clair, who took over command of Fort Ticonderoga on June 12.

The following day—a Friday—the fleet carrying Burgoyne's army set sail from St. John's, in Canada. A week later, he issued a wordy Proclamation, in which he threatened to unleash his Indian forces if the civilian population opposed him (a move that many of his own officers, and Carleton, considered a mistake). On June 25, his men began arriving at Crown Point, where bad weather delayed them for several days, before they recommenced their journey down the lake.

On the next day, July 2, the advance guard under Brigadier General Simon Fraser seized the outlying

larly shoes) and food, as well as the perennial problem of the expiring enlistments of his Continentals. There were also signs of serious rivalries and cliques developing among his senior officers, some of whom had performed better than others at Germantown (and elsewhere), and—in various combinations—among the Continental Army and Navy, the Pennsylvania State Navy, and the New Jersey militia. By the end of November, the Maryland and Virginia militia had gone home and the New Jersey militia had been recalled even before it had arrived.

Washington's plan to starve Howe out of Philadelphia ended with the loss of the forts, and his main hope for a victory—which he believed was every bit as badly needed as it had been in the winter of 1776—now rested on Howe coming out to attack him. In fact, Howe did just that, emerging on December 4 to assault Washington's main encampment at Whitemarsh, the two armies skirmishing at Edge Hill. Howe decided not to press home the attack

*Views of Fort Ticonderoga
from Lake Champlain.
These show Fraser's
Advance Corps landing at
Three Mile Point, just north
of Ticonderoga. (National
Archives of Canada)*

Above: *Fort Ticonderoga from Fort Independence. A contemporary watercolor by one of Burgoyne's engineers after the capture of the forts. The piers of the bridge across the lake (which the British had removed to allow vessels to pass) are clearly visible. (Fort Ticonderoga Museum)*

Right: *Mill and blockhouse at Skenesboro. Skenesboro (now Whitehall) possessed sawmills, iron foundries, and shipyards, and was used by Arnold to build the fleet that stopped Carleton on Lake Champlain. (British Museum)*

Left: *Captain Pierre St. Luc de la Corne had been prominent in Indian affairs since the 1720s and had a history of organizing war parties for both the French and the British. Described as a courtier away from battle and a savage in it, he was credited with the Fort William Henry massacre, Braddock's ambush, and persuading Burgoyne not to act over the McCrea affair. His two sons-in-law commanded the Native Americans and Canadians at Bennington. (National Archives of Canada)*

defenses on Mount Hope. Three days later, the British had hauled artillery to the top of nearby Mount Defiance, which overlooked both forts, but which St. Clair had insufficient men to hold. On July 6, St. Clair decided to evacuate (sparking accusations of treachery), sending the women and sick by boat to Skenesboro, while the garrison took the military road south to Castleton. A burning building alerted the British and by 9:00 a.m. both groups were being hotly pursued. At 3:00 p.m., British gunboats arrived in Skenesboro; troops were landed and after brisk skirmishing, they pursued the Rebels to Fort Ann.

Meanwhile, Fraser and Lieutenant General Friedrich Von Riedesel had left Mount Independence to catch St. Clair's main body, which was heading for Castleton. The Rebel rearguard was found by Native Americans during the night, and at dawn on July 7, Fraser drove back the enemy pickets and attacked. The action was hard-fought and Fraser—outnumbered three-to-two—was in danger of being defeated when Von Riedesel arrived with the leading elements of his Brunswick corps and forced the Rebels to retreat. As was so often the case, the Royal forces were too exhausted to pursue the enemy, but did have the satisfaction of taking over 300 prisoners.

Back at Fort Ann, another desperate action had seen 190 Regulars narrowly escape a force of 600 Rebels, but the latter were forced to burn the fort and

Right: *Colonel Barry St. Leger (1737–1789) was of Huguenot descent. Given the local rank of brigadier general and charged with restoring Royal authority in the Mohawk Valley before joining Burgoyne at Albany, his refusal to believe Fort Stanwix had been repaired prevented him taking a more substantial artillery train and contributed to the failure of his mission. (The Courtauld Institute and The National Trust)*

retreat thirty miles. In ten days, Burgoyne had captured Fort Ticonderoga—along with 200 ships, 100 guns, and tons of supplies—and had driven Schuyler's forces all the way back to Fort Edward. It was at this point that things began to go badly wrong for the Royal commander.

Schuyler sent reinforcements forward, but without knowing the exact whereabouts of either St. Clair or Burgoyne (both he and St. Clair were now being accused of treachery by the increasingly angry New Englanders). St. Clair reached Fort Edward on July 12, giving Schuyler 3,000 Continentals and 1,000 militia, but a quarter of these were sick and all of his guns were stuck at Fort George without transport. Washington sent Schuyler another 600 Continentals, but if Burgoyne advanced on Albany in strength, there was little hope of stopping him.

At Skenesboro, Burgoyne had increasing problems with the length of his supply lines and faced a choice of continuing to Fort Edward (over twenty miles through swamps), or returning to Ticonderoga and heading down Lake George, leaving only a ten-mile journey by road. Shortages of wagons and horses—both the result of poor preparation in Canada—forced him to choose the former route, but by the

time he moved forward again, Schuyler's men had blocked roads, flooded farmland, removed livestock and burned crops. Heavy rain made things even worse and it took Burgoyne three weeks to reach Fort Edward, his army arriving on the east bank of the Hudson River on July 29. Schuyler had evacuated Fort George and withdrawn to Saratoga, providing more ammunition for his detractors, but once again saving his army.

Meanwhile, Brigadier General Barry St. Leger had left Montreal on June 23 and arrived at Oswego on July 25, where he was joined by Sir John Johnson and Joseph Brant with almost 1,000 Iroquois, and advanced against Fort Stanwix (at a creditable ten miles per day, in terrain little better than that facing Burgoyne's army). On August 2, his advance guard just failed to prevent 200 men entering the fort with six weeks' provisions and when he arrived with his main body the following day, he was shocked to find substantial repairs had been made and the garrison numbered over 500 men, rather than the sixty he had expected. With his artillery too weak to batter the fort into submission, he was forced to commence a formal siege. Having seen the small size of St. Leger's army, the garrison resolved to fight on.

Below: *Brigadier General Nicholas Herkimer (1728–1777) at Oriskany (August 6, 1777). Seeing that his men were being "rushed" by Indians as they reloaded, Herkimer ordered them to fight in pairs, with one man always ready to fire. Ten days later, he died from a botched attempt to amputate his injured leg. He was a central figure in the Mohawk Valley's Palatine German community and had tried to negotiate Brant's neutrality a month earlier. (Trustees of the Utica Public Library)*

On August 5, St. Leger learned that a relief column—800 militia under Colonel Nicholas Herkimer—was on its way and dispatched 500 Loyalists and Native Americans to intercept it. The ambush took place around a ravine near Oriskany. However, the trap was sprung prematurely and although the leading and rearmost elements of Herkimer's column were all but wiped out, the center held and fought on. As a result of a combination of heavy casualties and a message that the garrison had left the fort and was ransacking St. Leger's camp, the Native Americans fled back to Stanwix, ending the battle. With under 200 men left, the mortally wounded Herkimer reluctantly agreed to retreat, but the losses inflicted on his opponents destroyed their resolve to continue the siege of Fort Stanwix.

Despite the proximity of Burgoyne's army, Schuyler had already sent Arnold to relieve the fort. Arnold produced a ruse that convinced the Native Americans he had 3,000 men and they went on a drunken rampage that forced St. Leger to abandon the siege. His remaining forces escaped just before Arnold arrived on August 23.

After two weeks at Fort Edward, Burgoyne sent Fraser over the river to harass Schuyler. Unaware of St. Leger's retreat, but knowing that Howe would not

Right: *Colonel Peter Gansevoort (1749–1812) came from a prominent Albany family, and served under Montgomery in Canada, then commanded at Fort George, before being promoted colonel of the 3rd New York at the age of 28. It was at the head of this regiment that he distinguished himself at Fort Stanwix. (Munson-Williams-Proctor Institute of Art)*

Left: *Lieutenant Colonel Marinus Willett (1740–1830) had served briefly at Fort Stanwix during the French and Indian Wars, as well as at Fort Ticonderoga and Frontenac. A rabble-rousing Son of Liberty in New York City, he had commanded the St. John's garrison during the invasion of Canada. He subsequently fought at Monmouth, then retired, but was persuaded to command militia levies during the Loyalist/Indian raids of 1781. (Metropolitan Museum of Art)*

Right: *Brigadier General John Stark (1728–1822) lived up to his Scots-Irish ancestry—brave and resourceful on the battlefield and fiercely independent away from it. Having resigned from the Continental Army, he accepted command of the New Hampshire militia only on condition that he took no orders from Congress or Continental officers. (Independence National Historical Park)*

now arrive, Burgoyne sent an expedition into neighboring New Hampshire to find wagons, horses, and recruits; as the men departed, on August 11, their orders were changed, redirecting them to a depot at Bennington. The mission was a disaster: the German commander spoke no English; the behavior of the Indian contingent alienated any support that existed; and large numbers of Rebel militia had been mobilized and (by sheer coincidence) were concentrating in the Bennington area. By August 16, the Royal forces were surrounded and outnumbered; in a brief struggle, barely fifty of the 850 men escaped and a German contingent sent to evacuate them arrived too late and was itself badly mauled. The disaster cost Burgoyne almost fifteen percent of his strength and

with more Indians departing each day, he now had fewer than 5,000 men. He briefly considered retreat, but decided to continue.

Two days before Bennington, Schuyler was replaced by Gates; his new command, now based at Stillwater, was growing as Burgoyne's was shrinking and by September 1, he had over 8,000 men, including militia. One week later, Gates advanced three miles to Bemis Heights, a heavily wooded plateau crossed by numerous ravines, that commanded the only road to Albany, twenty miles to the south. Here, his chief engineer, Taddeusz Koskiuszko, constructed an impressive fortified camp, as the opposing armies moved closer, groping for each other in the dense, roadless forests. By September 9, Gates also had the benefit (though not necessarily control) of hordes of militia threatening Burgoyne's left and rear; one group captured Fort George and narrowly failed to retake Fort Ticonderoga.

On September 12, Burgoyne crossed the Hudson and advanced along the Albany road, but at barely three miles as day as the Rebels had blocked the road and destroyed the bridges. Seven days later, he learned that Rebel riflemen were three miles away, with Gates's main force half a mile in their rear, and resolved to attack them. On September 19 he did just that but was fought to a standstill around Freeman's Farm.

Left: *"The Massacre of Jane McCrae". The story of McCrea's murder and subsequent scalping by Native Americans is well known. What is less well known is that a later exhumation of her corpse revealed three bullet holes but none of the head injuries supposedly inflicted. There was also an eyewitness, a Mrs McNeil, cousin of Simon Fraser, who made no mention of a scalping in a long list of complaints to the general. Years later her granddaughter confirmed the story that Jane had in fact been shot accidentally by a Rebel patrol that had fired on the women's Native American escorts.*

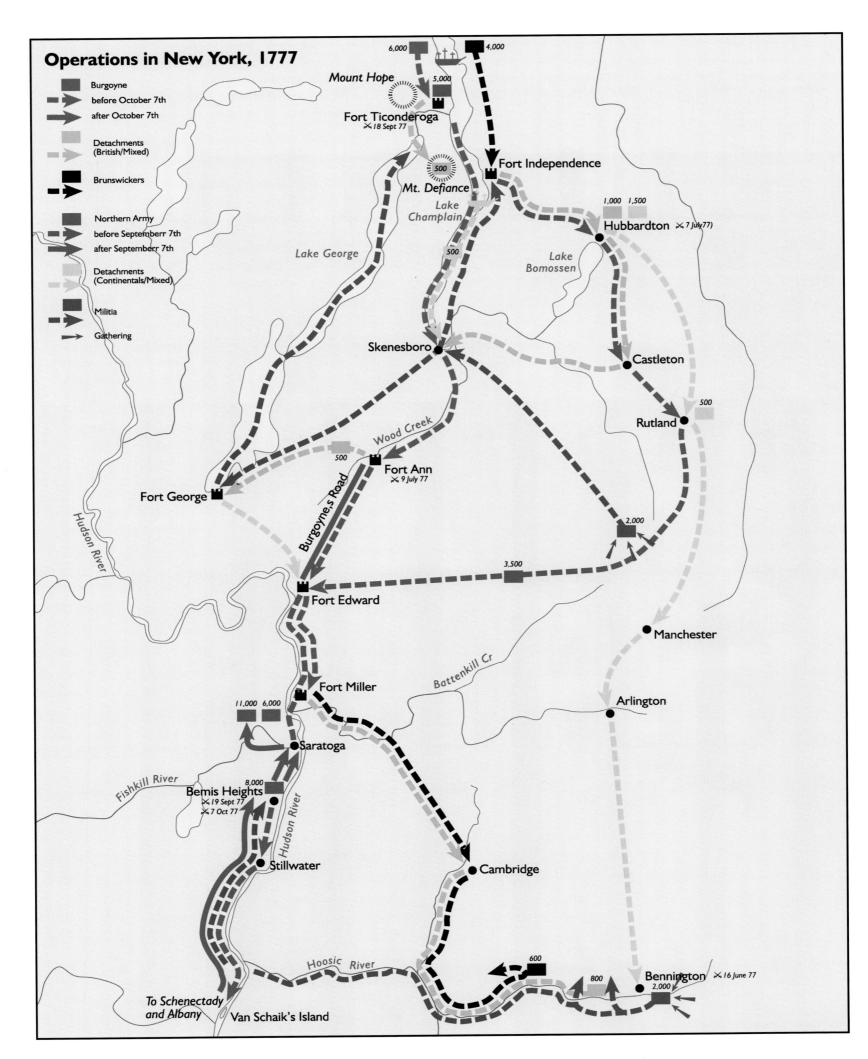

Operations in New York, 1777

Burgoyne

before October 7th

after October 7th

Detachments (British/Mixed)

Brunswickers

Northern Army

before September 7th

after September 7th

Detachments (Continentals/Mixed)

Militia

Gathering

Mount Hope

Fort Ticonderoga ✕ 18 Sept 77

Mt. Defiance

Lake Champlain

Lake George

Fort Independence

Hubbardton ✕ 7 July 77

Lake Bomossen

Castleton

Skenesboro

Rutland

Wood Creek

Fort Ann ✕ 9 July 77

Burgoyne's Road

Fort George

Hudson River

Fort Edward

Manchester

Fort Miller

Battenkill Cr

Arlington

Saratoga

Fishkill River

Bemis Heights ✕ 19 Sept 77 ✕ 7 Oct 77

Hudson River

Stillwater

Cambridge

Hoosic River

To Schenectady and Albany

Van Schaik's Island

Bennington ✕ 16 June 77

The next day, Gates's army was down to just forty rounds per man, but Burgoyne's men were in no position to resume their advance and his engineers supervized the building of redoubts and other defenses along a two-mile front. Gates also strengthened his lines, as more militia and Continentals arrived, but also had to deal with Arnold's insubordination and eventually relieved him of command.

On October 3, Burgoyne's army learned of the victory at Brandywine and that Clinton was heading upriver from New York City. However, food was becoming scarce as the militia cut communications with Ticonderoga and ambushed foragers. Burgoyne called frequent councils of war, but remained indecisive; he would not countenance a retreat, but had no feasible plans for attack. Finally, on October 5, he proposed a combined reconnaissance in force and foraging expedition, to be developed into a full-scale attack if circumstances looked promising.

On October 7 a combined reconnaissance and foraging party went forward but was quickly halted and then thrown back by Rebel forces. That night, Burgoyne ordered a withdrawal, blaming Von Riedesel's Brunswickers for the defeat and abandoning over 300 wounded for lack of transport. The next day, Gates was informed of the retreat and sent militia and artillery across the river to reinforce the contingent massing at Saratoga. Almost as soon as the

Above: *Major General Friedrich, Baron von Riedesel (1738–1800) was only 38 during the Saratoga campaign and his able and energetic leadership belied the reputation for slowness his countrymen have since acquired. Riedesel was a dutiful subordinate, but also knew when to defer to more experienced junior officers, such as Simon Fraser. (Fort Ticonderoga Museum)*

FREEMAN'S FARM (FIRST SARATOGA): SEPTEMBER 19, 1777

Burgoyne divided his force into three columns, with the left under Major General William Phillips, the right under Fraser, and the center under his own command. The columns set off at 9:00 a.m. and by noon had crossed a major watercourse (the Great Ravine). Gates was informed, but having no maps (and not having reconnoitered) decided to wait behind his defenses. Around 1:00 p.m., the center column was halted when its advance guard was badly mauled by the Rebel riflemen under Colonel Daniel Morgan—sent forward by Arnold who was disgusted by Gates's inactivity. Morgan was then taken in the flank by some of Fraser's men and retreated.

Burgoyne's column continued to advance to a clearing known as Freeman's Farm and formed line with Fraser on his right. Around 2:00 p.m., the British center was attacked by 1,000 Continentals under Brigadier General Enoch Poor, while Morgan's riflemen began picking off British officers and gunners. Fraser counterattacked and drove Poor back, but the fighting intensified: bayonet attacks were repelled by heavy fire from the Continentals, but they in turn were struck by Burgoyne's artillery when they left the woods to form up for a counterattack. By 4:00 p.m., the Regulars had suffered such heavy losses that their line was shrinking and threatening to break.

On Burgoyne's left, there was no opposition. At the first sound of firing, Phillips had gone to join Burgoyne, leaving Von Riedesel in command. As the gunfire grew heavier, Von Riedesel became concerned at the lack of communication and marched some of his command to the sound of the guns. At the vital moment, his Brunswickers hit Poor's right from the rear, almost certainly saving Burgoyne's center from collapse. German artillery then threw back the Continentals with canister fired at pistol range and Poor's men dropped back into the woods around 5:30 p.m., as darkness fell. Over on the right, Arnold had brought forward more troops under Brigadier General Ebenezer Learned, and they covered Poor's left as it, too, fell back.

By 6:30 p.m., the battle was over; Arnold's brigades had lost 100 dead, 325 wounded, and 40 missing; officially, the British lost 160 dead, 364 wounded, and 42 missing, but one report mentioned more than 500 injured. The Rebels had missed the chance to capture Burgoyne's artillery and baggage on the river road, but had handled the Regulars well in a standup fight in open ground.

BEMIS HEIGHTS (SECOND SARATOGA): OCTOBER 7, 1777

Burgoyne's plan involved a probing advance by Fraser and Von Riedesel with 2,000 men, while a picked group of marksmen, Native Americans, and Loyalists circled to the west in an attempt to locate the left flank of Gates's defenses. Another council of war, a meeting with the Native Americans and heavy mist, delayed the start until 10:00 a.m. and when the column finally set off, it took thirty minutes to cover the first 800 yards. A further halt was called while foragers collected grain and staff officers climbed on to the roof of a hut to observe Gates's lines; the front and flanks were covered by skirmishers, but the line was thinly held and there were huge gaps.

Gates, who now had over 11,000 men (including 6,000 Continentals), assumed that the advance was a decoy and reinforced the river defenses, but also sent forward Morgan, supported by Poor, Learned, and some artillery. Poor and Learned were spotted around 3:00 p.m., as they suddenly emerged from the woods and hit Burgoyne's left and center. Morgan, meanwhile, had circled around Burgoyne's right, drove it off a small hill with the bayonet, and then repeatedly outflanked it as it attempted to make an orderly withdrawal.

Burgoyne saw disaster looming and rode back to organize the defense of his camp, just as his center was overrun by militia. Fraser formed a rearguard, but was mortally wounded as he tried to rally the crumbling line. It had taken less than a hour to rout Burgoyne's entire force and the survivors withdrew to a nearby redoubt, from where they repulsed a number of overly impetuous attacks led by Arnold (now on the field and, according to some accounts, riding around like a madman) and Poor.

Frustrated by this setback, Arnold galloped over to his left where Morgan and Learned were attacking the works covering the right and rear of Burgoyne's camp, held by a group of Brunswickers and some Canadians. Morgan's men found a piece of dead ground and pinned down the defenders of the main redoubt from in front, while Arnold overran the Canadians and charged around the left flank of the German-held redoubt. In the process, he was wounded in the same leg as at Quebec and had to be carried to the rear. More Continentals arrived, but with Arnold gone, their attacks lacked coordination and leadership, and petered out as dusk fell.

Burgoyne had lost 900 men, including 278 dead; Gates lost about 200, of whom just thirty were killed, from almost 8,000 men engaged by the end of the day.

Royal forces moved out, torrential rain turned the road into a quagmire and the column covered less than a mile an hour. Burgoyne halted, hoping Gates would attack in the rain, but merely wasted another ten hours. At 4:00 p.m. on October 9, the Royal army moved off again, but had to abandon the baggage.

On the following day, Burgoyne crossed the Fishkill River and halted in Saratoga, while working parties went ahead to repair bridges. Gates, who had done nothing until that morning, rapidly overtook his opponent and reached the Fishkill at 4:00 p.m. Assuming Burgoyne was still moving north, he gave orders to cross the river the next morning; however, Burgoyne had dug in, still entertaining dreams of catching Gates in the open. On October 11, as Gates's army waded into the Fishkill in thick fog, a deserter warned them of the trap just in time, and the Rebels moved around Burgoyne's camp and surrounded it.

With artillery and riflemen firing into the camp from all directions, and down to only 3,500 men, Burgoyne called a council of war on October 14, to consider his options. There was unanimous support for capitulation and an officer was sent to Gates under a flag of truce. A ceasefire was agreed until 10:00 a.m. on October 15. Believing a relief force might be near, Burgoyne played for time, demanding the full honors of war; eventually, Gates agreed to a

surrender on condition that Burgoyne's force be returned to England and not serve in North America again. Burgoyne insisted on the word "convention" instead of "capitulation" and Gates, who had just heard that Royal forces from New York City had captured the Hudson Highland forts, agreed at once. Burgoyne tried to wriggle out of the agreement, but his officers persuaded him to accept and at 10:00 a.m. on October 17, the remaining 6,000 of the 10,000 men that he had brought from Canada marched out with the honors of war and set off on the 200 miles to Boston.

Further south, Clinton had been left with no orders regarding Burgoyne. On August 6, Burgoyne had indicated that he expected to be in Albany by August 23, and it was not until the end of September that Clinton realized all was not well. On October 3, he had set off up the Hudson River with 3,000 men and three frigates. Opposing him were 1,200 Continentals and some militia around Peekskill, and two forts—Clinton and Montgomery—with 500 men, commanded by George and James Clinton (who were brothers, but were not related to Sir Henry, although all were New Yorkers). The river below was fast-flowing, narrow, and blockaded by a log boom and chain that was guarded by two 24-gun frigates and some smaller vessels. Convinced that this was a foraging

Above: *The wounding of Simon Fraser (October 7, 1777). As the British line collapsed, both Arnold and Morgan recognized that Fraser was the only man capable of organizing further resistance and ordered riflemen to shoot him (something any British officer would have regarded as tantamount to murder). Shot through the stomach, Fraser died the next morning and at his own request, was buried in the Great Redoubt. (National Archives of Canada)*

Left: *Arnold is wounded while storming the redoubt held by the Brunswickers. (Anne S. K. Military Collection)*

Right: *View of the British Lines from the west bank of the Hudson. A contemporary print, apparently drawn from life, showing the Great Redoubt (actually three separate works) with the main camp, baggage park, and the hospital beside the pontoon bridge. The group of figures ascending the hill on the right is Fraser's funeral party. (Fort Ticonderoga Museum)*

Right: *Brigadier General George Clinton (1739–1812) was a radical lawyer who had challenged Schuyler in the New York assembly. Better suited to politics than the rigors of active service, he had no illusions about his limitations. Despite losing the Hudson forts and failing to protect Esopus, he won a reputation as an effective wartime governor, serving six consecutive terms and opposing Loyalist and Indian raids from Canada throughout 1779 and 1780. (Art Commission of the City of New York)*

raid, the Clintons did not call out the militia or speed up work on the defenses. On October 5, Clinton landed at Verplank's Point and made a feint at Peekskill; the following day, he crossed to Stony Point and stormed both forts. Below him, the Royal Navy captured the Rebel flotilla and broke through the boom, then headed upriver and captured Fort Constitution, opposite West Point, without a fight.

Clinton was now aware that, even if Burgoyne did reach Albany, he would need supplies. He set up a depot in Fort Clinton and summoned more troops, six months' supplies, and more transports from New York City, but was then forced to return as the senior British officers there had all fallen ill. Further progress was entrusted to Major General John Vaughan, who continued upriver to see if he could either contact Burgoyne or supply him via the Hudson. On October 16, Vaughan reached Esopus, some forty-five miles from Albany and barely seventy from Burgoyne. However, all attempts to contact Burgoyne failed and with Rebel troops massing on both river banks, Vaughan withdrew to New York City on October 17.

On November 6, the Convention Army (as Burgoyne's force was now known) arrived in Cambridge where it was forced to endure conditions so poor that Burgoyne had to spend £20,000 of his own money to keep his men fed. Staggered by Gates's generosity, Congress immediately reneged on the treaty, using the flimsiest of excuses, and ships sent to collect the troops in December were barred from Boston. On January 3, 1778, Congress resolved to detain the Convention Army until the Government ratified the treaty—knowing that such an implied recognition of independence would be prevented by the king. In fact, George III ordered Clinton to ratify it, whereupon Congress claimed the order was forged and demanded a witness to the king's signature!

Despite his claims to have been depending on Howe (by early October he was even asking Clinton for orders), Burgoyne had planned to avoid sharing the glory by capturing Albany on his own. Germain, through his ignorance of North America and failure to give complementary instructions to Howe and Burgoyne, was guilty by omission. In applying his orders to the letter, Howe did no wrong—and, indeed, had warned against expecting his help, as he saw Washington as the real threat to Burgoyne—but his indifference to Burgoyne's fate does him no credit.

The Saratoga campaign was the first in which the Regulars had been bested consistently by the Continental Army; it also disproved the theory that hordes of Loyalists were waiting to rise up against Congress. And once again, the weather had saved the Rebel forces from an early defeat that would have changed the course of fighting.

EUROPE

Word of Saratoga reached Paris on December 5, 1777—rather fortuitously, as the abandonment of Fort Ticonderoga and the loss of Philadelphia had damaged the Rebel cause—and King Louis XVI declared his recognition of the United States of America the next day. Yet despite celebrating Gates's victory as if it had been theirs, many in France feared that overt support might backfire if a reconciliation occurred—an outcome that, for different reasons, both Congress and the British government suggested might be increasingly likely. However, having just agreed proposals for naval operations against the West Indies, Louis and his foreign secretary, the Comte de Vergennes, decided to meet Franklin and a formal treaty of alliance was signed on February 6, 1778.

London learned of Burgoyne's defeat when a letter from Carleton arrived on December 3. Burgoyne's official dispatch reached England on December 15 (with a secret copy for his patron, the Earl of Derby, in case Germain censored the original). Denied a court of inquiry, Burgoyne presented his case in the House of Commons, condemning Germain's orders as too precise; Howe did the same, complaining that they were too vague! Public opinion favored Burgoyne (blaming Howe or Germain, according to political leaning), but in truth, all three had made mistakes in promoting—or failing to stop—a plan that was infeasible, given the lack of manpower and inherent logistical difficulties.

Another effect of the increased European interest in, and support for, Congress was the growing availability of dockyard facilities to Rebel privateers, allowing them to operate outside the western Atlantic. One of the first to enjoy success in European waters was Captain Lambert Wickes commanding the brig *Reprisal,* which had brought

Benjamin Franklin to St. Nazaire late in 1776. In January 1777, Wickes cruised the English Channel, taking five prizes into St. Nazaire. From their sale, he bought and fitted out a schooner and, together with another brig, the three vessels captured eighteen ships off the Irish coast, before being spotted by a British warship and chased back into St. Nazaire. As France was still neutral, Wickes was ordered to leave after formal British protests, and on September 14, the *Reprisal* escaped and headed for America, but was lost with all hands in a gale off Newfoundland.

In July, the Continental Navy sent Lieutenant John Paul Jones to Portsmouth, New Hampshire, to take command of a newly built sloop, the *Ranger.* His orders were to sail to France, where it was understood the Rebel commissioners would procure a new frigate for him to command. It was November 1 before Jones finally set sail, with ten officers and 140 men. In December, he arrived at Nantes with two prizes and set off for Paris, happy at the prospect of being rid of the poorly designed and constructed *Ranger,* and looking forward to his new command, the frigate *L'Indien,* being built in Amsterdam.

Above: *General James Clinton (1733–1812) served alongside his younger brother as a militia captain in the French and Indian Wars and fought in Canada under Montgomery. Promoted to brigadier general in August 1776, he served under his brother George in the Hudson Highlands and received a bayonet wound during the storming of Fort Montgomery. He was later commander of the Northern Army, and led a brigade at Yorktown. (Independence National Historical Park)*

1778

"Assure Congress of my friendship"

LOUIS XVI OF FRANCE

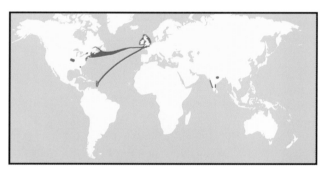

RED INDICATES FIGHTING, INCLUDING PRIVATEERING ON SHIPPING LANES

Flag raising at New Providence, January 28, 1778. (U.S. Marine Corps)

The fourth year of the war brought a new dimension to the struggle: the involvement of a major European state—France. In 1776, Congress had sent Benjamin Franklin—and later Silas Deane and Arthur Lee—to Paris, ostensibly to negotiate a trade agreement. However, Congress knew perfectly well that such a treaty would involve French recognition of the United States as a sovereign nation and this, in turn, would almost inevitably mean war between Great Britain and France.

The draft agreement presented by Franklin (often known as "the Plan of 1776") contained little of interest to the French court. Believing that the Rebels had no chance of winning, the aim of the French ministry was to prevent any reconciliation and to prolong the war so as to cause maximum damage to the British economy. The three commissioners engaged in polite, but pointless negotiations with French diplomats who were unwilling to commit their nation to a conflict in which their erstwhile ally might realign itself and join with the British against them. However, Trenton and Princeton illustrated a resolve, and Saratoga and Germantown an ability, to win, that gradually overcame these doubts. Equally, the French court was concerned that the British might be stunned into a peace deal that left France at the economic and political mercy of a reunified British Empire.

On February 6, the French king signed two treaties—the Treaty of Amity and Commerce (broadly a mutual agreement not to grant more favorable commercial rights to any other nation) and a separate Treaty of Conditional and Defensive Alliance, providing that the United States would not ally with Great Britain if France entered the war. The conditional aspect of the second treaty was that it only

Right: *Benjamin Franklin (1706–90) was widely regarded as possessing one of the best minds in America and was well known to French society before Congress sent him to Paris in 1776. He was singled out by Vergennes as the only one of the three Commissioners with whom he would deal, and Franklin's popularity did much to encourage covert aid from France prior to 1778. (National Archives)*

Opposite page: *King Louis XVI of France (1754–1793) had a sound knowledge of the dynastic diplomacy of Europe, despite being only 21 on his accession to the throne. Patriotic and conscientious, he was eager for revenge against Great Britain and played a prominent role in the development of "Hortalez & Cie". (Musée de Versailles, Paris)*

became binding once France and Great Britain were at war. If that became a reality, the French would make no attempt to regain possessions in North America that had been lost in 1763. Finally, neither side would cease fighting until independence had been secured for the United States, and neither would make peace with Great Britain unless both agreed. Given the relative power and influence of the two signatories, France had been remarkably generous—mainly so as to avoid being seen as greedy and opportunistic. The French did not want to antagonize the other European powers, whose sympathy and benign neutrality were essential to success.

The treaties also averted a major—and potentially fatal—crisis in the supply of war materials to the Rebel forces, as the spurious trading house *Roderigue Hortalez & Cie* (a cover organization for the French government) had no more money or credit left. That would have been catastrophic for Congress as this route had provided equipment worth five million *livres* by September 1777, and just one shipment

in April of that year (200 cannon, thirty brass mortars, 200,000 pounds of powder, and tents, clothing, and small arms for 25,000 men) had equipped its armies for the campaigns of 1777.

EUROPE

In March, Louis XVI ceremonially received Franklin, Deane, and Lee as accredited representatives of a sovereign, independent nation. The British response was to revive the negotiations adjourned indefinitely at the end of 1776. In February, the North ministry had renounced the right to tax the American colonies other than to regulate trade and had dispatched a commission, under the Earl of Carlisle (who was also head of the intelligence services at that time) to negotiate an end to the War. Recalling Washington's fit of pique at being addressed as plain "Mr." the Rebels were to be addressed in any style they chose, and complete withdrawal of Royal forces from the Colonies could be offered. Only the acceptance or acknowledgement of independence was not open for discussion. These were radical concessions—the King only accepted them grudgingly—and they sparked some panic in the French court when its agents in London reported them. Unfortunately, what might have made progress in 1776 was unacceptable in 1778 and Carlisle's deputation would achieve little.

France's entry into in the war (there was no official declaration of hostilities until late in 1779) led to increased diplomatic and economic pressure from Great Britain on the United Provinces of the Netherlands. A seventeenth-century treaty provided that the two nations would assist each other if attacked, but the treaty was not invoked. Instead, The Netherlands government invoked an equally ancient treaty that supported a "free ships, free goods" policy and defined contraband (war materials destined for one belligerent that could be seized by its enemies, even in neutral ships). The treaty specifically excluded naval stores, due to the difficulty of proving military (rather than civil) use, but the British ignored this provision and seized scores of Dutch vessels—forty-two in October alone—although they paid for their cargoes, thereby preventing the Dutch from selling such items to the enemy.

One matter in which the British succeeded in changing Dutch policy was over the fate of the frigate *L'Indien*, the ship being built in Amsterdam for John Paul Jones. The Dutch were forced to sell the vessel to the French government and Jones could not persuade the French to give it to him, so he went back to the *Ranger* in January, with orders to disrupt British commerce. On February 13, one week after the treaty of alliance was signed, *Ranger* weighed anchor and put into Quiberon Bay for extensive alterations. At Brest, he was escorted past the waiting British ships by a French frigate on April 10, and set off to raid an English port, with the idea of taking hostages whom the British government might exchange for the many American seamen in British prisons. Jones headed north into the Irish sea, then past the Isle of Man and up to the Firth of Clyde, before heading back to the Irish Sea. After an abortive attack on a vessel in Belfast Lough, he attacked the town of Whitehaven on April 23. However, while Jones was spiking the guns of one of the defending forts, some of his crew got drunk in a nearby pub; one man dashed through the town warning the inhabitants and Jones and the

remaining men were forced to flee. Little material damage had been done, but the psychological effect was enormous.

At 10:00 a.m. the following day, he attempted to kidnap the Earl of Selkirk from his home in Kirkcudbright Bay. Unfortunately, the earl was away and when Jones abandoned the plan, his crew demanded to be allowed to plunder the house (Lady Selkirk graciously handed over the silver, but Jones felt the action smacked of piracy, bought it back

Two illustrations of the action between Ranger *and* Drake *(April 25, 1778). While Jones was cruising the waters around the British Isles, he encountered the British sloop* Drake *which he captured in an hour-long action, losing just eight men against his opponent's 40. (Anne S. K. Brown Collection)*

Right: *Admiral Augustus Keppel (1725–1786). The dispute between Keppel and Palliser continued until 1783 and, though an extreme example, gives some idea of how intense such professional and political disputes could become within the armed forces. When Keppel was exonerated by a court of enquiry in 1783, crowds lit bonfires, looted Palliser's house and pulled the gates of the Admiralty building from their hinges. (National Maritime Museum)*

from the crew and returned it after the war). At daybreak on April 25, he returned to Belfast Lough, having disguised the *Ranger* as a merchantman, and fought a bloody action with the sloop Drake which he captured and brought back into Brest on May 8. Although his raid on Whitehaven and capture of the *Drake* were well publicized in America, no official recognition of his exploits came from Congress and he spent the rest of the year vainly trying to get the Dutch to release *L'Indien*, still at Amsterdam and almost ready to sail. (In fact, the Dutch did not release the ship until they themselves had entered the war, and then the French government sold it on and it ended up under the command of the incompetent Alexander Gillon of the South Carolina navy.)

Despite the loss of *L'Indien*, Congress maintained friendly relations with the Dutch and made the most of public disaffection with Great Britain, distributing propaganda throughout the Netherlands via its agent, Charles Dumas, a Dutchman of French ancestry and acquaintance of Benjamin Franklin.

Unsurprisingly, Congress made the most of Dutch disaffection, distributing propaganda throughout the Netherlands via its agent, Charles Dumas, a Dutchman of French ancestry and acquaintance of Benjamin Franklin. France was also active diplomatically, forming strong links with the "Patriot" party (the official opposition to the Statholder, who was pro-British) and encouraging Dutch merchants to ignore British protests. This was not difficult, as most Europeans—including people in Great Britain

and Ireland—saw the conflict as none of their concern. Indeed, only those working in ports saw any evidence that a war was being fought. Yet the geographical proximity of Great Britain and France, and their political rivalry, forced both nations to maintain a large part of their naval forces in home waters. Now that France had entered the fray, it was inevitable that those fleets would clash.

On April 13, the Comte D'Estaing (a former army officer and colonial governor, whose promotion had provoked jealousy among his subordinates) sailed for North America from Toulon with twelve ships and three frigates. French spies arranged for the British Admiralty to receive information indicating that D'Estaing's destination was Brest, where the main French fleet was stationed. With no idea where D'Estaing was, on June 15 the Admiralty sent Admiral Augustus Keppel with twenty-one ships and four frigates to blockade Brest and prevent the junction of the two fleets. When D'Estaing's real destination became clear, thirteen ships were sent to North America under Vice-Admiral John Byron.

Two days later, the British fleet sighted two French frigates and some smaller vessels. With no previous fighting having occurred between British and French forces, the situation was one of some delicacy. Keppel ordered a general chase and one frigate and a lugger were captured that afternoon; however, the other frigate—the *Belle Poule*—refused to surrender and the British frigate *Arethusa* opened fire. The action lasted several hours, and the *Belle Poule* eventually withdrew, with 102 dead and wounded from a crew of 230; the *Arethusa* had badly damaged masts and rigging, but suffered only forty-four casualties from her complement of 198. The importance of this relatively minor action was that the French saw June 17 as the official start of the war with Great Britain (as distinct from the alliance with the United States).

On July 8, Lieutenant General le Comte d'Orvilliers emerged from Brest with thirty-two ships and orders containing just a simple instruction to remain at sea for a month, which he assumed implied that he should avoid battle, except under the most favorable circumstances. On July 9, Keppel—who had returned to Spithead at the end of June—re-emerged with thirty ships, looking for action, and the two fleets spotted each other around midday on July 23.

D'Orvilliers was to leeward of Keppel, but managed to get all but two of his ships to windward overnight. However, this left Keppel between the French and their home and reduced them to only twenty-seven ships (the two exceptions having returned to Brest, while three others were unfit for action). D'Orvilliers managed to keep Keppel beyond range for three days, until dawn on July 27 revealed the two fleets less than ten miles apart, a hundred miles off Île d'Ouessant (Ushant).

Both fleets were initially on the port tack and

heading northwest, but managed to maneuver themselves into two clumsy lines on opposite tacks, but approximately parallel courses. Keppel's van passed beyond range of D'Orvilliers's first three ships, but the fourth opened fire as the two lines passed each other slowly. When the smoke cleared, Keppel's line was in confusion and the French wore and passed it again, this time to leeward, allowing the bottom deck guns—the heaviest—to fire at the masts and rigging of Keppel's ships (the standard French gunnery tactic, in contrast to the British who aimed at the hull). Realizing the significance of the move, Keppel ordered line of battle but Vice-Admiral Hugh Palliser, who commanded the rear squadron, failed to respond and then ignored a written message delivered by frigate. Sunset prevented any further fighting and by dawn the fleets were almost twenty miles apart. Having suffered more damage than the French, the British sailed back to Plymouth, and D'Orvilliers did not pursue.

Although this was the last major naval action of 1778 in European waters, the resultant in-fighting among senior officers of the Royal Navy lasted until 1783. Keppel (who owed his rank to earlier Whig governments and, like many opponents of the North ministry, refused to serve against Americans) blamed Palliser, a supporter of North, for throwing away the chance of victory; Palliser retaliated with a claim that a maneuver by Keppel's flagship (the *Victory*) constituted cowardice. Palliser, who was later reprimanded without any formal charges being made, used his membership of the Board of Admiralty to have Keppel court-martialled. The controversy quickly became a major issue of public debate and affected the conduct of naval operations on more than one occasion, only being resolved by Keppel's acquittal in 1783.

PENNSYLVANIA

The entry of France into the War did not come as a surprise to the Royal commanders in North America, although it did result in a major shift in strategy. At the start of 1778, they controlled more of North America than they would at any other stage of the war, but now this theater had slipped down the list of priorities for the North ministry. The flow of men was dramatically reduced and thus removed many of the offensive options previously available. In fact, the force in North America—the largest Army presence anywhere outside the British Isles—was now more likely to become a source of manpower for all operations west of the Azores. In any event, there was a growing feeling that the men who had failed in 1776 and 1777 should not have a third chance. Carleton and Howe had both tendered their resignations toward the end of 1777; both had been accepted and they were recalled to England early in 1778. Carleton was replaced by Major General Frederick Haldimand and Howe by Clinton; because both handovers were prolonged, there was no offensive activity in the first half of the year, and an atmosphere of *ennui* and lethargy prevailed.

Shortage of men, along with other factors, had revived interest in making more use of Loyalists, in the idea of a campaign in the South (including the Floridas, anticipating Spanish involvement), and in amphibious raids on New England, the last two intended particularly to damage Rebel commerce. In January, the king had indicated his support for these ideas, even proposing a complete withdrawal of land forces from North America in order to achieve them. The Earl of Sandwich, First Lord of the Admiralty, concurred with this view, but Lord Jeffrey Amherst (a veteran of the French and Indian Wars and now de

Above: *Portsmouth, New Hampshire. One of several New England coastal towns that became heavily involved in the war. Rebel privateers operated from the harbor throughout the War and the 74-gun ship* America *was built in the dockyard. (Library of Congress)*

The following three officers were instrumental in training the Continental Army, each in his own way contributing to its increasing capabilities and its growing confidence in those capabilities.

Right: *Major-General Friedrich Wilhelm Augustus von Steuben (1730–1794) was born in Magdeburg, raised in Russia and served in the Prussian army during the Seven Years' War. Having served briefly as an aide to Frederick the Great, he was recommended for a commission in the Continental Army and became its Inspector General. With a handpicked company of 100 men (who later became Washington's bodyguard), Steuben instructed the Continental Army in European methods of drill, amending and blending British, French, and Prussian doctrines to meet the needs of North America. However, it must be acknowldedged that the Continental Army already possessed military qualities before he arrived, and still lacked some when he had finished. His real value was his experience of the Prussian staff which was an unique institution at that time. (Independence National Historical Park)*

facto commander-in-chief of the British Army) warned of the possibility of Rebel attacks on the Caribbean. Nevertheless, when Germain wrote to Clinton in March, he included detailed instructions concerning all of these ideas.

Howe had never been keen on using large numbers of Loyalists as troops, still less to control areas captured by the main army, arguing that the best he had experienced was equivocal neutrality. He had also argued for maintaining one large force, to act against Washington's main army, rather than dispersing the troops around North America, as an increased reliance on Loyalists would require—though he did not seem to have appreciated that such a force had to justify itself with decisive victories. He had shown little interest in the South and his

Left: *Timothy Pickering
(1745–1829) was a
serious student of military
matters and a colonel of
militia, who attracted
Wahington's attention and
became a staff officer. In
1777, he succeeded Gates
as adjutant general and
served at Germantown. In
1775, he had published an
Easy Plan of Discipline for
a Militia which was based
on the English Norfolk
Discipline and was widely
used in the Continental
Army until replaced by Von
Steuben's regulations.
(Independence National
Historical Park)*

experience of amphibious operations during the French and Indian Wars had left him skeptical as to their worth, compared with the considerable risks involved.

Clinton, however, was more amenable to the idea of amphibious assaults (the planning of which was undoubtedly one of his main areas of expertise) and expeditions to the South—despite his previous expe-rience at Charleston. Such an expedition would also be easier to supply from the Caribbean and could rely on the support of the West Indies squadron (although nobody appeared to realize at the time that the same argument applied to the French). He also concurred with the idea of abandoning Philadelphia, which had proved difficult to supply, even with con-trol of the Delaware River and the aid of the Royal

Navy. Germain ordered him to adopt a more dispersed strategy if he was unable to destroy Washington's army within the coming campaign season.

During the winter, Washington's army at Valley Forge, eighteen miles northwest of Philadelphia, had largely disappeared as enlistments expired, leaving a hard core of veterans. However, those veterans had spent the winter months being trained by Major General Frederick von Steuben, who had incorporated the most appropriate elements of British, French, and Prussian drill and tactics to the needs of an army composed of Americans. Logistics were still in a des-

perate state (in May alone, Clinton's forces destroyed forty-two Rebel ships and much-needed stores in raids along the Delaware River) and the Continental Army was still far short of its paper strength. Washington increasingly used militia to perform guard and garrison duties on the more remote posts, in order to free his regiments for combat, but this lack of men, above all else, kept him on the defensive for the first months of 1778, despite proposals for attacks on Philadelphia or New York City.

Although neither army was on the offensive, it was equally clear that the peace talks were going nowhere. With insufficient ships to remove all the

Right: *Colonel Henry Knox (1750–1806) was, like Pickering, an avid reader of military books and owned The London Book Store in Boston, whose customers included many British officers. A loyal and able administrator, Knox served under Ward as a volunteer during the early part of the siege. He later impressed Washington sufficiently to be made commander of the Continental Artillery. In this capacity, he organized the transfer of the cannon from Ticonderoga that forced the British to evacuate Boston and developed the artillery arm of the Continental Army to a level of efficiency that matched anything in Europe. (Independence National Historical Park)*

Left: Charles Lee. There are no known portraits of the enigmatic and mercurial Lee, but this caricature, believed to have been made from life, is said to capture his likeness.

Loyalists, as well as his own troops, Clinton was left with the likely prospect of a fighting withdrawal overland from Philadelphia to New York City. Believing that he would need all the men he had, he decided not to dispatch troops to St. Lucia or the Floridas until after he had reached Manhattan.

Clinton's army left Philadelphia in the early hours of June 18, and crossed the Delaware. In addition to a massive baggage train (not entirely the fault of the civilian contingent) the troops had to carry all of their provisions, as the New Jersey countryside had been denuded by the campaigns—and subsequent plundering—of 1776. His chosen route was intersected with marshes and streams and the militia destroyed the bridges ahead of him and constantly harassed his flanks and rear.

Washington and his officers held a council of war to discuss a possible attack. Clearly, it suited the

Right: *Brigadier-General Anthony Wayne (1745–1796) had served in most of the major campaigns by 1778, including the invasion of Canada. He had briefly commanded Fort Ticonderoga (where he put down a mutiny at pistol point) and had led the Pennsylvania Line at Brandywine, Germantown, and Monmouth. It would be misleading to say that Wayne epitomized the junior generals of the Continental Army, since he was uniquely impressive. (Independence National Historical Park)*

Rebel cause to let Clinton return to New York City, where his army was shut up and could easily be observed, although Washington insisted that the army shadow Clinton in case he invaded the Hudson Highlands. Lee, recently exchanged after his capture at White's Tavern, in December 1776, argued that since Clinton was doing what they wanted, there was no point in risking battle in such circumstances unless success was certain. However, Greene, Wayne, Von Steuben, and La Fayette all pressed for an attack. Initially, Washington merely sent another 1,500 more men to harass Clinton and moved the

rest of his army into a better position. However, he then became more aggressive and on June 28 gave Lee the best units of the Continental Army and ordered him to attack Clinton's rearguard. A hard-fought action left neither side with any clear-cut advantage, and Clinton continued his withdrawal.

Washington's army was too exhausted to pursue Clinton, and in truth the latter was better prepared for a second round of fighting, had it occurred. However, Clinton could not afford to spend long sparring with his opponent, as his army was running short of food, only a day's rations remaining by the

MONMOUTH COURT HOUSE: JUNE 28, 1778

Lee had no idea of the size or disposition of Clinton's forces and Washington's orders were less than specific. Leaving camp around 7:30 a.m., Lee learned that the main British column—8,000 men under Cornwallis—had not moved, and he sent Brigadier General Anthony Wayne ahead. At 10:00 a.m., Cornwallis marched out of the village of Freehold, leaving 3,600 men as a rearguard; Lee's men passed through the village and, around noon, were attacked by British cavalry.

Clinton now sent Cornwallis back in strength, and Lee ordered Wayne forward to meet the British, while he and La Fayette tried to outflank their right. Unfortunately, Wayne advanced too far and Lee found himself facing a large enemy force with his own right flank exposed. At this point, a Rebel artillery unit retired to replenish its ammunition, leading other units to withdraw as well. About 1:30 p.m., Lee ordered his troops to move back to Freehold to avoid being outflanked, then issued a further order to retreat to a ridge overlooking a large bog (known as the east morass). By 2:00 p.m. his entire command was falling back in confusion.

Washington now arrived on the field, his obvious rage at the sight of the retreat silencing the normally vocal Lee. Using the knowledge of a local officer, Washington positioned his own troops on the ridge behind the east morass, incorporating Lee's units as they arrived. He now had 12,000 men waiting for Clinton, who had formed his 7,000 men into two lines and was advancing confidently.

Clinton initially forced back the Rebel left, but several regiments of Continentals formed up behind a hedgerow and held out for a vital half-hour, allowing more troops to come up. Fresh artillery covered the front of the Rebel positions and more took post on Coomb's Hill, overlooking Clinton's left and enfilading his entire line. Three major attacks by the elite of the British infantry were thrown back within the space of thirty minutes and at 4:00 p.m., Clinton brought up sixteen guns, precipitating a two-hour artillery duel that did little damage.

At 6:30 p.m., Clinton began to withdraw; Wayne forced back elements of the enemy rearguard, until it was reinforced, in turn, the British grenadier battalions making three charges and losing their commanding officer. There was more hard fighting as the British fell back across Weamaconck Creek, but the fighting ended around 7:30 p.m. and Clinton slipped away under cover of darkness.

Washington lost between 500 and 600 men (including nearly forty dead from sunstroke, temperatures having reached almost 100° Fahrenheit); Clinton's losses were upwards of 1,200, including over 400 Hessian deserters. Lee was charged with disobeying orders, showing disrespect to his commander-in-chief, and ordering a shameful retreat. He was suspended from command for a year, but never served again.

time it reached Sandy Hook, from where it was ferried back to New York City by Lord Howe's fleet. Washington moved to White Plains from where he observed Clinton, but did not respond to attempts to lure him on to less favorable ground.

Monmouth was the last major battle in the northern theater, although Clinton attempted to make the most of the remainder of the campaign season, and the troops that he was about to lose to other theaters. September saw British raids on Old Tappan, New Bedford, and Little Egg Harbor, while a substantial thrust into New Jersey brought much-needed forage, even if it failed to bring Washington to battle. However, a proposal to attack Boston with 6,000 men was rejected by Lord Howe (wary of losing ships and trained crewmen, who were even harder to replace than soldiers), despite the support of Carlisle.

In November, Clinton reluctantly sent 5,000 men to the Caribbean, 2,500 to Georgia, 1,000 to the Floridas, and 500 to Halifax in Nova Scotia, leaving just 15,000 in New York City and 4,000 at Newport. He had already written to Germain stating that these detachments would force him to abandon New York

City, and in October he again offered his resignation, arguing that he had too few troops to achieve anything of consequence. Germain persuaded him to stay, but feared Spain's entry into the war would prevent any substantial reinforcement of Clinton—and might possibly require him to give up more of his existing forces (he did eventually receive 3,000 men, but they were all recruits). Clinton was now forced to place more military reliance on the Loyalists, whose leaders insisted—as ever—that Rebel morale was about to collapse. But Clinton could see no evidence of this and, to his credit, also resisted their growing demands to lay waste the countryside and starve the rebellion to death, claiming that such behavior was unbecoming of a great nation.

At the same time, Rebel morale was high, despite considerable difficulties with pay and supplies, the perennial problem of enlistments (Washington had under 6,000 men by the end of the year), and the disaster at Newport. The commissary and quartermaster's departments had been improved by Greene and a series of magazines and depots were now appearing across the interior of the country, out of reach of

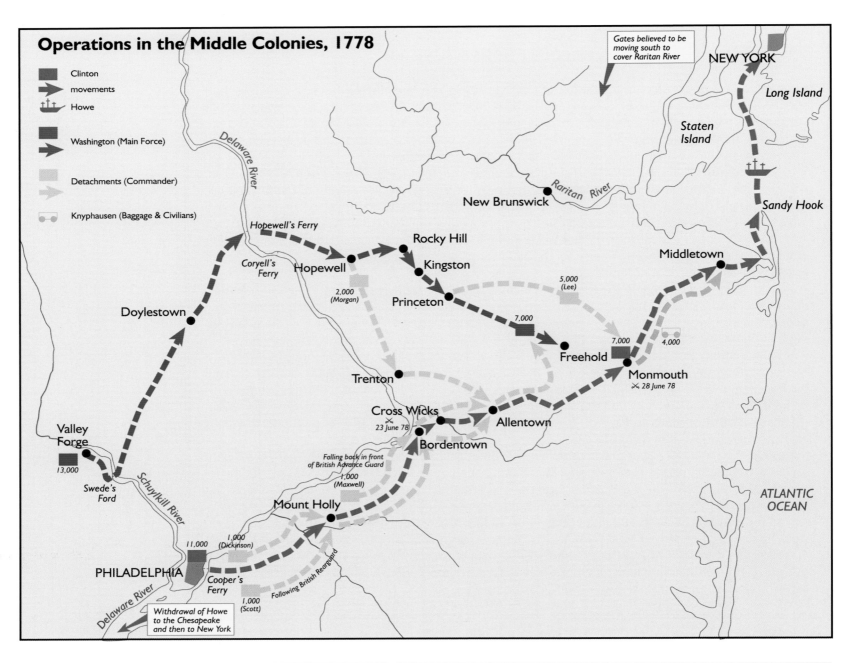

Operations in the Middle Colonies, 1778

Clinton
movements
Howe

Washington (Main Force)

Detachments (Commander)

Knyphausen (Baggage & Civilians)

Gates believed to be moving south to cover Raritan River

NEW YORK

Long Island

Staten Island

Raritan River

New Brunswick

Delaware River

Hopewell's Ferry

Coryell's Ferry

Rocky Hill

Middletown

Sandy Hook

Hopewell

Kingston

5,000 (Lee)

Doylestown

2,000 (Morgan)

Princeton

7,000

7,000

4,000

Freehold

Monmouth
✕ 28 June 78

Trenton

Valley Forge

13,000

Cross Wicks
✕ 23 June 78

Allentown

ATLANTIC OCEAN

Swede's Ford

Schuylkill River

Bordentown

Falling back in front of British Advance Guard

Mount Holly

1,000 (Maxwell)

PHILADELPHIA

11,000

1,000 (Dickinson)

Cooper's Ferry

1,000 (Scott)

Following British Rearguard

Delaware River

Withdrawal of Howe to the Chesapeake and then to New York

Royal forces. The only dark cloud for 1779 was the situation in the South.

RHODE ISLAND

Meanwhile, D'Estaing had arrived in Delaware Bay on July 8, hoping to surprise the fleet of Lord Howe who was supporting his brother in Philadelphia, but only to find that Howe had returned to New York City. D'Estaing headed north, but Howe was alerted and placed guns on Sandy Hook, commanding the western side of the entrance into the harbor, then moored seven ships in such a way that they could enfilade any fleet entering the main channel, and placed others in position to catch the enemy in a crossfire if they attempted to cross the bar, a couple of miles outside Sandy Hook. In the end, the bar itself proved the deciding obstacle; when D'Estaing arrived, the tide was full, but he did not believe that the water was deep enough for his largest ships. After heading south to mislead his opponents, he sailed northeast toward the British base at Newport, Rhode Island, where Washington had sent 2,500 Continentals and over 7,000 militia under Sullivan, Greene (himself a Rhode Islander), and La Fayette. Opposing the Allied forces were 1,500 British, 2,800

Hessian, and 700 Loyalist troops, plus 1,000 sailors and marines from the five frigates and numerous other small craft at Newport (most of which had been scuttled in a vain attempt to block the entrance to the harbor).

The plan was for Sullivan to invest the eastern side of Newport, while D'Estaing landed 4,000 soldiers and seamen on a neighboring island and then ferried them over to besiege the town from the north. On July 30, D'Estaing moved into Narragansett Bay and landed his men on Conanicut Island—a relief to the French troops, many of whom had scurvy after fifteen weeks at sea. On August 8, Sullivan—who disliked the French—crossed over to Rhode Island before D'Estaing was in position, and when Lord Howe appeared off Point Judith, just seven miles from Narragansett Bay, two days later, D'Estaing seized the opportunity to re-embark his men head out to engage the British.

As he left the bay, with the wind from the northeast, D'Estaing (who had fewer vessels, but more guns) was to windward of Howe and so had the advantage of the weather gauge. Howe headed out to sea, hoping that the wind would shift to the southwest and transfer that benefit to his fleet; unfortunately, it changed little and both fleets sailed on through the day and into the night without altering

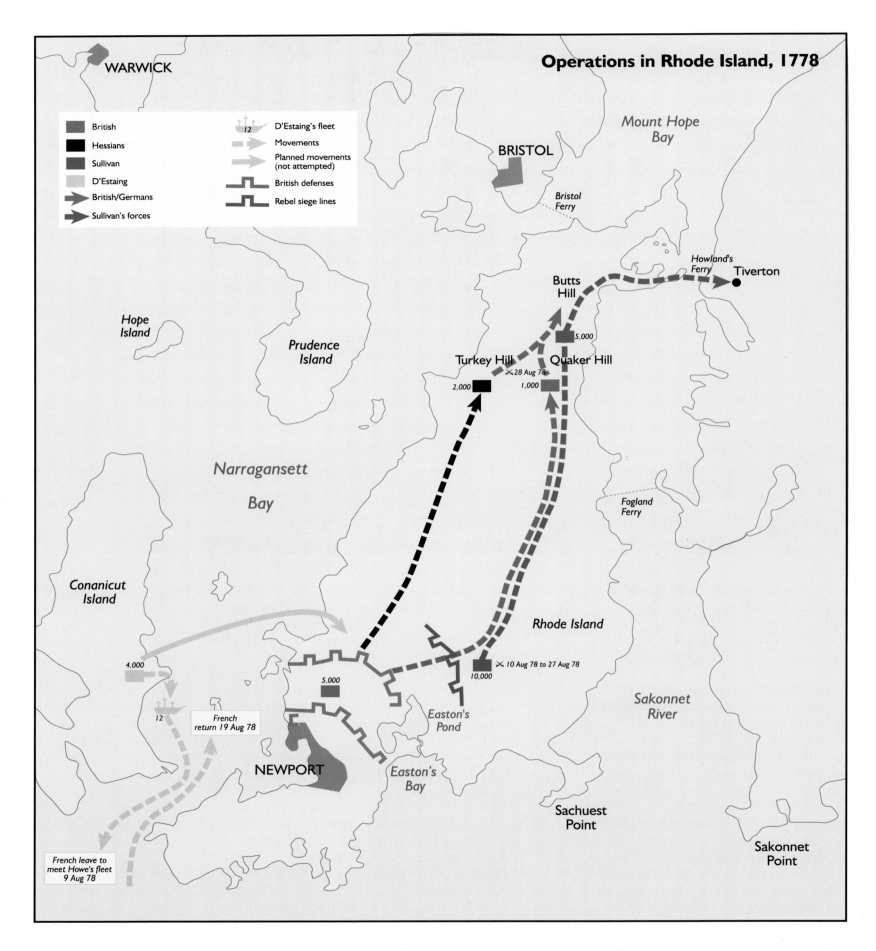

Operations in Rhode Island, 1778

their relative positions. Howe then shifted to a northerly course and as D'Estaing maneuvered into position some three miles astern of the British line, a storm began that continued throughout the following day, scattering both fleets and dismasting D'Estaing's flagship, the 90-gun *Languedoc*. Completely dismasted and with her tiller out of action, she was attacked by one of Howe's smallest ships, but was saved by darkness and the arrival of several other French vessels.

Admiral of the Blue Flag.
Son of John Viscount Barrington.

Left: *Admiral Samuel Barrington (1729–1800). In a highly creditable naval and amphibious operation, Barrington's swift and decisive attack on St. Lucia as soon as he had the resources to do so, ensured success and provided an object lesson for others (National Maritime Museum)*

While Howe returned to Sandy Hook to mend the damage to his own fleet, D'Estaing was forced to anchor and carry out running repairs at sea. He returned to Newport, but with such serious damage that he needed to find a port, and sailed for Boston, despite the protestations of Sullivan (whose men had advanced to within fifteen hundred yards of the British fortifications). On August 31, Howe arrived off Boston, but did not try to pass the fortified islands in the outer harbor and returned to New York City. Back at Newport, Sullivan knew that he had no chance of taking the town without French aid — especially as most of the New England militia had left in disgust at D'Estaing's "betrayal"—and was forced to carry out a fighting withdrawal.

While it is easy to understand—and appreciate as militarily correct—that D'Estaing's first priority was the condition of his ships, the whining New Englanders ensured that bad reports of the French were sent to Boston. La Fayette, who now felt a conflict of interests, almost fought a duel with one of Sullivan's officers. Washington attempted to placate Sullivan, publicly blaming the effects of the storm for the abandonment of the siege, while Congress passed a resolution thanking the French for their assistance. Washington asked Sullivan to maintain a united front, but the latter accused the French of abandoning their ally, and despite clumsy attempts to retract the statement, the damage was done. D'Estaing would never return to Newport.

Although D'Estaing's officers behaved well, bigotry prevailed and four riots occurred in September and October (although one related to bread shortages), involving local sailors, in which a number of Frenchman were killed.

THE CARIBBEAN

Another consequence of French intervention was the extension of the conflict to other parts of the world outside Europe and North America. The most crucial of these was the Caribbean, the wealthiest region in the world at that time. Pound for pound, commodities such as sugar, coffee, and cocoa were on a par with gold or silver; indeed, in 1763 Great Britain had contemplated giving back Canada to France in return for two of the lesser "spice islands." These islands were also important strategically; the trade winds of the Atlantic Ocean made them more accessible than North America to merchant ships from Europe (despite being farther away); many islands also had superb natural harbors that provided secure naval bases, although even those that did not were considered valuable. The islands were also close enough to North America to provide alternative employment for ships and soldiers outside of the "campaign season" (which was largely dictated by hurricanes, just as military activity in India and the Far East was dictated by the monsoons).

Geographically, the islands lay in a long curve running from northwest to southeast, and finally due south toward South America. The last section was known as the Windward Islands and it was here that ships arriving from Europe usually made land; not surprisingly, the islands formed a focal point for naval activity, eight of them changing hands during the War. In 1778, however, the French held Guadeloupe, Martinique (which contained the main naval base, at Fort Royal), and St. Lucia (which overlooked Fort Royal and hence had strategic significance for both sides). Between Guadeloupe and Martinique was Dominica, which was British, though only until word of the alliance arrived from Europe in September, when it was promptly seized by troops from Martinique in a surprise attack—the garrison being unaware that hostilities had commenced

The senior Royal Navy officer in the West Indies was Rear Admiral Samuel Barrington, based at Barbados, whose small squadron was augmented in December by eight naval vessels and 5,000 troops from New York City. By coincidence, this reinforcement had sailed on November 4, the same day that D'Estaing had left Boston for the Caribbean. D'Estaing

reached Martinique on December 9 and Barrington's reinforcements arrived at Barbados the next day.

Barrington promptly sailed 100 miles to St. Lucia and anchored in Grand Cul de Sac inlet, on the west side of the island, on December 13, seizing high ground north of the inlet and the batteries protecting it. The next day, he landed the bulk of his troops and by sunset they had captured La Vigie, a tall, steep hill that dominated the northern half of the island, and the capital, Morne Fortuné (immediately renamed Fort Charlotte). The speed of the operation had forced the French garrison to abandon all their powder, stores, and artillery.

Soon after the capture of Morne Fortuné, lookouts spotted D'Estaing's fleet, which had sailed from Martinique that morning with 7,000 troops. Barrington spent the night preparing his defenses, placing one of his ships and three frigates at the north end of Grand Cul de Sac to prevent D'Estaing sailing between around the British line and attacking the transports. His remaining six ships were anchored in a line that stretched south and slightly outward, with his flagship, the *Prince of Wales*, holding the most exposed post at the southern end of the line.

On the morning of December 15, D'Estaing's fleet sailed along Barrington's line from north to south, each ship firing as she passed, but causing little damage as the slight breeze did not allow his ships to get close enough to the British. He repeated the maneuver later in the day, again with no effect, and then shifted his attention to the land defenses. Anchoring in a small bay to the north, he disembarked his 7,000 troops and personally led three assaults on La Vigie, before being forced to withdraw with casualties of forty-one officers and around 800 men.

Before D'Estaing could mount another attack by sea, Barrington had strengthened the shore defenses at each end of his line and brought his ships closer to shore. Having spent ten days searching in vain for a weak point in Barrington's defenses, D'Estaing returned to Martinique, forcing the garrison to capitulate.

Below: *Action at St. Lucia (December 15, 1778). Barrington's ships are anchored across the bay known as the Carenage, as D'Estaing's ships attack from the left. (National Maritime Museum)*

INDIA

In the 1770s, India was not a nation, but a land of princes—some powerful, most petty—who were linked, or divided, by longstanding dynastic alliances. The decline of the Mogul Empire over the previous century had coincided with the growth of European involvement in the subcontinent, as first the Dutch and Portuguese, and later also the British and French, had gained a foothold in the region by forging alliances with local rulers. At the start of the Seven Years' War, the British East India Company, founded in 1600, and the French Compagnie des Indes Orientales, set up in 1664, wielded the greatest influence. The former represented the interest of the British government, as well as its own, and was enormously wealthy, wielding political control over the three "Presidencies" of Bengal (Calcutta), Madras, and Bombay, with overall control exercised by the council of Bengal from 1774. The latter was based mainly around Pondicherry on the Coromandel coast in the southeast; during the previous war, it had seen every one of its forts (also known as factories) captured by the British, only to have them all restored at the Treaty of Paris.

As a theater of operations, India differed from North America, Europe, and the Caribbean politically and militarily. Uniquely, the fighting in India involved large native forces with their own political agenda, while the troops of the European powers were often subordinated to their commanders. Those armies were huge—often with thousands of horsemen and many guns (sometimes of huge caliber)—yet the fighting man seldom comprised more than ten percent of the horde. There was little or no military infrastructure outside the cities, and armies lived off the land, moving at the speed of the slowest bullock cart. The serious fighting was usually left to mercenaries, drawn either from the more warlike tribes of northern India, or the increasing numbers of European-trained and regimented sepoys.

The main threat to the British came not from the French themselves, but from a man named Hyder Ali, who was the ruler of Mysore (initially in fact, but also later by right) and believed to be a descendant of Mohammed. In the 1760s, Hyder Ali had captured Madras during the First Mysore War, and extracted a peace deal that included a promise of British aid if he was attacked by another state. However, when Mysore was attacked by the Marathas (previously allies of both the British, against Hyder Ali, and of Hyder Ali against the British) in 1771, the British failed to help him, and when word reached India that the French and British were once more at war, he forged another alliance with the Marathas.

In May, Warren Hastings—recently appointed the first British governor-general in India—had sent East India Company troops from Bengal to reinforce the Bombay contingent, in order to deal with the Marathas, who were openly consorting with a Frenchman called St. Lubin. He had arrived in Poona in 1777, ostensibly at the order of the French court, to negotiate an alliance based on concessions at the port of Choule (thirty miles south of Bombay), in return for 2,500 French troops and the wherewithal to train 10,000 sepoys.

Although the ruling Maratha political group preferred British assistance, Hastings was taking no chances. Realizing that the only force he could spare was at Oude, a 500-mile march from Calcutta and then several weeks voyage to Bombay, transportation by sea was out of the question. He decided that the troops would march almost 800 miles westward, across India, as this would not only save time, but would also have a psychological impact. The troops had left Calpee in May, with orders to make the fastest progress they could. However, they became bogged down in local hostilities with Rajput princes in Bundelcund and were barely halfway to Bombay by October. A new commander made swifter progress, but in November the column was halted once more by the need to negotiate a treaty with the Rajah of Berar, a dissident Maratha ruler who opposed the Poona factions.

In July, Hastings had his expectations of hostilities between Great Britain and France confirmed. The French presence in India was not insignificant: there were small garrisons at each port and Pondicherry had been largely rebuilt after its destruction during the Seven Years' War, although it could not properly support a fleet of warships (the nearest French naval base was several thousand miles away on Île de France). Hastings was determined that the war should not provide the French with the chance to halt the rise of British influence and he ordered the immediate seizure of all French interests and dispatched troops from Calcutta to Madras to seize Pondicherry. Meanwhile, other troops from Bengal quickly captured Chandernagore, upriver from Calcutta, while on the west coast, Bombay troops occupied Mahé, just north of Calicut and within Mysore (thus giving Hyder Ali the excuse he needed to support the French and remove his British foes from the Carnatic for good).

On August 8, Major General Sir Hector Munro, with a force consisting of East India Company troops (native and European), British Regulars, and local forces, arrived outside the walls of Pondicherry, having marched down the coast. At the same time, two ships and three frigates of the East India Squadron, under Commodore Sir Edward Vernon, arrived off the coast and proceeded to blockade the port. Soon after Vernon's arrival, a French squadron appeared, consisting of one ship, two frigates, and several smaller vessels. Vernon gave chase and an indecisive engagement took place on August 10. The French took refuge in Pondicherry harbor, but when Vernon reappeared they left swiftly and sailed for Île de France, leaving the Indian Ocean to the Royal Navy. Now besieged by land and sea, Pondicherry held out for two months, before surrendering on October 15.

1779

*"If Great Britain will persevere,
America must soon be conquered"*

MAJOR ROBERT ROGERS

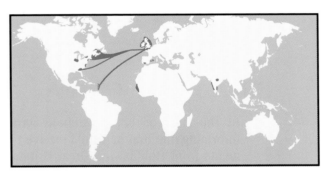

RED INDICATES FIGHTING, INCLUDING PRIVATEERING ON SHIPPING LANES

John Paul Jones's response, on September 23, 1779, to Captain Richard Pearson's demand that he surrender the Bonhomme Richard *to the* HMS Serapis *is legendary. His ship in flames Jones shouted back, "I have not yet begun to fight," and proved it by forcing Pearson to surrender. Two days later the* Bonhomme Richard *sank. Jones removed his prisoners and crew to* Serapis *and on October 3 sailed into Trexel.*

At the start of 1779, the major concern for the North ministry in London was the likely entry of Spain into the War, which had been threatening for almost a year. In the weeks between the signing of the Franco-American alliance and the outbreak of actual hostilities between Great Britain and France, Spain had offered a deal: neutrality (and diplomatic pressure on France to avoid hostilities) in return for Gibraltar. The offer was rejected and on April 12, in great secrecy, France and Spain signed the Convention of Aranjuez, under which France would help the Spanish to recover—among other things—Minorca, Mobile and Pensacola, and Gibraltar (the last being a prerequisite of France making peace). However, not wanting to be seen siding with colonial revolutionaries, Spain did not sign any treaty with the United States and, as the conflict progressed, the Spanish devoted as much energy to denying Americans access to the Mississippi River as they did to retaking the Floridas from the British.

With France pressing for military intervention by its Bourbon ally, the British received another offer: the Spanish would try to talk the French out of the war, if the British gave up Gibraltar, accepted the United States as de facto independent during peace talks, and all parties retained the territory they controlled currently (a condition that would have had extreme implications for the United States). Both offers were rejected and, on June 16, the Spanish ambassador left London.

GEORGIA

At the start of 1779, Germain wrote to Clinton, informing him that he would receive 7,500 reinforcements from Halifax and Great Britain, bringing his total strength to 29,000 (excluding Loyalists). This would give him 9,000 men for garrisons in New York and Rhode Island, 8,000 for amphibious raids, and a field army of 12,000 to be used either to bring Washington to a decisive action, or failing that, to drive him deep into the Hudson Highlands. The other pillars of British strategy would be the restoration of civilian government to areas that had been secured by Royal forces, and a war of movement (i.e. raids).

In November 1778, Congress had ordered General Benjamin Lincoln, the newly appointed commander of the Southern Department, to invade East Florida and remove the threat posed by the garrison at St. Augustine under Major General Augustine Prevost. Although Washington had retained more of his Continentals through the winter than he would in any other year of the War, Lincoln received little support, the militia assigned to him either deserting or refusing to march, and the invasion never materialized. In fact, it was the British who took the initiative in the South, with Lieutenant Colonel Archibald Campbell and Commodore Hyde Parker landing 3,500 troops near Savannah at the end of December.

Within six days, they had captured the city after being led through a weak point in the defenses by a local slave, and had inflicted 550 casualties against four dead and five wounded.

On January 3, Campbell and Parker announced the reinstatement of civilian government, with an elected assembly and a Royal governor. However, within days of their proclamation, the local militia announced that anyone who did not join them would be considered Loyalists. The military situation immediately began to deteriorate and, once again, Loyalists found themselves left to their own devices after declaring themselves. Rebel troops from North Carolina forced Campbell to abandon Augusta (which he had captured on January 31) and, on February 3, a detachment sent by Prevost to seize Beaufort had to be evacuated by ship. On February 14, 800 Loyalists from South Carolina were defeated at Kettle Creek, while pro-British Creeks were dispersed by Georgia militia on the Ogeechee River. Those Loyalists not now under arrest found their allegiance strained by plundering and compulsory requisitioning by Royal forces—especially those advancing from Florida, under Prevost. Campbell returned to Great Britain, disgusted at both the behavior of the troops and the reticence of some local commanders to give up military law and restore civilian authority.

On March 3, Prevost scored a much-needed victory over the North Carolina militia at Briar Creek, but despite more militia returning home, Lincoln still had superior numbers when he crossed into Georgia on April 23. Prevost responded by invading South Carolina, but spent too much time looting plantations and missed the opportunity to seize Charleston (despite himself identifying its capture as an act that might make Congress sue for peace). Yet when he finally arrived there, on May 9, the governor of South Carolina, John Rutledge, offered to surrender in return for the whole of South Carolina being regarded as neutral for the remainder of the War (an offer prompted in no small way by the British threat to confiscate the slaves of anyone supporting the Rebel war effort). Prevost insisted on unconditional surrender, but was forced to retreat by the approach of Lincoln, who was repulsed by Prevost's rearguard in a skirmish at Stono Ferry on June 20. Prevost escaped by sea and the extreme heat temporarily halted further campaigning.

At the same time, a major amphibious raid was under way in Virginia, involving 1,800 British, German, and Loyalist troops, with naval support, under Brigadier General Edward Mathew and Commodore Sir George Collier. Leaving New York City on May 5, they arrived at Portsmouth and in two weeks destroyed supplies, ships, and dockyard facilities at Fort Nelson, Norfolk, Suffolk, and Gosport. Encouraged by the response of the local population, Collier requested permission to establish a post at Portsmouth, but Mathew had orders to return north as soon as their task was completed, in order to reinforce a planned attack into the Hudson Highlands.

The force re-embarked on May 24 and was back at Sandy Hook five days later. When he heard of the raid, Washington demanded that all depots be moved inland and away from navigable rivers.

As he would do again, in relation to Virginia, Clinton had abandoned the idea of a permanent base around which Loyalist activity could be encouraged, in favor of cutting-out expeditions which, while economically damaging, did nothing to restore Royal authority. (It is interesting to compare Germain's proposition, involving 4,000 troops, with some degree of permanence, with what actually occurred.) Clinton, however, did realize that the British position in Georgia was vulnerable if Royal forces failed to gain control of South Carolina and, moreover, did so quickly and in great force. Unfortunately, a variety of factors conspired to prevent this happening: Washington's ability to remain in the New York City area, adverse weather locally, overoptimism regarding the number of men Clinton would receive; and, finally, the presence of the French fleet.

After his refit at Boston, D'Estaing had sailed for the West Indies (a move that became the norm for both British and French fleets at the end of each campaign season in North America) but in late August he left the Caribbean to return to American waters. He came back at the invitation of John Rutledge and Brigadier General William Moultrie—hero of the attack on Charleston in 1776—who wanted naval support for their plan to recapture Savannah.

Having had proposals for a spring attack on either Halifax or Newfoundland rejected by Washington, D'Estaing decided to help Rutledge and Moultrie. He arrived—unannounced—on September 8, with twenty-two ships, eleven frigates, and 100 transports, but bad weather hindered the landing of his 5,000 troops, who were not all ashore until September 16. He was soon joined by Lincoln, with 1,500 Continentals and 4,000 militia, and between them they invested the city, but relations were poor, Lincoln's men being banned from entering the French camp.

Prevost, who was now in charge of all Royal forces in the south, had 2,500 men (mostly Loyalists) in the city and thirteen naval vessels, but while the French were landing, another 800 Regulars arrived, giving him the confidence to reject D'Estaing's summons to surrender. Moultrie urged an immediate attack, but D'Estaing and Lincoln both rejected the idea and decided upon a formal siege. The work of disembarking the siege artillery took until October 3 and the delay made D'Estaing—usually ultracautious—eager to press on, fearing the arrival of hurricanes or, worse, a British fleet. Despite protests from French and Rebel officers, he insisted that a major assault must be made on October 9. However, when it did take place, the assault was uncoordinated and was repulsed with heavy loss.

Lincoln wanted to continue the siege, but nine days later, D'Estaing re-embarked his forces and sailed back to the West Indies on October 20. Once again, D'Estaing had been too slow and had been forced to gamble in order to compensate for that failing. Yet although the attack itself was unsuccessful,

---

SAVANNAH – OCTOBER 9, 1779

The attack, involving 3,500 French and over 1,000 of Lincoln's men, was preceded by a five-day bombardment that destroyed 430 houses. The plan was to attack at dawn (5:00 a.m.) in seven columns—one (French) through wooded marshes west of the city that came within fifty yards of the British defenses; one (militia) making a feint along the road approaching Savannah from the southeast—the British left—and five (three French and two Continentals) against the southwestern section of the defenses, around Spring Hill.

The semicircular line of defenses built by Prevost's engineers had been largely untouched by the bombardment. A large work called the Sailors' Battery guarded the wooded marshes on his right, with a small warship providing a crossfire, while two redoubts covered the road on his left. A strong redoubt stood on Spring Hill, covering 500 yards of flat ground that Prevost anticipated would be used by regular troops, and lesser works were dotted all along the line.

The two flank attacks both failed, the French losing their way in the swamp and emerging to find themselves exposed to heavy fire. In the center, matters were even more disastrous: it was 4:00 p.m. before the French were in position, and one French column (which D'Estaing led forward before the other two had deployed) was shot to pieces as it crossed the open ground. Having witnessed this, the other two columns were less than keen to advance and neither made much progress, but one column of Continentals fought its way into the Spring Hill redoubt and planted its flags on the parapet, although several officers were shot down trying to keep them flying.

With most of their officers gone, however, the Rebels were forced to retire by a counterattack led by Regulars (whom Prevost had kept in reserve, using Loyalists to man the defenses). At this point, Rebel cavalry under Count Casimir Pulaski (a Pole serving in the Continental Army), was supposed to charge into the British lines, but the preceding infantry had not cleared the abattis. Nevertheless, the Pole led the charge and his men were shot down trying to hack a way through with their sabers. A fresh column of militia attempted to attack the British right, but also got lost in the woods and withdrew.

The action, which was fought mainly in heavy fog, cost the Allies over 1,000 killed, wounded (including D'Estaing himself), and captured, while Prevost's casualties were about 120. The vast majority of the losses occurred in the fighting around Spring Hill, which had lasted about two hours.

it did contribute to Clinton's decision to abandon Newport in order to provide more manpower for operations in the South. The next time Rhode Island provided a home to large numbers of troops, they would be French.

NEW YORK

In New York City, Clinton was bemoaning the late arrival of the promised reinforcements, aware that—even by May—the various colonies had not completed their promised quotas of men and supplies for Washington's main army. Clinton did not feel confident about taking Washington on directly, but decided to move into the Hudson Highlands, threatening the latter's communications with the Northern Department. On June 1, he seized Stony Point and Verplanck's Point (as he had done in October 1777), which controlled the important King's Ferry, twelve miles from West Point. Having failed to entice Washington away from West Point, Clinton fell back to New York City, and tried to force his opponent's hand with more amphibious operations—this time via Long Island Sound (a popular area for raids by both sides) into Connecticut. Between July 5 and July 11, Collier and Major General William Tryon (the Royal governor of New York) destroyed New Haven, Fairfield, and Norwalk; they were about to attack New London when they were recalled to recover a serious setback.

On Clinton's withdrawal, Washington had ordered Brigadier General Anthony Wayne to look at recapturing Stony Point and Verplanck's Point. Several officers reconnoitered Stony Point, including Washington

Right: *View of Savannah. This watercolor by Pierre Ozanne, a draftsman attached to D'Estaing's fleet, gives some idea of the French mastery of siege warfare. (Library of Congress)*

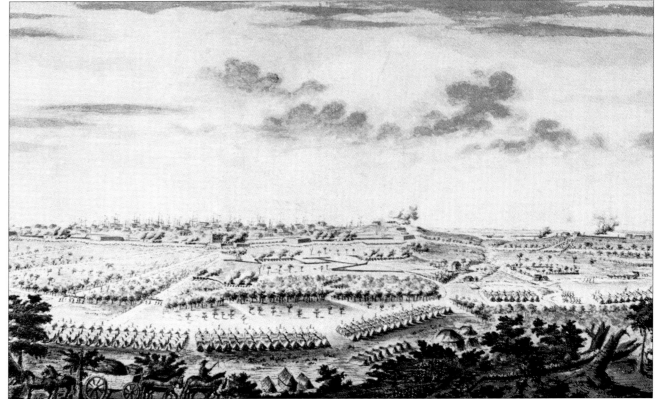

STONY POINT – JULY 15-16, 1779

Around noon on July 15, Wayne was inspecting the 1,350 men of his newly formed light infantry brigade at Sandy Beach. Suddenly, he marched them off the parade ground and took them southward on a fifteen-mile route march and, by 8:00 p.m., they were a mile and a half from Stony Point. From this point, Wayne enforced strict security: only a handful of officers were told of their destination; all civilians (and even dogs) were rounded up and held until after the attack; and a ring of trusted men prevented deserters from betraying their position.

Over 150 feet high, surrounded by tidal marshes, and possessing eight batteries and an enclosed fort, Stony Point seemed impregnable. However, the 600-man garrison was too small and many of the outer defenses and connecting trenches were unfinished.

Wayne organized his men into three columns: one attacking from the north, next to the King's Ferry landing point; a second advancing from the south, where there was less depth to the defenses; and a third, supported by light cavalry, making a feint against the center of the outer works. The two main columns would be preceded by twenty men with axes to clear away obstacles, and an advance guard of 150 men. Only the men in the third column were allowed to load their muskets—the others were to rely solely on the bayonet.

With Wayne leading the southern force (the strongest), all three groups set off at 11:30 p.m. and the two assault columns both contacted the enemy around midnight. The axemen cleared away the abattis (sharpened tree branches) from the first line of defenses and moved on to the second. Wayne was hit in the head, but carried on, while several other officers were wounded while encouraging their troops forward.

At this point, the British commander charged down the hill with half of his men, believing that the center column was the main threat. Realizing his error, he tried to retreat to the fort, but was cut off and captured by Wayne's column. Other isolated groups attempted to hold out, but with Wayne's men constantly yelling "The fort is ours!" (as they had been instructed) the noise and confusion prevented any organized resistance and the post was in Rebel hands in under thirty minutes.

Wayne lost 15 dead and 83 wounded; the British 20 dead, 74 wounded, 58 missing (presumed escaped), and 472 prisoners. The Continentals showed not only exceptional discipline and valor, but also extraordinary clemency in sparing the garrison—contemporary rules of war permitted the slaughter of anyone taken bearing arms during a night attack. The first five men into the fort were awarded "prizes" from $500 to $100 and the material captured was valued and the sum divided among the attacking force.

Above left: *Count Casimir Pulaski (1748–1779) was a Polish nobleman who had fought the Russians and later fled to France when his country was partitioned. On arriving in America, his cavalry experience recommended him to Washington as the man to take charge of the newly formed Continental cavalry arm. However, his lack of English and unwillingness to take orders from Washington caused immediate problems and he resigned as chief of cavalry. It was entirely in character that he should be mortally wounded leading a pointless charge against the British defenses at Savannah. (Independence National Historical Park)*

himself (whose visit, despite an elaborate disguise, was reported in the New York City newspapers within days) and, although the British were aware of the interest being shown in the post, it was decided to make a night attack which, if successful, was to be followed up by a similar attack on Verplanck's Point.

Although Stony point was captured in less than half an hour, it proved impossile to carry out the attack on Verplanck. Tryon arrived with more troops, Washington ordered the works at Stony Point to be leveled and withdrew upriver. One of Collier's ships later sank the vessel taking the twelve cannon captured in the assault to West Point. However, one month later, Major Henry "Light Horse Harry" Lee almost emulated Wayne with a similar exploit against Paulus Hook, opposite New York City. The attack was initially successful, capturing most of the defenses and part of the garrison, but the remainder refused to surrender and as dawn broke, reinforcements could be seen approaching. Lee withdrew with 150 prisoners, having inflicted another fifty casualties, against a loss of two dead and three wounded.

Farther north on the coast of Maine, however, one of the great Rebel disasters of the War had been unfolding. In June, Regulars and naval units from Halifax had established a base at Castine, in Penobscot Bay, intending to provide a safe haven for Loyalists, a base for privateers and a source of much-needed timber for ships' repairs, as well as denying those same facilities to the enemy. Massachusetts—

of which Maine was then a part—responded immediately, without consulting Congress and dispatched Brigadier General Solomon Lovell with 1,000 militia (including an artillery contingent under Paul Revere) and most of the Massachusetts Navy, under Commodore Dudley Saltonstall.

Arriving on July 25, the ships failed to force an entrance into the harbor, and could only manage to land troops nearby on July 28. Despite numerical superiority, Lovell began formal siege operations. On August 13, a Royal Navy squadron under Collier arrived and captured two of the Rebel ships; the remainder fled up the Penobscot River without a fight and, having been beached, were burned by their crews, who fled into the woods, along with the militia. The "battle" crippled Massachusetts financially and Saltonstall was court-martialled and dismissed. The British retained the post at Penobscot for the remainder of the war, but the event illustrated how easily isolated Royal forces could be threatened if the enemy achieved local control of the sea. However, if the lesson was noted, its impact was almost certainly dissipated by the incompetence of the Rebels and the knowledge that a French fleet would never leave the Caribbean for more than a few months in late summer and early autumn.

Toward the end of August, Clinton had received 4,000 reinforcements and another 1,000 arrived at the end of September. However, these were all recruits whose sole contribution was to introduce

sickness into the existing garrison, putting over 5,000 men temporarily out of action. Meanwhile, Clinton had been forced to send 2,000 men to reinforce the garrison of Canada and had cancelled an expedition to South Carolina in order to keep 4,000 more troops, under Cornwallis, available to move to the Caribbean to protect Jamaica. Depressed, he abandoned any further attempt to bring Washington to battle, withdrew the garrison of Rhode Island and once more tendered his resignation. The decision to abandon Rhode Island was heavily criticized, but it released 5,000 troops and several warships at a time when Clinton was desperately in need of them.

The new naval commander in North America (superseding the able Collier) was Rear Admiral Marriot Arbuthnot, a man not much given to decisiveness and certainly not the person Clinton would have chosen for the job. In so far as he favored any activity at all, Arbuthnot wanted to operate in the South, rather than be cooped up in New York City and Rhode Island. However, when Clinton suggested a winter campaign in the Carolinas, Arbuthnot demurred (citing the bad weather to be found in the region during that season) and only reluctantly agreed once D'Estaing's failure at Savannah was known. On December 26, Clinton and Arbuthnot sailed from Sandy Hook with 7,600 troops, with the aim of capturing Charleston.

THE WESTERN FRONTIER

In the summer of 1778, a Virginia militia officer, Colonel George Rogers Clark, had led a 200-man expedition west along the Ohio Valley from Pittsburgh, to attack the British post at Kaskaskia with the aim of putting an end to the Indian raids being controlled from Fort Detroit at the western end of Lake Erie. On July 4, he captured the post and, five days later, another at Cahokia; he then seized a small fort at Vincennes. In October, the British commander at Fort Detroit, Lieutenant Colonel Henry Hamilton (known as "the hair buyer" following rumors that he paid for scalps) realized the threat to British control in the region and set off with 500 Regulars, French militia, and friendly Native Americans, on a 500-mile march to Vincennes, which he recaptured at the end of the year, renaming it Fort Sackville.

On February 6, Clark set out to retake the fort with 200 men, despite the fact that it was now the depths of winter and he had no tents or food. He learned that Hamilton intended to winter at the fort with just thirty-five Regulars and resolved to attack at once before reinforcements could arrive. An early thaw compounded Clark's problems, forcing his men to wade through flooded countryside and he finally crossed the Wabash, two miles from the fort, on the night of February 20. He issued an ultimatum to the local inhabitants either to stay indoors if they supported him, or flee to the fort if they were Loyalists. Most remained at home, as Hamilton's arrogance had alienated the local population.

On February 23, Clark advanced under cover of darkness, in order to conceal his limited numbers. The garrison held out all night and into the following day, until Clark had four Indians (who had been captured with white scalps) executed in front of the walls. Hamilton immediately surrendered the fort and its eighty-man garrison; a returning patrol of forty men was also captured. Hamilton was sent to Williamsburg and imprisoned there. Lack of men and supplies prevented Clark from continuing on to Fort Detroit.

At the opposite end of Lake Erie, the Iroquois, led by "rangers" (British officers attached to the Indian Department), had targeted the agricultural heartlands of the western areas of the middle colonies that supplied much of the food and provisions for the Continental Army. In July and November 1778, they had raided the Wyoming Valley in Pennsylvania and the Cherry Valley in New York. The ensuing massacres had cost the lives of 265 inhabitants and many farms and settlements had been destroyed.

Congress demanded retribution and Washington produced a plan to invade the Iroquois lands, destroy their towns and take hostages as a guarantee of future good behavior. In April 1779, an expedition under Colonel Goose van Schaick attacked and burned the main village of the Onandagas, near modern-day Syracuse and returned without losing a

Left: *Joseph Brant (1742–1807) was born Thayendanegea, but grew up in the home of William Johnson (who later married Brant's sister, Molly) and by 1774, was personal secretary and interpreter to Guy Johnson (Sir William's nephew and successor as Superintendent of Indian Affairs). Disillusioned by the losses at Oriskany, Brant became more independent and launched his own raids into Pennsylvania and New York, although he was far from the bloodthirsty savage of Rebel propaganda (and was not even present at what was supposedly his worst atrocity—the Wyoming Valley "Massacre"). (Independence National Historical Park)*

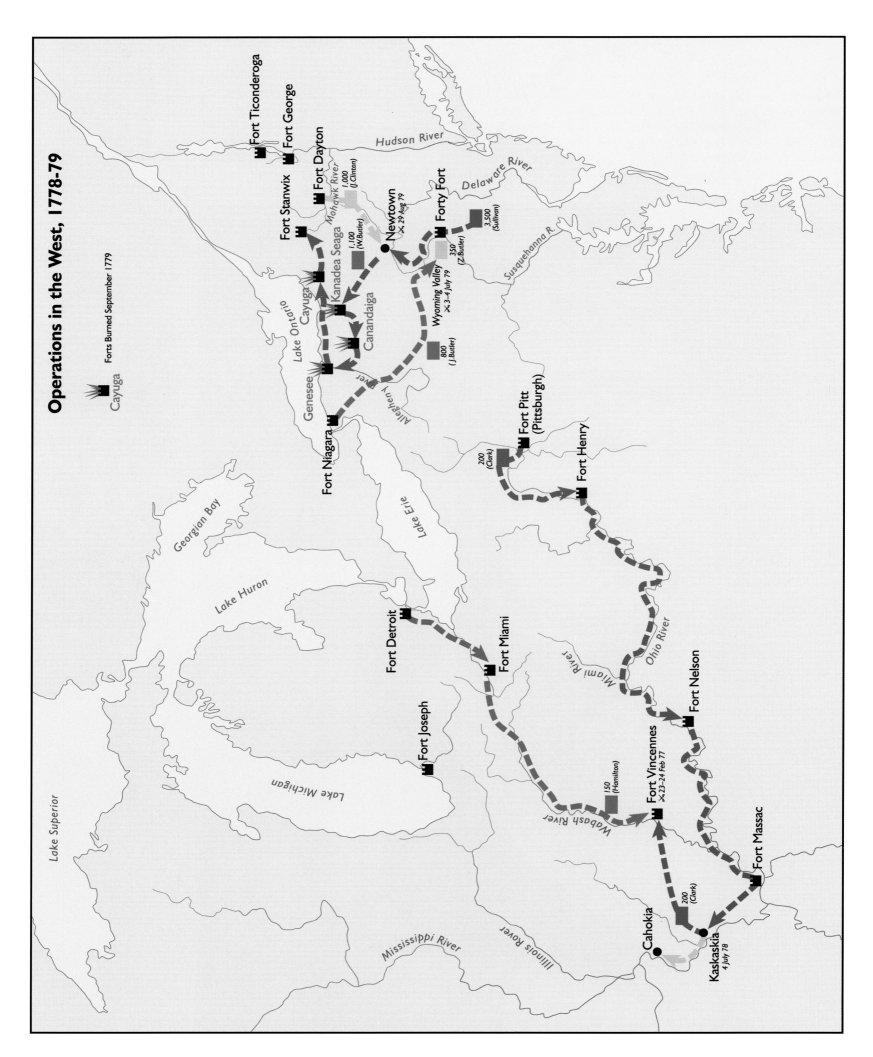

Operations in the West, 1778-79

man. While this was going on, Sullivan gathered 2,500 Continentals and marched north to join 1,500 militia under James Clinton, while a third column—600 men led by Colonel Daniel Brodhead—moved from Fort Pitt up the Allegheny River to rendezvous with Sullivan and Clinton at Genesee. From there, the combined force would attack Fort Niagara.

Sullivan set off up the Susquehanna River on July 31 and reached Tioga eleven days later, where he built Fort Sullivan. After destroying the village of Chemung, he continued north and met Clinton on August 19. Together, they approached the Seneca village of Newtown, where 200 Regulars, 200 Loyalists, and 600 Native Americans (under the Butler brothers, John and Walter) were waiting in ambush, but Sullivan saw them and outflanked them in a fight lasting six hours.

On August 31, Sullivan burned Catherine's Town and passed up the east side of Lake Seneca, destroying the Seneca capital of Kanadeaseaga. He then moved on to Genesee, where a group of his riflemen were ambushed, two of them being captured and tortured to death. The next day, when they were found, their comrades destroyed all 130 dwellings in the village and torched the surrounding fields. Unfortunately, with no sign of Brodhead (who had returned to Fort Pitt having run out of supplies), Sullivan felt unable to follow the culprits to Fort Niagara and headed back east, firing more cornfields en route.

LOUISIANA

Even when it had been officially neutral, the Spanish government had been eager to use the war to cause problems for Great Britain. In North America, this policy was directed from Louisiana, which stretched from the Gulf of Mexico to Canada, by its governor Bernardo de Galvez (who was to prove far more pro-Rebel than the Spanish authorities). The colony was still predominantly French, having been ceded secretly to Spain in 1763, and De Galvez had to overcome considerable hostility to Spanish rule. This he had achieved by marrying into a Creole family and encouraging trade with France, rather than the British, and encouraging white settlers—especially Loyalists fleeing Rebel intimidation. He also adopted the more conciliatory approach to the Indians used by the French and gradually won them over as well.

Between 1776 and 1779, De Galvez continued the policy of covert assistance to the Rebels, encouraging trade and giving refuge to at least one privateer. In February 1777, the clandestine shipment of military supplies was exposed, but De Galvez announced that they were for his own troops, declared them unfit and arranged for pro-Rebel "merchants" to buy them at auction. Later that year, he sent boats filled with supplies (including considerable quantities of gunpowder) to Fort Pitt, and later to Clark at Vincennes.

In 1778, Congress authorized James Willing to seize property and expel troops and Loyalists from the British settlements along the Mississippi. When Willing arrived in New Orleans, De Galvez placed him and his men under Spanish protection, and dealt firmly—even arrogantly—with British protests (though he also showed sympathy to Willing's Loyalist victims, returning property he considered stolen rather than legitimate spoils of war). However, Willing soon became an embarrassment, turning many neutral American settlers to the British cause and causing the British to strengthen the defenses in West Florida. Eventually, De Galvez sent him north, carefully keeping him away from the British settlements he had plundered.

News of the declaration of war by Spain reached Louisiana in July, along with orders to seize the British posts along the Mississippi and in West Florida. At the same time, De Galvez had to defend New Orleans from a planned attack by 1,500 troops from Canada and another 1,500 from Pensacola. On July 13, he called a council of war, which unanimously recommended strengthening the defenses of New Orleans as a first priority.

De Galvez, however, believed that attack was his best means of defense. Keeping his plans from the council (as he also had the news of the declaration of war), he assembled a small fleet and was about to sail for Manchac when a hurricane struck on August 18, sinking all of his vessels and destroying his supplies. Yet by August 27—only four days later than planned—he left New Orleans with 650 men (a mixture of veteran Spanish regulars, new recruits, militia, free blacks, and French and American volunteers) and ten guns. On the way, he acquired another 750 recruits, including 150 Indians, but by the time he reached Manchac, on September 6, a third of his men were sick. It was only now that he told his troops of their mission: to capture Manchac, Baton Rouge, and Natchez.

On September 7, Manchac fell immediately to a dawn assault by the militia; not expecting an attack, most of the garrison had transferred to Baton Rouge and the fortifications were incomplete. Baton Rouge, with its ditch eighteen feet wide and nine feet deep, palisade and *chevaux de frises*, would be harder. It was manned by 400 Regulars, 150 militia, and blacks, with thirteen cannon, against De Galvez's 384 regulars and 400 others, although his ten guns were more powerful.

With supplies dwindling, and so many sick, De Galvez needed to take Baton Rouge quickly. He deceived the garrison by having his militia, blacks, and Indians make a show of digging trenches at the most obvious point of attack. Meanwhile, he quietly placed his artillery close to the opposite side of the fort, where their fire damaged the walls to such an extent that on September 21, the British commander, Lieutenant Colonel Alexander Dickson, surrendered not only Baton Rouge, but also Fort Panmure, at

Right: *King Carlos III (1759–1788) was not keen to start a war with Great Britain as his nobility were pro-British and anti-French and he himself did not wish to appear to be dominated by his nephew, Louis XVI. (Museo del Ejercito, Madrid)*

Natchez. In less than one month, De Galvez had captured every British post on the east bank of the lower Mississippi and had discouraged the British from attacking New Orleans from West Florida, although a minor effort was made from Canada against St. Louis in May, 1780.

EUROPE

At the start of 1779, with French diplomats attempting to bring Spain into the war, French generals and admirals were taking part in the obligatory ritual of planning an invasion of England. The Comte de Vaux gathered over 30,000 men at Le Havre and St. Malo, along with 400 transports to carry them, while preparations were made to combine the French and Spanish fleets to escort this armada across the English Channel. Such activity was impossible to keep secret; there were mass evacuations of civilians and livestock along the south coast of England, and Plymouth harbor was blocked with booms and sunken vessels.

On June 4, two months after the signature of the secret Spanish-French alliance, D'Orvilliers left Brest with thirty ships and sailed south, in order to avoid any blockade that the British might impose once Spain declared war and to rendezvous with the Spanish fleet. On July 23, after six weeks' cruising off Cape Finisterre, he was eventually joined by thirty-four Spanish ships. The combined fleet then sailed for the Lizard, at the southwest tip of Cornwall. Entering the Channel, the combined fleet captured a convoy of fifty-five merchantmen (carrying cargo worth £1.5 million and almost 3,000 crewmen) and managed to miss Admiral Sir Charles Hardy, who had been sent to look for them with thirty-five ships. Hardy then proceeded to cruise southwest of the Scilly Isles, while the combined fleets anchored off Plymouth on August 16 (capturing a British ship whose captain mistook them for his own fleet). However, this was the extent of the combined fleets' achievements, due to a last-minute change in plans.

The French had originally intended to capture the Isle of Wight (including the naval base at Spithead) to provide an anchorage for the fleet and a base close to the English coast. But when D'Orvilliers arrived back in the Channel, he was informed that this had been changed and he was now to land near Falmouth. Despite his protests that there was no natural anchorage available, he was overruled; however, an easterly gale, lasting several days, blew many of his ships back toward the Atlantic. Aware that Hardy was in the area, D'Orvilliers tried to find him and give battle, while he still had a two-to-one advantage. Unfortunately, by the time the British were sighted, they were back in the Channel, where they slipped past the combined fleet and were back in Spithead by the end of August. D'Orvilliers was ordered back to Brest and arrived there on September

Left: *Admiral Comte D'Orvilliers commanded the French fleet of 30 ships at Brest. In 1779, he was supposed to join up with the Spanish fleet from Ferrol, but was five weeks late sailing and even then had to leave without most of his stores. (National Maritime Museum)*

14, to the relief of his crews and the troops, who had been at sea since June, and were now suffering from scurvy, smallpox, and typhus.

No sooner had he returned, than the invasion was effectively cancelled by the immediate recall of all the Spanish ships, which were to join the blockade of Gibraltar. Whatever effort the Spanish government had (or had not, as the case may be) been put into preparing the invasion force, the great Rock of Gibraltar, guarding the western entrance to the Mediterranean, was its main reason for becoming involved in the war. Rising out of the sea at the southern tip of Spain, and just fourteen miles from the coast of Morocco, Gibraltar had been captured during the wars of Marlborough and formally ceded in 1713. Its recapture had been a major goal of successive governments in Madrid.

On June 21, the British garrison—under the command of General George Augustus Eliott—learned that Great Britain and Spain were at war when the governor of San Roque, Lieutenant General Don Joaquin Mendoza, announced an end to all communication by land. Eliott had 7,000 men, including 1,500 Hanoverians, and more than 400 pieces of ordnance. However, the Royal Navy had only one ship, three frigates, and a sloop to oppose fifteen Spanish vessels at Cadiz, and many more at Algeciras and the Moroccan port of Ceuta.

The blockade began on July 5, when eleven Spanish ships were seen to the west; one attempted to intercept three British merchantmen, but was driven off by gunfire from the main defenses. Many more supply ships ran the blockade successfully, but never enough to meet the needs of the garrison; Eliott immediately instituted rationing and limited the use of ammunition.

Above: *French troops embarking. Some 30,000 troops had been assembled at Le Havre and St. Malo for the invasion of England —more than the number of Regulars in the whole of Great Britain. (National Maritime Museum)*

Right: *Admiral Cordoba commanded the Spanish fleet of 34 ships at Ferrol. His force did not rendezvous with D'Orvilliers' fleet off Cape Finisterre until July 23— twelve weeks after the original meeting should have taken place. By the time the combined fleets reached the Channel, they were so encumbered with dead and sick, and their hulls so fouled with marine growth, that they were forced to return to port. (National Maritime Museum)*

Left: *Admiral Sir Charles Hardy (1716–1780) had not been to sea for 20 years and owed his appointment to his good nature, his lack of involvement in politics, and the Keppel–Palliser affair. (National Maritime Museum)*

In February, Louis XVI had purchased a 900-ton merchantman—renamed the *Bonhomme Richard,* in honor of Benjamin Franklin—for Jones to command. Around the same time, La Fayette returned to France and, hoping to find employment nearer to home, began planning an amphibious attack on Liverpool, with Jones commanding the escorts; however, word leaked out and the city's defenses were reinforced, making the project no longer viable. Instead Jones began assembling a squadron to support the invasion of England by creating diversions in the north to draw British forces away from the south coast. When news reached him that the invasion was canceled, Jones decided to go ahead with his planned cruise around the British Isles and back to the Texel in Holland.

He sailed on August 14, taking several prizes before heading for the west coast of Ireland. Here, some of his crew deserted and he lost touch with the other ships of his squadron; but by September 1, he was off the northwest coast of Scotland and word of his presence was spreading like wildfire through Ireland and England. After several days cruising the Shetland Islands, Jones headed south and entered the Firth of Forth on September 16, to attack Leith. However, bad weather forced him to abandon the attack just as he was entering the harbor and he continued down the coast, spreading alarm and terror wherever he was seen. By September 23, his four ships arrived off Flamborough Head, after failing to entice enemy shipping out of the River Humber.

FLAMBOROUGH HEAD – SEPTEMBER 23, 1779

That afternoon, a convoy of forty-one ships from the Baltic, escorted by the frigate *Serapis* and the sloop *Countess of Scarborough,* came into view. Both Jones and his opposite number, Captain Richard Pearson, decided to engage, the one to remove the escort, leaving himself free to plunder the merchantmen at will, the other to buy time for his convoy to escape. As Jones signaled his other ships to form line of battle, they deserted him and around 6:00 p.m., he approached the *Serapis* under a British flag.

Challenged by Pearson, Jones hoisted the American ensign and the *Serapis* responded with a broadside at around 7:20 p.m. Within minutes, two of Jones's old guns had exploded, leaving him virtually disarmed. Aware that he was outgunned, Jones attempted to grapple with the *Serapis* and board her, but failed, so he rammed his bow into the stern of the *Serapis*, at which point it appeared that the *Bonhomme Richard* had struck.

In fact, Jones had not yet begun to fight: he backed his topsails in order to clear Pearson's vessel and moved upwind; at the same time, Pearson dropped back to get broadside on to the *Bonhomme Richard*. Jones then moved ahead and attempted to cross Pearson's bow and rake the *Serapis*, but he was too close and the tangle of damaged rigging and masts, and a sudden gust of wind, trapped both vessels together, side by side, facing in opposite directions with the muzzles of their guns almost touching.

This negated the superior gunnery of Pearson's crew and Jones proceeded to cut them down with musket fire and hand grenades from the *Bonhomme Richard*'s complement of French marines. Pearson tried desperately to break free by dropping anchor and using the wind and tide, as his guns kept firing into the enemy ship, despite the danger of fire from the flashes. By now, virtually nobody was left alive on the lower decks of the *Bonhomme Richard* or the upper decks of the *Serapis* and both ships were on fire. Jones looked for help from his other three ships, but although one was busy overcoming the *Countess of Scarborough*, the other two were merely spectators. In fact, the *Bonhomme Richard* was now sinking and Jones released the prisoners from the hold to man the pumps.

Pearson, however, also had problems: a grenade caused ammunition to explode below decks and a last-ditch attempt to board the *Bonhomme Richard* was driven off. With his mainmast about to collapse, Pearson surrendered at around 10:30 p.m. and was escorted aboard the *Bonhomme Richard*, where Jones took him below for a glass of wine.

The battle had lasted almost four hours. Both ships were wrecked and each side lost over 120 men. Jones transferred to the *Serapis,* sending his wounded to the other vessels, and watched the *Bonhomme Richard* sink beneath the North Sea.

Left: *Captain Sir Richard Pearson (1731–1806) was knighted and given command of the newest frigate in the Royal Navy as a reward for the action, since he had done his job and permitted every ship in the convoy to escape Jones's squadron. (National Maritime Museum)*

Opposite page: *Action off Flamborough Head (September 23, 1779). The fight between Jones'* Bonhomme Richard *and Pearson's* Serapis *was probably the most dramatic single-ship duel of the entire war and was watched by crowds of spectators from the nearby cliff tops. (National Maritime Museum)*

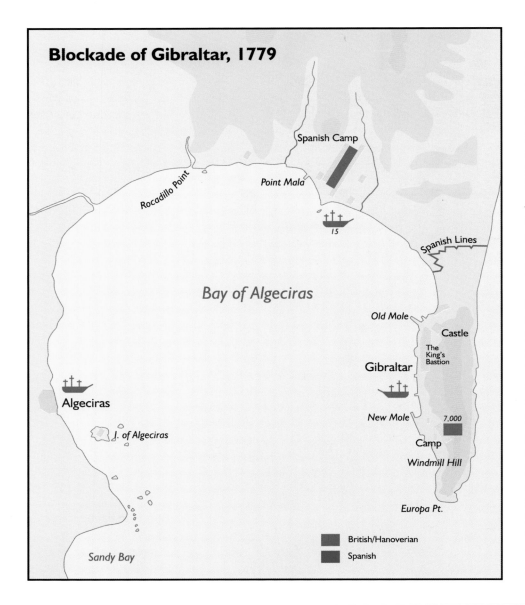

Blockade of Gibraltar, 1779

Spanish Camp

Rocadillo Point

Point Mala

15

Spanish Lines

Bay of Algeciras

Old Mole

Castle

The King's Bastion

Gibraltar

Algeciras

I. of Algeciras

New Mole

7,000

Camp

Windmill Hill

Europa Pt.

Sandy Bay

British/Hanoverian

Spanish

As other British ships searched for Jones and his squadron, he sailed straight to the Texel, which embarrassed the Dutch, who were still neutral and under pressure from Great Britain to arrest Jones as a pirate and seize his prizes. Indeed, the Danish government did exactly that, returning three vessels captured and sent to Norway by the *Alliance*. It was several months, however, before Jones was able to exchange his 500 prisoners for an equal number of his compatriots, after which he transferred to the *Alliance* and left the Texel on December 27, arriving off Ushant four days later. A fruitless search for enemy shipping ended with him putting into Corunna for repairs and provisions and then returning to Lorient.

The second half of 1779 also saw Anglo-Dutch relations worsen. In July, the British ambassador to the United Provinces of the Netherlands formally requested the military aid that had been guaranteed by the seventeenth-century treaty. If the fact that no reply had been received from the Staats-General (the Netherlands parliament) by the end of the year did not indicate the likely answer, another incident certainly did. On November 16, 1776, the governor of St. Eustatius, a Dutch island in the Caribbean, had fired an eleven-gun salute in response to a greeting from the privateer, *Andrea Doria*, as it entered the main harbor. This explicit recognition of the flag of the United States (see illustration, page 91) had angered Great Britain, which had demanded the recall and punishment of the governor. But in September, he was exonerated and returned to the island.

THE CARIBBEAN

Just days after the surrender of St. Lucia, Byron arrived in the West Indies from New York City and superseded Barrington as senior officer of the West Indies squadron. The French enjoyed superior numbers (D'Estaing now had twenty-five ships and several frigates), but were not much disposed to aggressive action after the mauling at St. Lucia, so there was little activity in the Caribbean until June. Then, D'Estaing captured the island of St. Vincent (just south of St. Lucia) while escorting a convoy bound for Brest past the British-held islands and into the western Atlantic and, on June 30, he sailed for Grenada. He arrived on July 2, landed troops that

evening, and accepted the garrison's surrender two days later.

For two days, D'Estaing's fleet and transports lay at anchor in St. George's Harbor, on the southwest tip of the island, when sails were spotted at dawn on July 6. It was a British fleet under Byron, with twenty-one ships, a frigate, and twenty-eight troop transports. Believing that D'Estaing had fewer ships and that he was in some disorder, Byron left three ships to protect the convoy and signaled "general chase." However, the French quickly formed line and Byron's van was exposed to the fire of every enemy, three of his ships being dismasted.

Around noon, D'Estaing regrouped and attacked the damaged British ships, which had become isolated, but they all escaped (one sailing all the way

Right: *Vice Admiral The Hon. John Byron (1723–1786) was known to his crews as "Foul Weather Jack" due to his habit of running into stormy seas. (National Maritime Museum)*

to Jamaica). D'Estaing had 860 casualties against Byron's 530, but Byron's ships sustained more damage and he was forced to put in at St. Kitts to effect repairs.

Described as the worst British naval defeat since 1690, the action off Grenada was precipitated by Byron's overconfidence and his misreading of the "clustering" of the French fleet prior to forming line of battle (a standard procedure). D'Estaing, by contrast, had protected his recent conquest, but had missed the opportunity to capture, or sink, at least three ships that would have been difficult to replace.

INDIA

The officers of the Bombay Presidency were not pleased with Hastings's choice of allies among the various Maratha rulers and wanted to make their own alliances. Accordingly, they sent 4,000 men

Above: *Capture of Grenada (July 4, 1779). While Byron was busy escorting a convoy bound for England out of the Caribbean, D'Estaing landed troops on the island of Grenada and captured 30 merchantmen anchored in the main harbour. (National Maritime Museum)*

(including nearly 600 Europeans) to capture Poona, but the army had not been ready to leave until the end of 1778, and when it did finally move inland it advanced at barely a mile a day, harassed constantly by rockets, musketry, and cannons. At the same time, the enemy—led by Madajee Scindia and Tookajee Holkar—was raising 50,000 men.

Eventually, the bedridden commander of the Bombay force, Colonel Egerton, ordered a withdrawal. Within twenty-four hours, the remaining 2,600 men found themselves surrounded and their baggage captured. Despite losing 350 men (including a suspiciously high number of "missing"—i.e. deserters), the troops continued to retreat in good order and finally took shelter in the village of Worgaom, which they fortified. Believing retreat impossible, Egerton and two civilian advisers negotiated the Convention of Worgaom, by which the Marathas allowed the survivors to return to Bombay in return for the restoration of the lands they had held in 1773; in addition, the force Hastings had sent from Oudh was to be sent back.

The Bombay government promptly dismissed the commanders of the force, repudiated the Convention, and continued with its military preparations. The Bengal Presidency did the same and Hastings ordered the Oudh contingent, now under Colonel Goddard, to continue to Bombay. Goddard covered 300 miles in twenty days, reaching Surat on February 26, and proceeded to open negotiations with the various Maratha factions.

The most powerful of those factions was based in Poona and led by Nana Furnawese. Unfortunately, Rugonath Rao (also known as Ragobah), the Peishwar of the Marathas, had escaped from Poona where he was being held hostage. His arrival in Goddard's camp, put an end to any negotiations with Nana Furnawese. He immediately made overtures to Hyder Ali for an alliance to drive the British out of India for good. To make matters worse, as the by now meaningless negotiations dragged on, the Madras Presidency—which had most to fear from the involvement of Hyder Ali—made the mistake of sending two precious battalions to join Goddard, leaving itself desperately short of trained men.

Aware that it needed to do something to protect its interests in India against the French and their allies, in the spring of 1779 the North ministry dispatched a fleet of six ships under the command of Rear Admiral Sir Edward Hughes. Several ships were sent from France, under Commodore le Comte Thomas d'Orves, at the same time, but for various reasons, they did not reach the Indian Ocean until 1781.

1780

"We fight, get beat, rise and fight again"

MAJOR GENERAL NATHANIEL GREENE

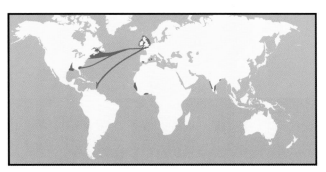

RED INDICATES FIGHTING, INCLUDING PRIVATEERING ON SHIPPING LANES

The siege of Charleston. (Anne S. K. Brown Military Collection)

THE CAROLINAS

On January 30, Clinton and Arbuthnot arrived at Tybee Island, near Savannah, having been forced past Charleston by a storm so fierce that one vessel ended up off Cornwall. By February 10, enough vessels had come in to justify the resumption of the campaign, and the fleet headed north and began forming up on James Island. Lincoln was under political pressure to hold Charleston (which had displayed extreme ambivalence to the Rebel cause when confronted by Prevost a year earlier) in order to deny the British a base in the Chesapeake. In any event, he could not have withdrawn due to lack of transport. At the end of a forty-day siege, Lincoln was left with no option but to surrender. For various reasons he was denied the honors of war—an act that would not be forgotten by the Continental Army.

The surrender of Charleston saw British control re-established over most of South Carolina. More than 200 prominent citizens of Charleston congratulated Clinton on his victory and several leading politicians returned, thus appearing to vindicate the policy of using military force to restore civil government in a way that met most of the demands made by the Colonists in 1775 (causing New England politicians to doubt the determination of their colleagues in the South).

Clinton, however, wanted to restore civil government by degrees and also made the mistake of abolishing parole (i.e. agreements not to bear arms against Royal authority) insisting that civilians take an oath of allegiance and provide active support instead. This lack of discrimination, criticized by Cornwallis and Arbuthnot, alienated the largely apathetic and neutral populace—many of whom considered their parole no longer binding—and undermined the policy of conquest followed by reconciliation. It also compelled the British commanders to rely on small Regular forces, which proved inadequate for the job, and Loyalists, whose presence introduced a growing element of bitterness on both sides.

Clinton left for New York City on June 8, with 4,000 men, having unwittingly bolstered the number

---

CHARLESTON: MARCH 1–MAY 12, 1780

Clinton advanced slowly, having lost most of his horses and entrenching tools in the storm, but by mid-March he had captured Fort Johnson and controlled the southern side of the harbor. On March 29, his advance guard crossed the Ashley River twelve miles upriver from Charleston and gradually surrounded the city, commencing siege works on April 1. A week later, Arbuthnot brought seven ships past the fortifications on the north side of the harbor and by April 13 the heavy artillery had been landed and was in action. Over the next few days, detachments from Clinton's army secured the areas around the Ashley and Cooper Rivers, effectively cutting off Lincoln from reinforcements, and escape.

On April 19, Clinton's men were within 250 yards of the Rebel defenses, despite the heat and sustained artillery fire from the defenders. Convinced that defeat was inevitable, Lincoln called a council of war at which he and his officers agreed that the army should be saved; unfortunately, they were overruled by the civilian council, one of whom threatened to incite the population to attack Lincoln's men if they decided to withdraw. Despite this, on April 21, Lincoln offered to surrender if permitted the honors of war; Clinton refused.

At dawn on April 24, a sortie by 200 defenders overran the outlying British trenches, inflicting over sixty casualties and suffering only three. The following night, a sudden panic in the British lines resulted in seven dead and twenty-one wounded, despite there being no evidence of enemy activity. As the besiegers came closer, enemy fire intensified but, by May 6, a "wet" ditch in front of the defenses had been almost completely drained, while Lincoln's men were down to one week's supply of fresh provisions. On May 7, Arbuthnot's sailors and marines captured the fort on Sullivan's Island, with 200 defenders. The following day, the British began a heavy bombardment and Clinton sent Lincoln a summons for unconditional surrender.

By May 11, the besiegers were thirty paces from Lincoln's defenses and red-hot shot was setting fire to houses in the city. Around 2:00 p.m., Lincoln accepted Clinton's terms and surrendered the city, with all troops, ships, military stores, and installations. The sailors and Continentals were to be held prisoner, the militia paroled and allowed home. Two days later, an explosion in a powder store killed up to 200 people and cost Clinton 3,000 muskets badly needed to arm the Loyalists.

This was the largest Rebel defeat of the War and the largest number of prisoners lost by American forces until 1862. The siege cost Lincoln 90 dead and 140 wounded from a reported 5,500 men (in reality the garrison numbered about 3,300), and Clinton 76 dead and 189 wounded from 12,500. On May 29, Tarleton destroyed the remaining Virginia Continentals at Waxhaws—reputedly killing many of them after they had surrendered and spawning the expression "Tarleton's Quarter," soon to be heard all across the South.

Right: *Vice Admiral Marriot Arbuthnot (1711–1794) was in charge of the port of Halifax, Nova Scotia from 1775 to 1778, before being appointed to command the American station in 1779. Old, lazy, unreliable, and vulgar, he barely cooperated with Clinton during the siege of Charleston, yet refused to allow any of the prize money to be shared with the Army. He later allowed the French to occupy and fortify Newport, refusing to assist Clinton in attacking them before they had completed the task. Poor tactics and indecisive leadership prevented him from destroying the French fleet at The Capes in March 1781, and left for England in July to be replaced by Graves. He became an Admiral of the Blue in 1793. (National Maritime Museum)*

Left: *Major General Benjamin Lincoln (1733–1810) had been a town clerk, a magistrate and a farmer, before becoming a major general of militia. Although more accomplished as an administrator than a general, he was a brave and respected leader and was recommended for a Continental commission by Washington in 1776. The following year, Lincoln played a prominent role in the defeat of Burgoyne by disrupting British supply lines, while his tactful handling of Stark made possible the latter's victory at Bennington. Sent to command the Southern Department, he led the American contingent at the abortive siege of Savannah, and was captured at Charleston, but was exchanged for Phillips and Von Riedesel. He led the American wing of the army on the march to Yorktown and accepted the British surrender. (Independence National Historical Park).*

Right: *Lieutenant Colonel William Washington (1752–1810) had planned to become a clergyman, but joined the Virginia Continentals and was wounded at Long Island, and again at Trenton. In 1780, he moved south with the remnants of three cavalry regiments and fought in the Charleston campaign, where he was beaten in a series of clashes with Tarleton. He was wounded again, and captured, at Eutaw Springs. (Independence National Historical Park)*

Below and opposite page: *View and map of Charleston, South Carolina. Four years of peace, prosperity and privateering had taken its toll on the patriotic fervour of Charleston's inhabitants. Despite the presence of men such as Moultrie, there was little desire to repeat the defiant exploits of 1776. (National Maritime Museum)*

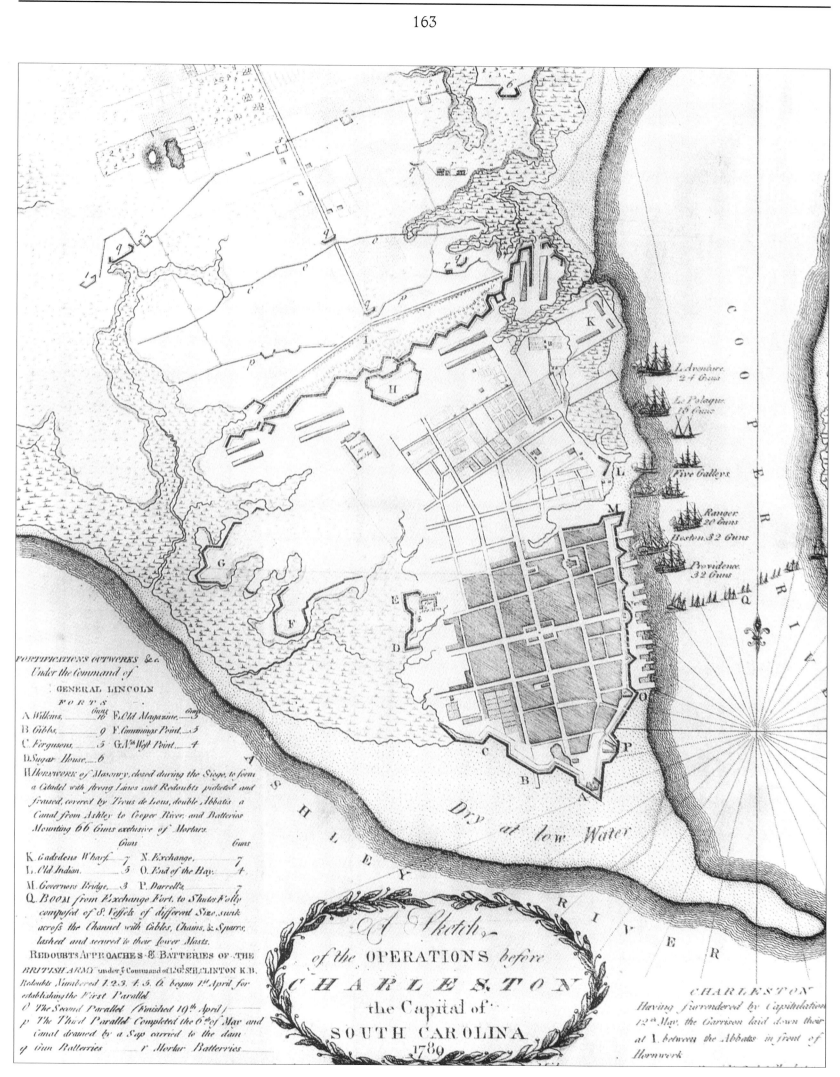

FORTIFICATIONS OUTWORKS &c.
Under the Command of
GENERAL LINCOLN
FORTS

		Guns			Guns
A	Wilkins	10	E	Old Magazine	5
B	Gibbs	9	F	Cummings Point	5
C	Fergusons	5	G	No. West Point	4
D	Sugar House	6			

W. Hornwork of Masonry, closed during the Siege, to form
a Citadel with strong Lines and Redoubts picketed and
fraised, covered by Fœus de Loup, double Abbatis a
Canal from Ashley to Cooper River, and Batteries
Mounting 66 Guns exclusive of Mortars.

		Guns			Guns
K	Gadsdens Wharf	7	N	Exchange	7
L	Old Indian	5	O	End of the Bay	4
M	Governors Bridge	3	P	Darrell's	7

Q. BOOM from Exchange Fort. to Shutes Folly
composed of 8 Vessels of different Size, sunk
across the Channel with Cables, Chains, & Sparrs,
lashed and secured to their Lower Masts.

REDOUBTS APPROACHES & BATTERIES OF THE
BRITISH ARMY under ye Command of Lt. Gl. Sr. H. Clinton K.B.
Redoubts Numbered 1. 2. 3. 4. 5. 6. begun 1st April for
establishing the First Parallel
O The Second Parallel (Finished 19th April)
p The Third Parallel Completed the 6th of May and
Canal drained by a Sap carried to the dam
q Gun Batteries ____ r Mortar Batteries

A Sketch
of the OPERATIONS before
CHARLESTON
the Capital of
SOUTH CAROLINA
1780

CHARLESTON
Having surrendered by Capitulation
12th May, the Garrison laid down their
at V. between the Abbatts in front of
Hornwork

of potential enemy recruits. He left Cornwallis with little more than 2,500 men, facing the possibility of the arrival of a French fleet, but otherwise optimistic about the prospects of retaining control of South Carolina.

Meanwhile, Congress had appointed Gates to replace Lincoln as commander of the Southern Department (although Washington had recommended Greene). His command included 1,400 veteran Delaware and Maryland Continentals under Brigadier General Baron Johann de Kalb, who had planned a cautious advance into North Carolina, where there was more support from the civil population. Gates, however, overruled him—believing that immediate action was needed to restore morale after Charleston—and marched toward the British post at Camden, through poor countryside, controlled by Loyalists.

Unknown to Gates, who believed Cornwallis had withdrawn from Camden, Cornwallis had returned with reinforcements on August 13. Two days later, he set out on a night march, determined to attack Gates at dawn. Gates called a council of war, perhaps hoping that it would recommend a withdrawal, but his officers said nothing, possibly realizing that it was too late. If so, that realization was prophetic: the next day Gates' army was crushed and scattered to the winds.

Despite having cleared South Carolina of Continentals and opened the way to North Carolina, Cornwallis still faced the problem of pacifying a large area with few men and a poor supply system, as well as large numbers of sick. But it was the growing difficulty of predicting levels of local support that concerned him most. Despite his best efforts to prevent premature risings by Loyalist militia (which he found politically unreliable and militarily inefficient, 1,300 men—barely 300 of them armed—were defeated and dispersed at Ramsour's Mill, North Carolina, while a series of bitter engagements in South Carolina showed that the back-country was far from under control.

Cornwallis decided to advance into North Carolina, both to provide a nucleus of Regulars on whom the Loyalist militia could rally and to secure South Carolina and Georgia from further invasion. He set off on September 9, and reached Charlotte on September 26, his western flank guarded by Loyalist militia and picked marksmen under Lieutenant Colonel Patrick Ferguson. Unfortunately, this force was wiped out by a group of rifle-armed, mounted frontiersmen at King's Mountain on October 7.

Opposite page: *Battle of Camden, South Carolina (August 16, 1780). A contemporary map, showing the dispositions of the armies of Gates and Cornwallis. (Library of Congress)*

CAMDEN: AUGUST 16, 1780

Gates formed his line in a narrow defile, about a mile wide, between two swamps. Cornwallis, despite having an unfordable creek at his back and no room to maneuver to his front, was completely confident. After two hours skirmishing, both lines were complete by dawn, and Gates awaited Cornwallis's advance at his command post, 600 yards behind the front line.

The battle began in heavy fog, with a brisk exchange of artillery fire. Gates's adjutant general spotted an opportunity for the Virginia militia, on the extreme left of the Rebel position, to attack a column of Regulars as it deployed from column into line. However, in the time it took the officer to ride back to Gates and obtain authorization, the opportunity had gone and only a few skirmishers were sent out, to little effect.

At this point, the Regulars advanced, firing and cheering, at which the Virginia militia fled without letting off a shot, followed almost instantly by the North Carolina militia who were holding the center of Gates's line. Instead of pursuing the militia, the Regulars wheeled left and rolled up the Rebel line. At the same time, the Loyalist regiments that made up the Royal army's left wing advanced against a brigade of Maryland Continentals, who held off repeated attacks, unaware (because of the fog and smoke) that they were now alone.

De Kalb now called for the reserve, another brigade of Maryland Continentals whose commander (along with Gates) had been swept away in the flight of the militia, to come up and support his left. Cornwallis directed his Regulars at them and, despite rallying twice after being driven back by the British fire, the reserve was driven from the field. This left De Kalb's men completely isolated, but the Bavarian refused to retreat without orders from Gates and fell, mortally wounded, when the British Legion cavalry hit the rear and flanks of his command.

Only a handful of Maryland and Delaware Continentals withdrew as a unit, while Tarleton pushed on and attacked Gates's baggage train at Rugeley's Mill. The rest of Cornwallis's men were too exhausted to pursue their beaten foe. By nightfall, Gates had arrived in Charlotte, some sixty miles away, on a "borrowed" horse. Two days later, Tarleton destroyed the partisan band under Sumter, at Fishing Creek.

Only 700 of Gates's men reached Hillsboro; almost 900 were killed and 1,000 captured (excluding another 450 men lost at Fishing Creek two days later). Cornwallis lost 68 dead and 256 wounded. As late as 1900, the action at Camden was cited as the most complete defeat suffered by an American army.

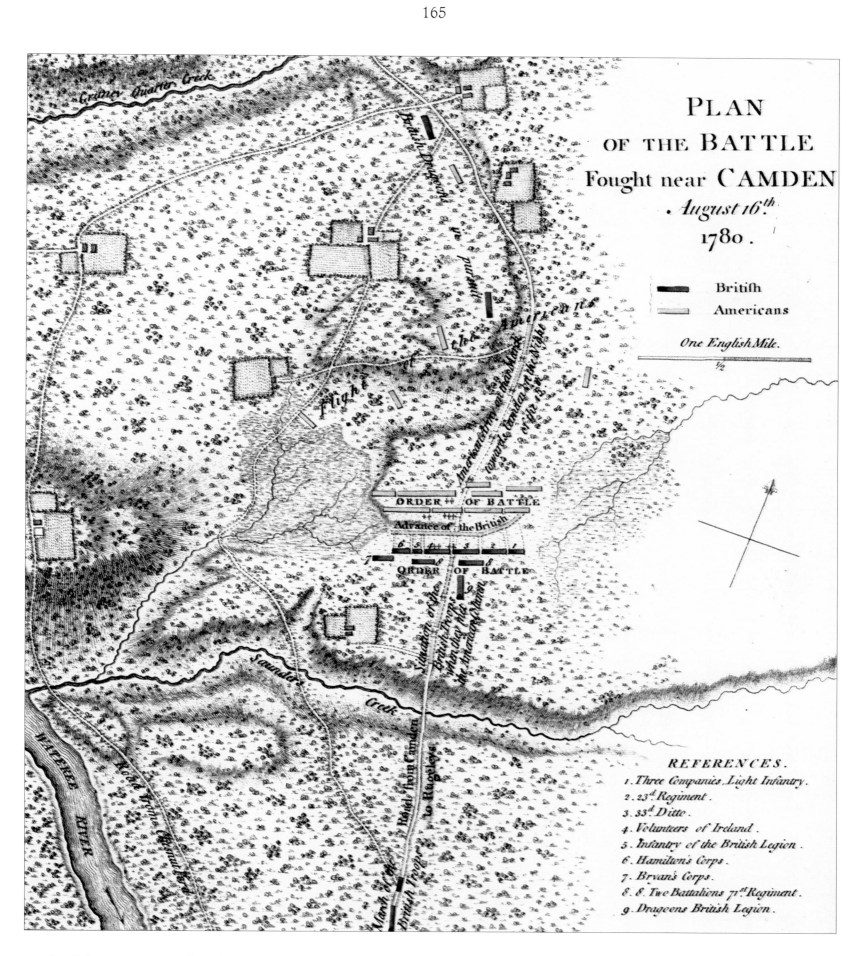

PLAN
OF THE BATTLE
Fought near CAMDEN
August 16th
1780.

Britiſh
Americans

One Engliſh Mile.
½

REFERENCES.
1. *Three Companies Light Infantry.*
2. *23d Regiment.*
3. *33d Ditto.*
4. *Volunteers of Ireland.*
5. *Infantry of the British Legion.*
6. *Hamilton's Corps.*
7. *Bryan's Corps.*
8. 8. *Two Battalions 71st Regiment.*
9. *Dragoons British Legion.*

The defeat cost Cornwallis a large portion of his valuable light troops and forced him to abandon his invasion of North Carolina. Clinton criticized him for ignoring the lessons of Trenton and Bennington. However, the size of the area to be pacified made such detachments a necessity and, in truth, they had proved successful to date in the Carolinas and Georgia, including fortified posts up at Augusta, Granby, Orangeburg, Motte, Watson, and Ninety-Six. Fortunately, the Southern Army was in no better condition; Gates was dismissed on October 5 and Greene finally appointed, although he did not

Left: *Lieutenant Colonel Francis, Lord Rawdon (1754–1826) was from a noble Irish family and had served with distinction at Bunker Hill before becoming a staff officer. He later commanded the Volunteers of Ireland, a Loyalist unit composed mainly of Rebel deserters. In 1780, Rawdon resigned as adjutant general to Clinton (who disliked him intensely) and served under Cornwallis, taking charge of the post at Camden and showing calm leadership in a dangerous position. (Anne S. K. Brown Collection)*

Right: *Major General Baron Johann de Kalb (1721–1780) was the son of Bavarian peasants, but managed to obtain a commission in the French army, and fought in the War of the Austrian Succession and the Seven Years' War. In 1768, he undertook a secret mission to North America to report on the military infra-structure, and returned in 1777, with La Fayette. Initially overlooked by Congress, he was later chosen as La Fayette's deputy for the abortive invasion of Canada in 1778. Over six feet tall, he possessed temperate habits and considerable endurance. Wounded eleven times at Camden, he died three days later. (Independence National Historical Park).*

arrive until December 2. He found matters in a poor state and wrote to Washington indicating that if the Royal forces chose to prosecute a war of posts, rather than marching into the field, he had no artillery and insufficient provisions and transport to dislodge them.

Determined to challenge Cornwallis's control of South Carolina, Greene hid in the back-country while his army recovered, sending out a large detachment under Morgan and, in the absence of any cavalry, relying on local mounted partisans for intelligence (although not all of the latter accepted his authority and acted in concert with him). Gradually, control of the South was slipping from Royal hands in a vicious civil war, making Cornwallis even more certain that the way forward was to invade North Carolina and cut off supplies to the Southern Department from the northern colonies.

RHODE ISLAND

Once the Franco-Spanish invasion of England was abandoned, the French government wanted to use the troops elsewhere and decided (thanks to persist-

ent lobbying by La Fayette) to send 6,000 of them to North America. However, much to La Fayette's chagrin, command of the force was given to General Jean-Baptiste Donatien de Vimeur, Comte de Rochambeau, who had never been to North America and spoke no English, but was a capable commander with tact and intelligence, who warmed to the task of cooperating with a foreign ally. Rochambeau agreed to accept the command, provided he received at least six regiments (plus a "legionary" corps) and artillery. However, France's shortage of merchant ships saw the force reduced to just 5,000 before it even sailed.

In the late spring, escorted by Commodore Charles Louis d'Arsec, Chevalier de Ternay, with seven ships and five frigates, the force left Brest and headed for Newport. After ten days at sea, Rochambeau opened his sealed orders, noting that he was to be subordinate to General Washington, and that he and his troops were to serve only under Washington. On July 12, the fleet arrived at Newport in heavy fog, to an extremely muted welcome. Using an interpreter, Rochambeau convinced the local community that his force was substantial—with additional men and ships on the way—

Above: *The death of Kalb at the Battle of Camden. (Anne S. K. Brown Collection)*

Right: *Lieutenant-Colonel Banastre "Bloody Ban" Tarleton (1754–1833) joined the Army in 1775 and served in the 16th Light Dragoons and the 79th Foot, before taking command of the British Legion during the Monmouth campaign. His actions in the South made his name synonymous with cruelty and after several flamboyant successes, his over-confidence led to the defeat at Cowpens. (National Gallery, London)*

Left: *Lieutenant Colonel Henry "Light Horse Harry" Lee (1756–1818) had graduated from Princeton and was about to leave to study law in England when war broke out. He was commissioned into the Continental light dragoons and after distinguishing himself during the 1778 campaign, he was promoted and given command of a legionary corps. In 1780, this unit became one of the Continental Army's two "partisan" corps and served in the South, where it wore a uniform very similar to that of Tarleton's British Legion. (Independence National Historical Park)*

and that it was there to fight. More impressive, however, was the appearance and bearing of the French officers—quite unlike the effeminate fops of popular image. One, the Chevalier de Chastellux, spoke English and became Rochambeau's liaison officer with Washington.

Eager to employ Rochambeau's corps, Washington asked that Rear Admiral Louis Urbain de Bouenic, Comte de Guichen, who had arrived in the Caribbean in March to replace D'Estaing, would sail north to join De Ternay in an attack on New York City. De Guichen, however, chose to remain in the Caribbean and escort a convoy bound for France. Meanwhile, Rodney, who knew of De Ternay's arrival

at Newport and assumed De Guichen would head north to join him once the convoy was safely away, decided to challenge the French. Leaving the Caribbean at the end of July, he arrived at Sandy Hook with ten ships on September 14.

Rodney's arrival came as a surprise—and not all together a pleasant one—to his colleagues at New York City. Arbuthnot had been reinforced by Rear Admiral Thomas Graves with six ships and a frigate, and had taken his entire force to Rhode Island (despite having refused to go there with Clinton in mid-August, in order to attack Newport before the French could improve its defenses). He remained at anchor, observing the entrance to Narragansett Bay,

Right: *Major General François-Jean de Beauvoir, Chevalier de Chastellux (1734–1788) was third-in-command of Rochambeau's corps and, being fluent in English, his commander's unofficial liaison officer. After distinguished service in the Seven Years' War, he wrote on military, scientific and philosophical matters, and the theater, and was the first Frenchman to be inoculated against smallpox. He later wrote a famous book* Travels in North America. *(Independence National Historical Park).*

until September 13, when he moved back to Long Island, hoping to intercept De Ternay if he left to winter in the Caribbean. As Rodney was senior to Arbuthnot, he assumed command; leaving Arbuthnot to watch for De Ternay, he ordered Graves to position himself to intercept the French should they elude Arbuthnot and stationed frigates along the South Carolina coast to protect British shipping and deter Rebel privateers.

However, Rodney found Clinton unwilling to assault Newport without a formal siege, fearing that further weakening the garrison of New York City would invite an attack by Washington. Moreover, Clinton was already committed, in October, to sending 2,500 men under Major General Alexander Leslie to raid Virginia and establishing a base in the Chesapeake. Clinton, meanwhile, was pinning his hopes on negotiations with Arnold, who now commanded West Point, the key to the Hudson Highlands. However, Clinton's adjutant general and intermediary in the negotiations, Major John André, was unluckily captured on September 23, and subsequently hanged as a spy. Arnold, learning of the capture by chance, fled, leaving his wife behind along with Clinton's chances of making progress in the region. Having also failed to persuade Clinton to send more men to Martinique, Rodney left for the West Indies on November 16.

Throughout the year, Washington had remained quiet: the late arrival of the French and the shortages of men and money (exacerbated by the growing demand for both in the South) had pre-empted offensive action, other than an unsuccessful raid on Staten Island by Lord Stirling, in January. Washington was therefore particularly keen for the French to act in the North, thus supporting his main army against that of the enemy, rather than in the South. Rochambeau, however, rejecting plans to attack New York City and to invade Canada, agreed to a gentle outing for his men in support of an attack on the British posts at Kingsbridge and northern Manhattan; but the strengthening of British naval forces along the Hudson forestalled this operation.

THE FLORIDAS

Once De Galvez had captured the British posts on the lower Mississippi, he turned his attention to the two British ports in West Florida, Mobile and Pensacola. With the annual South American treasure convoy passing through the Gulf of Mexico on its way to Spain, these bases constituted a menace. Such was the perceived importance of the mission that the Spanish King, Carlos III, had personally chosen De Galvez over other officers in Cuba, citing his experience, his knowledge of the country, the enemy, and the Choctaws (the leading tribe in the region), and the respect he enjoyed within Congress.

Immediately he had received word of the declaration of war, De Galvez had prepared plans for taking Mobile and Pensacola. On his return from Baton Rouge, he had begun gathering supplies—including confiscated British goods—and converting British vessels captured on Lake Pontchartrain and the Mississippi into troop transports. He also wrote to Diego José Navarro, Captain General of Cuba, requesting two ships, six frigates, other vessels, and 4,000 troops. Navarro refused, suggesting that he either capture Mobile and Pensacola by naval bombardment, or by attacking overland, via Mobile. De Galvez knew that the entrance to Pensacola Bay was guarded by 36- and 42-pounders; he also knew that an attack overland through the swamps would be disastrous. Accepting that Navarro could not—or would not—provide troops and artillery, De Galvez scaled down his plans and decided to attack Mobile only. He sent one last request to Navarro, this time for 2,000 men, to arrive by mid-February: he received 567.

Below: *West Point. The fortifications at West Point dominated the navigable stretch of the Hudson River and were, in the words of Washington, the key to America. Had Arnold succeeded in surrendering the post to Clinton, it would have caused untold damage. (National Archives)*

On January 11, De Galvez reviewed his 754 men as they embarked at New Orleans aboard his flotilla of twelve vessels, which included a frigate, a *galiot* (or sloop), and two brigs. Having reached the mouth of the Mississippi on January 18, they had to wait ten days for good weather before entering the Gulf. On February 6, the fleet was scattered by a storm, but all twelve arrived off Mobile three days later and entered the bay on February 10.

Entering the bay, however, proved problematic: two ships grounded on a sandbar; one was freed, but the other was trapped and hit by a storm the next day and had to be abandoned, along with another vessel. Nevertheless, the rest anchored safely and De Galvez salvaged the guns from the wrecks and placed them on Mobile Point, commanding the entrance to the bay. On February 20, as he got ready to attack Mobile itself, Navarro's reinforcements arrived, giving De Galvez over 1,000 troops, against just 300 British. He landed his men on the south bank of the Little Dog River, under covering fire from the 24-pounder on the frigate. On February 28, he crossed the river, encamped about 2,000 yards from Fort Charlotte, and began negotiations with the British commander, Captain Elias Durnford.

Asked to surrender, Durnford—in the belief that De Galvez had lost 700 men in the two shipwrecks—replied that his position was the stronger, and therefore it would be dishonorable for him to do so. Siege operations were then begun, although Durnford found time to present De Galvez with wine, chickens, fresh bread, and mutton, in return for which Durnford received wine, citrons and oranges, biscuits, corn cakes, and cigars.

The two commanders then began corresponding on the subject of respect for private property:

Right: *Lieutenant General Bernado de Galvez (1746–1786) was the archetypal colonial soldier-diplomat. De Galvez was one of the few Spanish officials—military or civil—who was both in a position to give direct aid to Congress and willing to do so. More sympathetic to the idea of colonial autonomy than most Spanish officials, he recognized the war as a chance to avenge past defeats and damage Spain's only European competitor in the Americas. He also played a prominent role in postwar Spanish-American relations, first as an adviser to King Carlos III and later as Viceroy of New Spain (where he succeeded his father). (Museo del Ejercito, Madrid)*

Durnford had burned down some houses to prevent the Spanish using them as cover for their siege batteries; De Galvez promised not to use private residences as cover, if Durnford would agree not to burn any more. This caused some confusion, Durnford assuming that De Galvez would not attack from the residential side of the fort, and De Galvez denying this (in any event, Durnford released him from the promise).

By March 9, the Spanish had brought up their guns and, at nightfall, began digging the approach trenches. At dawn the next day, Durnford opened a damaging fire, but by March 12, the first parallel was finished and a siege battery established that opened a breach in the British fortifications by sunset. With this, Durnford surrendered the 300-strong garrison and 100 or so civilians and blacks who had helped to defend the fort—and not a moment too soon for De Galvez, as his Choctaws reported a relief force of 1,100 men from Pensacola had now reached the Tensaw River, almost in sight of Mobile.

The column, led by Major General John Campbell, who commanded the post at Pensacola, turned around and headed straight back on learning of the surrender. De Galvez was upset that the limited reinforcements from Cuba had prevented him from ambushing the relief column, as this would have guaranteed the fall of Pensacola. Yet if he moved swiftly, he might catch the post in a state of disorganization from the column's return.

The garrison at Pensacola included 1,300 Regulars and Germans, 600 hundred militia and frontiersmen, 300 armed blacks, and 300 British sailors. De Galvez had about 1,300 men at Mobile and was aware that more would be needed to take Pensacola. In fact, Navarro had sent an expedition to Pensacola on March 7, but the ships could not get in close enough to silence the heavy guns and had returned to Havana. De Galvez, presuaded that Pensacola could only be captured from the sea, asked Navarro for more men and also for two frigates as he had no warships with guns larger than 8-pounders.

De Galvez learned that eleven British naval vessels and nine armed merchantmen had arrived at Pensacola, and when no reinforcements had arrived from Cuba by May 4, he left a small garrison at Mobile, sent the rest of his men back to New Orleans, and sailed to Havana to obtain the forces he required. In Cuba, the council of war approved his plans and allocated 3,800 men and provisions for six months, with another 2,500 men from Mexico, Puerto Rico, and Santo Domingo. On October 16, he set sail from Vera Cruz with seven ships, five frigates, three smaller vessels, and forty-nine transports, but a hurricane, lasting three days, scattered his fleet; with one vessel sunk and others badly damaged, the attack on Pensacola was postponed to the following year.

MARTINIQUE: APRIL 17, 1780

Rodney sighted the French fleet on April 16, beating up against the wind toward the channel between Martinique and Dominica. He ordered a general chase in order to overhaul the enemy and, as the sun set, formed line of battle on a parallel course, heading northwest. His plan was to concentrate his own forces and use them to attack one part of the French line, rather than the traditional tactic of opposing lines, with each ship engaging its opposite number.

Early the next day, De Guichen reversed course and headed south-southeast on the port tack. Rodney then signaled his captains to close the intervals between their ships, in order to concentrate their fire against the enemy rear. At that time the two lines were sailing on parallel, but opposite, courses, out of gunnery range of each other, with the British holding the weather gauge (as they invariably did, since it allowed them to be more aggressive).

By 8:30 a.m., the British line was opposite the French rear and Rodney signaled "line abreast," at which each of his ships turned toward the enemy immediately, in order to draw closer to the enemy. This left the leading British ship, now at the right of the British line, engaging the rearmost French ship, while the last ship in the British line was just forward of De Guichen's center.

De Guichen ordered his ships to wear together, reversing his line, so that his leading ships were heading toward his threatened rear. Rodney countered by heading up on the opposite course and sailing parallel, but beyond range, concentrating his line on the new French rear. Shortly after 10:00 a.m., he ordered his ships to wear again, bringing both fleets on to parallel courses, heading north by west, with his compact line concentrated opposite the French rear.

At 11:00 a.m., his line steered to port in order to bring the French ships within range, and fifty minutes later, each ship was ordered to steer for its opposite number—i.e. the closest enemy ship—the shortened British line resulting in each French vessel being outnumbered. However, having only recently arrived on station, Rodney (who was aloof at the best of times) had had little chance to get to know his captains, and several officers—including two rear admirals—misunderstood his orders. Rodney's flagship, the *Sandwich,* closed and fought successfully against three French vessels (firing seventy-five rounds per gun and sustaining three hits below the waterline), but the leading British ship and the six behind it headed for their equivalents in the French line, instead of attacking the nearest enemy with overwhelming numbers.

More than four hours later, the French broke off, having sustained the heavier casualties—222 dead and 537 wounded, to 120 killed and 354 injured among Rodney's crews—but having inflicted the greater damage, raking the British as they bore down on the enemy.

Above: *A view of Pigeon Island and Gros Islet Bay on St. Lucia. The island of St. Lucia occupied a vital strategic position, as it allowed the British to observe the comings and goings at Fort Royal, Martinique, the principal French base in the West Indies. (National Maritime Museum)*

THE CARIBBEAN

In March, Rodney arrived in the Leeward Islands, closely followed by De Guichen (who, like Rodney, had been a successful commander in the Seven Years War). When De Guichen reached Martinique, he decided to attack either Barbados or St. Lucia. On April 13, he embarked 3,000 troops and, with twenty-three ships, headed north as escort for a convoy going to Santo Domingo. Lookouts on St. Lucia informed Rodney of De Guichen's departure, and he followed with twenty ships—his entire fleet.

Rodney had missed what he would always consider was the greatest opportunity for decisive victory in his entire career. Furious at his subordinates, he ordered his fleet to make repairs at sea, and chased De Guichen to Guadeloupe, where the Frenchman put into port. Rodney then returned to St. Lucia and kept watch for any moves to return to Martinique. De Guichen carried out his own repairs at Guadeloupe and then attacked St. Lucia.

Sailing around Martinique, the French approached St. Lucia from the northeast on May 9. Two weeks of constant maneuvering followed, mostly beyond range, but on two occasions a sudden change in the wind saw parts of each fleet engaged. Eventually, Rodney went to Barbados and De Guichen to Fort Royal, Martinique. The latter had deliberately avoided a full-blooded action, but had inflicted sufficient damage on Rodney's ships to keep them in port for some time (though six of his own ships were also out of action for several weeks).

Worn out and having lost a son in one of the minor engagements, he wrote to Paris, asking to be relieved of the command of such a large fleet.

Meanwhile, twelve ships and 12,000 troops had left Cadiz on April 28, under Admiral Don José Solano, to protect Spanish colonies and possibly capture some British possessions. Learning of their approach, Rodney put to sea on June 7, hoping to intercept the Spanish east of Martinique, but Solano had sailed to the north of Guadeloupe in order to approach Martinique from the west. De Guichen, with fifteen ships, met him near Guadeloupe on June 9, and together they returned to Fort Royal.

Unfortunately, Solano's force was so racked by disease (an estimated 5,000 died) that he refused to cooperate with De Guichen, insisting instead that the latter escort him through the Bahama Channel so that they could proceed in safety to Havana. For his part, De Guichen had orders to return to France and decided it was time to go. On July 5, the two fleets and their transports weighed anchor in Fort Royal and De Guichen escorted Solano's ships to eastern Cuba, before proceeding to Haiti to collect a convoy. At Haiti, he found messages from La Fayette and the French minister to the United States urging him to come north and participate with Washington in a joint land and sea operation. But De Guichen sailed instead for Cadiz on August 16, taking nineteen ships to guard ninety-six merchantmen. With nobody left to fight, Rodney sailed north to New York City.

On his return, Rodney found that exceptionally strong hurricanes had swept through the islands in

October, wreaking particular havoc on Barbados, destroying two ships and nine smaller vessels, and damaging many others. With wood for repairs in short supply, he was happy to see Rear Admiral Sir Samuel Hood appear, bringing spars and timbers, as well as other supplies, together with eight more ships.

EUROPE

As the war dragged on, it began to affect the commercial and political fabric of every maritime trading nation in Europe that sought to benefit from the insatiable needs of the armies and navies of the belligerents. Unlike France and Spain, who became involved to serve their own ends, the other nations feared the financial cost of becoming embroiled in the fighting, yet had they had to protect their sources of revenue from the increasingly desperate acts of belligerents trying to prevent vital supplies reaching the enemy. By 1780, matters had reached a point where these neutral maritime nations felt a need to band together to protect their rights.

In the late eighteenth century, however, those rights were unclear, each nation's view being determined by individual need and tradition. It was generally agreed that belligerents could seize war materials (known as contraband), while neutrals could continue ordinary trade with one or both sides. But what constituted contraband (since it was now clear that weapons and ammunition alone were not enough to sustain war), and was it protected if the

carrying vessel belonged to a neutral? The first question was dealt with by a series of treaties, each defining contraband according to the philosophies of the signatories. The second was answered by the doctrine that the right to seize was predicated upon the destination of the cargo, rather than the ownership of the vessel. This traditional view naturally appealed to powerful belligerent nations, such as Great Britain, but not to neutrals such as the Netherlands, whose economy survived on meeting the shipping needs of other countries, and Russia, which had no merchant fleet and had to transport her goods in the ships of other nations. By the 1770s, the neutrals were promoting a new doctrine: "free ships, free goods."

In 1780, they found a champion in Empress Catherine II of Russia. In 1775, it had been assumed that Catherine would be pro-British, but she had been appalled at the way Parliament had dealt with the Colonies and predicted that Great Britain would lose them. She refused a British approach for the loan of 20,000 troops, and after France had entered

Above: *Admiral Luc Urbain de Bouexic, Comte de Guichen (1712–1790) had entered the French navy in 1730, but had risen slowly in rank. In 1779, he had served as a rear admiral in the action off Ushant, and had been chosen to take a large French fleet to the West Indies in 1780. Although he only escaped annihilation off Martinique due to the incompetence of several of Rodney's captains, he later displayed skill in opposing a more powerful enemy and prevented Rodney from achieving any major victories. (Musée de Versailles, Paris)*

the war, she considered that Great Britain should cut her losses and make peace, even at the cost of recognizing an independent United States.

Catherine, however, had no wish to see Great Britain crushed—especially by the French, who had recently encouraged the Turks to attack Russia. She also saw herself increasingly in the role of mediator, thereby adding to Russia's prestige. Yet while the British persisted in trying to "recruit" her, the French encouraged her neutrality and desire to protect the rights of neutrals on the open sea—which benefited France, who needed the services of neutral ships, whereas Great Britain had a large merchant fleet and a large navy to protect it.

Unsurprisingly, the British viewed enemy goods on neutral ships as fair game (and interpreted contraband very broadly to include naval stores such as timber, hemp, and pitch). France took the opposite position and in 1778, had affirmed the "free ships, free goods" doctrine. Ironically, the catalyst for

action was the seizure of Russian goods aboard eight British ships by a Rebel privateer, prompting Catherine to propose that Russian and Danish ships patrol the North Sea to protect merchantmen (for which read British merchantmen).

For his part, the Danish foreign minister, A. P. Bernstorff (himself virulently anti-Rebel), drafted much broader terms of engagement that unwittingly favored France and the United States, which was not what Catherine wanted. However, when Spain (which had a large navy and a large merchant fleet, and aimed to blockade Gibraltar) entered the war, she proclaimed her intention of following the same line as Great Britain—except that neutral goods on enemy ships would also be seized. Within days, the Spanish had arrested vessels belonging to several neutral nations, including a Dutch ship with a Russian cargo and a Russian merchantman.

These actions horrified Spain's ally, France, which lobbied for the resurrection of Bernstorff's

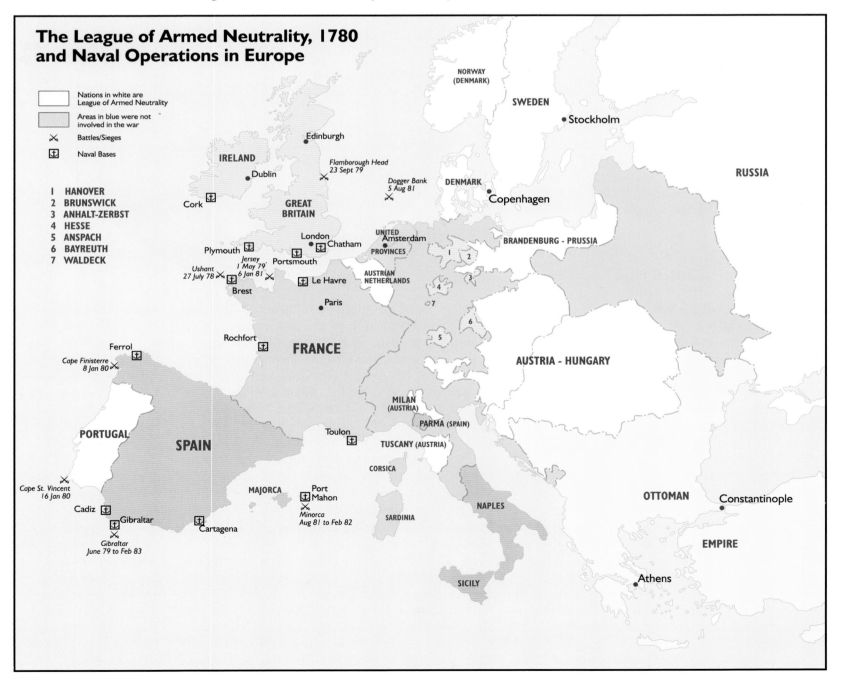

The League of Armed Neutrality, 1780 and Naval Operations in Europe

Nations in white are League of Armed Neutrality

Areas in blue were not involved in the war

✕ Battles/Sieges

⊞ Naval Bases

1 HANOVER
2 BRUNSWICK
3 ANHALT-ZERBST
4 HESSE
5 ANSPACH
6 BAYREUTH
7 WALDECK

proposals, and also raised a third issue of neutral rights: did a blockade require an actual line of ships, or did a mere declaration justify the seizure of any merchant ship in the area? Catherine drew up a declaration embodying the neutrals' view of neutral rights (taken almost verbatim from Bernstorff's proposals), and addressed it to Spain, France, and Great Britain as the official position of the Russian Empire. The Declaration of Armed Neutrality was issued at St. Petersburg on March 10 (February 28, according to the Russian calendar of the time) and contained four principles: that neutral ships could sail freely from port to port, including along the coasts of belligerent nations; that goods (other than contraband) belonging to belligerent nations could not be seized from neutral ships; that contraband was to be narrowly defined and did not include naval stores (timber being one of Russia's biggest exports); and that a blockaded port must be closed off and obviously rendered dangerous to enter. It was accepted immediately by France and later—with much French prodding—by Spain, but not by Great Britain.

On July 9, Denmark signed a convention with Russia to form the League of Armed Neutrality, joined by Sweden on August 1 and, subsequently, by the Netherlands, Prussia, Portugal, and Austria. Theoretically, the existence of the League favored the neutrals, and the Allies, but was bad for Britain. In practice, things were different: Bernstorff struck a deal with Great Britain, ending the shipping of naval stores in return for the removal of contraband status from salt fish, a major Danish export. Although diplomatic pressure from Spain and Russia saw Bernstorff removed from office, neither Denmark nor

Sweden made much effort to enforce the Declaration.

Another signatory, the United Provinces of the Netherlands, actually suffered as a result of joining the League. The Netherlands was a republic, governed by the Staats-Generaal (a legislative body comprising representatives of her seven provinces), but with a hereditary titular ruler, the Staatholder. Willem V was a cousin of George III and extremely pro-British; he had little constitutional power, but in practice could veto anything, as every decision of the Staats-Generaal had to be unanimous and he needed only to persuade one of the provinces to support his views. Highly urbanized, with her wealth based on trade, banking, and financial services, a two-party political system mirrored the Tories and Whigs—a conservative pro-British aristocracy and a rural peasantry supporting the Staatholder, while the opposition (or "Patriots") were pro-French, anti-British, urban middle-class professionals and merchants.

The once-feared Dutch navy was a shadow of its former self but there was still a sizeable merchant fleet and the War led to an upsurge in commerce, particularly via the island of St. Eustatius in the Caribbean. It also brought confrontation with Great Britain, technically an ally, and by March the British ambassador, Sir Joseph Yorke, presented a third demand that the treaty of alliance be honored. When the three-week deadline expired, Great Britain still did not declare war, but announced that the Dutch would be treated just like other neutrals, with no attention paid to the maritime treaty and its "free ships, free goods" clause.

With pressure increasing from Russia and John Adams (now in Amsterdam) to join the League of

Above; *The Moonlight Battle (January 16, 1780). On his way to the West Indies, via Gibraltar, Rodney captured a Spanish convoy of 22 ships on January 8. When the Spanish squadron blockading Gibraltar came into sight, eight days later, his coppered ships gave chase and, in a one-sided action, six of the 11 enemy ships were captured (although two of these were later lost in shallow water near the coast). (National Maritime Museum)*

Armed Neutrality, the Dutch held out—in vain—for Catherine to guarantee protection for their colonies, while the Staats-Generaal voted to improve the navy. However, time ran out and with British privateers steadily exterminating the Dutch merchant fleet, the country was dragged into a war that would be disastrous for her lucrative financial sector. In September, the British captured a draft treaty of alliance between the Netherlands and the United States. Although it was unauthorized by either party, its disclosure forced the Dutch to join the League, and led to a British declaration of war on December 21.

Meanwhile, in France, Jones was ordered to return to America in the *Alliance,* taking 16,000 "stand of arms" (a "stand" being a complete set of musket, cartridge box, bayonet, and cross-belts) and 120 bales of uniform cloth. Delayed by repairs, Jones went to Paris—where he was greeted as a hero—to encourage the French government to sell his prizes, so that he could pay his crew. He was forced to return empty-handed when a mentally unstable French officer in his squadron seized the *Alliance* and sailed for America.

Eventually, the French government loaned Jones a former British sloop captured off the Carolinas, in which he sailed from Lorient on September 5, with 11,000 muskets, 10,000 uniforms, and 800 barrels of gunpowder. Delayed by storms, Jones spent a month at Groix before putting back to sea on October 7. Unfortunately, he promptly ran into a storm that wrecked vessels and drowned men all along the coast of Brittany, but with excellent seamanship, he managed to return to Groix on October 12. After two months of repairs, he sailed again, on December 18, for Philadelphia, on what would be his final voyage in command of a Continental Navy vessel.

Meanwhile, the North ministry was also busy providing aid for Gibraltar and Minorca. On December 29, 1779, Admiral Sir George Brydges Rodney—a distinguished commander from the Seven Years' War—had left Plymouth with twenty-two ships, fourteen frigates, and other small vessels, to escort a massive convoy of merchant ships to the West Indies, via Gibraltar. On January 8, off Cape Finisterre, this force spotted a Spanish convoy taking stores to Cadiz and captured all twenty-two vessels, which were then sent to Gibraltar with prize crews.

Eight days later, Rodney had just passed Cape St. Vincent when he observed a Spanish squadron of eleven ships and two frigates, under Admiral Don Juan de Langara. The Spanish ships formed a line of battle and headed southeast for Cadiz, but the hulls of Rodney's ships were newly coppered and they closed the gap, before passing between the Spanish and the shore. In what later became known as "the moonlight battle," fighting began around 4:00 p.m. and within two hours one Spanish ship had exploded and another surrendered. The action continued until 2:00 a.m., by when another three Spanish ships had

struck, four more had escaped, and two had been driven ashore.

Along with his prizes, Rodney headed for Gibraltar, where news of the two actions had arrived in both camps. The Spanish ships at Algeciras remained behind a protective boom, as first the prizes from January 8, and then Rodney's main force, entered the harbor through heavy seas and head winds (Rodney himself not arriving until January 26). As supplies and more troops were disembarked, other vessels headed for Minorca, returning on February 13, at which time Rodney departed for the Leeward Islands. A small British force returned to the Channel, on the way intercepting a French convoy bound for the Indian Ocean, capturing one ship and three merchantmen.

With Rodney gone, the Spanish fleet at Algeciras resumed the blockade and the siege recommenced. In March, rationing was reintroduced and with few vessels successfully running the blockade, scurvy appeared among the defenders and the civilian population. Around the same time, rumors began that the Spaniards were preparing to send fireships into the harbor, where the British now had one ship, a frigate, two other small ships, and some armed transports, in addition to various small merchant vessels. On the night of June 6, the first of nine Spanish fireships was spotted drifting down upon the anchored British vessels. However, the Spanish crews abandoned their vessels too soon, giving the British time to attach lines and tow the fireships away from the harbor. Seven were beached—providing the garrison with a huge amount of wood—and two drifted harmlessly out to sea. At the end of June, the single British ship was attacked by four Spaniards and badly damaged; she was ordered home and slipped through the blockade.

As the summer wore on, secret peace talks between Great Britain and Spain collapsed, as the British position worldwide worsened. In addition, the French promised aid for the siege of Gibraltar and the Emperor of Morocco joined the Allies (the principal effect of which was to end a valuable source of intelligence and supplies via the British consul in Tangier). Smallpox now broke out, although the scurvy outbreak was contained in October, after a Danish ship carrying citrus fruit was forced into the harbor. However, the blockade was tightened when a Spanish gunboat mounting a 26-pounder "bow chaser" appeared and not only harassed shipping but also had the speed to come in close, fire at the fortifications under cover of darkness, and escape.

INDIA

In July, Hyder Ali invaded the coastal plain of the Carnatic with almost 100,000 men in order to avenge the British refusal to fulfil their treaty promises to help him when Mysore had been invaded by the

Marathas in 1772. Eager to assist the French in their plan to remove the British from India, he proceeded to attack British garrisons in the interior, seizing Arcot (capital of the Carnatic) and recapturing Pondicherry.

Having split their forces between Madras and Guntur, farther to the north, and sent aid to Bombay, the British were in no position to oppose him. Hyder Ali sent his son, Tipu Sahib, to attack the force at Guntur, which he overwhelmed with ease and virtually wiped out before Sir Hector Munro, in overall command at Madras, could arrive with help. In just three weeks, Hyder Ali and his son had taken most of the British posts in the Carnatic.

At this point, Hastings recalled Major General Sir Eyre Coote from Calcutta. Coote, a veteran of the Seven Years' War, was now fifty-three and in poor health. However, he retained his military capabilities and was still an outstanding and dutiful commander. He left Madras with 7,500 men and fifty-two guns and proceeded not only to relieve the forts being besieged by Hyder Ali, but also to recapture those he had taken—Chingleput, Carangooly, Wandiwash, and then Permacoil.

Above: *General Eyre Coote (1726–83) first saw military action in India as a major with Robert Clive's Calcutta expedition, culminating in the victory at Plassey in 1757. He served with distinction in the Seven Years' War, defeating the French general Lally at Wandewash (1760) and Pondicherry (1761), but his most notable victory was the checking of Hyder Ali's onslaught on Madras during 1780–82*

Left: *Warren Hastings (1732–1818) joined the East India Company at the age of 17 and although primarily an administrator and diplomat, was a member of Robert Clive's 1756 expedition to recapture Calcutta from the Sirajh-ud-daula, Nawab of Bengal. After the battle of Plassey in 1757, Hastings returned to civilian duties, and became the first governor-general of British India in 1773. Aiming to consolidate and protect British possessions in the subcontinent, his policies included strengthening the buffer state of Oudh. He is credited with saving the British Empire in India.*

1781

"Oh God! It is all over"

LORD NORTH

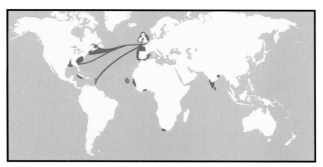

RED INDICATES FIGHTING, INCLUDING PRIVATEERING ON SHIPPING LANES

The Battle of the Capes (March 16, 1781)

NEW YORK

In December 1780, Rochambeau's senior naval officer, De Ternay, died and was succeeded by Chevalier Destouches, who initially declined an invitation from Washington to participate in a plan to capture Benedict Arnold (then in Virginia). Eventually, he sent one ship and two frigates, which soon returned empty-handed. Then on March 8, he finally agreed to make a more concerted effort and the entire squadron sailed for the Chesapeake, along with 1,200 troops. Arbuthnot was informed, but did not set off in pursuit until thirty-six hours later.

Frustrated by French inaction (which was actually more a symptom of their concern at the mutinies over pay and enlistments that rocked the Continental Army in January), Washington met Rochambeau at Wethersfield, on May 22. They discussed whether to deplete the Northern Department to reinforce the Southern Department (where the enemy was strongest), or to await the arrival of De Grasse and attack New York City (where the enemy were at their weakest since 1775). The latter offered a more immediate prospect of success, but no decision was possible without knowledge of what De Grasse planned, which Rochambeau would not divulge. However, Rochambeau did agree to join Washington at Peekskill; the French left Newport on June 9 and reached White Plains on July 6, inducing Clinton to ask Cornwallis to send troops back to New York City.

In mid-June, it was thought that De Grasse would arrive in the North by late July, but on August 14 Washington learned that the French fleet would only come as far up as the Chesapeake and would only be available until mid-October. All plans to attack New York City were now canceled and it was agreed that 2,500 Continentals and 4,500 French would head for Virginia to trap Cornwallis, leaving 4,000 Continentals to guard the Hudson Highlands.

On August 19, the two contingents crossed the Hudson River at King's Ferry and marched south in three columns. With many Allied staff officers still unaware of the real destination, the force gathered at Chatham on August 28, to make Clinton believe their target was Staten Island. The following day, the Americans marched through Brunswick and Boundbrook and the French through Morristown; and on 30 August, the ruse was exposed as the columns headed toward Princeton. On September 1, the artillery and engineers began loading their equipment on to boats at Wilmington, while the main body began crossing the Delaware River. The Continentals bypassed Philadelphia, but the French were allowed to pass through and spent two days being fêted by politicians and public alike. On September 5, Washington was relieved to learn that De Grasse was in the Chesapeake waiting for him and three days later both armies had reached Head of Elk.

Back in New York City, Graves, who supported Clinton's idea of a base in the Chesapeake, had replaced Arbuthnot, who had returned to England. In August, Graves returned from an abortive attempt to intercept a French convoy outside Boston to find a letter from Rodney informing him that De Grasse and Hood were heading his way. By chance, Hood had taken a more direct route and arrived in Chesapeake Bay on August 21; finding nothing, he headed for Sandy Hook to join Graves and arrived on August 28—the same day that Commodore Comte de Barras, recently returned from France, left Newport with eight ships, four frigates, and eighteen transports, in order to join De Grasse.

THE CAROLINAS

While Cornwallis was having problems pacifying the back-country of the Carolinas, Greene was finding it difficult merely to feed his men and maintain order. He sent some of his best troops westward, under Morgan, to find provisions and threaten Augusta, while Lee's legionary corps was instructed to coordinate the activities of partisan groups, such as those led by Marion and Sumter. The rest of Greene's army moved to Cheraw on the Pee Dee River.

These arrangements enabled Greene to counter any move by Cornwallis: if the latter decided to chase Morgan, Greene could join Marion or Lee to threaten Camden and Charleston. If he went for Lee or Marion, Greene could join Morgan at Augusta. If Cornwallis attacked him, Morgan and Lee could come to his aid, and the entire force could withdraw into the back-country, as Washington had in New Jersey in 1776.

Cornwallis accepted the challenge, once again detaching a large number of valuable light troops to attack Morgan, who was loitering on the western flank of any advance into North Carolina. Morgan retreated to a defensive position and his opponent—Tarleton—charged after him, like the true cavalryman he was. Without giving his men time to recover from a forced march, Tarleton formed them up and threw them at Morgan's position near Hannah's Cowpens, on January 17.

Morgan had drawn up his detachment in three lines, the first comprising skirmishers and sharpshooters, the second consisting of militia (with orders to fire three volleys and then "break"), and the third made up of veteran Continentals. Suffering losses from the riflemen, and given false encouragement by the withdrawal of the militia, Tarleton's command charged the Continentals, who broke the Royal forces and drove them from the field. Tarleton lost 110 dead and over 700 captured, including 200 wounded, out of 1,150 men (some of Cornwallis's regiments later refused to serve under Tarleton, they had so little confidence in his abilities). Morgan lost twelve dead and sixty wounded.

Cornwallis set off after Morgan, but his substantial baggage train slowed him down on the poor roads. At Ramsour's Mill, he managed to have his men's shoes repaired, at which point he ordered all the baggage and tents burned. The next few weeks were spent chasing Greene—now reinforced by Morgan and Lee—across North Carolina in what became known as the "race for the Dan" (another name for the Roanoke River). Greene eventually won by misleading Cornwallis as to his likely crossing place, and then crossing by boat on February 13. Cornwallis turned south in order to find supplies and entered Hillsboro on February 22, where he called for Loyalists to join him. The response was poor and one of the few units established was massacred after mistaking Lee's legion for Tarleton's.

Greene came back across the Dan on February 23 and Cornwallis left Hillsboro to follow him, two days later. Having assiduously avoided battle for so long, the recent arrival of substantial reinforcements now left him outnumbering Cornwallis by two-to-one and he determined to make use of them. The action at Guilford Court House was one of the most dramatic of the war. Cornwallis drove a superior enemy from good defensive positions, but at such cost that his little army was crippled.

Cornwallis remained on the battlefield for three days, before marching to Cross Creek near Cape Fear, where he expected to receive support from local Loyalists. Once again, though, the response was dis-

appointing and, unable to cross Cape Fear River, he set off for the British post at Wilmington. His choice was now to move south and help Rawdon, or march to the Chesapeake; disappointed in South Carolina as a seat of war, he chose Virginia.

On April 25, Cornwallis left his sick and wounded at Wilmington and marched to Halifax, where he learned that Greene had returned to South Carolina to mop up the isolated Royal garrisons. However, on May 12, news of Rawdon's victory at Hobkirk's Hill led Cornwallis to believe that he could now afford to join Phillips in Virginia (only later did he discover that Rawdon had been forced to abandon Camden and three other posts).

Greene, meanwhile, returned to South Carolina hoping that he would find it easier to feed his army, now that the militia had gone home. He determined either to capture the British posts (thereby forestalling the process of pacification), or else force Cornwallis to come south to save them. His first target was Camden and, on April 19, he occupied Hobkirk's Hill with 1,500 men. His opponent, Lieutenant Colonel Lord Rawdon, had only 900 men, but on April 25 he advanced on Greene's camp at night, hoping to surprise the Rebel army.

Greene tried to outflank Rawdon, but his army was not up to the task and was chased from the field. Undeterred, he looked for arms and food, while Rawdon was forced to withdraw to Charleston and other posts were left to be captured: Orangeburg (May

GUILFORD COURT HOUSE: MARCH 15, 1781

After receiving reinforcements totalling 550 Continentals and over 1,000 militia, Greene took up a strong position near Guilford Court House. He adopted Morgan's tactics from Cowpens, forming his men in three lines, about 500 yards apart: a rail fence defended by North Carolina militia, flanked by light troops and facing open farmland that the enemy would have to cross; more experienced Virginia militia in dense woods to break up the British formations and provide cover for the defenders; and finally, 1,500 Continentals on a low ridge looking over more open fields.

Around 1:00 p.m., the Royal army crossed Little Horsepen Creek and deployed; the men were tired after a twelve-mile march and had not eaten or slept under cover for two days. They advanced on the first rail fence, taking a volley from the defenders and returning their fire before rushing on with the bayonet. The North Carolina militia fell back into the woods, pursued by the Regulars and Hessians of Cornwallis's first line.

As the triumphant line moved into the woods, they came into contact with the Virginia militia. Both sides soon split into small groups and hand-to-hand fighting occurred; a Hessian unit pushed back the light troops on the Rebel left for some distance, virtually removing them from the battle. After a half-hour, the Virginia militia fell back.

The Royal forces once again followed up and emerged from the woods to find Greene's third line waiting ominously behind another set of rail fences. Two regiments of Regulars charged across the fields and up the slope, but were thrown back by a disciplined volley that caused heavy casualties. On Cornwallis's right, the Foot Guards pushed back one unit of Maryland Continentals, but another hit the right flank of the Foot Guards, while cavalrymen under Colonel William Washington (a distant cousin of the commander-in-chief) rode them down from behind. The situation was now so desperate that Cornwallis was forced to order his gunners to fire into the mêlée, knowing that they would hit their own men as well as the enemy. Fortunately, this halted the Rebel counterattack; seeing the large gap in his line, Greene ordered a retreat and his army fled from the field, abandoning its artillery.

Cornwallis attempted to pursue his enemy, but his army was too shattered. He had lost over 500 men—one-quarter of his force—against enemy casualties of 79 dead and 185 wounded. Once again, a decisive victory had eluded a Royal commander and once again the British Regulars had shown extreme courage in the face of superior numbers and a secure defensive position, and paid for it with their lives.

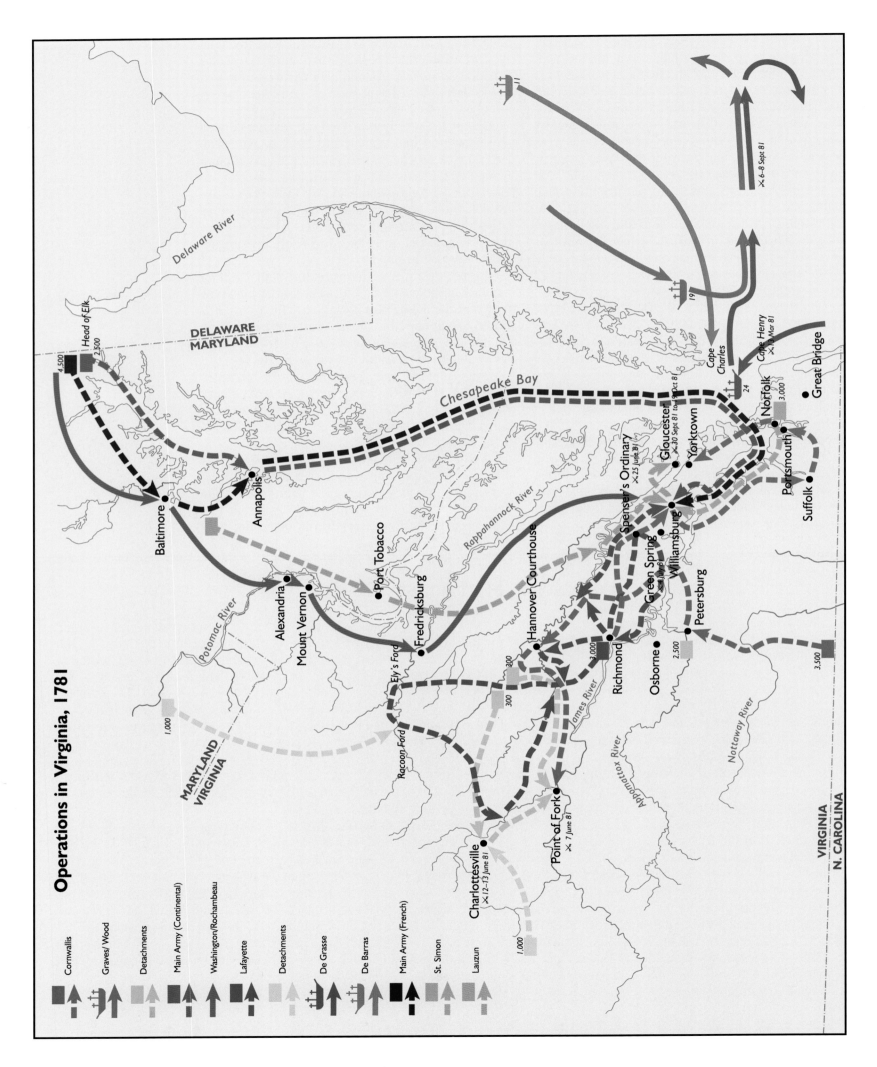

Operations in Virginia, 1781

10), Fort Motte (May 11), and Augusta (June 5). Greene then besieged Fort Ninety-Six, but Rawdon received reinforcements from Britain and was able to march them inland to relieve the post (though several men died en route due to the heat). Once again, Rawdon retired to the coast—this time followed by hordes of Loyalist refugees—then returned to England because of ill-health, being captured by the French on the way.

On September 8, Greene attacked a British force similar to his own (about 2,200 men) at Eutaw Springs. In a protracted, seesaw battle, Greene had victory snatched from his grasp when his starving men captured the British tent lines and looted them. The mixture of Regulars and Loyalists rallied and drove Greene from the field, but at considerable loss to themselves. The British then withdrew all of their outlying posts to Charleston and Savannah, but Greene did not have enough men to besiege either city, and the fighting gradually died out. He also made considerable efforts to attract Loyalists; his views that they were everywhere contrast with Cornwallis's comments that they could not be found.

In fact, the post at Wilmington, North Carolina, supported and sustained quite a large and successful force during the summer and autumn of 1781, until the Regulars evacuated the town on November 18. A typical example was the raid on Hillsboro, on September 13, when 1,000 Loyalist militia under Colonel David Fanning captured the North Carolina Assembly. Unfortunately, they were then ambushed by Continentals on the return journey, and had to abandon Fanning—who was badly wounded—on the field.

VIRGINIA

The year began for Virginia with a visit from Benedict Arnold, now a major general in the British Army, who had entered Hampton Roads on December 30 and spent New Year's Day moving up the James River. He disembarked at Westover on January 4 and entered Richmond the following day, destroying much of the town. He then withdrew to Portsmouth to establish a naval base, in accord with Clinton's instructions. Although Thomas Jefferson complained that Arnold had been virtually unopposed, Arnold felt that matters were reaching the point where he needed reinforcements.

His view was at least partially confirmed when, in February, a French ship and two frigates arrived from Newport to act in concert with 1,200 Continentals under La Fayette, whom Washington had sent south to capture Arnold. The ships left without achieving anything and poor roads prevented La Fayette from arriving until March. However, a larger French squadron, under Destouches, had left Newport on March 8, in another attempt to catch the traitor.

On the day after the action at Guilford, Arbuthnot and Destouches sighted each other, off the Virginia Capes. Heavy seas, drizzle, and a westerly wind pre-vented either side entering Chesapeake Bay, so at 7:00 a.m. Arbuthnot signaled his ships to set more sail and form line of battle. As the British turned about, the French formed line and headed into the Atlantic; by 1:00 p.m., when the weather had worsened and the wind shifted to the northeast, both sides were in line ahead heading east-southeast. At 2:00 p.m., Destouches executed a 180-degree turn around the British line, giving the French the unusual advantage of the weather gauge (this meant that they could use their lower-deck guns, while the British could not). A confused fight followed in which Arbuthnot lost 30 dead and 73 wounded, and Destouches 72 dead and 112 wounded. Destouches had outmaneuvered and outfought Arbuthnot, only to return to Newport (literally saving Arnold's neck). Arbuthnot wanted to pursue Destouches, but his three leading ships were too badly damaged. The French arrived back in Rhode Island on March 26, while Arbuthnot returned to New York on April 6 and then blockaded Newport.

Below: *Major General William Phillips (1731–1781) joined the Royal Artillery in 1746 and served with distinction at Minden and Warburg. He arrived in Canada in 1776 and served as Burgoyne's second-in-command in the Saratoga campaign. Exchanged for Lincoln in 1780, he was chosen to command raiding forces against Rhode Island and Virginia, but died of typhoid fever at Petersburg. (Frick Art Reference Library, New York)*

Right: *Lieutenant Colonel
John Simcoe (1752–1806)
joined the 35th Foot in
1771 and fought at Bunker
Hill. He was wounded at
Brandywine and
subsequently took
command of the Queen's
Rangers. He was captured
in 1778, but exchanged
the following year. An
independent officer, whose
judgment was widely
trusted, he was more
professional and less
"showy" than Tarleton.
After the war he became
governor of Canada.
(Metropolitan Central
Library, Toronto)*

On May 20, Cornwallis arrived in Petersburg with less than 1,500 effective men, only to find that Phillips had died on May 15, leaving Arnold in charge. Cornwallis sent Leslie to carry out Clinton's instructions to fortify Portsmouth, but moved his headquarters to Williamsburg as he had heard that the nearby port of Yorktown might provide a better base and anchorage.

Meanwhile, La Fayette—who had originally been sent to Richmond at the end of April to capture Arnold and prevent future British raids—had withdrawn to Hanover when Cornwallis entered Virginia, leaving southern and western Virginia at the mercy of the Royal army. Cornwallis ordered Tarleton to capture the Virginia Assembly at Charlottesville, and sent Lieutenant Colonel John Graves Simcoe to destroy stores and disperse the militia mobilizing under Von Steuben at Point of Fork. Tarleton missed capturing Jefferson by minutes, while Simcoe's men had similar ill fortune with Von Steuben, but managed to trick over 1,000 militia into abandoning large quantities of powder, wagons, and cannon.

On June 10, La Fayette joined up with Wayne, whose 1,000 Pennsylvania Continentals boosted his own force to nearly 4,000 men. As Cornwallis marched into Williamsburg on June 25, La Fayette attacked the British rearguard, under Simcoe, at Spencer's Ordinary. Cornwallis eventually arrived with reinforcements, but the battle had shown the quality of La Fayette's troops. The following day, two letters arrived from Clinton criticizing Cornwallis for entering Virginia and demanding he return 3,000

Left: *Camp of the Convention Army, Charlottesville, Virginia. Once Congress had decided to circumvent the Convention of Saratoga, it resolved to keep the Convention Army in captivity, moving—usually in midwinter—from Massachusetts to Virginia. In 1781, the threat of rescue by Cornwallis saw the men moved again, to Maryland. When the survivors were released at the end of the war, barely half of the rank-and-file remained, the rest having either deserted, escaped, or died from cold or hunger. (British Museum)*

Left: *Rear Admiral Thomas Graves (1725–1802) was from a famous naval family. Despite being court-martialed in 1756, he still attained flag rank in 1779, and went to New York where he later succeeded Arbuthnot as commander of the American squadron. On September 6, he failed to prevent De Grasse reaching the open sea, then allowed him to keep control of the entrance to the Chesapeake. Although he worked much closer with Clinton than had Arbuthnot, his caution prevented a relief force from reaching Cornwallis in time. (National Maritime Museum)*

men to protect New York City from the anticipated attack by Washington and Rochambeau. Still having found no suitable site for a permanent base in the Chesapeake, Cornwallis decided to fall back to Portsmouth and embark as many men as he could on the transports available.

As he ferried his baggage across the James River, Cornwallis prepared a trap for La Fayette, hiding his men in dense woods, approached only by a causeway across the swampy ground near Green Spring. La Fayette was enticed forward by information from two "deserters" but became suspicious and went to warn Wayne, whose advance guard was skirmishing with Tarleton's horsemen. As the latter withdrew, Cornwallis's Regulars burst from the woods and opened fire on Wayne's Pennsylvanians, who fled, abandoning three guns. La Fayette covered the retreat with his light infantry, but only night and the poor ground saved his command from being caught by Tarleton. Once again, a Rebel force had been beaten, but not decisively.

Cornwallis retired to Suffolk, where he received a request from Clinton to march into Pennsylvania and establish a base in Chesapeake Bay, while Clinton

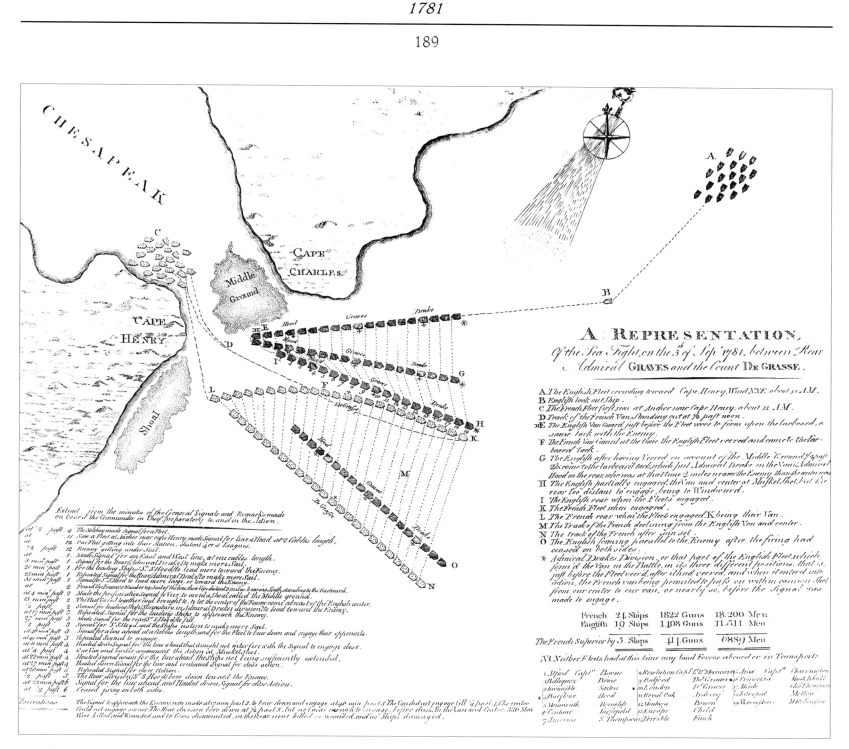

attacked Philadelphia or Newport. As his remaining men and horses were embarking at Portsmouth, another letter from Clinton arrived, enclosing a rare direct order for Cornwallis to occupy Old Point Comfort, in Hampton Roads, with all available troops. Unfortunately, Old Point Comfort was wholly unsuitable, both as a fort and an anchorage, and Cornwallis decided instead to fortify Yorktown and Gloucester. He left O'Hara to level the defenses at Portsmouth, sent Leslie to Charleston to replace the sick Rawdon, and moved his army to the former tobacco port at the junction of the Chesapeake with the York and James Rivers.

As Cornwallis's men began digging in the August heat, De Grasse arrived in the Chesapeake and anchored in Lynnhaven Bay. Leaving four ships to blockade Yorktown, De Grasse ferried St. Simon's corps up the James River, to reinforce La Fayette, and sent smaller ships up the Chesapeake to meet the troops moving down from New York City. Around

mid-morning on September 5, lookouts thought they saw De Barras, but later realized it was Graves's and Hood's twenty ships. At 11:00 a.m., Graves ordered his captains to form line of battle and headed for the Chesapeake.

Despite having 2,000 crewmen ashore foraging, De Grasse was determined to fight. At 11:30 a.m., he abandoned his shore parties and ordered his fleet to sea, eventually emerging in reasonable order. The French had twenty-four ships against nineteen and, although these were slower sailers—not being copper-bottomed—they had heavier guns and were in better repair.

At 2:00 p.m., De Grasse emerged from the Chesapeake, at which Graves changed course from southwest to roughly parallel to the enemy, which left the weakest British ships opposing the best of the French (to make matters worse, Graves's and Hood's squadrons used different signal codes). At 4:05 p.m., with the fleets ten miles off the Virginia Capes, the

Above: *Plan of the battle of September 6. (U.S. Naval Academy, Hampton)*

first shots were fired. The action lasted two hours, with almost all of the fighting around the van and center. Graves lost 90 killed and 246 wounded, while De Grasse, with over 200 casualties, had all but dis-abled five British ships.

More importantly for De Grasse, both fleets were now heading away from the Chesapeake. They remained in visual contact for two more days, until De Grasse turned back to the Chesapeake on the evening of September 9, having drawn Graves away from the bay and allowed De Barras to enter. On the morning of September 11, De Grasse returned to see De Barras in Lynnhaven Bay, as did a British frigate, which reported the fact to Graves. Having had one ship sink after the battle, Graves returned to New York City to effect repairs.

Meanwhile, La Fayette and St. Simon ensured that Cornwallis should neither escape nor discover what was happening, as the arrival of Lauzun's cav-alry on September 12 had canceled out his superiori-ty in mounted troops.

On September 14, Washington and Rochambeau arrived at Williamsburg, while De Grasse's frigates ferried Lincoln's division and the French down from

Head of Elk. On September 28, the Allies left Williamsburg and marched to within two miles of Yorktown, skirmishing with Cornwallis's light troops. The following day, the Allies formed a cres-cent-shaped line, with Washington's forces taking the post of honor on the right.

As the British and German rank-and-file marched off to Williamsburg, then to prisons in Virginia and Maryland, Clinton arrived off the Virginia Capes with 7,000 reinforcements. He had originally believed that Cornwallis could hold out until the end of October, but once he realized that the earl was Washington's target, a council of war on September 24 recommended immediate assistance. Despite the arrival of three ships under Rear Admiral Robert Digby, the Royal Navy was not happy and wanted more time to effect repairs, following the action against De Grasse on September 6. In fact, it was October 19 before any relief force left Sandy Hook for the Chesapeake.

Washington wanted to follow up his victory quickly with an attack either on Charleston or Wilmington, before De Grasse departed. The latter, however, was not keen to remain and would only

YORKTOWN: SEPTEMBER 30–OCTOBER 19, 1781

Cornwallis had built a defensive wall around Yorktown, with ten redoubts, fourteen batteries with sixty-five guns, a fort ("the hornwork") guarding the Hampton Road, and a covered way allowing troops to move safely within the perimeter. Across the river, Gloucester was also fortified, with four redoubts, three batteries with twenty guns, and a stockade.

On September 30, the Allies found several external earthworks abandoned and the enemy inside Yorktown. Under heavy gunfire, the Allies converted these works to face Yorktown and then began constructing their own, producing 6,000 stakes, 2,000 fascines, and 600 gabions while their siege trains were brought up from Williamsburg. At Gloucester, Virginia militia were reinforced by Lauzun's legion and 800 marines from the French fleet. On October 3, Tarleton led what would be the garrison's last foraging expedition, resulting in the largest cavalry engagement of the War, between his legion and Lauzun's.

On October 6, the first parallel was begun, to the southeast of Yorktown and no more than 800 yards from the outer defenses. The next day, they were entered with great ceremony by La Fayette's light infantry division. By October 9, four redoubts and five batteries had been added, with surprisingly few casualties, and on the following night several British ships were set alight and sunk. On October 11, the second parallel was started, just 350 yards from Yorktown.

On the night of October 14, picked French troops and Continentals stormed Redoubts 9 and 10, lying outside the main British lines. The Royal army was now in desperate straits and a sortie on the night of October 16 matched the bravery of their foes, but produced few results. A final attempt to escape across the river to Gloucester was defeated by a fierce storm on the following night.

As dawn broke, more than 100 guns began firing into Yorktown. Around 10:00 a.m., Cornwallis requested a twenty-four-hour truce in order to discuss a surrender. Aware that help might be on its way, Washington could not afford protracted negotiations and, on October 18, terms were agreed by both sides. The next day, O'Hara surrendered his sword to Lincoln and 7,247 troops and 840 naval personnel laid down their arms, in addition to 243 pieces of artillery, 300 horses, and 100 flags.

Above: *The Nelson House. The house of Secretary Thomas Nelson (uncle of Governor Thomas Nelson, one of the signatories of the Declaration of Independence) shown in 1796, still displaying damage from the siege. At the right is a flèche, an open-backed arrow-shaped work, built to protect a weak point in a defensive line. (Virginia State Library)*

Right: *The Surrender at Yorktown. This preliminary oil sketch shows a much more interesting view than that on the opposite page, with Lincoln and O'Hara bareheaded (as they would most likely have been) and the unusual version of the "stars and stripes," with red, white and blue bands. (Detroit Institute of Fine Arts)*

agree to escort a troop convoy to North Carolina (though even this was canceled). On November 4, he left for the Caribbean with St. Simon's division. Lincoln advised Washington not to attack Charleston without naval support and Washington contented himself with sending St. Clair's brigade to reinforce Greene, then sent Lincoln north with the rest of the army, while Rochambeau's corps wintered in Virginia. On December 22, La Fayette took ship for France, and took no further part in the War as an officer in the Continental Army.

THE FLORIDAS

After the hurricane of October 1780, De Galvez returned to Havana to argue for another expedition. Initially, the council suggested that he delay proceedings until March, but on hearing of an unsuccessful British attack near Mobile, on January 7, approved a more immediate strike against Pensacola.

On February 28, De Galvez sailed from Havana with 1,300 fresh troops (to which would be added the contingents at New Orleans and Mobile) and a small fleet of one ship, two frigates, and two smaller vessels, as well as transports. The senior naval officer was Captain José Calbo de Irazabal, but De Galvez was given command of both the army and navy contingents.

Despite the fact that three British frigates were patrolling the seas around Cuba, the fleet headed straight for Pensacola and, on March 9, sighted the long sandbank (known as Santa Rosa Island) in the mouth of the bay. That night, De Galvez landed his grenadiers and light infantry and led them into the unoccupied fort on Siguenza Point. Next, the Spanish landed artillery and constructed a battery, from which they drove off the two frigates that guarded Pensacola Bay.

As the ships began entering the bay, the leading vessel grounded, was freed, and then withdrew out into the Gulf. The next two days were spent landing supplies on Santa Rosa Island and creating a secure base. Several ships were lightened in anticipation of another attempt to enter the bay, but Calbo was unwilling to try, given the sandbars, the lack of a pilot, and the guns of Fort Barrancas Coloradas (Red Cliffs), which commanded the entrance. De Galvez

Above: *The Surrender at Yorktown. Trumbull's famous painting shows Lincoln accepting the British surrender from O'Hara watched by virtually all of the Allied commanders. (Yale University Art Gallery)*

Above: *Washington and Rochambeau at Yorktown. Washington (second from left) surveys the York River, with La Fayette (at left) and Rochambeau (third from right). Note the dead horses on the beach, killed prior to the abortive escape attempt on the night of October 16/17. (Colonial Williamsburg)*

knew that he had to bring his fleet into the bay in order to take Pensacola, whatever Calbo might think. Shaming the latter—and offering a challenge to the British—by hoisting his rear admiral's pennant in one of the smaller vessels (which were from Louisiana and so under his direct command), De Galvez sailed into the bay and across the bar. Three more small ships followed, successfully evading the fire of Fort Barrancas Coloradas, and anchored beside the battery on Siguenza Point.

De Galvez sent a map of the channel to Calbo who, despite the pleas of his subordinates, watched the remaining ships cross the bar the next day, then promptly sailed back to Havana claiming that his work was completed. Within two days, the troops from Mobile and New Orleans had arrived and joined the Havana contingent on the mainland, giving De

Galvez a healthy superiority of 3,500 men against Campbell's 1,100 British. Campbell, however, also had the services of Choctaws, Creeks, Seminoles, and Chickasaws, who were led by white "officers." During March and April, most Spanish casualties were inflicted by this group, who harassed the invaders as they transferred from Santa Rosa Island to the mainland, and tried to get close enough to study the British fortifications. On March 26, they also caused two parties of Spanish soldiers to mistake each other for the enemy, leading to several casualties.

On April 19, unidentified ships were sighted, which proved to be a squadron from Havana, carrying 1,600 troops, with another 700 aboard four French frigates. Again, the guns of Fort Barrancas failed to prevent the enemy entering the harbor, and once the troops had been landed, De Galvez had over

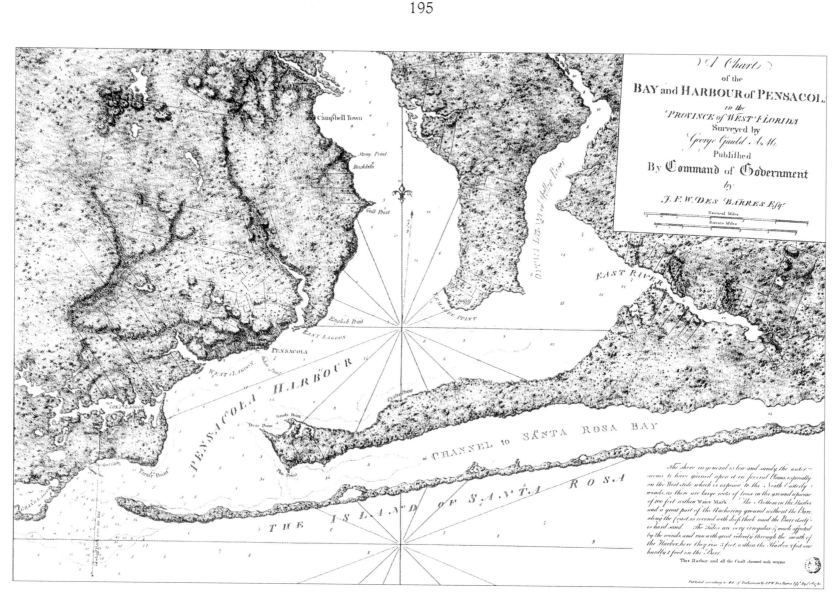

Above: *Map of Pensacola Harbor. The map clearly shows how the island of Santa Rosa dominates the entrance. (National Maritime Museum)*

7,000 men. On April 28, hundreds of men began digging a covered trench leading to a small hill that dominated part of Campbell's defenses. By May 1, a battery of six 24-pounders was emplaced on the hilltop, overlooking a crescent-shaped redoubt in front of Fort George, the key to the British positions.

The working parties then continued digging until the trench reached a higher spot, called Pine Hill. Here, the Spanish were emplacing another battery, on May 4, when Campbell's guns opened fire and infantry made a sortie from Fort George. Although the British captured Pine Hill, seriously wounding four Spanish officers and spiking four cannon, no long-term damage was done and within days both batteries went into action. On May 7, a planned assault was abandoned when it was learned that the attack had been betrayed.

The following day, however, a lucky hit on a powder magazine caused an explosion that killed around ninety men and destroyed the crescent-shaped redoubt. Spanish light troops rushed into the work while the dust and smoke were still hanging over the ruins; a new battery was constructed inside it and artillery brought forward. Shortly after noon, the new battery opened fire on the central British redoubt of Fort George, wounding another thirty men.

At 3:00 p.m., Campbell requested a temporary cessation of hostilities until the following noon, while surrender terms were discussed. At 1:00 a.m. on May 10, Campbell surrendered the town and harbor of Pensacola, Fort George, Fort Barrancas Coloradas, and all of West Florida, together with 1,113 troops, four mortars, 143 guns, six howitzers, 40 swivel guns, 2,100 muskets, 8,000 flints, and 298 barrels of powder, as well as other material. Spanish losses were 74 dead and 198 wounded, mostly in the British sortie and the capture of the crescent redoubt. Campbell's troops were taken to Havana, but then promptly returned to New York City (prompting complaints from Congress that the men were now free to fight against the United States).

Having witnessed at first hand the ineffectiveness of Fort Barrancas Coloradas, De Galvez immediately began improving the defenses of Pensacola by removing its armament and siting them nearer the channel, in a better position to hit approaching vessels. He also built a fort at Siguenza Point on Santa Rosa Island, aware of what such a work could have done to prevent his own attack. Likewise he acknowledged the effective role played by Campbell's Native American allies and issued orders that they should be made welcome. The new commander of the post was Arturo O'Neill, while the civil law of

Above: *View of Pensacola Harbor. Despite the odds against him, Campbell had high hopes of holding out until relief came. The explosion in the main magazine left him with no option but to surrender to De Galvez. (British Museum)*

Louisiana (known as the Code O'Reilly) became the law in West Florida.

Honors were showered on De Galvez: Pensacola Bay was rechristened Bahia de Santa Maria de Galvez, and the victor was named governor of West Florida as well as Louisiana. In addition, he was ennobled as a *conde* (or count), receiving a crest for his coat of arms and the motto *"Yo Solo"* ("I alone") as his motto. Although plans to invade Jamaica were under way, De Galvez was forced to return to New Orleans by an uprising among the residents of Natchez, who had been encouraged by Campbell to overthrow Spanish rule, although agents of Congress were also at work, letting the British fight the Spanish and then claiming Natchez as part of the United States.

The rebel leader was a Swiss, John Blommart, one of several men given commissions in the British Army by Campbell in order to legitimize the rebellion. Blommart attacked Fort Panmure with 200 men, but the Spanish commander was expecting the assault and refused a summons to surrender. However, one of Blommart's men impersonated a Spanish messenger and persuaded the commander to yield up the fort.

Blommart promptly hoisted the British flag over the fort (instead of the Stars and Stripes proposed by the pro-Congress faction). He sent the Spanish prisoners to Baton Rouge, and placed Anthony Hutchins, a former chief magistrate of Natchez, in charge of civil affairs. However, the loss of Pensacola left the rebels holding the only British post in the region, and on hearing that Spanish troops were coming from New Orleans, many of the insurgents either sought refuge with friendly Indians, or simply went into the

wilderness, where many of them died. Campbell initially denied any involvement, but later admitted his role.

When De Galvez reached New Orleans, he studied reports of the uprising. Despite the various broken paroles, and the loss of (one) Spanish life, there were no executions and although the ringleaders were imprisoned, they were later released. With the Mississippi once more under Spanish control, De Galvez left for Havana, leaving his deputy, Estevan Miro, in charge.

Farther up the Mississippi, while De Galvez was assembling the force to attack Pensacola, the Spanish commander at St. Louis sent 120 Indians and militia to attack the fort and trading post of St. Joseph, on the St. Joseph River, some 200 miles east of the Mississippi. On February 12, they surprised the garrison and spent the next twenty-four hours destroying supplies. A more interesting outcome of the raid was the resulting claim by Spanish negotiators at the peace talks, two years later, to a massive belt of land east of the Mississippi, stretching from Canada to the Gulf.

THE CARIBBEAN

When Great Britain declared war on the Netherlands, a ship immediately left England with orders for Rodney to seize all Dutch possessions in the Caribbean. On January 27, they reached him at St. Lucia and three days later he sailed for St. Eustatius with twelve ships, having left six others to watch four French ships at Fort Royal.

On February 3, Rodney captured St. Eustatius, whose governor and garrison of sixty men were unaware that war had been declared. In addition to a frigate and five smaller privateers, Rodney seized 130 merchant ships in the harbor and warehouses packed with goods estimated at more than £3,000,000. The neighboring islands were also taken, and twenty-three merchantmen that had sailed three days earlier were pursued and captured. The Dutch flag remained over the port for some time and several more merchant ships were taken. When the news reached London, Rodney was raised to the peerage; in Amsterdam, John Adams reported that there was also rejoicing at the court of the pro-British Stadholder.

Rodney spent three months on St. Eustatius. He was furious with the inhabitants and decreed that all residents—including British and neutrals—were to be treated as prisoners of war, and that all property now belonged to the king, regardless of what it was or who owned it. (The French, however, were well treated, being sent to French islands with their household goods and house slaves.) All of the warehouses were destroyed or had their roofs removed and business records, which might have been used to file claims for compensation, were confiscated. More than 100 Jewish men were deported without their families, including one who was a refugee Loyalist from Newport and had already been robbed twice by Rebel forces.

At the time, Rodney probably saw an end to the financial problems that had plagued him most of his life, but in the longer term he profited little personally. His reputation was tarnished and he aroused much indignation in Europe by confiscating private property and imprisoning civilians. Ironically, he probably helped the enemy: despite his precautions, most of the goods were purchased at auction by French or Spanish agents for less than if they had been bought from the merchants of St. Eustatius. Most damaging of all was the accusation that the three months spent on the island had cost him the chance to defeat the French and allowed De Grasse—newly arrived from France—to slip into Fort Royal, from where he would eventually head north to the Virginia Capes. As a final cruel twist, the convoy carrying most of the prizes back to England was captured by the French, just off the Scilly Isles, and the French recaptured the island and subsequently returned it to the Dutch.

In April, De Grasse made plans to seize St. Lucia and in an action off Martinique, forced Hood, outnumbered, to withdraw toward St. Eustatius. De Grasse then landed 1,200 troops at the northwest tip of St. Lucia, but could not capture the fortifications and the British retained their important lookout post next to Martinique.

At the same time, De Grasse had also sent two ships and 1,300 troops to seize Tobago, off the coast of South America. Concerned by information that Rodney had left St. Eustatius and was taking on fresh water at Barbados, De Grasse set sail with the rest of his fleet to rescue them, on May 25. In fact, Rodney had heard of the French attempt to take Tobago and had sent six ships to reinforce the island's defenses, but they had arrived too late and had to flee from an encounter with De Grasse's entire fleet. Rodney then headed for Tobago and arrived on June 4, only to learn that the garrison had surrendered two days earlier.

On July 7, Rodney wrote to Thomas Graves (now commanding at Sandy Hook) that a French fleet might soon be heading north. He suggested that Graves rendezvous off the Virginia Capes with a squadron he was sending under Hood. Unfortunately, the dispatch was captured and Graves did not become aware of the situation until mid-August, by which time Rodney's poor health had forced him to return to England, handing over command in the Caribbean to Hood. At a crucial time, the Royal Navy had lost its ablest commander, leaving one of the least talented—Graves—in overall charge.

Below: *Capture of St. Eustatius (January 27, 1781). Despite its wealth, the island was only six miles long and three miles wide; Rodney's fleet can be seen in the harbour. (National Maritime Museum)*

Right: *Death of Major Pierson. The French troops under Baron de Roullecourt had seized the centre of St. Helier and were holding the governor of the island hostage when Pierson launched his counter-attack. Roullecourt was hit almost immediately and on his death, the French surrendered. (Tate Gallery, London)*

On August 5, De Grasse left Haiti with twenty-six ships and five frigates, carrying 3,200 troops under Major General Marquis de St. Simon. Adopting an indirect course, to confuse the British and rendezvous with reinforcements, he sailed north between Florida and the Bahamas. Five days later, Hood also sailed north, with all fourteen serviceable ships of the twenty-one left him by Rodney.

EUROPE

The year opened with a French attack upon the island of Jersey. Some 2,000 troops embarked in stormy weather and set sail from Brest under Baron de Rullecourt. Half of the transports were blown back into port and others were wrecked, but 800 men were landed on the island in the early hours of January 6. The main contingent seized St. Helier and captured the lieutenant governor, who surrendered the island; however, the senior officer of the garrison, Major Pierson, refused to acknowledge the capitulation and surrounded the French in the marketplace, where they surrendered when their own commander was killed.

Since the abandonment of the invasion of the British Isles, naval action in European waters had centered on the seizure of merchant shipping. One of the largest hauls was made by the French Admiral La Motte-Picquet who, on May 2, encountered the convoy bringing back the spoils from St. Eustatius. After driving off the naval escort, he captured twenty-two of the thirty merchant vessels before the appearance of eight British halted his spree. He sailed triumphantly into Brest with two-thirds of the booty Rodney had shipped to England.

The commercial war also impacted on the Netherlands, where the declaration of hostilities by Great Britain was met, quite literally, with dancing and singing in the streets (leaving Congress's envoy, John Adams, hopeful of securing Dutch recognition of the United States and, more importantly, a loan). However, the Dutch navy had only twenty ships—mostly old and small—and could not enter the English Channel to join the French and Spanish fleets. The early encounters were minor actions—usually ship-to-ship—and virtually all ended in victory for the Royal Navy, the exception being the single fleet action, which occurred in the North Sea.

On August 5, Vice Admiral Hyde Parker (one of the officers scolded by Rodney after the battle off Martinique) was escorting a convoy from the Baltic when his path crossed that of a Dutch squadron convoying merchant ships to the Baltic, just off the Dogger Bank. Both squadrons included old, decaying ships and some of Parker's vessels mounted fewer than their standard number of guns. After three hours, neither side had achieved an advantage, although Parker's convoy had got through to the English coast, while the Dutch convoy was forced

back into the Texel. In terms of numbers engaged, it was probably the bloodiest battle of the war, with almost 500 casualties on each side.

In December, a French convoy carrying supplies for the invasion of Jamaica left Brest escorted by De Guichen with twenty-one ships (five of which would continue on to the West Indies, while two more headed for the East Indies). Waiting for the convoy was Rear Admiral Richard Kempenfelt, with twelve ships and several frigates, a force that De Guichen should

have been able to avoid, had he not allowed his ships to get ahead and to leeward of the convoy (leaving it at the mercy of the British). Ignoring the warships, Kempenfelt captured fifteen transports before sunset, and, soon after dawn the next day, disappeared before De Guichen could bring him to battle. A few days later, a storm scattered the convoy, leaving only two warships and two merchantmen fit to continue, the rest seeking refuge at Brest. Despite his success, Kempenfelt's action led to criticism of the Admiralty in Parliament for failing to assign him enough ships to have secured a decisive victory in such an important mission.

Meanwhile, at Gibraltar, Vice Admiral George Darby had brought a convoy of 120 vessels, carrying a year's provisions for the inhabitants and the garrison, into the harbor without opposition. The Spanish were so furious that they began firing on civilians, as well as soldiers and sailors: in just six weeks 56,000 shot and 20,000 shells turned the residential areas

into a ghost town, forcing Eliott to hang looters on the spot. On April 20, Darby returned to England, taking most of the women and children, and the heavy bombardment continued throughout the summer as the Spanish used the good weather to advance their batteries and trenches closer to the Rock. They now had 21,000 men against Eliott's 6,000, but while they were planning their first major assault, Eliott attacked first.

At 2:00 a.m. on November 27, Eliott led almost half the garrison into the Spanish lines, achieving complete surprise. The Spanish abandoned their fortifications to the British, who spiked guns, demolished walls, and fired stores. As Eliott's men withdrew, they blew up the main magazine, scattering burning debris over a wide area. The Spanish set about rebuilding their siege lines and life for the garrison returned to the normal routine of death, damage, and disease (between April 1781 and January 1782, 122 men were killed, and 400 wounded).

AFRICA

In the eighteenth century, it took up to six months to sail from western Europe to India and the East, making it vital to have staging posts along the route. The first of these was the Portuguese Cape Verde Islands, off the west coast of Africa; next was the Dutch colony at the Cape of Good Hope; then, off the east coast of Africa, were the French islands of Madagascar, Île-de-France, and La Réunion. Île-de-France was essential for control of the Indian Ocean, but was, in turn, reliant on the Cape Colony for food. In addition to the major ports and bases, the British, French, and Dutch all had fortified trading posts along the west coast of Africa, from which slaves, gold, and ivory were exported to the New and Old Worlds.

With so many demands from the West Indies, North America, and India, the British had few ships or soldiers to protect their own possessions, much less capture those of the enemy. In 1779, the French had seized some of the British settlements in Senegal and the Gold Coast captured during the Seven Years' War. When the Netherlands entered the war, however, her possessions became legitimate military objectives. In May, a single British ship attacked the Dutch port of Commendal, but was forced to withdraw, having failed to find anywhere to land troops. Shortly after, several Dutch ships captured the British Gold Coast fort of Secondee.

On March 13, Commodore George Johnstone (who had little seagoing experience) left England with five ships, eleven smaller vessels, and several hundred troops, to capture Cape Colony. On April 16, he put in at Porto Praya to take on water and supplies. Unaware that the French had sent five ships after him, Johnstone allowed his captains to anchor wherever they chose, with no plan of defense and 1,500 troops and sailors ashore. At this point, the French squadron, under Admiral Pierre de Suffren de Saint Tropez, arrived, also seeking water and not expecting to encounter the enemy.

Suffren immediately decided to attack, sailing into the bay and anchoring his own flagship in a position to engage the largest British ship (both 74s, named *Héros* and *Hero* respectively). Unfortunately for Suffren, of his other four ships, one anchored so close to him that he could no longer fight his opponent, another lost its captain to a stray British shot and drifted seaward, and the other two failed to enter the bay. After an hour's fighting, Suffren headed back out to sea; Johnstone followed, but steadily fell behind until sunset found him some distance to leeward of the island and, with the troop transports unguarded, he decided to sail back to Porto Praya, while Suffren headed south.

Johnstone remained at Porto Praya for two more weeks, surrendering any chance of reaching Cape Colony before Suffren. When he finally arrived off the Cape, he found Suffren waiting for him, the French troops ashore and the defenses ready. After capturing five merchant vessels, Johnstone sent three ships on to India and returned to England. Suffren sailed on to Île-de-France, where he joined the Comte d'Orves. On December 7, they left for India, escorting a convoy of troop transports and supply ships (whose cargoes included presents from Louis XVI to Hyder Ali).

INDIA

The Comte d'Orves finally appeared off Fort St. George near Madras at the end of January. Coote, knowing that Hughes's squadron was wintering at Bombay, feared that the French might try to land troops, but D'Orves had none and also needed supplies and replacement items. He anchored briefly at Pondicherry, but when Hyder Ali begged him to put troops ashore, he refused and eventually returned to Île-de-France.

Coote was also short of supplies (especially meat) and in February he moved his army to Fort St. David at Cuddalore, where he was forced to wait five months before a shipment of grain finally arrived

from Madras. With many of his men sick, Coote had to deal with an attack by Tipu Sahib in early June, which he successfully repulsed. Coote then tried to raise the siege of Thiagar, which was surrounded by Hyder Ali's main army, but could not make any headway against the superior numbers of the Mysore army. Eventually, Hughes arrived from the Malabar coast, bringing provisions and two battalions, which gave Coote a stronger force with which to engage Hyder Ali.

At the end of June, Coote was ready to leave Fort St. David and march to Chillumbrum. Having failed to capture this town, he moved on Porto Novo, just south of Cuddalore, where supply ships from Madras landed more provisions for his men. Coote was aware that Hyder Ali was between him and Cuddalore, with a large army, but could gain no more information on his deployment, as the plentiful Mysorean cavalry controlled the countryside surrounding the British camp.

In mid-July, Coote once again took the field, quickly capturing Wandewash. Through August and September, his force—now over 12,000 following the arrival of more sepoys from Bengal—proceeded to capture enemy forts at Tripassore, Polilur, and Sholinghur. These successes restored British morale and prestige, but were not decisive and when ill-health forced Coote to return to Calcutta in October, he was no nearer to removing Hyder Ali from the Carnatic.

PORTO NOVO: JUNE 1, 1781

At 5:00 a.m., Coote's 8,500 men set off toward Cuddalore. He sent his enormous baggage train (guarded by two cavalry regiments, a sepoy battalion, and seven cannon) on ahead, keeping it between his main body and the sea, to avoid the coming engagement. The rest of his force marched out on to the plain in two lines, either side of the road. The first line consisted of two native cavalry regiments, three European and five sepoy infantry battalions, and thirty guns, under Sir Hector Munro. The second line, commanded by Major General James Stuart, had four sepoy battalions and twenty-six guns.

Before his army had covered much more than a mile, the enemy position was sighted and Coote ordered his men to halt, just within range of Hyder Ali's guns. As the men waited under the hot sun, they had to endure a hail of fire, to which they could not reply as they were desperately short of ammunition. Coote and his staff reconnoitered Hyder Ali's position, which included a line of redoubts to the west of, and cutting across, the Cuddalore road. His right occupied some high ground overlooking the road, and his left was just beyond it, in front of a line of sand dunes that ran north–south, parallel to the sea.

Coote estimated that Hyder Ali had around 60,000 men, many of them cavalry and including 620 Europeans, most of whom were French officers. Having ascertained that there was space between the dunes and the sea, Coote formed his men into columns and began moving first to his right, and then to his left, around the back of the dunes. With his movements concealed by the sandhills, he brought his first line of troops to an opening in the dunes opposite Hyder Ali's left rear, while his second line occupied some hills overlooking the enemy redoubts.

Once his artillery had moved into position, Coote re-formed his first line and marched out through the dunes, covered by fire from Stuart's guns, as Hyder Ali desperately tried to remove his own infantry and artillery from the now useless line of redoubts. As his men formed a new line, facing east, in front of the advancing British, waves of cavalry charged Coote's line, but were driven off each time. Hyder Ali then sent infantry and cavalry against Stuart's positions, in an attempt to turn the British left, but met stubborn resistance. The Mysoreans lost their commander, Meer Sahib, early on and subsequent attacks were broken up by enfilading fire from a small British schooner.

Meanwhile, Munro had continued to advance against Hyder Ali's new position, and forced the Mysorean infantry back. As they broke and ran, Hyder Ali, who was watching nearby, finally realized that the battle was lost and left the field. Coote moved forward to occupy the enemy positions. After two days' rest, Coote proceeded to Cuddalore.

1782–3

"An Army without the hope of getting back America should not stay in it"

MAJOR GENERAL JAMES ROBERTSON

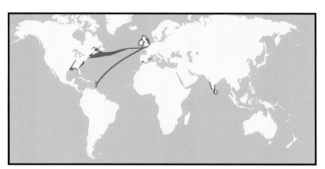

Observer v. Jack *(May 29, 1782). Many of the smaller ships engaged in the commerce war changed hands several times during the conflict: here HM Brig* Observer—*formerly the Massachusetts-built privateer* Amsterdam—*engages the American privateer* Jack – *already captured previously by the British and later retaken by the French – off Halifax.*

The American Revolution

204

NORTH AMERICA

The War did not end with the capture of Yorktown. Fighting continued around the globe—including North America—for another eighteen months, as the European protagonists looked for last-minute military and economic gains and jostled for the best bargaining positions at the peace negotiations. Indeed, in that respect the war became more earnest, especially for the British who were looking to offset the inevitable loss of the Thirteen Colonies and avoid being in the same position as the French at the previous Peace of Paris, in 1763.

There were still substantial Royal forces in both the Northern and Southern theaters, and of course there was still a garrison in Canada. However, the North ministry had been replaced and the emphasis was increasingly on a peaceful withdrawal.

In the South, these forces were now completely confined to coastal enclaves, although the strong defenses of Charleston and Savannah kept them relatively safe from any attack made exclusively by land.

An attack on Georgia by Wayne's Continentals achieved little at first, partly due to the perennial problem of enlistments expiring, but also because the numbers of Loyalist militia and Native Americans mirrored the problems Cornwallis had faced in the Carolinas. As the year progressed, however, the inability of the Regulars in Savannah to protect the back-country led to Rebel atrocities, which in turn encouraged desertions among the Loyalists. With Wayne still too weak to attack Savannah and the garrison too inadequate to venture out (both sides had only 3,000 men), an impasse existed.

Leslie had decided, nevertheless, to exercise his discretion to evacuate and the city was abandoned on July 11 (the delay being necessary to gather the 10,000 tons of shipping needed). This left the local Loyalists dumbfounded and angry, as they considered the position invulnerable; such a view was echoed by the Royal governor, Sir James Wright, who argued that 500 Regulars would suffice to remove Wayne and restore control. In fact, 1,300 troops had already been withdrawn from Savannah to reinforce the West Indies.

Greene, who was now having to impress men to keep up numbers, was still to weak to attack Charleston and limited his operations to the prevention of foraging by the garrison and the isolation of Loyalists. Charleston was evacuated on December 18 and around the same time a decision was made to abandon the Floridas as part of the peace deal (although a Spanish governor was not in place until June 1784).

Meanwhile, Carleton had arrived in New York City in May to relieve Clinton as commander-in-chief. One of his first acts was to try to resolve the Huddy–Lippencote–Asgill case: Huddy, a Rebel prisoner of war suspected of murdering Loyalist civilians, was hanged by Lippencote—a Loyalist officer, acting under instructions from the ruling Loyalist body in New York City. Washington retaliated by placing Asgill, a Regular officer, drawn by lot from the Yorktown prisoners, under arrest and threatening to hang him in retribution. Carleton pointed out that the far more widespread (and institutionalized) ill-treatment of Loyalists and the trial of Lippencote, despite ending in an acquittal, allowed Washington—who had been criticized by Congress, French officers, and politicians, and even officers in his own army—to release Asgill.

Carleton also discovered that he had been misled by the new government in London: he had been given *carte blanche* to attempt to find a peace deal acceptable to Congress and to inform Washington openly of his plans to disengage from North America (although Washington, perhaps overconfident after Yorktown, was eager to strike another blow and, conveniently or not, expressed doubts over British intentions).

Carleton, assisted by Admiral Robert Digby, considered various options for peace, including a political union similar to that existing with Ireland. However, in August, he learned that negotiations had opened in Europe with the distinct possibility of concessions on the thorny issue of independence. He immediately submitted his resignation, strongly suspecting that he had been removed from Europe to allow more favored generals to be promoted. His resignation was accepted at the end of 1782 and plans made to replace him with Grey, but peace was signed before this could happen. In the end, he was left to organize the departure of thousands of Regulars and Loyalists from New York City, a task that took almost a year due to the lack of shipping and the need to evacuate southern garrisons.

Washington was entirely dependent on a French fleet for any offensive action he planned for 1782. In July, he informed Rochambeau that he was prepared to consider attacks against either New York, or Charleston, depending on how late in the year the fleet arrived. He even considered an invasion of Canada, if that fleet brought more troops with it. Although his Continentals now numbered 13,000, he

Above: *Washington enters New York City. Following the British evacuation, Washington and the Continental Army entered New York City. (Anne S. K. Brown Collection)*

Above: *View of south prospect of New York. This would have been the scene during the British evacuation of New York toward the end of 1783. The last ships left on November 25, having completed the evacuation of the 10,000-strong garrison and over 7,000 Loyalists.*

was still 6,000 understrength and had learned that his enemy had more Americans under arms in regular formations than he had.

At the end of July, De Vaudreuil arrived from the Caribbean with thirteen ships and 2,300 troops. This gave an immediate naval superiority over the Royal garrison, which had only three small ships of the line and a few smaller vessels. However, the French believed that Washington was not ready for an all-out attack on New York and when a British fleet, under Admiral Hugh Pigot (brother of the diminutive Robert, of Bunker Hill fame), arrived shortly afterward, numbers became even. The French also learned that Carleton had sent more men to the Caribbean and De Grasse ordered De Vaudreuil to return. The plan to attack New York City was scrapped and Washington was forced to disperse his men in order to keep them properly fed and supplied. Nevertheless, in doing so he managed to organize a mock amphibious assault on the city, which impressed observers.

Thereafter, Washington's most serious problems were administrative ones and his battles were fought in Congress. His army went into winter camp at its new headquarters at Newburgh, where, in March 1783, discontent at pay and conditions surfaced among officers and enlisted men, following rumors that Congress wanted to discharge them before settling their dues and grievances. A group of officers, including devotees of Gates, circulated their demands in two pamphlets known as the Newburgh Addresses. Washington's quiet appeal to the officers and urgent warnings to Congress defused the situation, but there were also a number of smaller disturbances among recruits and departing veterans.

Following the signing of the peace treaty, in September, the Continental Army was demobilized. On December 4, Washington made an emotional farewell to his officers and then, on December 23, resigned as commander-in-chief in front of Congress. A month earlier, on November 25, the last Royal troops had left New York City; as an act of defiance, they had greased the flagpole in the main fort and their final view of America was of their bemused opponents struggling to raise the Stars and Stripes.

THE CARIBBEAN

De Grasse set off from Martinique on January 5, to capture Barbados. On the way, he anchored in Basse Terre Roads, off St. Kitts, on January 11, and landed 8,000 men. The British garrison withdrew to a remote corner of the island, but the civil population surrendered to him and, on January 20, he also captured the neighboring island of Nevis. The following day, Hood put in at Antigua, about fifty miles away, to take on supplies and 2,400 troops. Two days later, he set sail intending to round the southern tip of Nevis and be in Basse Terre Roads by daybreak on January 24, anticipating, because of the geography of the Roads, that he could attack and overwhelm the eastern end of De Grasse's line before the rest of his fleet could enter the fray. Unfortunately, the two leading British ships collided and the delay for repairs resulted in the French sighting Hood's fleet before it had rounded the southern tip of Nevis.

Dawn on January 25 saw both fleets standing to southward, De Grasse consequently assuming Hood was retreating. However, Hood cleverly slipped

between the French and the island and stole their anchorage: his rear engaged De Grasse's center, while his van and center anchored. With French troops still besieging the British garrison, De Grasse could not simply sail away. The following day, he twice sailed his fleet past Hood's, each ship firing in turn, with his own flagship, the *Ville de Paris,* remaining on station the longest during the first pass. The firing was so heavy that observers on shore could see nothing but flags and pennants above the smoke.

Hood held firm, but unfortunately, the troops he had brought were insufficient to help the garrison and De Grasse waited offshore for the matter to be decided on land. The British surrendered on February 12, at which point the French engaged Hood with shore batteries, and on the night of February 13, his ships cut their cables and slipped out to sea, leaving lights burning on buoys tied to their anchors. Although Hood had not been able to rescue the garrison on St. Kitts, he had bought time for Rodney to arrive from England with sufficient forces to equalize the British and French fleets, at thirty-six and thirty-five ships of the line respectively.

Franco-Spanish strategy for 1782 included an attack on Jamaica to be launched from Haiti, involving the forces of De Galvez and De Grasse, and a massive convoy of supply ships on its way from Brest (replacing the one dispersed by Kempenfelt off Ushant). Rodney knew of this plan and the imminent arrival of the convoy, but faulty dispositions around Martinique allowed the transports to enter Fort Royal on March 20. However, this still left De Grasse with the problem of slipping 150 merchantmen safely past Rodney's lookouts on St. Lucia and on to Haiti.

With the British so close to Fort Royal, it was impossible for such a huge fleet—which could sail no faster than the slowest merchantman—to gain any significant headway on its opponents. Consequently, De Grasse decided to hug the western coasts of the Windward Islands and then the Leeward Islands as he moved north. This would keep him in touch with friendly forces, as the French held Dominica, Guadeloupe, and St. Kitts, and the Spanish the island of Puerto Rico. He left Martinique on April 8. Rodney was soon aware of this and put to sea with his entire fleet. Around 2:30 p.m., his lookouts had spotted the French.

The last thing De Grasse wanted was a general action, but by the following morning it was clear that Rodney was going to catch him. He sent the transports to Guadeloupe for safety and then attempted to draw Rodney away from them by sailing into the channel between Guadeloupe and Dominica. In this way, he hoped to use the superior speed of his ships (due to their sleeker design) to evade Rodney, return for the transports and then continue to Haiti. However, during this maneuver, he saw that the eight ships of the British van (commanded by Hood) had outstripped the remainder of Rodney's fleet and was isolated. De Grasse could not resist such a tempting target, and sent half his ships to attack Hood.

The French passed the British van twice; wary, however, of the new British carronades (which were deadly at close quarters), they remained at such a distance that their own fire did no serious damage. The French resumed their course and over the next two days built up a substantial lead over the British, until two unfortunate collisions (one involving his

Above: *Action in Frigate Bay, St. Kitts (January 25–26, 1782). In a two-day action, Hood (attempting to relieve the besieged garrison) outwitted De Grasse, occupying the French fleet's anchorage after luring them out into the open sea. De Grasse attacked Hood's ships at anchor, but could not break the line. Unfortunately, the British garrison on the island was forced to surrender on Febuary 18 and Hood slipped away under cover of night. (National Maritime Museum)*

own flagship) left the *Zelé* badly damaged and forced De Grasse to send her back to Guadeloupe towed by a frigate.

Rodney decided to set a trap for De Grasse and lured him back by sending four of his own ships after the *Zelé* and another vessel, the *Magnanime*. De Grasse promptly bore down toward the damaged ship and ordered the rest of the fleet to follow. Rodney maneuvered his fleet into an orderly line and prepared for battle, recalling the four pursuing ships once he was ready. In contrast, De Grasse's line was in poor order, as he was not anticipating battle. More importantly, there was little wind (and that variable), making it difficult to maneuver, and De Grasse also held the weather gauge, which meant that he could not escape. The two lines approached on opposite tacks. The two lines approached on separate tacks but a sudden shift in the wind gave the British the opportunity to break the French line and isolate individual enemy ships.

Rodney, no longer young or in good health, did not attempt to follow up his victory. His ships needed considerable repairs to their masts and rigging and he remained off Guadeloupe until April 17, before heading for Jamaica. Hood went after the French, taking another four prizes, but criticized Rodney in the belief that greater vigor would have led to the capture of twenty ships and virtually removed the French navy from the Caribbean. De Grasse (the first French naval commander to be captured in battle) blamed his defeat on the poor spirit and inaction of his captains, contrasting them with the superior discipline, neatness, and order of the British (a fact confirmed by John Paul Jones, who was with the French fleet).

This was the last significant action in the Caribbean. On July 22, Rodney sailed for home, having been replaced by Pigot. The French and Spanish abandoned the idea of attacking Jamaica and De Grasse returned to England as a prisoner of war, his defeat at The Saintes having eclipsed his contribution to the victory at Yorktown.

EUROPE

In London, the North ministry was slowly losing power; Germain resigned on February 10 and, on February 27, the government was defeated on a proposition that the fighting in North America should be brought to a speedy conclusion and the war effort focused on the Bourbon enemies. In fact, North and Germain had long recognized this and had prosecuted the War accordingly, but were always handicapped by the knowledge that the king would not countenance independence for the Colonies in any form, which would have been an inevitable consequence of taking this strategy further.

Yet despite these chill winds of reality, many Loyalists and their supporters argued either for

Opposite page, bottom:
Capture of the Ville de Paris, Battle of The Saintes (April 12, 1782). Aided by a change in the wind that threw the French line into disorder, Rodney defied convention and broke De Grasse's line, isolating his flagship, the Ville de Paris. De Grasse and his 110-gun ship were captured, the largest prize taken by either side throughout the war. (National Maritime Museum)

THE SAINTES: APRIL 12, 1782

Despite his weak position, De Grasse trusted that the fleets would make a single, parallel pass—the French heading south-southeast and the British north-northeast—at a safe distance. At 7:30 a.m., the French van passed across the front of the British line, giving a desultory and ineffectual fire, but the British ship *Marlborough* fired the first broadside just before 8:00 a.m. De Grasse realized that his rearmost ships would end up being engaged by Rodney's entire fleet in succession, while his van and center were out of the fight. He decided to steer for the still water in the lee of Dominica, to frustrate Rodney's intentions to engage him closely, and twice made a signal to wear.

Unfortunately, just after 9:00 a.m. the wind changed and forced the French to turn slightly toward the British line, creating several gaps in the French line. To Rodney, this was an unmissable opportunity, but in order to take advantage of it, he had to break with traditional fighting tactics. He immediately broke his own line by taking his flagship, the *Formidable*, through the French line, and five more ships followed him; the vessel immediately ahead and the sixth astern of him also cut the French line, splitting it in three.

By now, Rodney's fleet was also in three groups, but had the advantage of the weather gauge. As they cut the French line, each British ship raked its opponent and the shock prevented the French re-establishing their line. At 11:15 a.m., Rodney signaled his leading ships, which had continued northward, to tack and at 12:30 p.m. ordered close action. The one-to-one fighting suited the British because of their superior rate of fire and their deadly short-range weapon, the carronade. Following tradition, the British aimed at the hull and the French at the rigging, so the French were better placed to maneuver in the light wind and at 1:00 p.m., they were observed heading to leeward in disorganized groups. No longer bound to keep the line, the British pursued them, although Rodney never gave the signal for a chase. In fact, he slackened sail on the *Formidable* and several captains followed his example.

De Grasse suffered very heavy casualties (probably well over 3,000), due to the British carronades and the fact that he was also carrying troops for the invasion of Jamaica; British losses were 243 dead and 816 wounded. Three French ships were dismasted and captured, then a fourth (a captured British vessel carrying all the siege artillery for Jamaica); and finally, just before sunset, the *Ville de Paris*, with De Grasse aboard, was taken. One of the prizes later blew up, killing 460 Frenchmen and the sixty-man British prize crew. Most of the French fleet escaped to Cap François, where they met up with the convoy from Guadeloupe; another six vessels arrived in May, having diverted to Curaçao.

greater effort—believing victory to be just around the corner—or else a more drastic approach (one German officer suggested laying waste the entire eastern seaboard for up to ten miles inland). Various newspapers announced that 50,000 men and twenty ships would recover the Colonies in two campaigns, although where these ships and men were to come from was not explained. Other suggestions included evacuating New York and focusing on Georgia and the Carolinas, effectively denying a very large (and economically very advantageous) chunk of territory to the enemy and retaining it for Great Britain.

On March 20, North resigned, having learned that the traditional Tory supporters, the country gentlemen, would no longer back him. Despite his personal loathing of the Whigs, the king was forced to turn to them to form the new British government, which they did under Lord Rockingham seven days later. The new brooms immediately swept clean, abolishing the American Department and replacing all generals and admirals who were friends of the North ministry—a move that led to embarrassment after Rodney's victory at The Saintes and forced the government to reward him extravagantly on his return. They had sent Carleton to replace Clinton with orders to reinforce the West Indies from the North American garrison and had advised him to tell Washington of the intention to wind down and evacuate. Rockingham died in July, but was succeeded by Lord Shelburne, who pursued a strategy of dividing (if not

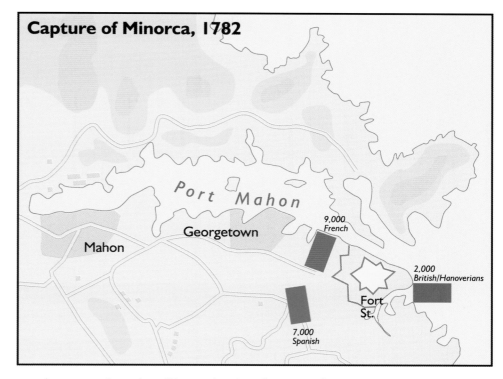

Capture of Minorca, 1782

exactly conquering) the Allies and using the natural suspicion of Bourbon motives among the Colonists to make the best of a bad situation.

Meanwhile, in the Mediterranean, the French had captured the last British outpost on Minorca during February, enabling them to transfer 9,000 troops to the siege of Gibraltar. In May, the Duc de Crillon (a French officer in Spanish service) arrived to take

command of operations and immediately began preparations for a combined land and sea assault. Throughout the summer, the Allied navies prepared their secret weapon—ten former line of battle ships modified as "floating batteries" that could withstand anything the British guns could throw at them and be able to move in close enough to destroy the defenses.

On September 11, two days before the assault, Lord Richard Howe had set sail from England with thirty-four ships, various other vessels, and over 100 merchantmen. After weathering heavy storms off

GIBRALTAR: SEPTEMBER 13, 1782

On September 12, the Franco-Spanish fleet assembled at Algeciras: in support of the floating batteries were over forty ships of the line, and numerous frigates, xebecs, and bomb-ketches (more than ninety vessels in all, carrying at least six admirals). For the troops there were special landing craft and over 300 transports. Such was the certainty of success that the Comte d'Artois, brother of Louis XVI, the Duc de Bourbon, along with an estimated 80,000 spectators, arrived to watch.

The assault began the following morning—a Friday—with the floating batteries, manned by 5,200 men, being towed into the harbor in a light northwesterly breeze. As they did so, over 160 guns and mortars in the Spanish land batteries opened a heavy fire. The floating batteries were anchored between 900 and 1,200 yards from the defenses and opened fire, initially with considerable effect, around 10:00 a.m.

The British, however, had their own secret weapons: one was an innovative gun carriage, specially designed by the senior artilleryman of the garrison, that could fire downward; the other was red-hot shot that not only pulverized its target, but also set it on fire. Having had to wait while the kilns reached the appropriate temperature (during which time conventional fire had had little visible effect on the enemy vessels), at around noon, the first red-hot cannonballs struck home. By 2:00 p.m., the *Pastora*, flagship of Admiral Moreno, was smoldering, while the largest floating battery, the twenty-one-gun *Talla Piedra*, commanded by the Prince of Nassau, was set alight. With a strong southwesterly wind fanning the flames, the fire was soon raging out of control. As the crew was ordered to abandon ship, the other floating batteries were also set alight, one by one, with the same consequences. The Allied land batteries maintained a constant fire throughout the night, but the seaborne assault was over and Eliott had boats sent out to pick up the survivors of the floating batteries. At dawn, seven of these vessels could be observed still blazing in the water; the other three had either been sunk or had blown up. Bodies and wreckage littered the water: it was estimated that over 2,000 Allied seamen had been killed, and another 350 captured, many of them badly injured; British casualties were around thirty dead and 100 wounded.

On the afternoon of September 14, large numbers of French and Spanish infantry marched down to the siege lines across the isthmus, and transports packed with more troops could be seen across the water at Algeciras. The defenders stood to, anticipating all-out attack, but the Duc de Crillon called it off at the last minute, believing it had no chance of success. During the two-day assault, the defenders, with fewer than 100 guns, had fired 8,300 rounds and used 750 barrels of gunpowder; the Allies had fired over 30,000 rounds from nearly 300 guns.

Left: *Defense of the King's Bastion, Gibraltar (September 13, 1782). Commanded by Admiral Bonaventura Moreno, the floating batteries carried 142 36-pounders at the ready and another 70 in reserve. Observers saw some of the crews being herded on board by cavalry prior to the attack. All of the batteries in the defenses had grates and furnaces for heating shot. Once the charge was loaded, a wet wad was inserted, then the red-hot ball and finally another wad to hold it in. The gun was then depressed and fired as quickly as possible to prevent the heat setting off the charge. (Beverley R. Robinson Collection)*

Below: *The firing of the Spanish battering ships during the night (September 13-14, 1782). The floating batteries were old ships, cut down on one side and with the other side reinforced with three layers of heavy*

timber and one of wet sand, to a thickness of three feet, and lined with cork. Overhead was an angled roof of cordage and wet hides, designed to protect the gunners from plunging fire by mortars and to deflect cannon-balls into the sea. The entire hull was served by a network of water pipes to combat fire, while bilge ballast provided stability. (Beverley R. Robinson Collection)

Above: *View of the north part of Gibraltar (September 13, 1782). Previous test firings of red-hot shot had met with great success, striking one of the main batteries in the Spanish siege lines and spreading fire everywhere. The Spanish responded with a two-day bombardment, in which their land batteries alone fired over 5,500 roundshot and 2,300 shells. (Beverley R. Robinson Collection)*

Above: *British vessels rescuing Spanish survivors (September 13–14, 1782). British gunboats under Captain Sir Roger Curtis cease offensive action and go to the assistance of the crews of the Spanish floating batteries. Over 350 men were saved as a result of this action. (Beverley R. Robinson Collection)*

Cape Finisterre and Cape St. Vincent, he entered Gibraltar harbor without a fight, the forty-nine ships of the Franco-Spanish fleet observing matters from their anchorage off Algeciras. They did attempt to follow Howe's fleet when he left to return to England, on October 19, but after indeterminate skirmishing off Cape Spartel they returned to port, leaving Howe to sail on in peace.

By October, the French and Spanish troops had withdrawn from the siege lines, to be replaced by militia, and Allied artillery fire had become sporadic. At the end of January, both sides learned that Great Britain had conceded Minorca and the Floridas to Spain, but had retained Gibraltar. The siege finally ended on February 2, after three years, seven months, and twelve days—the longest continuous siege in modern warfare—with British losses numbering 350 dead from enemy action, 500 more from disease, and just over 1,000 wounded. It was a failure that would severely limit the negotiating positions of the Allies in the peace talks.

Further south, in the eastern Atlantic, two British ships began seizing Dutch forts along the Gold Coast during the spring of 1782. An attack on Elmina in mid-February was repulsed, but troops were landed near Mouree in March. Within a month, they had captured Mouree itself, Commendal, Apam, Barracoe, and Accra, all of them major trading posts for slaves and ivory and a serious economic loss to the Netherlands.

INDIA

Aware that a French fleet was coming his way, and knowing that the French-held port of Pondicherry would not be able to support it, Admiral Hughes realized that the Dutch port of Trincomalee, on Ceylon, had the best harbor in the region. He decided to deny it to the enemy and dispatched a frigate to blockade it. He arrived with his fleet on January 4, and landed 500 sepoys and a similar number of sailors and marines. After fierce fighting, the Dutch finally surrendered on January 11 and Hughes returned to Madras, leaving a small garrison.

On February 15, the French fleet was seen approaching: it was now commanded by Suffren, the Comte d'Orves having died some ten weeks after leaving Île-de-France. Suffren had three 74s, seven 64s, two 50s (not including a British ship captured on the way), three frigates, and three corvettes; Hughes had two 74s, one 68, five 64s, and one 50, plus two frigates. Suffren called a council of war, but after nearly three months at sea, and with a large convoy to protect, only one of his captains advocated an attack, so he headed south for Pondicherry, which was held by France's ally, Hyder Ali. He knew, however, that he had to seize either Trincomalee or

Negapataam, the only suitable naval bases in the region and that to do so, he would have to fight the British fleet at some point.

After dark, Hughes put to sea and followed Suffren. During the night of February 15, the French warships became detached from the slow-moving merchantmen they were escorting, to the extent that, at dawn the next day, Hughes's nine ships had come between them, with Suffren's dozen ships about twelve miles to the east and the convoy almost ten miles to the southwest. Hughes immediately captured six of the transports (including the one bearing the gifts for Hyder Ali), put prize crews aboard and sent them back to Madras, while Suffren, forced to turn about, needed the rest of the day to catch up with the British fleet. By sunrise on February 17, the two fleets were six miles apart not far off Madras, with Suffren to windward and northeast of Hughes. The wind was light and northerly, and Hughes took the port tack and sailed east, anticipating that the wind would move into that direction (as it normally did in that part of the world) and thus give him a windward position.

On this occasion, however, the wind did not shift and Suffren ran before it, closing on Hughes. Suffren, still to windward, then steered a parallel course until his van was abreast of Hughes's flagship (the *Superb*), which was in the center of the British line. Suffren planned to concentrate his fire on the rearmost ships of Hughes's fleet, by having the three leading ships of his own fleet circle around the British rear, so that the last three British ships would have enemy on both sides, while the first four were unopposed, but unable to help. His captains, however, did not obey his orders: only two rounded the British line to present their opponents with enemies to port and starboard, while the other French ships failed to come within pistol range and thus caused less damage with their broadsides than Suffren had planned. After two hours, the wind eventually shifted to the southeast and both lines tacked, allowing Hughes's van to rejoin the action, but by now dusk was falling and the action ceased. Hughes sailed to Trincomalee to carry out repairs and then returned to Madras in early March.

Meanwhile, Suffren continued to Pondicherry, where the survivors of the convoy awaited him, and then sailed on to Cuddalore. Here he landed 2,000 troops to reinforce Hyder Ali who, despite a few minor defeats, had besieged the town. The fresh troops, combined with the presence of Suffren (who effectively cut off any chance of relief from the sea), forced the surrender of Cuddalore on April 4.

Back at Madras, Hughes had learned of the surrender of Cuddalore and that Suffren was now heading south, surmising (correctly) that his objective was Trincomalee. Collecting reinforcements for the garrison at Trincomalee, Hughes put to sea on March 29 and rendezvoused with two new ships from England the following day. Suffren, who had been cruising the area in the hope of intercepting these reinforcements, had given up and sailed toward Ceylon. On April 8, the two fleets spotted each other, both heading south in a light northeast breeze. Over three days, Suffren gradually caught up with Hughes, whose priority was to reinforce the garrison at Trincomalee. On April 12, Hughes formed his eleven ships into line on the starboard tack, just off the coast of Ceylon, and headed west. Suffren was to windward and assumed a parallel course until noon, when he signaled his twelve ships to bear down together. The last ship in his line was ordered to maneuver to the leeward side of the rearmost British vessel.

As the French came within range, the British opened fire. Unfortunately for Suffren, the ships at each end of his own line then altered course in order to return fire, rather than closing in, as instructed, while his flagship, the *Héros,* and three others moved to within pistol shot of Hughes's center. The action continued for three hours, hard-fought in the center, but less so at the van and rear, as the firing took place at much longer ranges. Eventually, Hughes was forced to wear by the proximity of the coast and Suffren followed. The two sides anchored about five miles apart, the British having lost 137 dead and 430 wounded, the French 137 dead and 357 injured.

Both fleets remained at anchor for almost a week in order to effect running repairs. On April 19, Suffren sailed for Dutch-held Batacalo, about sixty miles south of Trincomalee, where he received provisions from the Dutch and watched for convoys coming from Europe. The capture of several merchantmen enabled him to provision his fleet for six months' service and saved him having to return to Île de France. Hughes weighed anchor on April 22 (having had more damage to repair) and took refuge in Trincomalee harbor, where he spent the next two months completing his repairs. On June 23, he left for Negapataam, just south of Cuddalore, which had been a major port of the Dutch East India Company and, like Trincomalee, had been seized on the outbreak of hostilities between Great Britain and the Netherlands.

Meanwhile, Suffren had paid a brief visit to Cuddalore and had learned not only of Hughes's whereabouts, but also that he would soon receive more reinforcements from England. Suffren immediately sailed for Negapataam, hoping to engage Hughes before these arrived, and on the afternoon of July 5, Hughes saw him approaching and put to sea. Dawn the next day found Hughes in the windward position as the two lines sailed south-southeast on the starboard tack, both now eleven ships strong after a squall had forced one of Suffren's vessels to limp away. As before, the fighting was fiercest around the two flagships in the center of each line, and lasted for two hours.

At one point, the wind backed into the southeast,

and both fleets had to fall away—the British to starboard, the French to port—in order to keep the wind in their sails. However, four British vessels and two French (one of them being the *Brillant*, which had earlier dropped to leeward of the French line after being partially dismasted) turned inward toward each other. Suffren managed to rescue the *Brillant*, but the captain of his other ship, the *Sévère*, ordered the crew to strike her colors. The crew, however, continued firing and rejoined the French fleet (Suffren subsequently sent the captain home). Once again, both sides had suffered heavily, with virtually every vessel damaged. Hughes broke off and remained at anchor for twelve days until his ships were in a fit state to reach Madras.

Suffren returned to Cuddalore, breaking up his frigates and English prizes, and even taking timbers from houses on shore, in order to effect repairs. After a meeting with Hyder Ali, he once again put to sea and sailed for Batacalo. On July 21, he met a convoy bringing six hundred troops, supplies, and two ships of the line and two days later set off to capture Trincomalee, which would provide the dockyard facilities he so badly lacked. Although Hughes had anticipated this and had left a small garrison at Trincomalee, he had remained at Madras until July 20 and thus allowed Suffren (now with fourteen ships of the line) to enter the harbor unopposed on August 25, and land troops and artillery. Six days later, the garrison surrendered and Hughes arrived,

too late, on September 2. The two fleets fought their second action off the Ceylon coast, but it was indecisive.

After Hughes had withdrawn to Madras, he moved on to winter in Bombay, in order to avoid the northeast monsoons that usually arrived in November and December, and which rendered most of the ports and harbors on the east coast unsafe for shipping. Although Trincomalee offered safe haven, Suffren did not feel that it had sufficient resources to keep his fleet and, after rapid repairs, he moved on to Cuddalore (losing another of his ships in a gale) in order to encourage Hyder Ali not to abandon the city, despite the lack of reinforcements.

Having accomplished this mission, Suffren made for Sumatra (held by the Dutch), where he remained for about six weeks before returning to the Coromandel coast. He then sailed back to Cuddalore, after learning of the death of Hyder Ali, and made contact with his son, Tipu Sahib, whom he was able to promise more troops, having had word of a convoy bringing three ships and 2,500 men. This convoy arrived in March; the troops, however, were led by General Charles Castelau de Bussy, once a talented commander, but now sixty-four years old, suffering from gout and probably unfit to be commander-in-chief of all French land and naval forces east of the Cape of Good Hope. Suffren promptly escorted Bussy and his troops to Cuddalore to reinforce the garrison, then returned to Trincomalee, but with orders from

TRINCOMALEE: SEPTEMBER 3, 1782

Suffren had already taken most of his men and guns back aboard, leaving a garrison to hold the port. Early on the morning of September 3, he stood out of the harbor with fourteen ships and a frigate, to challenge Hughes's twelve ships (another having just arrived from England). Unfortunately, Suffren had not separated the faster and slower sailers among his fleet and the French were in disorder as they left the harbor.

Meanwhile, the British—who were to leeward and initially heading east-southeast—altered course several times to draw Suffren further away from Trincomalee. The wind—originally southwesterly—soon died away and Suffren, with the weather gauge, spent most of the morning attempting to reach a point where he could bear down on Hughes. The French ships were still in a ragged line abreast at 2:00 p.m., by which point the fleets were about twenty-five miles off the coast. At 2:30 p.m., Suffren signaled his fleet to bear down and attack, angrily reinforcing the order with a signal gun. Unfortunately, the guncrews of his flagship misunderstood and discharged a broadside (usually the signal for all ships to commence firing) and many of his ships opened fire prematurely as a result.

Confusion reigned as Suffren's fleet attempted to conform, seven ships ending up in a bunch ahead of Hughes's van and too far to windward. Suffren intended to use the same tactics as at Madras in February, with two ships taking post to leeward and leaving the last two ships in the British line with opponents on each side. However, the captains of the two vessels remained to windward of the last ship in the British line, and when the vessel ahead came to its rescue, the French ships were driven off. In fact, only three of Suffren's ships, including the *Héros*, came within pistol shot of the British line, as ordered. Not surprisingly, they bore the brunt of the French losses on the day, as they faced not only the fire of their immediate opponents, but also that of the ships ahead and astern in the British line who formed a semicircle around them. The British lost 51 killed (including three captains) and 283 wounded, spread evenly throughout the fleet; the French lost 82 dead and 255 wounded, with 64 and 178 respectively from the three vessels in the center, all of which were partially dismasted.

Suffren then ordered the seven ships of his van, who had overshot their opposite numbers, to use their boats to tow themselves around in the nonexistent breeze. Around 5:30 p.m. the wind shifted to east-southeast and they were finally able to move in closer; but it was too late in the day and the fighting ended around 7:00 p.m. To make things worse, when Suffren arrived back in Trincomalee on September 7, one of his ships ran aground entering the harbor and had to be destroyed. In Suffren's defense, four of his captains had been in action for the first time and when four others applied to return home due to ill health, he let them go.

Left: *Admiral Sir Edward Hughes (1720–1794). Although Hughes was at a numerical disadvantage in three of the four actions fought against Suffren in 1782, the overall quality of his captains more than made up for it. Suffren, by contrast, was forced to command men who either did not understand his tactics, or else actively disapproved of them. (National Maritime Museum)*

Right: *Admiral Pierre Suffren de St Tropez (1729–1788). Though not opposed by the Royal Navy's best officers, Suffren did well to challenge British naval supremacy in the Indian Ocean and was acclaimed by his opponents as well as his fellow-countrymen. (National Maritime Museum)*

Bussy to remain there in case he was needed back at Cuddalore.

Elsewhere on the subcontinent, Hastings repudiated the Treaty of Worgaom early in 1782, and sent troops from Calcutta to Bombay. This force soon captured all the Maratha cities and, in May, the Treaty of Salbai was signed, allowing the British to turn their attention to Hyder Ali and his French allies. Hastings ordered the Bombay government to attack western Mysore, in order to draw him away from the Carnatic. As this force moved down the coast, it collected more troops at Calicut and then attacked Hyder Ali from the west, forcing him to send badly needed troops from Cuddalore and elsewhere, under his son, Tipu Sahib, to confront the British.

Early in 1783, another expedition set out under the command of Brigadier General Edward Mathew, an officer of the East India Company. Mathew captured Mangalore, some 450 miles south of Bombay, on the Malabar coast, and then attacked the province

of Bednur, which was surrendered by its Mysorean governor, Aiyaz Khan, in return for being allowed to serve under the British. Once again, Tipu Sahib (who now ruled Mysore after the death of his father in February) rushed troops across southern India from the Carnatic, capturing Mathew and most of his men, leaving only Mangalore in British hands. However, with most of Mysore's army in the west, Stuart (who had replaced Coote when the latter returned to Calcutta in October 1782) assembled a force to retake Cuddalore.

Meanwhile, during the winter, Hughes had been reinforced by five more ships of the line from England and his fleet now numbered eighteen sail. He returned to the Indian Ocean late in the spring of 1783 and, in May, escorted supply ships from Madras to an anchorage close to the camp General Stuart had established just south of Cuddalore, at Porto Novo. Here, Hughes anchored his fleet, having cruised the waters to the south and found no trace of the enemy.

By June 10, Suffren had been informed of the threat to Cuddalore and two days after leaving Trincomalee, he sighted Hughes's fleet at anchor. Hughes saw Suffren approaching, dispatched the supply ships to Madras, and set out to sea. At this stage, neither commander wanted a pitched battle and with Hughes away from the coast Suffren was able to continue to Cuddalore, where he took on 1,200 men to replace his losses from battle and disease. His crews now at full strength, he decided to attack Hughes, hoping to inflict sufficient damage on the latter's ships that he would have to seek refuge in a major port to effect repairs. Stuart's troops at Porto Novo would thus be forced to surrender or withdraw.

For two days, the two fleets jockeyed for position in the light and variable winds, but on the after-noon of June 20, the wind finally became constant. Both fleets were heading north on a parallel course, with Hughes's line formed on the port tack, until Suffren straightened his line and bore down on the enemy around 4:00 p.m. Each ship engaged its opposite number in time-honored fashion until fighting ceased just before 7:00 p.m. The British had lost 99 killed and 434 wounded, the French 102 killed and 386 wounded, although the amount of damage to the ships themselves had been limited (and certainly not what Suffren had hoped for). Neither commander wanted to continue the action, least of all Hughes who, in addition to his battle casualties, had 1,100 men down with scurvy and was desperately in need of fresh water. He was forced to return to Madras and, with the supply ships gone, Stuart had no naval support and no provisions.

Suffren now had complete command of the sea, but when Hughes returned to Madras, he found that word had just arrived that the Preliminary Articles of Peace had been signed in Paris five months earlier. He promptly informed both sides and all hostilities in India were halted.

Not unlike Greene in the southern colonies of North America, Suffren had won no major victories, but had severely weakened his enemy and thwarted his plans. Like Greene, his orders were sometimes ignored and his battle tactics could have been better, but he had kept the Indian Ocean open to French convoys and had supported valuable local allies. Without a secure base of his own, he had captured Trincomalee from Great Britain, thereby frustrating British designs on the Dutch East Indies (though this philanthropy did not extend to returning Trincomalee to the Dutch!). Although he had not greatly weakened the British presence in India, he had increased that of France.

Below: *Battle off Negapataam (July 6, 1782). Soon after the two fleets had engaged, a sudden shift in the wind threw both lines into confusion. Suffren's ships had the worst of the engagement, suffering approximately twice as many casualties as the British. (National Maritime Museum)*

Halifax, Nova Scotia. *These views show the harbour and defences of the capital of Nova Scotia and the site of the principal British naval base in North America during the eighteenth century. In addition to having the only Royal dockyard on the subcontinent, Nova Scotia was the only region from which the king's forces could mount a counterstroke against the Rebels, as Howe proved when he withdrew to Halifax from Boston and later moved his army down to Staten Island. At the end of the War, Halifax provided a port of entry for many of the 40,000 Loyalists who fled the United States. Above, south view; below, north view. (National Archives of Canada)*

PEACE ...
WITH HONOR?

Most histories of the American Revolutionary War imply that peace negotiations began in earnest soon after the surrender of Lord Cornwallis at Yorktown, in October 1781. Such a view, however, seriously underestimates the level of diplomatic activity that occurred from 1779 onward—indeed, almost from the moment that the European powers officially entered the war. It would also be naïve in the extreme to assume that the Allies shared a common negotiating position—even in regard to something as apparently fundamental as the independence of the United States. Each participant had its own agenda and pursued a military strategy designed primarily to secure the objectives contained therein; unsurprisingly, when it came to negotiating a peace, that agenda took precedence over all considerations of loyalty, regardless of what any treaty might say. For France and Spain, the goal was the restoration of national pride at Great Britain's expense and—quite literally—the regaining of lost ground from successive conflicts dating back to the wars of Marlborough. Just as Washington's soldiers were at first puzzled, then offended, by Anglo-French fraternization at Yorktown, so the ambassadors—and later the peace commissioners—sent to the courts of Europe by Congress invariably found themselves acting alone, and were often forced to place more reliance on the good faith of their enemies, than of their allies.

WHO WANTED WHAT

The actual aims of each protagonist changed frequently as the war—and later the negotiations—progressed. As France's national debt grew, the primary war objective of weakening Great Britain by securing an independent United States became less and less important (despite being guaranteed in their treaty of alliance). Instead, French diplomacy focused on traditional areas of Anglo-French rivalry—the West Indies and India—and, somewhat ironically, in ensuring that the British kept Canada, to avoid making the United States too large and powerful for France to compete with economically. Naturally, all this was kept secret; however, there was one overt French objective that did cause concern, involving the vestigial fishing rights around Nova Scotia and Newfoundland that had been retained in 1763 when Canada was ceded. These rights were shared with British fishermen (which defi-

nition included the American Colonists, as British subjects), but the French objected to sharing them with an independent United States as well—especially as most American fishermen were based in neighboring New England—and argued that independence automatically forfeited these rights.

Spanish demands were clearer, if not quite so realistic: Gibraltar, above everything else, then exclusive rights of navigation along the Mississippi River, the return of the Floridas, and control of the Gulf of Mexico.

In February 1779, a Congressional committee had outlined the minimum requirements for a negotiated peace, which Congress then proceeded to debate for another six months. The terms included the Northwest Territory and all of the lands to the east of the Mississippi River, together with a total British evacuation of the above areas (Canada and Nova Scotia were excluded from these minimum demands, but would still be claimed). In addition, the United States wanted fishing rights off Newfoundland and Nova Scotia; and free navigation of the Mississippi. The French Minister to Congress, Gerard (who also represented Spanish interests), persuaded Congress to drop the fisheries claim, but failed to gain agreement to Spanish demands for exclusive navigation of the Mississippi. John Adams was sent to France to negotiate with British representatives, but only if they acknowledged the United States as an independent nation. After receiving a decidedly cool reception in France (partly through being confused with his radical—and anti-French—cousin Samuel, and partly due to the popularity of Franklin), Adams settled in the Netherlands in the hope of acquiring financial support and recognition.

BEFORE YORKTOWN

Throughout the war, and particularly after the official entry of France and Spain, various peace plans were touted around the courts of Europe, mainly via spies and double agents (the latter including Franklin's friend and assistant, Edward Bancroft). Thomas Walpole, cousin of the Opposition leader, Horace Walpole, had made peace overtures to the French court in 1780 (entirely on his own authority, apparently), while Paul Wentworth tried to open negotiations in Paris in 1780 and in Amsterdam two years later. Another French proposal—interestingly,

Below: *Charles Gravier, Comte de Vergennes (1717–87) was France's foreign minister throughout the period of the American Revolutionary War. His hatred of Great Britain made him one of the leading proponents of French involvement, and while the independence of the United States was in no small part the result of his prodigious efforts to bring France into the war, so too was the massive increase in his country's national debt—one of the principal causes of the French Revolution. (Musée de Versailles)*

not from Vergennes—came via Viscount Mountstuart, son of George III's confidant Lord Bute, and British ambassador in Sardinia. However, it included independence for the New England colonies, so the king promptly rejected it.

Then there was the shadowy "Montagu Fox," who visited the Netherlands, seeking French backing for an anti-government revolution in Cornwall. Despite producing a string of documents (later exposed as forgeries) purporting to indicate similar activities by members of the Parliamentary Opposition, such as Lord Shelburne, it seems likely that "Fox" was acting for Lord North and attempting to create mistrust between France and Spain. Certainly Vergennes, who was extremely mistrustful of Spanish commitment to the war, accepted much of the "information" sent via the French ambassador to The Hague, at face value. His willingness to do so can possibly be explained by the arrival of two British agents in Madrid, whose activities were typical of the diplomatic "shenanigans" that proliferated after 1779.

Thomas Hussey, an Irish Catholic priest educated in Spain, but working in London, had befriended a minor civil servant and playwright, Richard Cumberland, who was a friend of Lord Germain. Somehow, Germain was persuaded to send Hussey and Cumberland to Spain to sound out the chances for a separate negotiated peace between the two nations. Two matters definitely not to be discussed, however, were any form of independence for the American Colonies, and Gibraltar. Indeed, Cumberland was not to go to Spain until Hussey (who was actually a double agent working for both Great Britain and Spain and who frequently managed to be paid by both governments for the same mission!) had ascertained that the Spanish would not mention either.

George III's intransigence on the question of independence shocked most Europeans, who felt that a treaty leaving both sides in possession of what they held currently, offered the fairest solution. Depending on timing, this would have left the British with New York, part of the Carolinas and Georgia, while New England and the middle colonies would form the basis of the United States—although such a fragmentary solution would have been equally unacceptable to Congress.

The Spanish, unaware of these limitations, were happy to talk, now that the planned invasion of England had been postponed indefinitely. Leading politicians, including Prime Minister Conde de Floridablanca, were unenthusiastic about the war in general and, anticipating a deal that involved Great Britain giving them Gibraltar, felt no loyalty either to France or the United States (whom Spain, with an eye to its own imperial status, had no intention of recognizing as a nation). Hussey knew all of this, but allowed Cumberland to believe the conditions had been met, and Cumberland arrived in Madrid to find he and his family fêted by an enemy country, while at the same time, John Jay, the Congressional envoy to Spain, had to endure endless red tape and court protocol to see anyone of significance. Nothing came of the Cumberland negotiations, but—to the delight of Floridablanca—a stream of reports reached an increasingly concerned Vergennes.

At the other end of the diplomatic scale; Maria Theresa (mother of the French queen, Marie Antoinette) offered to mediate early in 1779, but with preparations for the Franco-Spanish invasion of England under way, she aroused little interest from either side—a situation that continued until her death, in November 1780. Empress Catherine II of Russia made similar approaches, both before and after setting up the League of Armed Neutrality, including a suggestion that each colony be given a free choice (either independence or reversion to the status quo). This would allow France to honor its promise not to make peace without American independence, and with the Continental Army having suffered several reverses (including the surrender of Charleston) and France near to bankruptcy, Vergennes happily accepted.

In early 1781, the British responded with a proposal for a joint Austro-Russian mediation, aware that Joseph II (who had succeeded Maria Theresa) and his chief minister, Von Kaunitz, both hated the French. France and Spain naturally demurred and were extremely upset when Catherine not only agreed to joint mediation, but also accepted Vienna as the location. Although horrified, Vergennes accepted the opportunity to secure a settlement that fell short of the onerous terms of the treaty of alliance and informed Congress that, where appropriate, France would handle United States interests (with or without their approval). He then briefed John Adams on the likely need to compromise over independence for all thirteen Colonies, but Adams refused to cooperate unless total independence and sovereignty were agreed in advance and a representative of Congress invited to the negotiations. Yorktown effectively ended this mediation process, which would undoubtedly have foundered on George III's intransigence over independence in any event (even without a crude British attempt to bribe the mediators with offers of land). Nevertheless, the process—together with concurrent events in Philadelphia—exposed the growing French "flexibility" over the issue of independence.

In June 1781, Congress had appointed a new peace commission, comprising Franklin, Jay, and Adams, plus Henry Laurens (then a prisoner in England) and Thomas Jefferson (who would never actually make it to Europe in time). The commission would work to a much less stringent agenda, with sovereignty and independence the only non-negotiable demands. These reduced conditions were largely the result of a charm offensive by Gerard's more popular successor, the Chevalier de Luzerne, who simultaneously persuaded Congress that all other issues—even national boundaries—should be negotiated at the commissioners' discretion, but only with the prior "knowledge and concurrence" of the French government. Congress was now relying on France to look after its interests at the very moment the French were considering a separate peace with Great Britain that would have divided the United States into several parts, some of which would remain under British control.

AFTER YORKTOWN

Until Yorktown, the peace process had quite deliberately focused on the European protagonists, ignoring Congress and its representatives almost to the point of ostracism. After the surrender, however, the situation changed dramatically. Despite the efforts of the King, North's government began to collapse and although a last-minute effort was made to negotiate with Congress, it was done in a way that would have courted rejection when Rebel fortunes were at their nadir, let alone at the moment of tri-

umph. Facing the inevitability of independence, the king became so depressed that he made plans to abdicate.

On February 27, 1782, the Commons voted to cease hostilities between Great Britain and its former colonies, and less than a month later, North resigned. As his successor, the king chose Lord Shelburne (largely because he, too, was reluctant to recognize the United States, despite having sympathized with the Colonies during the earlier taxation crises), but he commanded insufficient support to lead a government and stood aside in favor of Lord Rockingham, leader of the antiwar party. Rockingham immediately arranged for Richard Oswald, a Scottish merchant known to be sympathetic to the Colonists, to commence discussions with the Congressional peace commission.

At that time, only one of the five commissioners, Franklin, was in Paris; Oswald enquired about a separate peace granting independence in return for the United States withdrawing from the conflict and leaving Great Britain to continue the fight against her European enemies. In reply, both Franklin and

Below: *John Jay (1745-1829). Initially opposed to independence, Jay later became President of Congress and was appointed minister to Spain in 1779 (a curious choice, given his anti-Catholic writings in opposition to the Quebec Act). He later joined Adams in Paris for the peace negotiations and helped to persuade Franklin not to trust Vergennes. (National Archives)*

Vergennes confirmed that the Franco-American alliance would not permit this. However, although aware of French opposition to the idea, Franklin then privately suggested that Britain offer to cede Canada to the United States, partly as a goodwill gesture and partly to aid the compensation of both Rebels and Loyalists who had lost private property.

In May, Oswald was joined by Thomas Grenville (the son of George Grenville, creator of the Stamp Act), who was acting on behalf of Charles James Fox, a powerful rival of Oswald's patron, Shelburne. This duplication illustrated the divisions within the British government, caused by Rockingham's poor health and consequent lack of firm leadership. Both men were offering substantially the same terms, which included recognition of independence (despite the continuing opposition of the King), but only after the treaty was signed and ratified—not before or during negotiations. Equally, the American commissioners would not be acknowledged as representing a sovereign nation. Territorially, matters would revert to the position in 1763. The first two points were unacceptable to Congress and the last was unaccept-

able to France, which had entered the War precisely to reverse that status quo.

Preferring to deal with Oswald, Franklin (now reinforced by Jay) outmaneuvered Grenville, who resigned and went home in July. Soon after, news arrived that Rockingham had died and Shelburne was the new Prime Minister. Oswald still had no brief to accept Franklin and Jay as representatives of an independent nation, while for their part, the two Americans saw that they stood little chance of support on this issue from France, let alone Spain, which had still not recognized American independence, and for whom Gibraltar was the only issue of any interest. Indeed, the Spanish were becoming uneasy about the possibility of a new neighbor for their empire in the Americas, to the extent that Congress had recently been pressurized into ordering Jay to end negotiations then taking place in Madrid over navigation rights along the Mississippi River: even an offer of exclusive rights for Spain on the lower Mississippi and a mutual guarantee of all Spanish and United States territory in America, was rejected. Jay now learned that Spain not only wanted control of the lower Mississippi but also wanted the western border of the United States set 500 miles east of the river, a claim that appeared to have French support.

Franklin and Jay were still bound to act only with the knowledge and concurrence of the French ministry, and to be governed by its advice and opinion. However, shortly after a meeting with Vergennes in August, they decided to ignore this instruction if they believed that it compromised the honor of the United States. They overcame the problem of making a separate peace treaty by providing that it would have no effect until Great Britain had also signed a treaty with France. As the French court became increasingly uneasy about the Americans, Vergennes decided to use La Fayette, now back in France, as a go-between, to reassure them. Meanwhile, he sent his undersecretary, Rayneval, to England for a meeting with Shelburne that lasted several days. The evidence suggests that nothing underhand either took place, or was planned, but when the Americans learned of the mission, they sensed that Vergennes was looking for a separate peace.

With Franklin now *hors de combat* through illness, Jay took the lead and, without consulting anyone else, sent Benjamin Vaughan, a pro-American representative of Shelburne, to go to England to speak with his principal. Vaughan successfully convinced Shelburne that the start of negotiations was entirely dependent on acknowledging the independence of the United States. He also impressed upon Shelburne that the United States wanted a share in the Newfoundland fisheries, the Northwest Territory and all the land to the east of the Mississippi, and free navigation of the Mississippi. At the same time, Jay produced a compromise on the immediate recognition of independence, suggesting that Great Britain recognize "the Thirteen United States" (rather than

Below: *John Adams (1735–1826). One of the five men chosen by Congress in 1781 to handle the peace negotiations, Adams had been charged with securing a peace treaty with Great Britain two years earlier, but had fallen foul of Vergennes. A gentle, honest and soft-spoken man, Adams had defended the soldiers involved in the Boston "Massacre" and after the War became the first US ambassador to Great Britain and later President. (National Archives)*

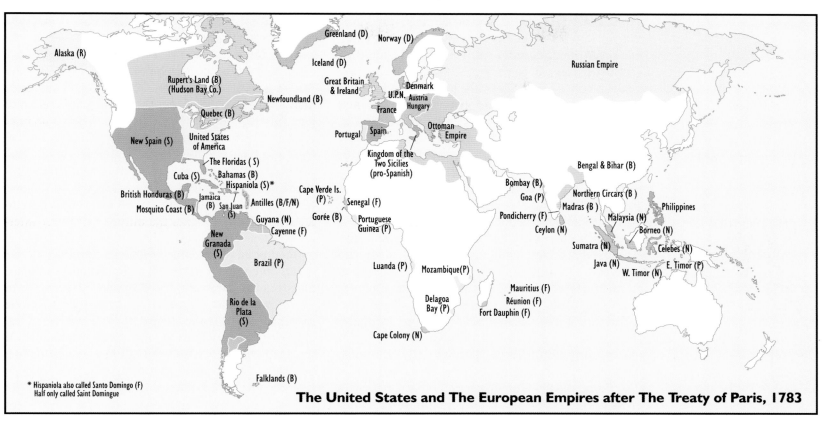

The United States and The European Empires after The Treaty of Paris, 1783

* Hispaniola also called Santo Domingo (F)
Half only called Saint Domingue

"the United States of America"—a term that left George III almost apoplectic with rage).

On September 19, 1782, Oswald received a new commission authorizing him to negotiate with the commissioners of the Thirteen United States and formal talks commenced on September 27, though whether they would have gone ahead had Shelburne known of the failure of the final Franco-Spanish attack on Gibraltar, is a moot point. In early October, Oswald passed on to London, with his endorsement, a draft treaty that had been put together by Jay and approved by Franklin. However, the atmosphere in London had changed considerably since Oswald had last been briefed, following the news from Gibraltar and the discussions with Rayneval. The Cabinet immediately instructed Oswald to remove the provisions relating to the Northwest Territory and certain of the fishing rights. All outstanding prewar debts were to be settled and all Loyalists compensated for any damage to, or loss of, property. Oswald, having effectively recognized independence, was strongly criticized and another representative, Henry Strachey, was dispatched to keep an eye on him.

Meanwhile, Vergennes, who was in constant contact with the British, was trying to speed up the peace process by having Luzerne suggest to Congress that it concede the claims relating to the fisheries and the Northwest Territory and agree to compensate Loyalists. However, Jay had been joined in Paris by John Adams; both he and Franklin, who had previously shown signs of becoming too close to the French court, supported Jay's draft. Shelburne, fearing that his weak government would fall, delayed the recall of Parliament until December, hoping to present it with a *fait accompli*.

Despite Shelburne's pressure, Jay, Adams, Franklin, and Henry Laurens (now released from prison) held out and the preliminary treaty was signed on November 30. It established the first boundaries of the United States, including the Northwest Territory and all the land to the Mississippi. Navigation of the Mississippi was to be free to Great Britain and the United States from its source to the Gulf of Mexico. Americans were given access to the fishing grounds, along with places to dry and cure their catches. Congress agreed to the payment of all legitimate debts and to urge all thirteen states to restore the property of peaceful Loyalists (though none ever did). There was also a secret clause that anticipated the possible outcomes of any Anglo-Spanish treaty. This allowed for Florida to be enlarged by moving its boundary with the United States farther to the north, should it be held by Great Britain at the cessation of hostilities, rather than by Spain.

The treaty was extremely favorable to the United States, granting all of its main demands—other than the ceding of Canada, which France would not have supported and which had never been considered essential—and creating a nation that occupied more than twice the area of the original thirteen Colonies, back in 1775. The ancestral homelands of thousands of Native Americans living in the Mississippi–Appalachian corridor, between the Great Lakes and the Gulf of Mexico, suddenly became "American" territory. This was doubly ironic: a war caused, in no small part, by British attempts to protect those lands had ended with the British simply handing them over—without the slightest consultation—to those claiming to fight for "liberty" and "freedom."

THE EUROPEAN RESPONSE

The speed and content of the Anglo-American agreement upset both Vergennes and the Spanish ambassador to Versailles, the Conde de Aranda (what their reaction would have been had they known of the Florida clause is probably best left to the imagination). The treaty would not be ratified until Great Britain had also agreed terms with France and Spain, but the positions of those two nations had been seriously—almost fatally—weakened. Franklin neatly sidestepped the Bourbon wrath by apologizing for any lack of consultation and playing on the need to avoid exposing any rifts between the Allies while negotiations with the British were continuing. In reality, the United States saw a much more secure future with its English-speaking cousins, whose liberal ideals and economic structure it shared, and was happy to court the protection of a Protestant British Empire as a safeguard against future expansion by Catholic France or Spain.

By comparison, the negotiations that took place between the European protagonists were highly complex. Spain would not make peace without Gibraltar, but this demand was complicated by the fortunes of war and the power of British public opinion on the subject. Indeed, Shelburne's government was almost brought down by the outcry that followed the disclosure that he and the king were willing to swap Gibraltar for one or two Caribbean islands.

However, the news of the defeat of the Franco-Spanish assault and the arrival of Admiral Howe's relief force now enabled the British to refuse even to discuss the matter. Vergennes could only encourage the Spanish to settle for retaining the Floridas, to which De Aranda agreed in order to speed up the peace process. Although this probably benefited Spain in the short term, it left Charles III and Floridablanca furious. Given their mutual animosity, however, De Aranda probably lost little sleep over Floridablanca, particularly once he had won over the king by explaining the problems of British public opinion and the consequent—and far more commercially important—gains Spain had made in the Americas.

On January 20, 1783, to the relief of the governments of all three nations, Great Britain signed a peace treaty with France and Spain. The French, to their delight, believed that they had achieved their principal aim of weakening Great Britain. The view from Paris showed that Great Britain had lost her North American Colonies and the remainder of her Empire had been shattered. In contrast, France had made some small, but valuable, gains in India; she had regained Senegal, which controlled the French side of the transatlantic slave trade (though the British had kept Gorée); they also regained the little islands of St. Pierre and Miquelon, off Newfoundland (captured by Britain during the war), and received nonexclusive fishing rights. In the Caribbean, she exchanged Tobago for Dominica. But France's former empire had not been restored, and many of the British losses were illusory, since few of them produced any automatic gain for France, and it would take time before those that did would begin to bear economic fruit. In fact, the long-term result, in terms of Anglo-French rivalry, was a pyrrhic victory: the war had left France with a level of debt that, combined with the exposure of French society to the ideology behind the struggle, would lead eventually to another, much bloodier, revolution within her own borders.

Spain had not regained Gibraltar and the damage to national pride over that fact alone made it difficult to assess the gains that had been made. The Spanish war effort almost certainly cost more than could be recouped from them. However, one major policy objective was achieved: the Floridas had been regained, which, with the retention of New Orleans, made the Gulf of Mexico virtually a Spanish lake. It also meant that whatever Great Britain and the United States might agree about the upper reaches of Mississippi River, for the final few miles—the most important as they led to the open sea and the rest of the world—both banks were firmly in Spanish hands.

The Netherlands, which never stood to gain much from the war, almost caused Vergennes more trouble than the British. In proportion to their size and economy, the Dutch suffered the heaviest losses out of all the Allies, a fact that generated a spirit of intransigence within the Staats-Generaal. Their demands included British recognition of the principle of freedom of the seas and the return of all captured territories in the East and West Indies, along with compensation for any private property damaged. Eventually, the Dutch found themselves isolated and gave in. The treaty between Great Britain and the Netherlands was the last to be signed between the European belligerents.

Despite having apparently lost the war—and a good many of her overseas possessions—Great Britain actually emerged from defeat creditably well. With so many important commercial contacts still based in London, the former Colonies soon resumed trade with the mother country. As a result, Great Britain now had the money and other resources—not least a much less overstretched army and navy—available with which to support other ventures.

Elsewhere in the world, little of value had been lost, while British power in India was now close to being unchallenged. Partly by good fortune, partly by pluck, and partly by playing on the uncertain friendship between the United States of America and its European allies, Great Britain had avoided the humbling so carefully planned in Paris and Madrid.

VICTORY
AND DEFEAT

Any discussion of the outcome of the American Revolutionary War usually focuses on how the British managed to lose. Yet this presupposes that Great Britain could possibly have "won" once the talking had stopped and the shooting had started. In contrast, all that was needed for Congress to succeed was that the British did not win—an outcome that appeared more and more likely over time, especially after 1778. The oft-cited British advantages of a professional army, the world's largest navy, larger population and vibrant economy, were more apparent than real, certainly in relation to a rebellion in North America. Long before fighting began, several politicians and military officers—not all of them sympathetic to the Colonists—had warned the king that a military solution was, if not impossible, then certainly fraught with enough imponderables and difficulties as not to be worth the risk.

POLITICAL CONSIDERATIONS

The first problem was Great Britain's ultimate aim: to restore civil authority (preferably to those friendly to the British government) and re-establish good relations—tricky enough in itself, let alone from 3,000 miles away and with a three-month time lag. This objective was based on the view that the overwhelming majority of Colonists were loyal and that they were being manipulated by a handful of radicals. Although much derided by modern historians, the North ministry could only act on what it knew, or was told by those on the spot; and there appeared to be much that supported this contention at the time. Perhaps the North ministry refused to accept the obvious, perhaps it just preferred to hear what it wanted to hear; yet it is hard to believe that men of reason and intelligence would have prosecuted such an expensive war—and one that made them increasingly unpopular—if they had known that there was no point. True, the rift owed as much to fundamental differences over the nature of the relationship between Great Britain and her Colonies, as to any specific act by the British government, or the ending of the laissez-faire attitude toward the law, taxation, and smuggling; yet, in 1775, the separatists were still very much a minority. In any event, the alternative—abandoning the Colonies—would have set a precedent, as well as leaving Canada, the Floridas, and the Caribbean exposed to future aggression.

The second problem was in matching the political goal with the military imperative of defeating Washington's army (although some moderate Whigs and Tories believed that a stalemate offered the best hopes for peace). There was a fine line to be trod between a comprehensive defeat that convinced the Rebels to give up, and utter humiliation—especially if accompanied by heavy losses—that would generate long-lasting resentment. Equally, anything seen as conciliation would have been interpreted as weakness, strengthening enemy resolve and offending those who had remained loyal (often at some personal cost).

Allied to the need to temper victory with mercy was the need to avoid excesses against the civil population (and not merely their persons—this was an age in which private property was almost as sacred as human life). In any event, laying the country waste would have been counterproductive militarily, as well as politically, since it would have deprived friendly forces of provisions and supplies. This would have made it difficult to keep troops in areas that had been reclaimed and gains would quickly have been lost.

Unfortunately, two factors conspired to ensure that this did occur. First, there was a strong lobby in favor of putting the Colonies to the sword and the flame, initially mainly among Royal Navy officers, but increasingly within the Army once an early peace had been ruled out and foreign intervention had weakened its strength in North America. Second, there was the natural propensity, given their impoverished backgrounds and lack of supervision, for the rank-and-file to plunder, exacerbated by the prevailing attitude that all Colonists were Rebels. Many loyal and neutral communities were driven into the Rebel camp, though it must be noted that acts of Congress and the Continental Army sometimes did the same. It is also worth bearing in mind that the worst excesses—those against people and not just property—were committed by Loyalists, usually avenging similar outrages committed by their opponents earlier on in the conflict. However, whatever their provenance (and authenticity), such acts provoked the inevitable Whig outrage on both sides of the Atlantic.

STRATEGY AND TACTICS

Another reason frequently postulated for British defeat is timidity and indecisiveness among the senior commanders, all of whom, at some point, have stood accused of mistakes, or lack of imagination. Such a view assumes that British defeats (in reality there were only two of real strategic importance in North America) lost the war; other factors make such a statement highly debatable. The same men also won some stunning victories, often against long odds, and the same accusations could be leveled at many of their opponents. Whatever their personal traits, the actions of these men were influenced pri-

marily by their knowledge of the enemy (or lack of it) and the level of local aid they might expect from Loyalists. Burgoyne's campaign illustrates that "action" did not guarantee success; indeed, it is hard to think of a British defeat that was not wholly, or at least partly, the result of "boldness" or incaution on the part of the Royal commander.

It has also been argued that those Royal commanders were not "the first XI." This is probably true—especially in the case of the Royal Navy, whose

Below: *Washington presents good conduct medals to Continental veterans at Newburgh. (Army Historical Society)*

appointments to the command of the North American squadron from 1779 were such that Clinton regarded them as a personal insult! However, it begs the question as to whether those who refused to serve on the grounds of health or politics would have done any better. Even this may be a moot point, as European intervention was anticipated from 1775, and as with other military resources, the best officers—again, particularly in the Royal Navy—were earmarked for the defense of the British Isles, or the Caribbean.

Political interference also influenced their performance and it is worth contrasting the position of the four Royal commanders-in-chief in North America (Gage, Howe, Clinton, and Carleton) with that of Washington. From the earliest, Congress tended to defer to him on military matters and, while he suffered as much from political intriguing as his opponents, he had a much greater say in the appointment of his subordinates. True, there was still some opposition to a standing army *per se*, but this was not personal and the benefits of a unified command within the Continental Army should not be underestimated.

Such lack of unity was reflected in the lack of a unified strategy among the Royal forces in North America. Initially, a simple blockade was considered, but there were never enough vessels of the right type (or of any type) to enforce this. In any event, a land-based presence was needed to defend Loyalist enclaves and the interior routes into Canada (not to mention providing victories to boost Tory morale at home and abroad). Once Boston was evacuated, the aim was to destroy the main Rebel army, after which, it was assumed, Congress would sue for peace. However, when the inconclusive victories of 1776 showed how difficult this would be, the "seaboard strategy" (seizure and occupation of as many as possible of the major ports throughout the Colonies) evolved.

Despite much subsequent (and contemporary) criticism, the seaboard strategy was partially effective and focused on British strengths and Rebel weaknesses. Three out of four Colonists lived within two days' ride—about eighty miles—of the sea and, in addition to international trade, most movements of goods between the Colonies themselves were by sea. The damage that resulted from Royal control of at least two, and usually three, of the major ports—Boston, Newport, New York, Philadelphia, Charleston, and Savannah—at any given time during the War, was not inconsiderable. In particular, control of the main ports in the South after 1779 isolated the Colonists from their most important market, the West Indies.

That said, such a strategy could never have delivered victory by itself, as it might have done in a European conflict, because none of the ports gave automatic control over the surrounding areas and only once—at Charleston—was a substantial garri-son captured at the same time. In the context of North America, the strategy also had two fatal flaws: the Army never had enough men to provide sufficient garrisons and the Royal Navy did not have enough ships to protect them from the annual arrival of the French fleet from the West Indies. As a result, the ports became virtual prisons for their garrisons and once the Allies learned how to cooperate, they were able to pick them off one by one.

Of the alternatives, Cornwallis's idea of seizing the back-country proved equally fallible, based as it was on the idea of hordes of Loyalists awaiting only the arrival of Royal forces to make themselves known, and the idea that a series of forts and other posts would be sufficient to control a region. In the end, it was the combined failure of his plan and the seaboard strategy that led to his downfall at Yorktown. More, perhaps, could have been made of the panic and economic chaos caused by the raids on the western and northwestern frontiers, but once again, ethics—and Rebel propaganda—proved a major barrier to increased use of this type of warfare. In any event, there were insufficient Regulars to back up the Rangers and Indians, and once Sullivan and others had visited similar destruction on the latter, enthusiasm for the war seemed to disappear.

In any event, after 1778, British strategy in North America was subject to the needs and dictates of a world war, in which Great Britain was outnumbered, both on land and sea, in virtually every theater of operations (except, ironically, North America). Prior to that date, the British had not only been able to focus completely on North America, but had been able to support that theater by stripping the defenses of the British Isles and the Caribbean. Foreign intervention dramatically reduced the naval resources available in North America (which, in turn, severely hindered the mobility of the Army) and brought a maritime dimension to the Rebel war effort that did not just counter the "seaboard strategy," but actually made it a recipe for defeat in detail.

Although the British defeated their European enemies more often than not in other theaters, it was the decisive actions of the French in Virginia, and the Spanish around the Mississippi, that finally convinced the British government it could not triumph (at least not over Congress and Washington—it was perfectly prepared to continue the struggle with France and Spain). Indeed, had European support been as committed, or as sustained, in other theaters—particularly Europe—the birth of an independent United States of America might also have heralded the death of an independent Great Britain.

One factor often overlooked in this context is that, unlike most colonial rebellions, the North American revolutionaries were almost exclusively whites of European stock, making it easier for them to appeal to the sensitivities and sensibilities of their European cousins. Despite the history of imperial rivalry between Great Britain and the Bourbon powers, the decisions of the French and Spanish courts to provide support must have been influenced by this factor; it is unlikely, given their own colonial status, that such support would have been given—or at least given quite so readily—to a revolt by non-whites.

Other supposed failings among the king's officers were arrogance and tactical inflexibility. Before Lexington and Concord, the Regulars did have a low opinion of the American as a soldier—an opinion widely shared by Americans and quite justified on the performance of the great mass of Provincial soldiery in previous colonial wars. There is no doubt that the events of April 19, 1775, came as a great shock and Gage was not alone in asking why the Colonists had never shown such spirit against the French, while Percy warned that anyone who still thought them cowards was in for a shock. It is certainly hard to think of a subsequent occasion when the Regulars underestimated their foes on the battlefield, although the Germans had to learn the same lessons the hard way at Trenton.

Tactically, there was little or no difference between the British Army and its Continental opponents. The Royal forces were invariably on the offensive in a country ideally suited to defense, with thick forests, ravines, rivers, rail fences or stone walls, and lacking the large flat open spaces in which to maneuver in line. While it might have been necessary to relearn the lessons of the French and Indian Wars, the Royal forces did so, and their tactics—including those of *la petite guerre*—were adopted and adapted by their enemies, not the other way around.

THE NUMBERS GAME

Aside from the political imperatives, there were two major restraints on the Royal commanders in North America, both of which inhibited strategic and tactical freedom: logistics and manpower. Of the two, logistics was the more fundamental, since it applied to whatever numbers of men the North ministry managed to deploy in North America. From the very start of the conflict it was clear that the Army would have to rely on the sea for all its equipment and supplies, particularly consumables (during the course of the war, this included several million loaves of bread, the condition of which after three months at sea is probably beyond the modern imagination). Given the time taken to cross the Atlantic and the actions of enemy privateers, much vital material did not arrive and the Royal forces must often have matched the ragged and starving image so often attached to their opponents.

In previous conflicts, logistics and supply had never been a problem, as the Colonists had supported the Army (much to their own profit, it must be said). Not only was that support not available, but now there were two armies competing for increasingly scarce supplies. Again, unlike the previous colonial conflicts, fighting moved away from the traditional land routes and waterways and—especially in the South—men found themselves in fertile, but completely uncultivated and often uninhabited country that could not sustain even relatively small forces. Such destruction of infrastructure and agricultural production as is inevitable in wartime added still further to the shortages faced by both sides.

In their seaboard garrisons, the Royal forces could be supplied by sea, to some extent, but items such as water, fresh food, and firewood had to be acquired locally and they never controlled enough territory around the seaports to guarantee those needs. To some extent, that problem was offset by the ability to offer hard cash to local farmers and merchants, whereas Congress was increasingly forced to rely on paper money and promissory notes. This was especially true around Philadelphia, though less so at New York, where geography allowed Washington's army to control civilian movements. Nevertheless, it did not usually take long for patriotism to give way to the more fundamental need to earn a living.

Even where supplies were plentiful, both sides had difficulty in distributing them by road, as there were acute shortages of wagons and draft animals (the latter being particularly valuable as virtually the only labor-saving devices available in North America at the time). As a consequence, both sides tended to operate close to waterways, which further restricted strategic options.

In terms of manpower, even before the war, Gage had appealed for more men, a sentiment echoed by each of his successors (except Carleton). Despite being the complaint of generals since time immemorial, the Royal commanders had a point. At no time did the Royal forces exceed 60,000 (including Germans and Americans), which sounds a substantial figure. However, it must be remembered that this was to subjugate—and then hold—an area of approximately 350,000 square miles (including the Floridas), while defending a similar area in Quebec, Nova Scotia, and the Great Lakes region. Indeed, it was doubly fortunate for the British that European intervention not only coincided with a slump in support for the Rebel cause among the Colonists themselves, but also served to increase the popularity of the war (and thus recruitment) in Great Britain.

As the more aggressive side throughout the war, the Royal forces tended to suffer higher casualties, while a diet high in salt and the warmer climate, even in the North, created large numbers of sick (typically twenty-five percent of effectives, but often higher in the South). Replacements had to come 3,000 miles, often falling ill themselves on arrival in the Americas. All of this was soon transmitted to Washington and his colleagues through an efficient civilian spy network and on more than one occasion Rebel commanders were able to anticipate enemy strategy, and even predict or eliminate specific movements, through their knowledge of enemy strength.

In contrast, although Washington himself thought the militia were a mixed benefit, consuming supplies and then disappearing just as the enemy arrived, nevertheless he did have recourse to them whenever he needed. They allowed his generals to field larger armies than the enemy, in an era when numerical superiority was beginning to count for more than quality of training. Their sudden appearance often threw the enemy into confusion and made forward planning difficult by concealing the actual numbers of Rebel troops available in a given area. They also provided something that the Royal commanders never had, namely the ability to control large areas permanently through intimidation, which effectively countered the growing reliance on Loyalists.

The real manpower problems for Congress lay with the Continental Army, riven by intercolonial rivalries and perennially short of men, even after the introduction of three-year enlistments. The Continental Army had to compete not only with high rates of pay in civilian life, as even unskilled labor grew scarcer, but also with the higher bounties paid by individual colonies to encourage enlistment in units designated for "home defense." The poor pay and conditions, and natural abrasiveness (one might even say "independence") of the rank-and-file, led to frequent mutinies, something that Washington's opponents never had to contend with. Desertion was another source of loss and although more usually associated with the Royal forces (especially the Germans), was actually far more common in the Continental Army. Those born outside of the Colonies (especially Irish Catholics) tended to be the least reliable and Washington was forced to halt the recruitment of British prisoners-of-war, due to the frequency with which they returned to their former colleagues. It was said that several minor engagements in the South were fought by armies composed almost entirely of deserters.

One of the great imponderables of the war is whether the British could have made better use of the human resources available locally and, if so, how might this have influenced the outcome. Recent research has cast doubt over John Adams's assertion that the population comprised equal numbers of Rebels, Loyalists, and neutrals (though it may have come close for the early years of the war); a more likely division over the course of the conflict was forty, twenty-five, and thirty-five percent respectively. However, this merely reflects political support—there is a huge difference between professing loyalty to a cause and risking one's life—as Congress also found.

The British "failure" to mobilize the Loyalists needs to be seen in the light of other factors. First, it took time—and scarce experienced officers and NCOs—to create efficient fighting units from scratch and the aim was to finish the war as quickly as possible. Second, all Americans were viewed alike, and their poor image as soldiers was applied indiscriminately (to which could be added the facility of inserting spies into the Royal forces). Few Loyalists would have accepted mass induction into the Army and few Regulars would have welcomed them. Third, the mass employment of Loyalists would have turned a rebellion into a civil war, leaving bitter feelings that would have hindered the primary British aim of restoring civilian authority—and normal relations—as quickly as possible. Equally, many Loyalists took the traditional American view that it simply was not their job and that war should be left to the professionals—it was, after all, what they were paid for. Finally, to be effective, Loyalist units needed the physical and moral support of Regulars, of whom there simply were not enough to provide this everywhere.

The same arguments apply to the other "local" sources of manpower—black slaves and Native Americans. Outside India, few European armies had experience of training non-white units at that time and, as with white Americans, there was a widespread view that they did not make good soldiers. In any event, Cornwallis and his colleagues rarely had the resources to overcome either factor, and the establishment of black units would probably have required the recruits to be sent hundreds or thousands of miles to a secure base, such as Charleston or New York, for equipping and training. In any event, the use of armed blacks would undoubtedly have hampered postwar reconciliation, as was shown by the response to Dunmore's actions in Virginia and the later threat to free and arm the slaves of Rebel plantation owners during the campaigns in the South (the South Carolina Assembly actually offered to remain neutral for the remainder of the war if the Royal forces exempted that colony from the threat). In reality, the employment of blacks as pioneers (military laborers) answered the most pressing local need, resulting from the paucity of combat troops and the inability of whites to cope with the Southern climate.

The use of Native Americans was equally controversial and, to some extent backfired against the British on two levels—first, in mobilizing pro-Rebel support on both sides of the Atlantic, and second in failing (despite considerable financial investment) to provide the expected military benefits. Despite their propensity for scouting and ambushes, the Native Americans did not take well to European warfare, and did not appreciate European discipline or the civilities of war. Given the successes of the raids into New York and Pennsylvania later on in the war, it is possible that better deployment along the frontiers would have done more harm to the Rebel war effort and drawn more of Washington's Continentals away from the main theaters of operation. However, their excesses (real and invented) handed Congress a major propaganda weapon—and no organization in the world was better equipped to make use of it.

Since the earliest days of political opposition to British policy, propaganda had played a huge part in

Whig strategy. While Gage and his successors were busy checking facts before submitting a considered report on recent events, a suitably lurid version was winging its way across the Atlantic to the Colonists' agents in London and friends in Parliament. A study of Whig pamphlets and speeches at the time, both in America and in Great Britain, shows typical court-room hyperbole, coupled with an amazing economy with the truth, particularly in misrepresenting the arguments and motives of the opposition. The use of the 3,000 churches in the Colonies, in particular, was a master stroke; the Whigs reasoned—quite right-ly—that few men would disagree with something told to them by a servant of God. Any clergyman attempting to present the Tory view from his pulpit was soon ousted by his flock.

Although Loyalists attempted to restore the balance later on in the war, by then their circulation was restricted to their own enclaves and they were merely preaching to the converted. The real damage—the creation of the idea of reasonable men fighting min-isterial tyranny and oppression—had been done. Indeed, the level of "innocence" portrayed eventually backfired on the Whigs: so much effort went into proving that the Regulars fired first at Lexington, that those militiamen who had traded shots with the troops found it difficult to make anyone believe them. At the end of the war, a Congressional commit-tee set up to investigate British "atrocities" (possibly the first ever war crimes tribunal) was forced to con-cede that most of the evidence they had heard was false and that what little remained too tainted to be usable in court.

It has been noted that the British assumption that the rebellion was the work of a few radicals, who had inflamed the masses with lies and misrepresenta-tions, is considered naïve, if not stupid, by modern historians. Yet the extent to which radical American Whigs "gilded the lily" and "got their retaliation in first" suggests they were fundamentally insecure with allowing the facts to speak for themselves. This, in turn, begs the question of who stood to benefit most from political—and, if necessary, military—con-flict between Great Britain and her colonies. British politicians and merchants are often accused of using the law to promote and protect their own financial interests, yet, given the benefits from the causes of the war and from supplying material to Congress, could not the wealthy merchants and lawyers of North America be accused of having similar motives?

CONCLUSION

Given the odds against her, Great Britain actually came out of the war in a surprisingly good position, both economically and politically, while her military failures were largely confined to North America. In fact, of all the belligerents, probably only the United States fared better in the long term. Once the peace

treaties had been signed, trade with North America soon resumed and was probably much less sporadic and much more profitable than it had been for most of the previous twenty years. Freed from the burden of administering and defending the North American Colonies, Great Britain finally saw them become a net contributor to her Exchequer—something that they had seldom been in the past (and possibly might never have been). In Canada, a rebellious and trou-blesome "English" minority had been expelled and replaced by Loyalists intent on creating a dynamic nation that would compete with their former home-land. Most of the British losses elsewhere in the world would be recovered—with interest—within a generation, while the empires of France and Spain

Right: The Declaration of Independence. "And for the support of this declaration, with a firm reliance on the protection of Divine Providence, we mutually pledge to each other our lives, our fortunes, and our sacred honour." Seven years after the signing of the Declaration of Independence, Great Britain recognizes its former Colonies in North America as a sovereign and independent nation. (National Archives)

were now in financial distress. But perhaps most importantly, British politicians had learned valuable lessons in handling colonial affairs that would make the second British Empire a much sounder and more successful institution.

It is worth considering the replies of one Captain Preston, a nonagenarian veteran of the action at Concord Bridge, to questions put to him by the historian, Mellen Chamberlain, in an interview in 1842:

Chamberlain: "Did you take up arms against intolerable oppressions?"

Preston: "Oppressions? I didn't feel them."

Chamberlain: "Were you not oppressed by the Stamp Act?"

Preston: "I never saw one … (and) certainly never paid a penny for one of them."

Chamberlain: "Well, what about the Tea Tax?"

Preston: "I never drank a drop of the stuff!"

Chamberlain: "Then I suppose you had been reading about the … principles of liberty?"

Preston: "We read only The Bible, The Catechism, Watts's Psalms and Hymns, and the Almanac."

Chamberlain: "Then what did you mean in going to the fight?"

Preston: "What we meant was this: … we had always governed ourselves and we always meant to."

H. CHARLES McBARRON

APPENDIX 1
THE ARMIES

The American Revolutionary War came in the middle of what is generally known as the "horse and musket" era of military history—a period in which European warfare was dominated by smoothbore muskets and cannon, and massed ranks of saber-armed cavalrymen. The tactics employed by the armies of the *ancien régime* appear ludicrous—even suicidal—to anyone familiar with modern warfare and the technology that accompanies it. However, those tactics had evolved over 150 years and—just as today—related directly to the weapons used by European armies, or rather to the virtues and limitations of those weapons.

The basic weapon was the infantry musket, an instrument of death that had changed in only two major respects since firearms first appeared in numbers on the battlefield, in medieval times. The first change was the introduction of a bayonet, which allowed the musket-armed soldier to defend himself; this had itself evolved from a simple knife, the handle of which was plugged into the muzzle, specifically a socket device that fitted around the outside of the musket barrel and enabled the musket to be fired when the bayonet was fixed. The other development was in the firing mechanism, where the matchlock (a piece of lighted cord that ignited the charge in the barrel by being applied to a hole at the breach end) had been superseded by the flintlock, which achieved the same result by striking flint against steel to produce a shower of sparks.

The musket was a smoothbore weapon, in other words there was no rifling inside the barrel to produce a spin when the bullet was fired. It fired a soft lead ball of anything from 0.69 to 0.75 in caliber and weighing about an ounce. Although the theoretical range of the musket was 150 yards—and a ball could still injure at 300—troops would normally open fire at no more than 50 or 60 yards. Anything more than 100 yards was a waste of effort, as a ball fired under normal circumstances would drop six feet over 120 yards.

Errors in loading, poor-quality powder, or a misfire (literally a "flash in the pan") meant that individual shots stood little chance of producing a worthwhile effect. For that reason, troops were trained to stand in dense ranks, shoulder-to-shoulder, loading and firing as fast as they could—from two to four times per minute—in order to produce a wall of lead. Even this relatively slow rate of fire could not be kept up for long, as powder residue often fouled the barrels, while the cumbersome loading process—involving up to fifteen separate movements—was tiring.

The need to operate in such tight formations, however, had obvious disadvantages: any form of movement required perfect timing in order to avoid confusion; and such bodies presented excellent targets for opposing infantry and artillery. Discipline was therefore essential and many hours of the soldier's life were devoted to drill. The normal speed of march was seventy-five paces per minute, which sounds desperately slow, but it proved no problem to maintain over rough, or uneven ground, making it easier to keep alignment and prevent gaps forming. Thus, the typical eighteenth-century battle consisted largely of groups of men on foot, moving about a battlefield slowly, but steadily, approaching the enemy, and then exchanging fire until loss of men, or morale, or both, caused one side or the other to flee. (It is worth noting at this point that bayonet fights were extremely rare, unless both sides had exceptionally high morale, or the side being charged had no means of escape.)

In order to maintain the cohesion necessary to move around the battlefield in good order, and to establish the *esprit de corps* that would keep men in line and obeying orders in the worst conditions, soldiers were assigned to a specific unit. In European armies, this would normally be a company of between 40 and 150 men and the company would provide the basic mechanisms by which he was fed, clothed, equipped, housed, and paid. According to the nationality of the army, a number of companies would form a battalion, and two (sometimes three) battalions would form a regiment—except in the British service, where only a handful of regiments had more than one battalion.

During the Seven Years' War, however, a new type of foot soldier had begun to appear on the battlefield. This was the light infantryman, who was the product of a need to have mobile units for reconnaissance and outpost duties. Very often, these troops were recruited from the wilder, more rugged parts of Europe, and were men accustomed to independence and living rough. Generally clothed in green or brown, so as to blend in with the background, and often armed with specialized weapons, they were a potent force if used properly.

The frontiersmen of western North America formed one such group; another comprised the German *Jäger*, or huntsmen. Both used a new type of weapon (at least new to the battlefield), namely the rifle. While the rifle had some impact on the American Revolutionary War, it was nowhere near as great as is often supposed—the weapon was never efficient enough, nor employed in sufficient numbers, to influence an entire battle. In fact, the weapon could be something of a liability, since the slower rate of fire (or rather of loading, as the rifling grooves inside the barrel quickly became fouled with burnt powder) and inability to accept a bayonet, left the rifleman vulnerable to musket-armed opponents. For that reason, riflemen were generally used for screening and outpost duties, and for skirmishing in front of the main battle line, picking off enemy officers and artillerymen.

Whereas the heathland of Europe and the dusty plains of India were perfect ground upon which cavalry could operate,

Left: *All armies in North America required large numbers of wagons and draft animals to move from one area to another, or simply just to feed themselves. Often animals were in such short supply that the only means of movement was by ship.*

the terrain in most of North America was not. In fact, the absence of cavalry was an important factor in promoting the looser infantry formations adopted in that theater of war. As a result, very few cavalry units were formed or sent to serve there, and those that were tended to be of a specific type—the light dragoon.

This category of cavalryman had evolved in the same way as the light infantryman—namely from the need for reliable men to perform outpost and raiding work. Closely linked to this type of soldier was the legionary corps, a mixed unit of infantry and cavalry proposed by the Maréchal de Saxe in his famous *Rêveries* that combined the solidity of infantry with the rapidity of cavalry.

By this time, artillery was also acquiring greater importance—and mobility—on the battlefield. Like the musket, the cannon of the day were smoothbore and fired various types of ammunition, but predominantly solid iron shot ("ball"), normally between 8- and 12-pounders. Again, like the musket, practical and theoretical range differed enormously and it was rare to open fire above 700 yards (if for no other reason than that it was difficult to observe where nonexploding shot fell—often the path of a ball could only be followed by watching where men collapsed). Guns tended to be placed on the flanks of an army, in order to enfilade the ground immediately in front of the troops, or else were positioned in the gaps between infantry units of the front line, to provide support in defense or attack.

Where the artillery did differ was in firing three different types of ammunition: solid shot, canister, and shell (also known as "common shell"). Roundshot was deadly against formed bodies of troops, knocking men down like skittles, and it was the weight of the roundshot fired by a gun that gave it its caliber (or example, 6-pounder). Canister was a tin container filled with musket balls and was used almost as a giant shotgun against massed targets; when fired, the tin broke up, releasing the balls in a fanshaped pattern. Shell was a hollow iron sphere filled with powder and fitted with a fuse cut to length so that it ignited the powder as near as possible to the target. Shell was more commonly fired from howitzers (short-barreled guns that fired at high trajectory and usually engaged targets hidden behind hills, buildings, or other obstacles), but the first firing of shells from conventional guns, in order to obtain extra range, was undertaken by British artillerymen during the Revolutionary War.

Engineering and medical services were also part of the military setup by this time, but drivers and others involved in what would now be called the "tail" of the army were still civilians and often created problems in terms of discipline under fire, on the march, or in camp.

THE CONTINENTAL ARMY

The enduring image of the American Revolutionary War is the humble, patriotic farmer, leaving

hearth and home to risk all for liberty. In fact, the brunt of the fighting was borne not by the militia but by the "Continentals"—regular soldiers who were drilled, disciplined, and taught to fight in the same way as their opponents. Although the Continentals did not win the war (the ultimate credit for that must probably go to the French and Spanish), they avoided defeat in a manner that the militia alone could never have done. Ironically, they came as close to the stereotypical image of King George's "paid hirelings" as the "Bloodybacks" themselves, and endured the same indifference, poverty, and ingratitude once they were no longer required.

In June 1775, Congress created the Continental Army by adopting the predominantly New England "Army of Observation" outside Boston, and appointing the Virginian, George Washington, commander-in-chief. The army was subdivided into territorially based commands—known as

Above: *Continental infantry in line await the enemy. The linear tactics used in the American Revolutionary War required discipline and good morale.*

departments—to handle administration and logistics more easily. The Northern Department covered Canada and upper New York; the Eastern Department took in New England; the Middle Department was responsible for the area from lower New York to Maryland; and the Southern Department covered Virginia, the Carolinas, and Georgia. In 1776, strategic requirements forced the

Below: *Light infantry storming a redoubt. Such troops were removed from their parent regiments and "converged" into special units that provided an army commander with elite shock troops or a dependable reserve.*

Above left: *An officer of a light cavalry unit. In the first years of the war Congress could not afford mounted units. Those that did exist were usually formed by the wealthier elements of society to emphasize their superior social status.*

Above: *Continental general and staff officers. Despite his reputation as a drillmaster, it was von Steuben's experience as a staff officer under Frederick the Great that proved most valuable to the Continental Army.*

Left: *Riflemen. Despite the popular image of such troops, it was usually the musket-armed infantry of the line who decided the battle. Toward the end of the war, Washington tried to reduce the number of riflemen in his army and replace them with musketeers.*

creation of two more: the Highlands Department guarded the stretch of the Hudson that was defensible against warships; and the Western Department protected the Virginia–Maryland–Pennsylvania frontier.

In 1775, the infantry comprised twenty-six regiments, or battalions, numbering over 20,000 men, plus a rifle regiment (the first truly Continental unit, incorporating men from several colonies). A further nine infantry regiments were eventually assigned to Canada and, apart from the riflemen, all personnel came from New England or New York. However, as other colonies raised long-term forces, the infantry arm expanded to 110 regiments—88 from the colonies themselves, plus 16 "additional" regiments (recruited from regions that crossed colony boundaries), and six "extra" regiments raised by Congress. Manpower was a permanent problem and, in 1778, various colonies absorbed the "additional" and "extra" regiments and then gradually reduced the number of regiments in their own establishments. In May 1778, a light company was added to each infantry regiment, and all light troops in the Main Army, under

Washington, were "converged" to form the corps of light infantry that stormed Stony Point and Redoubt 10 at Yorktown. In 1781, Congress faced reality and reduced the infantry establishment to fifty regiments and it remained at this number until the end of the war.

Infantry tactics emphasized firepower over "shock" action—the use of the bayonet—and from 1777 onward, manpower shortages prompted a shift from the regiment to the brigade as the principal tactical unit. In 1777, the Continental Army as a whole should have numbered 90,000, but there were only 16,000 infantry, instead of over 60,000. By February 1778, 20,000 men were enlisted, but through sickness and leave, barely one-third were available and 2,500 of those were on detached service in garrisons. In 1781, there were 10,000 infantry, but this was still 7,000 under strength.

There were no cavalry units until 1777, as they were considered an unnecessary luxury. However, political pressure compelled Washington to accept the creation of four regiments of light dragoons in 1777. Their role was to include intelligence-gathering and outpost duty, rather than shock action,

and in 1778 they were formed into a brigade under the Polish émigré, Count Pulaski. His resignation and the need to disperse the brigade because of the difficulty of finding forage meant that the regiments never served together again and reverted totally to reconnaissance, outpost, and escort duties, as Washington had originally envisaged. In 1781, the regiments were converted into four legionary corps by dismounting one-third of the men, and two "partisan" corps (formerly independent legionary corps that were half infantry and half cavalry) were added to the establishment. Some regiments reached a strength of 300, but seldom retained it for long.

The artillery arm consisted of one regiment and several independent companies in 1775, but increased to three regiments in 1777. These followed the European tradition in manning whichever types of ordnance—field, siege, or garrison—was required and units were rotated to ensure proficiency in all areas. In 1778, four 3- or 6-pounders were permanently attached to each infantry brigade, and a fourth regiment was raised. As a technical arm, the artillery needed a better class of recruit and was inevitably under-strength throughout the war. In 1781, there were only 800 gunners—over 600 fewer than were required.

Hospitals and medical services were also established, along with corps of artificers (tradesmen) and engineers (an all-officer unit, with individuals assigned to each department), and a permanent Congressional committee to oversee administration. At no time in the war did the British have anything to match Washington's Corps of Engineers (commanded by highly competent European mercenaries), or his specialist ordnance, quartermaster, and military police units.

The perennial bugbear was recruitment: in December 1775, with the enlistments of the "Army of Observation" due to expire, Washington had only 6,000 recruits for the 1776 campaign. Once the quota system was established, based on each colony's population, the existence of permanent regiments meant that colonies merely had to find replacements and not constantly raise new units. However, the sheer number of regiments diluted scarce resources and led to unhealthy competition for recruits. From 1778, consideration was given to a nationwide draft (i.e. conscription), but in the end this was left to the individual colonies. The quotas for 1780 amounted to 35,000 men, but even this proved impossible to achieve and the strength of the army sank year by year from a high of over 45,000 in 1776. After Yorktown, Congress looked for still more economies, but held back when Washington showed that the majority of Americans in military service were now Loyalists.

A typical recruit was in his early twenties (more than half were under twenty-two on enlistment), barely—if at all—literate or numerate, unskilled, unemployed, penniless, landless, and single. He rarely enlisted in the town of his birth, or even his place of abode, and his contribution to the "quota" often represented his only perceived value to the community. Enlistments varied from six months, or to the end of the year (July 1, 1776 for the riflemen), in 1775, to one year from January 1, 1776, and then "three years or the duration of the War". Unfortunately, the ambiguous wording of these enlistments sparked a mutiny among the Pennsylvanian and New Jersey troops.

On enlisting, the solider received a bounty from Congress; some colonies defied Washington and offered "top-ups" in order to attract more men and fulfil their quotas; there were also promises of land, while black recruits (who made up ten percent of the rank and file by 1778) were promised their freedom if they were slaves. Some men were genuine patriots, but most saw military service as a simple contract for the hire of labor. On the battlefield, however, the soldier fought for much the same personal reasons as his enemy—survival, self-esteem, peer pressure—rather than for abstract concepts such as liberty, duty, or country.

Socially, the officer corps was similar to its British counterpart and equally adept at taking offense and resigning, while some officers became too accustomed to independent action and often refused to take orders from anyone. The egalitarian approach of the rank-and-file electing company officers produced equal numbers of "popular" (i.e. easygoing) leaders and French and Indian War veterans. This sometimes generated astonishing levels of snobbery, for example when officers were seen performing their civilian trades, such as cutting their men's hair, or mending their shoes. As ever, political influence often counted for more than military experience in the early days, but Washington was permitted some say in who served under him and generally ended up with officers with whom he was happy.

It is difficult to establish how "patriotic" the officers were, as many had financial and political interest in the cause. As the War continued, the officer corps certainly grew in competence.

From 1777, the "native" officers were joined by foreign "advisers." Many were impostors and their demands for rank and pay caused resentment among their hosts, although a few—like the engineers Duportail and Kosciuszko, or Pulaski who briefly commanded the four cavalry regiments—provided valuable leadership in developing those services, such as the engineers, in which few Rebel officers had any expertise. One officer who has perhaps received too much acclaim is Von Steuben. Widely credited with turning the Continental Army into a redoubtable fighting force, it has to be said that it was not as bad when he arrived, nor as good when it emerged for the Monmouth campaign, as is often supposed. Nevertheless, he may be credited with establishing a system of drill and tactics that adapted the best European theory to the limitations and cultural diversity of North American practice.

Over the course of the war, the Continental Army became the first truly "national" organization of the United States, developing a bond that for the first time transcended colonial boundaries. In 1783, with the War clearly over, the Continental Army was reduced to eighty men at Fort Pitt and West Point. A peacetime establishment of 700 infantrymen and gunners, drawn from New York, New Jersey, Pennsylvania, and Connecticut was agreed for one year. This later became the 1st American Regiment, the first permanent unit of the US Army.

THE MILITIA

Those colonies with Royal Charters had the right to establish and maintain a militia, along similar lines to that in England. This required that every man between the ages of sixteen and sixty could be required to serve in the defense of the colony. In the case of non-Royal colonies, such as Pennsylvania and Maryland, different arrangements existed, usually involving groups of volunteers (often known as "associators"). As the colonies grew, it became necessary to place the first lines of defense ever farther west, in the less densely populated areas. Military operations in

Above: *Militia in line. Despite the preference of radical politicians for patriotic amateurs, Washington and others recognized that militia alone could never win the war.*

these regions resulted in long absences and caused economic hardship, so units of volunteers (or occasionally "drafts" of men from a particular area), would be sent to garrison remote outposts, or undertake raids into enemy territory. By the 1750s, such units had evolved into the famous "rangers" and Provincial regiments, but far from improving the military abilities of the militia, these quasi-regular units made local defense appear pointless. As the danger of French and Indian raids lessened, musters became the social events they had long been in Great Britain. Even at the height of the French and Indian Wars, some colonies used the presence of Regulars—and even the poorly disciplined Provincials—as an excuse to do nothing to defend themselves. This attitude explains the low opinion many British officers had of the fighting abilities of the militia in 1775.

After the surprise raid on the powder house at Charlestown, Massachusetts, the county of Worcester reorganized its militia, transferring one man in four—usually the youngest and fittest—into special units that could be ready at a minute's notice. The system was well received and had soon been copied throughout Massachusetts and, in time, the whole of New England. Eventually, other colonies developed similar systems, although the highly dispersed nature of the white population in the South meant that the militia there maintained an organization geared to the suppression of slave revolts.

Soon after the establishment of the "minutemen," another type of unit—the "alarm company"—was established. These incorporated the oldest and least physically capable men, who were

Above: *The vast majority of militia units were composed of infantry. However, there was a handful of corps that had traditionally trained and operated as gunners.*

only required to turn out if the enemy came into their immediate vicinity. In fact, the entire militia body received a considerable shakeup in 1775 and while its military capabilities may only have improved slowly, it soon became a much more serious and determined force. Typical of the standard expected was that of the New York militia which comprised all nonexempted males between sixteen and fifty, with men up to sixty impressed in times of danger (as, for example, the expedition to relieve Fort Stanwix). Each man brought his own musket and either a bayonet, tomahawk, or sword, with three pounds of powder and one of bullets. His section (one of four per company) met weekly for fours hours' drill; companies met once a month and regiments twice a year.

The "minuteman" concept was not new: similar organizations had existed as far back as the 1650s. However, the challenge of creating their own elite force, the concentration of experienced men, and the rooting out of Loyalists, boosted the morale of the militia as a body. The "minutemen" were given the best of the equipment available and, in stark contrast to the formation of detachments in the British Army (where drafting was an unmissable opportunity to remove the worst soldiers), the militia seems to have parted willingly with its finest. The individual companies were formed into regiments, with the men electing their company officers (who, in turn, elected the regimental staff and commanding officer). The dispersed nature of the population meant that company strengths and catchment areas varied and it was this, rather than the inflexibility of the Regulars, that led to units below company level—the platoon and the squad—acquiring a much

greater importance than they did in the professional armies of Europe.

By April 1775, the militia were by no means as inferior to the Regulars as is often made out and almost certainly had more combat veterans (possibly as many as one man in three) than their opponents, particularly among the company officers. Composed almost entirely of infantry—there were some mounted units in rural areas, and a few artillery units in some of the coastal towns and cities—they represented as much as twenty percent of the population of each colony, although ten percent was a more realistic figure if the local economy was to continue to function. Using tactics suited to individual, rather than collective, military skills, they harried Percy and Smith back to Boston and it was only the lack of a higher level of command that prevented the destruction of the British column. This shortcoming became even clearer when Boston was surrounded by 441 companies of militia the following day, and had still not been completely rectified by the time of the Battle of Bunker Hill.

As the war progressed, the role of the militia changed to one of supporting the Continentals on the battlefield and harassing the enemy away from it. As the conflict moved up and down the continent, various colonies raised "levies" who would serve for short periods in an emergency, such as Burgoyne's invasion from Canada. After July 1777, they were paid as Continentals while serving, but volunteers were still scarce and "drafting" was common. In general, their performance varied from awful (especially when acting alone) to adequate (usually when supported by Continentals or facing only Loyalist militia). There were notable exceptions, such as Bennington and the raids on Fort Ticonderoga that so inconvenienced Burgoyne, but arguably it is the rarity of such exploits that has made them so well known.

This "bulking out" prevented Royal commanders from assessing the true strength of their opponents and canceling perfectly viable operational plans. By the same token, the militia behaved in a highly pedantic manner, counting traveling time to and from mobilization points toward their thirty- or sixty-day "callout" periods and leaving the very moment the callout expired, regardless of enemy activity. When the enemy were not around, they were a liability, consuming scarce rations and failing to observe proper discipline in camp. However, they invariably fought well when defending their own homes, and some "levies" were considered good enough to be brigaded alongside Continental regiments.

By the end of the war, some militia contingents—especially in areas that had seen much military activity—contained men who had served together for years (even from the French and Indian Wars) as well as a growing number of former Continentals whose enlistments had expired. Some units were apparently christened "grenadiers" as an informal acknowledgment of their veteran status and the performance of the militia units attached to Greene's Southern

Army, and those at Yorktown, was creditable if unspectacular.

THE BRITISH ARMY

In 1775, the British Army had, on paper, 48,647 men, divided between two "establishments"— British and Irish—each being maintained by the relevant Parliament. However, actual numbers were far less: the Irish Establishment was supposedly 13,500 strong, yet had only 7,000 men; and of the 8,600 troops supposedly guarding North America, only 7,000 existed and noneffectives reduced that to nearer 5,000. As Cornwallis was surrendering at Yorktown, six years later, the Army had grown to over 110,000, of whom 56,000 were stationed in North America and the Caribbean. To this figure must be added 10,000 Loyalists and Indians currently under arms, 20,000 German Auxiliaries, the 40,000 militia in England and Wales, and another 20,000 or so in Ireland.

The infantry comprised three regiments of Foot Guards and seventy "line" regiments of foot, the latter numbered in order of seniority. The principal tactical formations were the battalion and the platoon (which were synonymous with the administrative units of the regiment and company) and all movement and firing were based on these formations. Over the course of the war, the line infantry expanded from seventy to 102 regiments (three more were "raised" after Yorktown by taking existing Loyalist units on to the British Establishment). It is worth noting, however, that of these, only one was raised between 1775 and 1778, when the war was solely with the Colonists. After France entered the conflict, recruiting improved: twelve regiments were raised in 1778 and another seventeen by the end of 1780.

Many of these regiments were raised "for rank", which meant that an appropriate person would undertake to recruit men, in return for a commission. The rank he achieved depended on how many men he could recruit. The king disliked this system, preferring to enlarge existing regiments, as he felt—quite rightly—that those "raising for rank" invariably appointed too many of their friends and relations to important posts within the unit, regardless of experience and ability.

Officially, there was no standard drillbook (and would not be until 1792) and it was not uncommon for several regiments participating in an exercise or a general's review each to carry out the same order in a different way, or at a different tempo (the Army had only begun to march in step in the 1750s). Initially, the rank-and-file formed up in a line three ranks deep. However, when the British abandoned Boston, in 1776, they also abandoned the three-rank line for one or two ranks. Over the course of the war, as numbers of Regulars dwindled and enemy superiority grew, it became necessary to cover more ground with the same (or even fewer) men, and a new formation, called "loose files", was developed, with spaces between each file and the rear rank men covering

the gaps in the front rank. This "thin red line" required discipline and coolness when facing denser enemy formations, but a string of victories—often against superior numbers—proved the efficacy of the system.

Throughout the war, *esprit de corps* grew by units being brigaded together for long periods: the 23rd and 33rd, for example, came together in 1779, fighting through the Carolinas and Virginia. As was customary in most armies of the time, the "flank" companies—grenadiers and light infantry—were detached to form "converged" battalions. This gave a commander an elite advance guard and reserve (Howe had four battalions of grenadiers and the same of light infantry), but stripped the battalions of their best men. In addition, their role almost guaranteed heavy losses that could only be replaced by further transfers from the parent regiment.

The other arm of the Army was the cavalry (the Royal Artillery and Corps of Engineers were not part of the Army proper), of which there were 6,689 men in twenty-eight regiments; four more were added after 1778. However, only two mounted units served in North America and both were light dragoons (as were all four of the new regiments). Their special duties—outpost work, reconnaissance, escorts, and messengers—involved greater individual responsibility; consequently, the men were better treated and regarded themselves as an elite. In both cases, the regiments were augmented by dismounted troops, partly as an economy measure and partly to create a legionary-style corps.

Unlike the infantry and cavalry, Royal Regiment of Artillery was controlled by the Board of Ordnance and made its own arrangements for almost everything (it even had its own customized naval transports). The regiment had emerged from the Seven Years' War with a reputation for innovation, aggression, and competence, but thirteen

years of peace had necessarily blunted these qualities. The four battalions comprised forty-eight companies, but as in most armies at the time, these contained only personnel. Guns (together with all accompanying vehicles and draft animals) were allocated according to availability and the task in hand. In the field, there was a move away from attaching smaller guns (normally 3- or 6-pounders) to each infantry battalion. Both Howe and Burgoyne set up artillery "brigades" to support each "wing" or division of their armies; however, in the South, the small numbers of Regular infantry and relatively few guns available meant that lighter pieces (6-pounders) were effectively being used as battalion guns.

Although a Corps of Engineers existed, there were too few to go around and those posted outside the British Isles were mostly tied up in fortresses, such as Gibraltar. Most of the "engineers" attached to the headquarters of senior commanders in North America were infantry officers with ability at mathematics and a talent for drawing (early in 1775, Gage had been forced to ask for two officers who could draw to reconnoiter the roads to Concord). Despite this, the individuals concerned appear to have performed adequately.

The Marines (they only became "Royal" in 1802) were the Royal Navy's private army, administered by the Admiralty and controlled by senior Navy officers, but ranked in the Army List between the 49th and 50th Foot. There were fifty companies, based either at Chatham, Portsmouth, or Plymouth, with detachments or individual replacements assigned wherever they were needed. The rank-and-file were volunteers and wore Army-style uniforms and equipment, but were trained to serve on warships and undertake amphibious operations. Service at sea also encouraged personal marksmanship and initiative, with sergeants often commanding the detachments on smaller vessels. Normally, there was no higher unit than the com-

pany, but in 1775, two battalions (complete with flank companies) were formed in Boston. After the evacuation to Halifax, they were broken up and dispersed around the fleet and the experiment was not repeated (although ad hoc "battalions" were formed from sailors and marines during the sieges of Rhode Island, Savannah, and Yorktown).

Compared to its European opponents, and even the Continental Army, the British staff organization was amateurish. As with transport and other logistical services, the staff was only organized at the outbreak of war. The two most important officers were the adjutant general and the quartermaster general. The former ensured that orders were passed down to regimental level, while the latter dealt with transport, supplies, organization, and movement. The last was critical, as it involved supplying maps, regulating the order and timing of the march, providing guides, and organizing billets at the end of each day. He was also responsible for constructing the order-of-battle from among the regiments supplied at the beginning of a campaign, ensuring that "posts of honor" were allocated properly and generally soothing military egos.

If the staff system was rudimentary, the transport system was even worse. Incredibly, few armies had military wagon trains, most relying on civilian contractors for the provision of wagons, draft animals, and drivers (as was also the case for food and clothing—and usually with similar results). Throughout the war in North America there were never enough wagons to move the Army.

Surprisingly, British hospitals were praised. Rush, a signatory of the Declaration of Independence, remarked favorably on the conditions (especially the availability of vegetables), adding that Rebel wounded were better off than in their own hospitals. It should be added that this was in 1777, when attempts at conciliation were still the order of the day and before the *Jersey* was brought into its infamous service in New York harbor (though to be fair, at the time of the worst conditions aboard that hulk, the Anglo-German garrison of New York was also starving).

Revolutionary folklore depicts British soldiers as illiterate, drunken criminals and doubtless some were. Others inevitably became so, in boring, hostile garrisons such as Boston. However, most were ordinary men—often skilled, sometimes literate—who joined primarily to avoid unemployment. Recruitment of enlisted men was almost nonexistent in the early years of the war and losses in North America in the campaigns of 1776 had to be replaced by "drafting" men from other units that were returning to Europe. Part of the problem was the poor image and treatment accorded to the soldiery. Taxpayers and their political representatives saw a peacetime army as an extravagance and a threat to liberty; only in Scotland was soldiering regarded as an honorable occupation and it is no coincidence that the only regiment raised before 1778 was Scottish (some proud Lowlanders refused to accept the bounty and the families of men who volunteered were looked after by their communities). Of the 15,000 men raised in 1778, two-thirds were Scots.

Eventually, the government was forced to offer short-term enlistments—three years, or the duration of the war, whichever was longer—instead of service for life. By the end of 1775, invalids and Roman Catholics were being recruited (despite the requirement for recruits to swear that they were Protestants) and by 1778 pardoned criminals and deserters were also acceptable. After 1778, recruiting became much more urgent, and the Press Act of that year led to the "able-bodied idle and disorderly" (voters and harvest laborers were exempted) being impressed in London and Scotland, to serve for five years. This produced few results—many men joining the militia in order to escape impressments—and it was immediately replaced by the 1779 Press Act, which offered better incentives to volunteers (for example, the right to set up in business after completing their service). This produced more recruits, since many of those expecting to be impressed decided to volunteer and claim the money. By 1780, 77,000 men had been raised; however, most of them had gone into the newly formed corps and the existing regiments were wasting away in various parts of the world.

In terms of the officer corps, the purchase system and patronage are often used to illustrate the faults of the British Army and Royal Navy, and to condemn a system that was actually far less rigid than its French or Prussian equivalents. The traditional English obsession with the threat of a standing army led to the officer corps being deliberately and inextricably tied into party politics. This, in turn, prevented senior officers, however wealthy, from progressing without patronage, while the inevitable quid pro quo condemned them to support policies or politicians they found personally offensive.

Despite the myth of the lazy aristocrat buying his way to the top, the officers of the British Army and Royal Navy were probably the most socially diverse in Europe. In fact, unlike most other European services, there was no requirement of "nobility" (denoted in France and Spain by the prefix *de* or à and in German service by *von*), just literacy, good health, good character, and adherence—at least nominally—to the Protestant faith. Even money was not essential: by the 1770s about one army commission in three had not been purchased and although their attempts to abolish purchase completely were thwarted by vested interests, the Hanoverian kings asserted increasing levels of control over the system. Commissions in the Royal Navy could not be purchased, but the senior service made up for this on the patronage front.

Socially, there were four distinct types of army officer: the titled aristocracy and landed gentry who, with the advantages of birth, money and "interest" (i.e. patronage), tended to reach the higher levels of rank; the lesser gentry, who lacked money and interest, but were often the protégés of senior officers and public figures; those from "army families" who were carrying on a family tradition, and who included many foreigners (chiefly Swiss, Germans, and Huguenots—all Protestant groups); finally, a surprisingly large number—around ten percent in peacetime—were former NCOs promoted as a reward for bravery or meritorious service.

Contrary to popular myth, the British system threw up as many geniuses as it did congenital idiots, with the great mass of the capable, average, and mediocre in between (as was the case in most nations). Finally, it is worth remembering that the senior officers who lost the American Revolutionary War emerged from a similar—in many cases, the same—society that produced the victors.

GERMAN AUXILIARIES

When news of the Battle of Bunker Hill reached Europe, three of the three hundred or so petty German princes offered to provide troops to augment the British Army (which, initially, were politely refused). There was nothing unusual in this: Great Britain had a history of using foreign troops to put down internal disorder in the British Isles (principally, the Jacobite Rebellions of 1715 and 1745) because of shortages of manpower in its own forces. Equally, many of the smaller states of Europe had no natural resources and no other source of income than their troops, and found such arrangements a useful way to keep their coffers filled and to reduce the tax burden on their own subjects.

During the course of the conflict, almost 30,000 men from six "German" principalities served in North America and without them—and several more thousand in the Mediterranean—the British government simply could not have fielded enough troops to defeat the Rebel army. These troops have become known collectively as "Hessians" (although only two-thirds were from Hesse-Kassel or Hesse Hanau) and had earned a reputation as monsters before they had even set sail from Europe.

These men, however, were not the first choice of the British government. The first request had been to Empress Catherine II of Russia, for the loan of 20,000 troops (on the basis that the Russians had no links with North America and, not speaking English, would be immune to enemy propaganda). Unfortunately, Catherine was still concerned about a possible war with Turkey, had little sympathy for the British government because of the clumsy way it had handled the colonial situation, and was under pressure from Frederick the Great, eager to pay Great Britain back for her perceived betrayal of Prussia at the end of the Seven Years' War. The next stop was the Netherlands, with whom the British had a longstanding treaty of alliance, and a request for the return of the Scots Brigade, a unit that had crisscrossed the English Channel often since William III had taken the English throne in 1688. However, the Dutch were wary of becoming involved in a conflict that might not only harm their commercial interests, but could also offend their powerful neighbors, the French.

These moves having failed, in August 1775, Colonel William Faucitt was sent to Hanover to collect five Hanoverian battalions (whom George III, as Elector of Hanover, had agreed to lend to himself) and was then to visit the rulers of Brunswick and Hesse-Kassel, whose troops had fought alongside the British in the Seven Years' War.

Below: *Hessian infantry. Over 30,000 German auxiliaries fought alongside the British army during the war.*

January 9, 1776 saw the signing of the first treaty, with Karl, Duke of Brunswick (Braunschweig-Wolfenbuttel), who agreed to provide a corps of 4,300 men trained, uniformed, organized, and armed along Prussian lines. In return, the Duke would receive from the British government a bounty of just over £7 per recruit. There was also what came to be known as a "blood money" clause, under which the Duke received a similar bounty for each man killed (except from disease), half that much for each man wounded, and one-third for any man disabled. If a unit was lost at sea or in battle, the British would pay the individual bounties, but also the cost of reraising the unit. In addition, the Duke himself would receive a subsidy of £11,500 per year until the corps returned to Brunswick, and a further £24,000 for each of the two years following their return. In all, the Duke sent 5,723 men to North America, of whom only 2,708 returned. Of the other 3,000, many had formed part of the Convention Army, which had been moved around North America to prevent rescue attempts, but also—covertly—to provide opportunities for the Brunswickers to desert.

Six days later, a second treaty was signed, this time with Frederick II, Landgrave of Hesse-Kassel. With a population of 300,000, Hesse-Kassel was probably the wealthiest of the minor German states in the Holy Roman Empire and had an army of 40,000 men. The principality had provided troops to Great Britain on five previous occasions and the British knew they were hiring some of the best soldiers outside Prussia. In return for a corps of 12,000 men (which was to serve only under Hessian officers), he received a bounty of over £15 per man on the same terms as the Brunswick treaty, but a subsidy of £110,000 per year until one year after the corps arrived back in Hesse-Kassel. There was no "blood money" clause, but the Landgrave's paymaster could pocket the pay of dead men who remained on the muster rolls until the next annual audit. Some 16,992 men were

Above: *Jägers. These rifle-armed troops were as deadly as their more famous opponents and generally much better disciplined and professional in their outlook.*

Right: *Brunswick dragoon. Only one of the German regiments sent to North America was a cavalry unit but even they operated dismounted because of the nature of the terrain.*

sent from Hesse-Kassel—a large number of them foreigners pressganged or kidnapped by the Landgrave's recruiting officers from other principalities. These genuine "Hessians" served throughout North America, always alongside British Regulars. Officially, just under 3,000 men deserted in North America, but up to 3,000 more either disappeared after being taken prisoner, or were discharged prior to leaving for Europe.

On February 5, the Landgrave's son, Duke Wilhelm of Hesse Hanau, agreed to supply 900 men, in return for £10,000 per year and a "blood money" clause. In all, the duchy supplied 2,422 men, who served mainly in Canada and under Burgoyne; only 1,400 returned home.

Then on March 17, a fourth treaty was signed, with Prince Frederick of Waldeck. All adult males in Waldeck were liable to compulsory military service (except for students) and the principality already had over 5,000 men in service with the Dutch army. However, the Prince scraped together another 1,225 men, for which he received approximately £140,000 (thirty crowns per recruit and an annual subsidy of 20,050 crowns). The Waldeckers spent most of the War in the Floridas and were captured at Pensacola, in 1781; and thanks to disease and battle casualties, less than half ever saw Europe again.

The last two treaties were signed in 1777. In February, Margrave Karl Alexander of Anspach-Bayreuth hired out 1,285 officers and men, for which he received over £280,000 by the end of the

War. In October, Prince Frederick Augustus of Anhalt-Zerbst, brother of Catherine II and ruler of one of the poorest states in Europe, agreed to supply 1,152 men from his tiny population of just 20,000. In return he received just over £100,000. His contingent served in Quebec City and returned home—minus 168 men—without seeing any active service.

Each of these contingents was paid at the same rates as British soldiers and received the same hospital and other benefits (such as they were), including free transportation to Europe for those disabled by wounds or illness. Except for the Hesse-Kassel contingent, the pay was given directly to the soldiers and not through the various princes, as the government wanted to ensure that none of it was withheld. Out of the six contingents, only in those from Hesse-Kassel and Hesse Hanau were the families of men serving in North America exempted from taxation.

An appraisal of the military value of the German contingents is difficult, as many of the troops spent most—in some cases all—of the war in garrison at New York, Rhode Island, or Quebec. German troops invariably served in forces ultimately commanded by British generals, and actions involving no British or Loyalist units were rare: when they did occur, however, it was invariably not a happy experience (as at Trenton and Red Bank; the only occasion in which a "mixed" detachment was commanded by a German officer was Bennington). However, they fought well at

White Plains and Fort Washington and the performance of the *Jäger* (whose shorter, but equally deadly rifles proved a match for their more famous opponents), was consistently impressive.

The trend among the German contingents was to follow the lead of Frederick the Great in all things military and this was true of the officer corps (at least in the main contingents, from Hesse-Kassel and Brunswick-Wolfenbüttel). The "native" officers usually came from the nobility, although this was a more elastic term than in most parts of Europe, due to the smaller populations of most German "states." The aspiring officer underwent fulltime professional training from the age of twelve or thirteen, either locally, or in Prussia. This lasted for about three years, and usually comprised schooling followed by a period of service in the ranks as *cadets*; alternatively, candidates could serve as a special category of NCO (known as *Junker*) until a vacancy arose. German officers were generally the most professional on either side, taking considerable interest in the welfare and organization of their men (the French—and still more so the British—were inclined to see such duties as beneath them and left such work to NCOs). Again, the size of the contributing states and their populations meant that a large proportion of officers were foreigners: one of the Hesse-Kassel commanders, Knyphausen, was born in Prussia, while Riedesel, who led the Brunswickers, was from Hesse).

Despite the reputations that preceded them, the German troops were soon recognized as human and German prisoners often received preferential treatment from the civilian population. Many worked locally while in captivity, some even married. They found much about America that both disturbed and attracted them and the thought that this was not their war was constantly at the back of their minds. It is not surprising that so many of them, having seen the life that could be had in North America, were not in a rush to go home at the end of the war.

LOYALISTS AND CANADIANS

The war was far from being the popular uprising of common perception. It is possible that up to thirty percent of the two million white Americans were at least passively loyal, and as many as 25,000 may have served alongside the Regulars throughout the conflict. Unsure of what to do with them, or how to use them, the British government and the Royal commanders in North America first left them exposed for too long, and then placed too much reliance on them.

In addition, throughout the conflict, Loyalists showed a peculiar inability to organize themselves. In part, this was the result of lack of support from official sources and intimidation by the Sons of Liberty and other pro-Whig groups. However, it perhaps owes something to the diversity of circumstances that led people to become Loyalists. Some were office holders, whose income was at stake; other "economic" Loyalists had major contracts with the British government (interestingly, those who did all became Loyalists, whereas those who had once had contracts but had lost them all became Rebels). There were those who accepted Parliament's right to tax the Colonies; those who believed in monarchy, or who feared God and honored the King; and those whose support was determined by family, friends, or enemies.

Loyal associations were formed in virtually every part of the Thirteen Colonies as soon as open resistance first appeared, and Gage, and later Howe, were inundated with requests for commissions to raise Provincial regiments. They were also asked for assistance, in the form of detachments of Regulars, to provide support until proper units could be organized, but with a shortage of troops everywhere and official reticence toward using Loyalists, nothing happened. As a result, many Loyalist groups were defeated and dispersed and many, particularly in the South, never forgot this "betrayal" by the authorities. Looting and plundering by British troops in New York and New Jersey cooled Loyalist enthusiasm there, also, and by the end of 1776, less than 3,000 Provincials were under arms. Three years later the figure was 8,000.

From the end of 1775, Loyalists were permitted to raise Provincial regiments for rank, as happened in Great Britain. The most productive areas for recruiting were the frontiers, despite the supposedly "independent" nature of those living there. However, many of them were former soldiers who had been given grants of land after the French and Indian Wars, or else were social or religious minorities, who frequently found themselves persecuted by the supporters of liberty (late in the War, a regiment was formed from Irish Catholics and another of former Jacobites). Others were tenants of benign landowners and formed units that were practically feudal levies, such as Johnson's Royal New York Regiment.

It is estimated that New York alone supplied 15,000 men for Provincial regiments (including nine complete regiments, several smaller corps, and much of the manpower for two other units) and another 8,000 militia. The remaining colonies furnished a similar number of Loyalists between them, although all of these figures probably include some duplication (as do the corresponding figures for the Continental Army and Rebel militias). In contrast, New York provided just four infantry regiments and two artillery companies for the Continental Army.

No fewer than sixty-nine Loyalist regiments were raised (or were at least subjects of serious recruitment attemps) during the course of the War. Over twenty of these corps saw action and took the field in strengths ranging from 200 to 500 men; in fact, almost two-thirds of all Loyalists who bore arms served in these units.

In May 1779, a new American Establishment was formed, with the aim of providing parity of service conditions and pay for Loyalist officers. At the end of the war, all five regiments were taken on to the British establishment. The majority of the units formed were infantry regiments, organized and trained in the same fashion as the Regulars, although cavalry and pioneer units also existed (but strangely no artillery). There were, too, smaller units of Rangers who operated in conjunction with the Indian tribes. However, the best units were the legionary corps commanded by two Regular officers, Banastre Tarleton and John Graves Simcoe. Simcoe's corps, The Queen's Rangers, had probably the best combat record on either side and enjoyed a brilliant reputation for its work in scouting and raiding, without attracting the odium associated with the vicious British Legion.

In addition to the permanent organizations, Loyalist militia were formed in almost every colony, with about as much success as the Rebel militia. In fact, the majority of Loyalist militias seem to have been concerned purely with obtaining retribution for past atrocities by their opponents.

After the war, 40,000 Loyalists fled to Canada and are widely credited to this day with establishing the economy and social fabric of that nation. In all, over 100,000 Americans fled the Thirteen Colonies, producing such a drain on the professions that Congress was forced to offer amnesties and coerce the more reluctant states to accept some of them back. All those who left obviously abandoned homes, and often personal property as well. The British government paid out in excess of £3.3 million in compensation to over 4,000 Loyalists who submitted claims; however, more than forty percent of those claimed less than £500 and only seven percent more than £5,000. Given that the vast majority of Loyalists clearly never bothered to claim at all, this suggests that the Tories were far from being the wealthy, Royal "placemen" and bureaucrats of popular history. In fact, half of those who claimed listed their occupation as "farmer" and another thirty percent were shopkeepers or artisans—both groups traditionally associated with the Rebel cause.

In Canada, there were 75,000 French-speaking Canadians and 3,000 English colonists; and both sides attempted—in vain—to secure the martial aid of the first group. Although a number of former French soldiers joined the Rebel army, the majority of French-speaking inhabitants wanted nothing to do with the heretics from the far end of Lake Champlain, even if they were not all that disposed toward fighting for King George. Most followed the lead of their *seigneurs* and priests in opposing the invasion passively and it was largely due to the mishandling of civilian relations by the Rebels that Carleton was able to raise eleven "French" companies of Quebec militia to defend the city against Arnold and Montgomery. Given the pro-Rebel sympathies of most of the English-speaking population at that time, it is even more surprising that six companies of "English" militia, and an artillery company, were also formed.

In theory, the *corvée*—a relic of French government—could be used to mobilize the male population for fighting or manual labor. Carleton, however, was reluctant to do so after the disappointing results during the Rebel invasion. In 1777, some 2,000 men were called out to provide bateau handlers and axe men for Burgoyne's expedition, but so many deserted that barely 300 crossed into New York. The arrival of French troops in North America produced a brief spark of interest, but once it became clear that France had no further interest in Canada, matters soon quietened down and remained stable until the end of the war.

NATIVE AMERICANS

Possibly the most contentious act committed by Royal forces during the war was the employment of war parties recruited from among the tribes inhabiting the lands bordering the Thirteen Colonies. In previous conflicts in North America, the French had overcome their lack of parity in regular troops by this method, as they enjoyed a better relationship with the tribes than did the British. In 1754, the British had formed a Department of Indian Affairs, divided into two districts that increasingly functioned as separate entities, with little attempt being made—either locally, or in London—to coordinate their activities. The northern district stretched as far south as Pennsylvania, while the southern district ran from Virginia to the Gulf of Mexico. Control was divided between the commander-in-chief in North America (who controlled the finances) and the two superintendents.

In 1775, the northern district contained over 8,500 warriors from forty tribes, including the Six Nations (Iroquois), the Seven Nations (mainly in the St. Lawrence Valley), the Great Lakes tribes, the Ohio tribes, the Illinois tribes, and the Wabash Confederacy. Of these, only the Six Nations had been allied to the French until 1760. The southern district had around twenty tribes, of which the five most important—the Choctaw, Cherokee, Creek, Chickasaw, and Catawba (known as the Five Civilized Tribes)—could boast some 13,000 warriors. The southern tribes were far more independent and isolated from one another, due to the geography of the southern district, with its many unconnected rivers and mountain ranges.

Not all of these tribes, however, were available to the British at any one time: the invasion of Canada at the start of the war had prevented the British from supplying and arming the Iroquois until later in 1776. Indeed, few tribes were able to sustain hostilities for more than two or three of the eight years of fighting along the frontiers. Once their raids into the Colonies became effective, either Congress, or the local colonial assemblies, would send punitive expeditions into the interior—most notably Clark's march to Vincennes, Sullivan's expedition in the Mohawk valley, and mounted raids from Georgia and South Carolina. The raids destroyed villages and agricultural land, leaving the tribes to freeze and starve, or else become a logistical burden on the nearest British post.

The use of Native Americans by Royal commanders was sanctioned by Lord Dartmouth in July 1775 (although they were first employed by the other side—the Massachusetts Provincial Congress having authorized a minuteman company of Stockbridge warriors in March of that year). However, it was not a universally popular move and many complaints were heard in Parliament that these "savages" were being used against fellow Englishmen. Of the senior officers in North America, only Carleton spoke out vociferously against their use, possibly as much from his own awareness of their military limitations as for humanitarian reasons.

By and large, Congress made as much propaganda as it could from the situation, while at the same time attempting to flatter, cajole, threaten, or bribe the tribes into remaining neutral. Ostensibly, this was for the humanitarian reason of avoiding the horrors of frontier warfare. In reality, there was little likelihood of recruiting them to join the struggle for independence, given the incursions and atrocities of white settlers, and the main objective was to deny the British another source of manpower. While Schuyler was busy recruiting 300 Oneidas and Tuscaroras (who later starved Burgoyne's army of intelligence after his own Native American forces had deserted him), the New Hampshire Assembly was offering £70 for male scalps and half that sum for women, or children over twelve years old.

The only year in which they served as part of a substantial army was 1777, when Burgoyne—against the advice of Carleton and other officers with experience of serving in North America—took 650 warriors, led by two former French officers, on his march south, while 1,000 Iroquois, under Joseph Brandt (Thayendanegea) went with St. Leger.

As regards their military value to the Crown, they were generally at their best when scouting or raiding; they did not accept casualties easily and would often break if engaged in a prolonged action with a determined enemy. At Oriskany, they sprang an ambush prematurely, and then fled the field when on the verge of wiping out the militia under Herkimer. Eventually, St. Leger was forced to retreat when the Iroquois became drunk and looted the camps of his few Regulars and Loyalists.

While Burgoyne's group provided him with useful intelligence on his enemy, and prevented Rebel patrols from doing the same, they became increasingly difficult and undisciplined when scalps and booty did not become available. They contributed to the defeat at Bennington and their very presence may have encouraged the militia to turn out in greater numbers, although this is arguable. Rather like the Hessians, the Native Americans were the victims of propaganda. While they undoubtedly did torture and kill indiscriminately at times, this was no worse than the treatment meted out to them by whites before the war.

Ironically, their most famous "victim"—Jane McCrea (the "Yankee Joan of Arc")—was most probably killed by a stray bullet from a Rebel patrol.

From the Rebel viewpoint, the Native Americans posed more of a menace in the North than they did in the South and there were several reasons for this. The bases from which attacks were launched were closer to the frontier (e.g. Fort Niagara) and also tended to have Regulars among the garrison. Leadership was offered by local Loyalists to a much greater extent. Equally, the enemy in the South was hardier. But the main difference was undoubtedly the group strength of the Iroquois and the leadership provided by Joseph Brandt. Yet even he became disillusioned with the war and the way that the British and Loyalists were using his men.

In 1775, many considered the Native Americans to be potential war winners; by 1781, they were considered a liability and were seldom employed for anything but raids after 1777. In fairness, their repeated underachievement throughout the conflict owes much to their misuse by senior commanders, who placed too much reliance on both their numbers and their reputation. In fact, when they were used properly and in familiar territory, they proved deadly.

THE FRENCH

The French army which served in the American Revolutionary War was probably one of the best that nation has ever produced. Defeated and demoralized in 1763, it was completely reorganized in the 1770s by the soldier-statesman De Choiseul and his successor Saint-Germain. In 1778, it had over 200,000 men from a population of twenty-five 25 million—paradoxically, this gave France the largest standing army in western Europe, yet the lowest ratio of soldiers to civilians (about one to 125 in peacetime and one per 65 in wartime—compared with one per 28 and one per 14 in Prussia).

Aside from the *Maison du Roi* (a larger version of the British Foot Guards), there were 112 infantry regiments, of which twenty-two were foreign (Swiss, Italian, Scots, Irish, and German, of which the last two contingents provided regiments for North America), totalling 172,000 men.

The cavalry arm numbered 46,000 men, comprising the mounted *Maison du Roi*, the *Gendarmerie de France* and the line cavalry (heavy horse, dragoons, and hussars). However, during the Seven Years War, various "legions"—mixed corps of light infantry and light cavalry—had been raised. In 1778, the navy decided to raise eight more for colonial service, composed of foreigners. In fact, only three were formed, but one of those—Lauzun's Legion—provided Rochambeau's only cavalry and generated great interest in North America, as well as fighting hand-to-hand with Tarleton's own legionary corps. Another legion, the *Volontaires de Luxembourg*, was transferred to

Dutch service and sent to assist in the defense of the Cape of Good Hope.

The artillery had recently been reformed, the system devised by the De Valières, *père et fils*, having been replaced by the new Gribeauval system, which standardized and lightened equipment and brought technical innovations (such as traversing carriages, so that coastal guns could engage moving targets). Now with 12,000 men in seven regiments—each capable of serving enough guns to support a field army—the artillery boasted 4-, 8-, and 12-pounder guns and 6-inch howitzers for field operations, and 18- and 24-pounder cannon, and 10-inch and 12-inch mortars for sieges.

The regular army was backed up by a three-tier militia. The Royal Militia comprised fifty-four regiments of infantry and thirteen of grenadiers (the latter often serving in the field in wartime). The men were drafted and remained available to be called up for six years, during which time they continued to live in their villages. The Bourgeois Militia was based in the towns and mainly fulfilled the duties of a police force. It consisted of middle-class men, who were excused taxes and all other forms of military service. The Coastguard militia (which was the responsibility of the navy) consisted of single men living near to the coast. Organized either into "watch companies" or "detached companies"—the latter being liable for five years' service and required actually to defend the coast—they were mainly gunners, but some dragoon companies were also formed.

Below: *Lauzun's Legion. The equivalent of the corps commanded by Tarleton and Simcoe, Lauzun's Legion was actually controlled by the French navy, but fought as part of Rochambeau's corps at Yorktown.*

Above: *Rochambeau and Washington issuing orders. This print shows a good selection of French army uniforms.*

Lengthy service abroad was unpopular with the metropolitan regiments, so there was a substantial colonial army (administered by the navy, which could cause bureaucratic problems). The colonists had wanted troops raised locally and led by local officers, which is—eventually—what they got, to the extent that officers did not require noble ancestry. During the war, the colonial forces in Africa, India, and the Caribbean rose to twenty-eight battalions, various independent companies, and twelve companies of artillery—in all, some 12,000 men on paper (about 9,000 in reality). Each colony also had its own militia, in which all able-bodied whites and free blacks and mulattoes had to serve.

The navy also had its own troops, namely the 100 companies of the *Corps Royale d'Infanterie de la Marine* and three companies of *Bombardiers de la Marine* who provided marines and gunnery instructors respectively, on French warships. Although they numbered over 12,000, detachments from army units still had to be assigned to some vessels (John Paul Jones was given 100 men of the Irish regiment, Dillon).

Enlisted men were volunteers, unless they were drafted from the militia, but only served for six, or at most eight, years (however, if a regiment was short of men, they tended to hold on to them). All recruits had to be Roman Catholics and in any regiment, roughly half of the men would come from the province whose name the regiment carried, while the other half would be from other parts of France. No foreigners were allowed to join the "French" regiments, but Frenchmen were increasingly allowed into the "foreign" regiments (where the pay was higher). In wartime, replacements would be drafted from the Royal Militia, which provided a third or depot battalion to each infantry regiment.

As in the British service, commissions in the French Army were usually purchased. This system was briefly abolished by Saint-Germain in the late 1770s, but the outcry led to it being reinstated in 1781. Before then, enlisted men who displayed bravery or leadership could be promoted (such men were known as *roturiers*), but the vast major-

ity of officers were drawn from the nobility. In the household regiments, such as the *Maison du Roi* (in which even the lowest *soldats* were noblemen), or the cavalry, this meant the leading families in French society. At the other end of the spectrum, infantry officers tended to be provincial noblemen, with little or no money and influence, for whom the army was the only route to fame and fortune, or at least a decent pension—if they survived.

Ironically, the higher nobility tended to adopt a more egalitarian view of officer status and it was the *petite noblesse* (who saw military commissions as their birthright) who felt most threatened by the *roturiers* and objected to them. From 1750, the *roturiers* declined from one-third of all officers, to virtually none. After 1781, proof of noble lineage was required for all commissions, leaving brave or talented rankers with no hope of advancement. Such attitudes hastened the advent of the French Revolution, particularly among those who had fought for "liberty" in North America.

The 1760s and 1770s saw a major debate on infantry tactics: one school supported the traditional approach of punching through the enemy's line with massed columns, the other favored the linear tactics of the Prussian army. The 1776 and 1777 regulations issued by Saint-Germain proposed a compromise, retaining the column for forcing a point in the enemy line, or an obstacle, but using the three-rank line as the principal combat formation. After Saint-Germain's death, the conservatives won back control, among them Marshal de Broglie, who attempted to prove the superiority of the traditional system in an exercise involving the force assembled to invade England. However, the linear system triumphed at every turn and one of its most enthusiastic supporters, Rochambeau, was chosen to command the advance guard of the invasion and later, when this was canceled, the corps destined for North America.

On arriving in North America, French officers expressed a desire to meet the British in combat, confident that their third rank gave them the extra weight needed to punch through the thinner enemy line. Yet when they had been given such a chance, at St. Lucia in 1778, five British light companies managed to hold several battalions at bay.

It was almost twenty years since French troops had left North America, and (as with the British army) most of the "forest-fighting" skills and the "picquet" or light companies attached to each battalion, had all been lost. However, the French did not lack up-to-date intelligence on military affairs in North America. In 1769, De Choiseul had sent a retired officer, Johann de Kalb, on a journey through the Thirteen Colonies to report on their military capabilities and relations with Great Britain. For political reasons, De Choiseul ignored the reports, but another of his successors, Marshal de Broglie, made sure they were used to support the pro-intervention argument at the French court.

During the war, the number of men committed overseas—especially to North America—was fewer than Congress had hoped. Worldwide, there were eleven battalions (5,000 men) serving overseas in 1778, but by 1782 the figure had risen to forty-nine battalions (over 20,000—of which 11,000 were sent to the Caribbean in 1781 and 1782). Some 4,000 men from the West Indies served under D'Estaing at Newport and Savannah, but the failure of those enterprises generated misgivings over further cooperation.

It was only when the planned invasion of England was abandoned that another expeditionary force for North America was proposed. Numbering 8,000, it was to be commanded by Rochambeau who would serve under Washington (to be treated as a marshal of France). The only conditions were that the corps could not be dispersed and could serve only under French officers. Lack of naval transport left 3,000 men stranded in France, but at Yorktown, Rochambeau was joined temporarily by 3,000 men from the West Indies.

THE SPANISH

The army of Carlos III was small by European standards: just 78,000 from a population of twelve million, a ratio that appeared slightly better than Great Britain (another nation in which the army had to compete for manpower with a large navy), but was actually worse, as one man in six was Swiss! This shortage of manpower and the size of the Spanish empire made it impossible to commit large numbers of regular troops abroad. Hence, the main functions of the army—frontier defense and internal security—were shared with the local population, either via the urban and provincial militias in Spain, or colonial units filled with men who enlisted for short periods in return for land grants.

This was also reflected in the officer corps. The Spanish Army followed the French in customarily drawing one-third of all officers from the ranks, while the remainder were mainly men of noble blood (*hidalgos*) who made up five percent of the population and were the equivalent of the provincial nobility in France. They received their commissions from the war ministry and attended one of the five military colleges. Cavalry officers were expected to be *grandees* (the wealthiest and most powerful nobles), but this was seldom required in the infantry. However, a large number of officers were foreigners—mostly Swiss and Irish, but also some French and Italians. Such men held a disproportionate number of senior regimental posts (even in Spanish units), as ex-rankers could not progress beyond captain and the *grandees* and wealthier *hidalgos* were given the senior posts.

The Spanish Army had also performed poorly during the Seven Years' War and underwent substantial modernization between 1765 and 1775, absorbing the tactical doctrines of their French neighbors. However, unlike the French (and most other European nations) they resisted "Prussianization" and especially physical punishment, which was abhorred both by officers and men. The result was a limited, but generally brave (often absurdly so), well-trained and capable force, with discipline based on religious devotion, rather than fear. Administrative improvements had also given the army an extensive and able corps of 350 staff officers, mainly based in Spain, but with a few personnel in Havana. These "officers of the pen" controlled army finances, pay, accommodation, and procurement, to such an extent that they were required to be consulted by "officers of the sword" (i.e. generals and military governors) when planning their campaigns.

Including household troops, there were thirty-six infantry regiments, of which eight were foreign (Swiss or Irish). Of these, only one—the Louisiana regiment—was permanently stationed in North America; De Galvez had barely 200 regulars when he took command in 1776; by June 1778 there were 437 and the following year there were 769. In fact, given the size of the Spanish Army and its European commitments, only in times of major civil unrest were numbers of regular troops ever sent out from Spain.

There were also twenty-one mounted regiments, of which one was light cavalry (similar to the British Light Dragoons regiments) and eight were dragoons, who maintained the dual function as foot and mounted troops to a greater extent than in most armies. None of these served outside Europe.

The artillery consisted of five battalions—roughly 5,000 men—with each battalion nominally serving around 240 pieces of ordnance of varying types and calibers, as in the British service. Again, French influence was apparent, the guns being based on the Vallières system, introduced in 1743 (the Gribeauval system was not adopted until after the war), but with more ornate metalwork. Calibers were, by the 1770s, unfashionably large, with field guns ranging up to 16- and 24-pounders; in addition, there were 8-inch howitzers, and 8-, 10-, and 12-inch mortars. Carriages were either painted red, or just oiled; interestingly, both the brass for the barrels and the heavy woods used to manufacture the carriages and vehicles, came from the New World.

As in most European armies, the engineers—the *Real Cuerpo de Ingenieros*—were all officers. There were 200, most based in Spain, but with individuals posted permanently to the islands and colonies. Generally competent, the service enjoyed a particularly high reputation for coastal fortifications, especially in the Americas.

In Spain, the *Milicias Provinciales* (similar to the Royal Militia in France) usually relieved regular units from garrison duty. There were forty-two single-battalion regiments on the mainland and three more on Mallorca and the Canary Islands. The men were drafted by lot, while the officers came from the local gentry. The *Milicias Urbanas* had around 20,000 men in 114 independent companies, divided among the thirteen main municipalities according to population (*Campo Gibraltar*, for example, had thirteen companies, many taking part in the famous siege). Between 1776 and 1778, De Galvez increased the militia in and around New Orleans from 136 to 302.

There were also 12,000 marines (*Infanteria de la Marina*), in twelve battalions, serving at the main naval bases at Ferrol, Cadiz, and Cartagena.

In the colonies, military organization was based on the *presidio* (fort) that usually defended a town or mission. The troops came from all ethnic groups (even Acadians displaced from eastern Canada, and German settlers) and throughout the eighteenth century attracted complaints from the clergy regarding poor morale, loose morals, and lack of equipment. The arrival of De Galvez improved matters considerably, at least in the Louisiana area, and units under his direct command invariably performed well. For example, during the attack on Mobile, he had 134 regulars (41 from Louisiana, the rest from Spain and Havana), 14 artillerymen, 26 carabineers (horsemen), 323 white militiamen, 107 free blacks, 24 slaves, and 26 Anglo-American volunteers.

THE DUTCH

The army of the United Provinces of the Netherlands, which was maintained largely as a protection against French invasion, took little part in the War. It included a large number of mercenaries, including eight battalions—around 5,000 men—from the German principality of Waldeck, and the famous Scots Brigade, originally composed of Scottish mercenaries, but now incorporating many of their Dutch descendants.

A few European regulars, along with local volunteers and militia, guarded the colonies and occasionally, as at Cape Town, they were reinforced by French troops, some of whom were transferred into Dutch service for the duration. Ironically, the only "Dutch" unit to see any serious action was the 3rd Waldeck Regiment, composed of German mercenaries, which was "loaned" to the British in 1776 and was captured at Pensacola.

APPENDIX 2
THE NAVIES

At the outbreak of the American Revolutionary War, the "age of fighting sail" was over two centuries old and the wooden sailing warship was about to reach its heyday. There were three basic types of warship, each of which had evolved over two centuries to fulfil specific tactical roles. The largest were up to 200 feet long, 50 feet across the beam, and had a draft of about 20 feet (usually maintained by lumps of metal and rock in the hold, to counter the force of the wind on the huge expanse of sail). Even relatively small vessels were expensive to build and construction of the largest ships took several years and might require as many as 2,000 trees.

The largest vessels were the "ships of the line" (ships), so called because they formed the opposing lines in fleet-sized actions of the period. This category was further divided, or "rated", by the number of guns carried—divided equally between port and starboard broadsides, although only one side could be operated at a time. Ships of the line usually carried their guns on two decks, although the larger navies also had a few three-deckers, which carried more guns, but were slower and less maneuverable—and usually had more space for senior officers, as they were mainly employed as flagships. Three-deckers mounted more than 90 guns (those built during the war usually carried over 100), while two-deckers mounted between 60 and 80 and, being cheaper to build and maintain, formed the backbone of most fleets; theoretically, vessels carrying less than 60 guns were no longer classified as "ships of the line", being too weak to fight the larger types, but were still used as such in remote theaters and for reasons of economy. As the eighteenth century progressed, the trend was toward larger two-deckers, which in turn made the original three-deckers obsolete and also forced designers to upgrade and enlarge them.

The second category was the frigate, which had a single lower gun deck and mounted between 20 and 40 guns. They were often as long as the smaller two-deckers, but narrower and thus faster, as reflected by their tactical roles— messengers, raiders, convoy escorts, and scouts. In extremely desperate circumstances, they would even stand in the line of battle, but normally they would use their speed and maneuverability to escape if they met a two- or three-decker. Originally armed with 8- or 9-pounders, by the start of the war, 12-pounders were increasingly becoming the standard armament, and the majority of frigates built during the war mounted 18-pounders, compared with 24- and 32- (French) or 36-pounders carried by two-deckers.

The third category comprised the sloops, brigs, cutters, corvettes, schooners, etc. that carried all their guns on their upper deck, and that performed tasks requiring speedy vessels with shallow draft. They were often used to escort prizes, attack lone merchant ships, or transmit messages, and carried much more rigging than ships or frigates, so as to make them faster. However, they were often not very robust and many were lost at sea; in fact, in heavy seas, they were vulnerable to capture, as they would often be overtaken by supposedly slower ships and frigates.

All vessels were either "in ordinary"—i.e. had their guns, stores, and upper masts removed in order to be refitted or repaired—or "in commission", which meant that they were fully rigged and armed (though not necessarily fully crewed, as commissioned ships could perform passive tasks, such as guarding harbor entrances, or as floating prisons and hospitals). As an example, the Royal Navy had 174 ships at the end of the war, but of these, only 90 were available for active service.

Despite the romantic appearance of majestic paintings of sea battles, in reality, the wooden sailing ship was simply a cramped, smelly, mobile fort. Unlike a landbased fort, when it was in action the crew had to sail the ship as well as fight it; handling the vessel, however, required only about ten percent of the crew on larger ships, and no more than twenty percent on smaller vessels. Another ten percent would be marines (or soldiers serving as marines), who kept order among the crew, provided landing and boarding parties, and cleared the enemy decks with small-arms fire in action. The rest of the crew were there to man the guns and these were usually victims of the Press Gang, as no respectable captain would jeopardize his ship by employing "landlubbers" in the rigging, or at the wheel and tiller.

In action, most nations had very basic rules of engagement—the Royal Navy's (in)famous Fighting Instructions were very much the exception—and tactics were usually predictable. In most cases, the weather was very much a factor, not just tactically, but also strategically; a prime example was the transfer of the Caribbean fleets to North American waters during the summer months in order to avoid the hurricane season, and then the return in the fall and winter to avoid the Atlantic storms. In battle, the two fleets would occupy relative positions known as the "weather gauge" (i.e. upwind of the enemy) or the "lee gauge" (i.e. downwind).

The former was the more aggressive position, having more room to maneuver and also, as the fleets got closer, "hiding" the wind from the enemy and blowing both sides' smoke back into the enemy's face. The major disadvantage was that in a heavy sea, the ships might be forced over by the wind to the extent that the gun ports on the lower decks facing the enemy would have to be closed to prevent flooding (although the same effect would also point the enemy's guns into the air and expose the lower hulls of his ships). The "lee gauge" was often considered the more vulnerable position, as the side holding it could not attack a weaker, or "shy" enemy. Being downwind, however, made it easier to escape; smoke could be used to mask movement; and all gun decks were clear of the water (and could also aim higher, in order to destroy the rigging of the windward vessels, slowing them down).

Both positions had their supporters, but in general the British preferred the wind gauge and the French the lee gauge. It is difficult to know whether the argument was responsible for their respective gunnery tactics, or vice versa. What is clear is that the British preferred to fire at the enemy hull, which would dismount the guns and cause casualties among the crew, but leave the ship in a fit condition to be sailed home if captured. The French (and Spanish) preferred to damage the enemy rigging, making it easier to outsail their opponents if they wished to retreat, or to surround and capture any ships that were completely dismasted.

These tactics in turn reflected national maritime strategy: the British wished to dominate the oceans and believed that the best way to do so was to destroy the enemy fleets. This was further underlined by the policy of "prize money" which was awarded to crews capturing enemy ships (although this policy could occasionally make senior officers put financial gain before military sense). By contrast, the French and Spanish fought from a position of weakness; they could not afford to lose ships and had to be ready to "live to fight another day" in order to keep the Royal Navy tied down and unable to influence land campaigns.

Once an enemy was sighted, be it a fleet or a single ship, and the decision made to fight, the crew would prepare for battle. Sails would be taken down or furled; livestock and valuables would be lowered into boats to be reclaimed later; furniture in the wardrooms would be folded down and stored; hammocks and bedding would be stashed in nets over the upper deck guns to protect the crews; and the guns would be cleared and run out. Most Royal Navy ships could be cleared for action in less than twenty minutes.

Battle tactics had changed little in the preceding seventy-five years and consisted of both sides forming line ahead, parallel to each other, either facing the same way, or approaching from opposite directions—the only difference being that the latter would produce a shorter action and the leading ships would usually take fire from every vessel in the enemy line. This tended to stifle initiative and simply produced large casualty lists for little or no result on either side. However, the Seven Years' War and the American Revolutionary War had witnessed the development of several ideas designed to circumvent the predictable stalemate of broadside-to-broadside battles. One was "crossing the T", when the faster fleet would sail around the end of the opposing line, concentrating its fire on the leading enemy ships. Another was "doubling" (which was used when the lines approached from opposite directions), whereby the leading ships would circle around the opposing line and maneuver into a position where an enemy vessel had an opponent on either side. A third tactic was "breaking the line", whereby one or more ships would pass through the gaps between enemy vessels, breaking up the opposing line into small groups that would then be overwhelmed by superior numbers.

The key to a ship's performance in battle was its captain; he determined how aggressive the ship would be and how closely orders would be obeyed. Any initiative would come from him—or his successor, should he be killed or incapacitat-

ed. Once engaged, a ship's crew would fire their guns as fast as they could, while marines in the "fighting tops" on the masts would pick off officers and men gathering to form boarding parties. Usually, one ship or the other would strike its colors, and the victor would send across a prize crew to take charge. On occasion, both ships would be so badly damaged that they would drift away and out of the fight. Sometimes, one ship would begin to sink; if both sets of rigging were entangled and the other ship could not get away, it was not unusual for both crews to stop fighting and attempt to save at least one of the vessels, so that both crews would have a safe haven (surprisingly few sailors ever learned to swim). The worst scenario was fire, which—if it got out of control—would inevitably reach the powder magazines, resulting in a massive explosion. In such cases, nearby ships would lower their boats, first and foremost to tow the ships away from the impending blast, and second to pick up any survivors.

Once battle was ended, damage was repaired; if this did not require the ship to put into a friendly port, any wounded would be transferred to a smaller vessel and sent home. The ship would then come back "on station" and await the next opportunity for action.

Above: *A fleet of wooden sailing ships on the move was an impressive sight that often belied the physical effort needed to maintain station in such a large formation.*

The principal military factor in the escalation of the American Revolution from colonial revolt into global conflict was the maritime strengths of the European protagonists. It has been suggested that the maritime struggle constituted a major paradox, in that it made a (if not *the*) vital contribution to the independence of the United States, without any major participation of Americans, on either side. However, the disruption caused to British supply lines and communications with North America cannot be underestimated. Perhaps a more genuine paradox was the contribution of the Royal Navy to limiting Great Britain's losses during the war, given that the conflict as a whole—and particularly the surrender at Yorktown that effectively ended—it was hardly the Senior Service's finest hour.

Below: *Two fleets in action. In such a heavy sea, the lower deck gun ports could be submerged causing a ship to founder and sink.*

THE ROYAL NAVY

In 1775, the Royal Navy was the largest in the world, with 131 ships of the line and 139 other vessels (by 1783 this total had reached 468 of all classes, of which 100—mainly frigates and smaller vessels—were committed to North America). It also possessed a plethora of senior officers who had gained valuable experience during the Seven Years' War. However, even more so than the British Army, the Royal Navy suffered from the politicization of its officer corps— though to nothing like the extent of the French navy, where senior posts were still awarded to court favorites. Given the political divisions generated by the causes of the war, this affected the service far more than it had in the Seven Years' War, or would do during the Napoleonic Wars. Many capable officers refused to serve against the Colonists—although most offered to fight later on, against the French and Spanish—and the government was forced to appoint politically acceptable, but less talented, men in their place.

In the context of technology, the British notoriously lagged behind both the French and the Spanish in terms of ship design. Such was the extent of the problem that there was enormous competition among junior officers to obtain postings aboard captured French vessels and a disproportionate number of them achieved great feats when combined with the greater aggressiveness of British captains. Even the larger three-deckers (first-rates, mounting over 100 guns) were smaller than their French and Spanish equivalents, although the 16 second-rates (over 90 guns) available in 1775, offered better economy and gave a tactical, and moral, advantage over the two-decker "80s" of the Bourbon navies.

British shipwrights were notoriously conservative, and although the British captured more

enemy ships than other navies—and thus had more opportunity to examine alternative designs—ships of the Royal Navy, class-for-class, remained smaller and slower than those of their opponents. Another factor was the innate conservatism of the Admiralty, which dictated—often quite literally—a set of rules known as "the establishments" that set the dimensions and armament of each class of ship. Deviation was discouraged and often prohibited, which was not a bad thing in itself, except that the limits set were too conservative in terms of size and tonnage. These were raised as the war continued, but it was only during the early years of the Napoleonic Wars that this handicap was finally eradicated.

Such problems were illustrated by the widespread use of two classes of ship—two-deckers armed with 50 and 44 guns, respectively—that were of little or no use. The "50" had become obsolete as a line-of-battle ship well before 1775, but had continued in service as a cheap alternative, having only 350 crew (against 500 in a "64"). They were also useful as flagships for squadrons composed of frigates and smaller vessels operating in the colonies and remote stations; for reasons of cost and safety, it was rare for larger ships of the line to serve on foreign stations in peacetime. In fact, they continued to serve and fight in the line in emergencies, where it was necessary to make up the numbers. By contrast, the "44" was completely useless, being incapable of fighting in the line, yet too slow and deep-drafted to be used as a frigate. Some attempts were made at justifying their continued production by reference to the need for larger ships that could navigate the large bays and venture inland along the major rivers in North America. Yet the "44" was too slow to catch enemy privateers (often just armed merchantmen and therefore quite fast), or escape the clutches of bigger ships that outgunned them.

On the smaller level, however, the British were ahead of their opponents. Frigates—the eyes of the fleet—were undergoing a revolution of their own. In 1775, the standard types carried either 18-, 12-, or 9-pounder guns as their main armament, with less than one in twenty carrying 18-pounders; by the end of the war, that proportion had improved

Above: *The character of a ship's captain often determined how aggressive and successful a ship was in action.*

to one in six and the Royal Navy was actually ahead of its opponents in this category.

The Royal Navy also countered the damage caused by shipworm, and the loss of speed from the accumulation of barnacles, by fitting thin copper sheets over the hull below the waterline. A program to copper every ship in the fleet was begun in 1778, but was not completed until after the War. However, the improvements in speed made a difference in a number of operations later on in the

Below: *One of the main functions of naval forces was to transport and put ashore large numbers of troops. This required as much discipline and training as going into battle.*

Below: *Privateers were used by all nations to disrupt enemy trade and commerce.*

conflict—although it could also prove to be a double-edged sword: on occasion, British ships failed to locate an enemy squadron they were chasing, having unknowingly overtaken it.

Another invention was the carronade, designed in 1774 at Carron, in Scotland. Nicknamed "the smasher" because of its effect, this short-range gun needed fewer crew and less space in which to operate. In addition, it was more accurate up to 400 yards (its maximum range and the sort of distance at which most naval combat usually occurred) and fired a 32-pound shot, yet weighed only as much as a 6-pounder cannon. This made it particularly useful for smaller vessels, but generally allowed ships to carry armaments in places where traditional long guns could not be mounted. First fitted to a warship in 1779, by January 1781 over 600 carronades had been fitted to 429 ships. At the end of the war, hardly a vessel did not have at least one, and many smaller vessels, such as corvettes, assigned to convoy duties, had been entirely rearmed with the weapon. Although ships carrying carronades were captured, the French and Spanish made little or no use of them, since both preferred engaging enemy

Below: *John Montagu, 4th Earl of Sandwich (1718–92) presided over the decline of the Royal Navy after 1763, demonstrating levels of corruption and negligence that were astonishing even by the standards of the eighteenth century.*

ships at longer ranges, and aiming at the rigging, whereas the British favored close action and aimed at the hull.

Paradoxically, the loss of supremacy by the Royal Navy provided more freedom for British privateers, as well as those of the enemy nations. Although the government was reluctant to authorize reprisals against the Colonies for political reasons (primarily the desire not to create hardship and bitterness by destroying the trade of fellow Englishmen, but also because of the implicit recognition of independence), it bowed to the inevitable. From 1777 to 1783, over 7,300 privateering commissions and letters of marque were issued, almost 2,300 of them against the Colonies. Over 2,600 British and Loyalist vessels were engaged, operating mainly from ports in the British Isles, the Channel Islands, the Caribbean, and Halifax in Nova Scotia. The privateers accounted for fifty-six percent of enemy prizes, with the entry into the War of the Dutch (whose merchant fleet numbered 16,000 vessels) providing the richest pickings.

Theoretically, Great Britain should have been able to crush the rebellion with its navy and marines alone. Unfortunately, the ships themselves had not fared so well: the cost of the Seven Years' War had been met, in part, by severe cuts in the Navy's budget, while at the same time, a series of men with little or no ability had held the vital post of First Lord of the Admiralty. Few new vessels had been built and many were so overdue for repair that they had become rotten and, to all intents and purposes, useless. In consequence, the service was completely unprepared for war generally and, more particularly, for the type of war that would need to be fought in North America. Once the French, and then the Spanish, entered the conflict and the British Isles was threatened, new ships were built, but it was a case of too little, too late.

THE CONTINENTAL AND STATE NAVIES

Although a very large (and growing) proportion of the cargo carried around the British Empire was transported in American ships, this did not translate into any military capability. A navy is not just a collection of ships and their crews; it requires a complex administrative and logistical infrastructure, involving dockyards with shipbuilding and repair facilities; special stores and materials (and warehousing to protect them); and a skilled team of bureaucrats to ensure that everything is in the right place, at the right time, and in the right quantities. It had taken Great Britain and France more than a century to develop systems that were less than perfect; Congress was hardly the type of organization to create one in a few months and it is perhaps surprising that so much was achieved, rather than so little.

As the war progressed, three distinct organizations appeared: the Continental Navy was brought into being by a decree of Congress and was based extensively on the Royal Navy. In November 1775,

Congress passed resolutions establishing the Continental Navy and the Continental Marines. By the end of 1775, a fleet of eight vessels had been assembled at Philadelphia, comprising two frigates, two brigs (including the *Andrea Doria*), and four smaller vessels. These eight ships, mounting 110 guns, were ordered by Congress to drive the Royal Navy (78 ships and over 2,000 guns) from the eastern seaboard of North America! In the end, they attacked the Bahamas and then withdrew to Rhode Island.

On December 13, 1775, Congress had authorised the building of thirteen frigates—one for each of the rebelling colonies. Five would have 32 guns, another five 28 guns, and three just 24 guns. These vessels would form the basis of the Continental Navy and despite the lack of experienced shipwrights in North America, they were well designed (possibly with French aid). Unfortunately, their history makes sad reading: six were either captured, or burnt on the stocks to avoid a similar fate; the other seven had all been sunk or captured by July 1781. Their record provides an interesting comparison with that of the privateers: with only three ships in commission in 1781 and two in 1783, the Continental Navy took 196 ships worth $6 million.

Soon after work had begun on the first frigates, Congress passed another bill authorizing several new projects, including three "74s" and five more frigates, all of 36 guns. Such plans were never likely to be fulfilled and in the end, only one "74" (the *America*) and one "36" (the *Alliance*) were ever built. The *America* was laid down in 1777 at Portsmouth, New Hampshire, and took five years to complete—albeit due to financial problems, rather than technical deficiencies. Eventually, she was given to John Paul Jones to command, but he never took her to sea as she was given to the French government in November 1782 (ostensibly to replace a French "74" lost in Boston harbor, but it must have been an excellent opportunity for Congress to rid itself of such an expensive "white elephant"). Ironically, the French retired it from service immediately because of its poor design—as the British did with the Continental frigates they captured. By the end of the war, a total of fifty-three vessels had served in the Continental Navy; of these, only two—the *Alliance* and the *Hague*—were at sea in 1783.

Various State navies had also been established (only New Jersey and Delaware did not have them) some predating the Continental Navy. In the main, they were charged with defending the coastline and inland waterways and therefore were predominantly made up of galleys and gunboats. However, South Carolina boasted a significant number of "cruisers" (frigates and smaller armed vessels) as did Massachusetts—at least until 1779 when seventeen ships were lost in the Penobscot Bay fiasco.

The last category, privateers, were by far the most numerous; by a resolution of Congress dated March 23, 1776, any private citizen could obtain "letters of marque" that granted them

licence to attack enemy vessels (warship or merchantman) and sell any captured ships, and their cargoes, for personal profit. This was a lucrative business, and men such as Abraham Whipple made fortunes. However, it was also extremely risky, in that such activities were regarded as little better than piracy. If captured, crews would not be eligible for exchange as prisoners-of-war and would languish in prison for the duration, unless they volunteered to serve on one of His Majesty's warships. Such activities also had a detrimental effect on the Continental and State navies, as the lure of prize money denuded the various seafaring communities of their best men and the prizes were sold in Europe – often allowing the British to buy them back.

Huge numbers of privateers were commissioned, although many only undertook one voyage. Nevertheless, it is estimated that around 1,700 letters of marque were issued by Congress and 600 by Massachusetts. The ships employed varied in size from 100 to 500 tons and carried up to 100 men and 20 guns, removing perhaps as many as 20,000 men of fighting age from the potential pool of recruits for the Continental Army and Navy, and the militia. In 1781, when privateering was probably at its peak, an estimated 450 ships, mounting 6,700 guns, were at sea. Over the course of the war, privateers captured about 600 British vessels, including sixteen warships, earning prize money estimated at $18 million (one privateer took $1 million in a single cruise to the Baltic).

Prior to the authorization of the Continental Navy, Washington had commissioned a small flotilla of six schooners and a brigantine to prey on British shipping during the siege of Boston, denying valuable cargoes to the garrison and obtaining much-needed supplies for his own troops. This force took thirty-five prizes, together with cargoes

worth over $600,000 before it was disbanded in 1777, following the British evacuation of the city.

Another "independent" fleet that deserves mention is the flotilla put together by Schuyler, Arnold, and others that halted Carleton's advance down Lake Champlain in October 1776. Arnold had four galleys built (only three of which took part in the battle), each carrying eighty men and mounting nineteen guns—a mix of 18-, 12-, 9-, and 2-pounders, and swivel guns. In addition, there were eight or nine gundalows (i.e. gondola—flat-bottomed rowing boats, pointed at both ends, with a twin-sailed mast), each with a 12-pounder "bow-chaser" and two 9-pounders amidships, carrying a crew of forty-five. (In contrast, the British fleet comprised a sloop with eighteen 12-pounders; two schooners, each with fourteen 6-pounders; a gundalow with seven 9-pounders; twenty gunboats, each with one cannon (calibers varied); and a 90-foot "radeau"—to all intents and purposes a raft—that displaced 422 tons and had a complement of 300 men, manning fourteen pieces of ordnance, including six 24-pounders.

Perhaps the most famous Rebel ship of the war was that given to John Paul Jones by Louis XVI—the *Bonhomme Richard* (formerly the *Duc de Duras*). The ship was an old East Indiaman, a class of vessel of large and stout construction, specifically designed to handle the long voyages between Europe and the Indies. Renaming the ship in honor of Benjamin Franklin, he armed it with six 18-pounders, twenty-six 12-pounders, and eight 9-pounders and made her the flagship of the small squadron that he took around the British Isles in 1779, culminating in the dramatic fight with the *Serapis*.

THE FRENCH NAVY

When France entered the war, she was better prepared for conflict than she had been for almost a century. This feat was all the more incredible as the French navy had been all but destroyed during the Seven Years' War, losing thirty-five ships of the line—over half of its strength—in a series of disastrous defeats. Reconstruction had begun even before the Treaty of Paris had ended the conflict, with the impetus provided by the appointment of the Duc de Choiseul as Minister of the Navy in 1761. One of the few men in France to have a complete grasp of the value of sea power at that time, he was determined to re-establish the French navy and, together with the fleets of Spain, create a

Left: *From 1778 the French navy provided a perfect illustration of how sea power could affect the outcome of a primarily land-based conflict.*

force that could meet—and defeat—the Royal Navy in any future conflicts. Within ten years, he had established a programme to produce eighty ships of the line and forty-seven frigates via public subscription, with individual provinces (departments) sponsoring "80s" (the first being the *Languedoc*) and major cities the "74s" (such as the *Bordeaux*), overseeing the construction of a large, modern fleet of ships and frigates, while the dockyards at Le Havre, Brest, Lorient, Rochefort, and Toulon were well stocked with the enormous range of materials needed to maintain wooden sailing vessels.

Fortunately for Great Britain, Choiseul fell from grace in 1770 and was replaced as Minister of the Navy during the last four years of Louis XVI's reign. As a consequence, the rebuilding programme was largely shelved, until the outbreak of fighting in North America rekindled interest. Between 1775 and 1778, virtually every ship in the fleet underwent repairs or reconstruction in preparation for the anticipated renewal of hostilities with Great Britain, and building recommenced—in 1775, France had one 110-gun ship, one "90", five "80s", twenty-six "74s" and twenty "64s", as well as six "50s" that could stand in the line in an emergency. At the outbreak of war between the two nations, another eleven ships—nine of them "64s"—had been added, giving France numerical parity with her foe; by 1782, there were seventy-three ships. However, this would not last for more than a year, as the British had greater capacity to build new ships, the manpower to crew them, and—above all—the superior economic resources to afford them (the finances needed to support the French fleet drove the nation deep into debt, eventually prompting her own revolution). For this reason alone, the French needed their Bourbon cousins in Spain to enter the war as well.

Just as her army at this time was one of the finest France ever produced, so the five years in which the French navy was involved in the war saw it reach its zenith in terms of the era of the sailing ship. In 1778, France had fifty-two ships of the line; by 1782, that figure exceeded seventy and was still growing. In the first four years, only one ship (and that a mere "64") was lost to enemy

action, although several others succumbed to storms and accidents, but no more so than their opponents. However, by 1782, this run of good fortune had come to an end. In that one year, fifteen ships were captured or sunk by the British, or lost to the sea (eight of them within a period of only ten days). The French navy simply could not sustain such losses and remain an effective fighting force; Vergennes and others knew this and the situation may well have encouraged the search for a peaceful settlement to the war.

In the same way that the British political system forced officers to become Tories or Whigs, so there was also a political dichotomy—albeit far more vicious and arbitrary— within the French navy. The officer corps was divided into the noble classes (the *Corps de la Marine*) and those of non-noble birth. Such a division obviously limited the career prospects of capable officers, but possibly of even greater detriment to the service was the tendency for the noble officers to regard orders as polite requests—something to be discussed rather than instantly obeyed. As in the army, attempts to change matters in the early 1770s were thwarted by the upheaval that followed the death of Louis XVI, and the nobility simply became more powerful. Both De Grasse and Suffren were troubled by insubordinate captains who, in addition to costing them victory in battle, created political problems for them back in France.

As if this did not cause sufficient problems, French naval officers generally spent less time at sea than their British counterparts. This was principally due to the cost of maintaining a large enough peacetime navy to allow officers to serve at sea and hone their nautical skills. The consequence was that shiphandling in general, and coordinated evolutions by groups of ships, were not performed to the same standard as in the Royal Navy. French fleets often looked ragged and untidy when forming line of battle, although on at least one occasion this served to mislead a British admiral into underestimating their numbers and good order.

The one area of real advantage for the French, however, was in the design of their ships. French naval architects studied more theory, including extensive instruction in mathematics, than those

of any other nation. As a result, there was a greater willingness to experiment and over time this led to a series of designs that produced warships that were faster, bigger, and more heavily armed than their British opponents. In fact, throughout the war there was a gradual, but obvious, move to faster and larger vessels within each class, increasing those advantages.

This is most clearly observed in the number of three-decker ships (which would generally carry 90 to 100 guns) in the French navy during the war, which became a major area of ship development for the remainder of the eighteenth century. In 1775, the Royal Navy had eight three-deckers—more than all of the other navies in the world put together. However, because such ships had no role to play in North America, the British built no more in the early years of the war. After 1778, the Admiralty needed as many ships as possible, as fast as possible, and so only one more was constructed by 1783. In contrast, the French had just two such ships in 1778, but in 1779 they laid down four new three-deckers, all of which were completed within a year and mounted 110 guns, while one of the original pair was uprated from 90 to 104 guns.

At the same time, the French also upgraded their stock of two-deckers—the "74s" and "64s"

Above: *Etienne François Choiseul, Comte de Stainville (1719–85). Choiseul was almost single-handedly responsible for the renaissance of the French navy following the disasters of the Seven Years' War.*

(unlike the British, the French had little faith in "50s" and only four served in the war, two of which were captured). By 1782, the faster, more heavily armed "74s" dominated, with thirty-two against just eighteen "64s", the latter being seen increasingly as more vulnerable to loss in battle, or at sea, as was also the case in British service. Such was the impact of the "74" on French thinking, that "64s" had been completely phased out within six years of the Peace of Paris.

The French navy had two main types of frigate—12- and 8-pounder—although both typically carried thirty or thirty-two guns. As the British found with their 9-pounder frigates, the weight of broadside of the *frigates de huit* left it too lightly armed to compete with other frigates and many privateers, and the type was quickly phased out in favor of the *frigates de douze* as the war progressed. By January 1780, there were fifty-one 12-pounder frigates, against only seven 8-pounder vessels. However, the following year saw the first French 18-pounder launched at Brest; this was followed by seven more before the war ended.

THE SPANISH NAVY

Prior to 1714, all Spanish warships belonged to the individual provinces. The new national navy proved to be considerably more efficient, but still left Spain trailing behind Great Britain and France throughout the eighteenth century. There was no professionally trained officer corps and the crews were often composed of convicts and landsmen— as might be expected of a service that still employed slaves to row galleys. Corruption and incompetence within the Ministry of Marine meant that naval stores were often in short supply, or in bad condition. With a poor naval tradition and a largely rural economy, there was little opportunity for such a state of affairs to improve.

By 1775, however, the Spanish possessed the third largest fleet in the world: one 12-gun ship, three "94s", seven with 76 to 80 guns, thirty-four with 70 to 74 guns, eleven "60s", and two obsolete "50s", as well as twenty-two frigates and twelve corvettes. This alone made it a vital component of the Allied war effort, since France could not hope to win a predominantly maritime conflict with Great Britain on her own. Together they outnumbered the Royal Navy by just enough (around forty percent, both by tonnage and numbers of ships) to give them a chance of victory. One example was the attempted invasion of England in 1779, in which thirty French and thirty-six Spanish ships were opposed by only thirty-five British, who had to seek refuge in port, leaving the Allied fleet in virtual control of the English Channel for several days

Whatever the failings of their crews, Spanish ships were of impressive construction, although the design (especially of the hull form) did not impress the Royal Navy, and while French designs were gradually incorporated, no Spanish ship was

ever copied. The quality of build, however, was due mainly to the large numbers of British and Irish shipwrights recruited to manage the dockyards and the availability of fine hardwoods from the Spanish colonies in South America. The use of these materials explains why Spanish ships generally lasted longer—often as much as sixty years, compared to twelve years (fifteen at most) for a typical oak-built vessel. Over one-third of the line-of-battle ships built in the eighteenth century were constructed in Havana to take advantage of these materials.

Spanish ships were generally much larger than British and French ships of the same class and armament. The standard ships were "70s" and "60s", which were weaker than the equivalent "74s" and "64s" in British and French service, both in terms of the number of guns carried, and their caliber. For example, Spanish "70s"—the equivalent of British and French "74s"—would typically have 24-pounders on the lower deck, instead of 36- or 32-pounders. Equally, Spanish frigates would carry thirty-four 12-pounders, yet would be the same size as a British frigate carrying a similar number of 18-pounders; it fact it was common practice, when the British captured Spanish frigates, to add more guns. This tendency to undergun their ships had obvious disadvantages for the Spanish in battle, although it put less strain on the hull and this probably also helped to extend the life of the vessel.

The most powerful ships were two-deck "80s", of which six were built between 1765 and 1775, and up to eight were in service at any one time during the War itself. Like the French, the Spanish had been slow to appreciate the value of the three-decker ship and had only built one before 1769. That year, however, saw the launch of the *Santissima Trinidad*, the largest ship in the world (which took part in the Battle of Trafalgar). Another two were completed before the end of the War and these gradually replaced the "80s".

Spanish frigates, as with other classes, were undergunned, but were considered excellent sailing ships. Again, the smaller armament contributed to the speed of the vessel.

THE DUTCH NAVY

For various reasons—economic, geographic, and demographic—the navy of the United Provinces of the Netherlands was completely unprepared for war in 1781. Economically, the eighteenth century had seen a decline in Dutch seapower and as other nations developed merchant fleets, the world's goods were no longer carried almost exclusively in Dutch vessels. With few natural resources to rely upon, the Dutch economy entered a period of decline after 1730, making it difficult for the Netherlands to afford the size and quality of navy that she had boasted in the seventeenth century. This problem was made worse by the fact that the trade lanes ran through the English Channel and so were vulnerable to pressure from both Great

Britain and France. Demographically, the Netherlands also had a small population base from which to provide crews for her warships (and little room for it to expand), whereas the populations of France, Spain, and Great Britain were burgeoning and had space in which to grow, both at home and overseas in the colonies. The shortages of money and people were exacerbated by the need to maintain a substantial army, in order to watch the border with France.

Politics also played a part. It suited the pro-British Stadholder and his supporters not to have a large fleet, which would have been seen as a threat to Great Britain, especially with the emergence of a pro-French party made up largely of merchants and the middle classes. On a more practical level, the United Provinces were just that—a loose confederation of seven virtually independent states— while the navy was divided into five separate admiralties. These organizations often argued vehemently and made any kind of policy or strategy in terms of naval affairs and administration virtually impossible.

The ships themselves generally followed British designs (due to the importation of British shipwrights at the start of the century) and tended to be small, partly because of the shallow nature of the river estuaries along the coast, and partly because the fleet was now intended to protect commerce, rather than fight the mass battles of its glorious past. However, as warships generally increased in size, the disparity became increasingly problematic: of the eleven ships in service at the outbreak of hostilities, only one was a "74" and the rest were "64s" and "54s" in the ratio of about 1:2, although generally the ships were heavily armed by comparison with British ships of the same class. After war was declared, a major building program was begun, aimed at delivering thirty-three new ships. However, only three of these were "70s" while one-third were "50s" (the rest being "60s"). In fact, there was never enough money or facilities to carry out the program fast enough. The number of vessels fit for service rose from eleven, at the end of 1780, to nineteen in April 1782, and might have exceeded twenty-five by the end of 1783 had the war continued, but how such a fleet would have been crewed and financed, is another matter.

Whatever the administrative and logistical shortcomings of the Dutch navy, it did serve to tie down forces that the British desperately needed elsewhere. In addition, these limitations were compensated, to some extent, by the population's natural affinity for the sea—a trait that they shared with the British, rather than the French and (perhaps least of all) the Spanish. The only fleet action, off Dogger Bank, in August 1781, was probably the bloodiest of the war, in relation to the numbers engaged, and both sides claimed a victory (although the British claim was probably more realistic). It was fortunate for the Royal Navy that the larger and better-supported French and Spanish fleets did not show the same tenacity, or with such consistency, as the Dutch.

BIBLIOGRAPHY

History is invariably written by the winners and rarely more obviously so than in this conflict. However, the Bicentennial was a watershed for revisionism among historians in the United States of America, and with the lack of interest in the conflict among British audiences, it is often surprising to find that the most sympathetic views of British policy and strategy are mostly to be found in American works.

The list below is not exhaustive and covers only those works referred to repeatedly by the author; various campaign histories—too numerous to mention, but generally found in the bibliographies of the works listed below—were also consulted for specific details.

REFERENCE AND GENERAL HISTORIES

Anderson, T. *The Command of the Howe Brothers in the American Revolution*
Bailyn, B. *The Peopling of British North America*
Bakeless, J. *Turncoats and Traitors: Espionage in the American Revolution*
Berger, C. *Broadsides and Bayonets: The Propaganda War of the American Revolution*
Black, J. *War for America: The fight for Independence, 1775–1783*
Blanco, R. (ed.) *The American Revolution, 1775–1783: An Encyclopedia*
Boatner, M. (ed.) *Cassell's Biographical Dictionary of the American War of Independence*
Burgoyne, J. *A State of the Expedition from Canada*
Clinton, Sir H. *The American Rebellion*
Clowes, W. *The Royal Navy: A History from Earliest Times to 1900* (Volumes 3 and 4)
Cumming, W. and Rankin, H. *The Fate of a Nation: The American Revolution through Contemporary Eyes*

Dickinson, H. *Britain and the American Revolution*
Dupuy, E. and Hammerman, G. *The American Revolution: A global war*
Farragher, J. *Encyclopedia of Colonial and Revolutionary America*
Greene, J. *Understanding the American Revolution*
Greene, J. and Pole, J. (eds) *The Blackwell Encyclopedia of the American Revolution*
Gruber, I. *The Howe Brothers and the American Revolution*
Hibbert, C. *Redcoats and Rebels*
Higginbotham, D. *The War of American Independence*
Lossing, B. *Field Book of the Revolution*
Mackesy, P. *The War for America*
Mahan, A. *Major Operations of the Navies in the American War of Independence*
—*The Influence of Sea Power upon History*
Miller, J. *Origins of the American Revolution*
Pearson, M. *Those Damn'd Rebels*
Purcell, L. *Who Was Who in the American Revolution*
—and Burg, D. *World Almanac of the American Revolution*
Rossie, J. *The Politics of Command in the American Revolution*
Seymour, W. *The Price of Folly: British Blunders in the War of American Independence*
Shenkman, R. *I Love Paul Revere, Whether He Rode or Not*
Ward, C. *The War of the Revolution*
Wickwire, F. and M. *Cornwallis and the War of Independence*

ARMIES AND NAVIES

Balch, T. *The French in America during the War of Independence*
Bilias, G. *George Washington's Opponents*
Bonsal, S. *When the French Were Here*
Chartrand, R. *Louis XV's Army* (5 vols)

—*The French Army in the American War of Independence*
Curtis, E. *The Organization of the British Army in the Revolution*
Eelking, M. von *German Allied Troops, 1776–1783*
Frey, S. *The British Soldier in America*
Galvin, Major General J. *The Minute Men*
Gardiner, R. (editor) *Navies and the American Revolution, 1775–1783*
Hogg, I. and Batchelor, J. *Armies of the American Revolution*
Lowell, E. *The Hessians: German Auxiliaries of Great Britain in the Revolutionary War*
Martin, J. and Lender, M. *A Respectable Army: The military origins of the Republic, 1763–1789*
Mayer, S. (ed.) *Navies of the American Revolution*
Neimeyer, C. *America Goes to War: A social history of the Continental Army*
Novak, G. *We Have Always Governed Ourselves: The War of Independence in the North*
—*Rise and Fight Again: The War of Independence in the South*
Royster, C. *A Revolutionary People at War*
Shy, J. *Toward Lexington: The role of the British Army in the coming of the American Revolution*
Syrett, D. *The Royal Navy in American Waters*
—*Shipping and the American War*
Wright, R. *The Continental Army*

MAPS

Barnes, I. and Royster, C. *The Historical Atlas of the American Revolution*
Marshall, W. and Peckham, H. *Campaigns of the American Revolution*
Nebenzahl, K. and Higginbotham, D. *Atlas of the American Revolution*
Symonds, C. and Clipson, W. *A Battlefield Atlas of the American Revolution*

INDEX

VIEW of *BOSTON*, the Capital of NEW ENGLAND; from

VIEW FROM *DORCHESTER NECK*, at Station A.

VIEW FROM *CHARLESTOWN*, at Station B

Roxbury